NEW OUTLOOKS IN PSYCHOLOGY

New Outlooks in Psychology

EDITED BY

G. Pat Powers

and

Wade Baskin

PHILOSOPHICAL LIBRARY

New York

CONTENTS

PREFACE

The last decade has witnessed the development of new methods of coordinating and synthesizing research in the broad field of psychology and related disciplines. Psychologists today face the challenge of intensifying their efforts and applying findings from many different areas of research to the solution of complex problems generated by technological advances which are rapidly reshaping the face of the physical universe and impinging from all sides on the destiny of man.

A few months ago we announced our intention of preparing for publication a substantive survey of new and promising developments in the general field of psychology and solicited contributions from a number of researchers who had distinguished themselves in their several areas of investigation. After laying down broad guidelines for the symposium, we expressed the hope that the collaborative effort would bring together much new knowledge and serve as a stimulus to further productive research in the social and behavioral sciences. We hoped that the projected volume would provide a much-needed conspectus of a discipline characterized by specialization and rapid progress. We asked each contributor to summarize the results of recent investigations in his area, to identify promising trends or lines of research, and to focus attention on developments which might contribute to the solution of contemporary problems. In some instances we asked specialists to adapt previously published materials to our design. In each instance we asked the contributor to modify the topic suggested to him so as to give himself sufficient latitude to move freely over familiar grounds and into peripheral areas, subject only to the restraints suggested by the nature of our undertaking. We suggested the adoption of a style appropriate to a generalist treatment of a technical subject since our intended audience included specialists in other areas as well as students and the hypothetical "general reader." We urged that primary stress be placed on emergent trends, exciting discoveries, and promising lines of investigation and experimentation.

We would like to thank all of those who have paused in their research long enough to accede to our wishes, and we hope that their efforts will be rewarded by the knowledge that they have helped to consolidate the gains of their science.

G. Pat Powers, Director of Testing
and Counseling
Wade Baskin, Professor

Southeastern State College

NEW OUTLOOKS IN PSYCHOLOGY

RECENT ADVANCES IN BRAIN CONTROL

JOSÉ M. R. DELGADO, M.D.
Yale University School of Medicine

Editorial Note

The brain remained for centuries beyond the range of the psychologist, who had to restrict himself to the study of the outward behavior of his subjects. One of the most significant advances of the twentieth century has been the elaboration of a new electrical methodology for the investigation and control of the human brain. We now have the means to investigate and influence our own intellect, according to Dr. Delgado. The exploration of the biological bases of social and anti-social behavior, he notes, "may be of decisive importance in the search for intelligent solutions to some of our present anxieties, frustrations, and conflicts."

Dr. José Manuel Rodriguez Delgado is Professor of Physiology at the Yale University School of Medicine. He has been at Yale since 1950, where he has developed methods for chronic intracerebral electrical and chemical stimulation by radio in colonies of rhesus monkeys.

Dr. Delgado was born in Ronda, Spain. He received his M.D. and D.Sc. degrees *cum laude* from the Madrid University Medical School in Madrid, Spain in 1940 and 1942. From 1940 to 1950 Dr. Delgado's work was centered in Madrid where he served as Instructor and Associate Professor at the Medical School. He was awarded a Spanish fellowship at the Yale School of Medicine in 1946.

Dr. Delgado is on the Editorial Boards of Psychosomatic

1

Medicine, the International Review of Neurobiology, and the Journal of Nervous and Mental Disease. He has been the recipient of many awards including the Ramón y Cajal Prize (Spanish Government) and was a Guggenheim Fellow in 1963-64.

•

RECENT ADVANCES IN BRAIN CONTROL

The human brain has evolved with a functional asymmetry which may be responsible for some of the conflicts of our present age. Apparently it has been easier for man to direct his attention outwards to the environment than inwards to deal with the complexity of his own mental structure, and easier to understand and manipulate Nature than to control his own behavior. In prehistoric times, and even today in primitive societies, man was and is at the mercy of the elements. When disaster struck and floods, pestilence, or hunger desolated the land, the only possible reactions were fatalistic resignation, appeal to supernatural powers, or despair. Modern civilization has progressed so much in the understanding and domination of the physical world, that relations between man and Nature have been completely transformed. Technology is reshaping the face of the earth, but the greatest change has taken place in the human brain which is now filled with new formulas, theories, and knowledge, and empowered with a new attitude of confidence towards natural forces which are no longer the masters, but are becoming the servants of man. The expanding sciences have directed most of our present intellectual and economic power towards industry, biology, electronics, atomic energy, outer space, and similar fields of endeavor, while only a minor fraction is devoted to inquiry into the roots of mental faculties. This unbalanced interest has an explanation. When observation and reason were the main tools for the acquisition of knowledge, philosophical speculation flourished. When the discovery of new methods permitted the scientific exploration of Nature, the study of subjects beyond experimental reach was neglected. Certainly, the disciplines of psychology and psychiatry have greatly expanded in our century, but a perusal of the literature shows that until one or two

2

decades ago, the brain was treated as a "black box" which could only be reached through the senses. Psychological investigations analyzed correlations between sensory input and behavioral output, but it was not possible to explore the processes lying in between which were hidden in the mystery of brain physiology.

During the last decade we have reached an historical turning point because of the development of methods which permit the coordination and synthesis of physical, physiological, pharmacological, and psychological research. As will be explained in the following pages, science has developed a new electrical methodology for the study and control of cerebral functions in animals and humans. Learning, emotions, drives, memory, consciousness, and other phenomena which in the past belonged only in the realm of philosophy are now the subjects of neurophysiological experimentation. In the last few years, the scalpel of the brain surgeon has modified psychological reactions and a wealth of wonder drugs has liberated many patients from mental institutions.

I am not so naive as to think that cerebral research holds all the answers to mankind's present problems, but I do believe that an understanding of the biological bases of social and anti-social behavior and of mental activities, which for the first time in history can now be explored in the conscious brain, may be of decisive importance in the search for intelligent solutions to some of our present anxieties, frustrations, and conflicts. Also, it is essential to introduce a balance into the future developments of the human mind, and I think that we now have the means to investigate and to influence our own intellect.

In support of these ideas, I shall present a brief outline of the evolution of the physical control of cerebral processes, followed by several examples of our incipient control of behavioral mechanisms, and I will end with a discussion of the principles and implications involved.

Historical Outline: *Theoretical and Methodological Evolution*
Animal Experimentation

For many centuries it was accepted that fluids or "animal spirits" were the cause of muscle contraction (Galen, 130 to *ca.*

200 A.D.), until the famous controversy between the schools of Luigi Galvani (1737-1789) and Alessandro Volta (1745-1827) focused the attention of nineteenth-century scientists and philosophers on the possible physical control of some manifestations of life. Contractions produced in a frog nerve-muscle preparation by touching it with a bimetallic arc were interpreted by Galvan as proof of the existence of animal electricity, while Volta believed that the electrical source was in the contact of two dissimilar metals. This controversy was resolved when Alexander von Humboldt (1769-1859) demonstrated that animal electricity and bimetallic electricity were co-existing phenomena. Leg movements evoked in frogs by the inanimate force of electricity proved that muscle contraction could be induced independently of the "principle of life" which had been considered the essential mover of all biological activities. The discovery that living organs could be influenced by instrumental manipulations directed by the will of a human being brought about a revision of the traditional concepts of vitalism which were challenged at that time by Emil DuBois-Reymond (1818-1896) and other scientists. The romantic mystery of the soul's "animal spirits" which had dominated biology for almost 2000 years now gave place to more prosaic chemical and physical laws, and even nervous activity could be investigated experimentally. DuBois-Reymond not only discovered many basic neurophysiological principles, including action current, polarization, electrogenesis, and propagation of the nerve impulse; he also provided the technical means for study of the two most fundamental processes of neural activity by inventing the galvanometer for the detection of electrical currents and the induction coil for faradic excitation of nervous tissue. At that time, the possibility of exciting the spinal cord and brain stem by other than physiological stimuli was violently debated, and the excitability of the brain was completely denied. Then Fritsch and Hitzig (1870) performed a beautiful series of experiments, applying galvanic stimulations to the exposed cerebral cortex of anesthetized dogs. Excitations of the posterior part of the brain failed to evoke motor effects, but in the anterior region contralateral body and limb movements were elicited. Weak currents induced discrete contractions local-

4

ized to specified muscle groups, while stronger currents increased the strength and spread of the evoked responses; if the intensity was further augmented, generalized convulsions appeared.

The scientific impact of these studies, and also the successful clinical localization of speech functions by Broca (1824-1880), promoted great interest in cerebral mapping, based on regional ablation and electrical stimulation studies attempting to pin precise functional labels to specific anatomical structures. Fortunately, there was much less speculation and much more experimentation in these studies than in the discredited phrenology, and, in spite of controversial issues, many of the facts discovered in the last century have remained important scientific contributions.

One of the main handicaps in these investigations was the need for opening the skull and exposing the brain. Operations were usually performed under general anesthesia which blocked pain perception but also blocked some of the most important functions of the nervous system. Emotions, consciousness, and intelligence were certainly absent in heavily sedated animals or in the isolated nerves of the squid, and for many years scientists directed their attention to sleeping brains and overlooked the complexity of awake minds. Textbooks of cerebral physiology were concerned with synapses, pathways, reflexes, posture, and movement, while mental functions and behavior were considered to belong to a different discipline.

Some pioneer efforts, however, were directed toward exploration of the waking brain, and techniques were devised for the introduction of wires through the skull in order to apply electrical currents to the brains of conscious animals. In 1898, Ewald had the idea of screwing an ivory cone into the skull of an anesthetized dog, and the following day, when operative anesthesia had worn off, electrodes were inserted into the brain through the ivory piece. A leash around the animal's neck contained stimulating wires, and a small dry cell battery carried by the observer served as the electrical source. Although the technique and results were primitive, a way had been found to investigate the brain in awake animals. The technique of intracerebral electrodes was dormant for many years until Hess (1932) developed his own method to explore the hypothalamus and other cerebral areas in unanesthetized cats. In a series of brilliant experiments, Hess demonstrated that autonomic functions, posture, equilibrium, movement, sleep, and even fear and aggressiveness may be influenced by electrical stimulation of specific cerebral structures. For the first time, it was revealed that psychological manifestations like rage do not depend exclusively on sensory inputs and physiological stimuli, but can be induced by electrical currents applied directly to the brain. Although these findings did not produce a significant impact on philosophical thinking, in retrospect they may be considered as important as the nineteenth century demonstration that the contraction of a frog muscle did not depend on circulating spirits, and could be controlled by physical instrumentation.

For two decades, the methods of Hess attracted only limited interest among biologists, but in the 1950s, there was a sudden expansion of the new disciplines of psychosurgery, psychosomatic medicine, psychopharmacology and physiological psychology, and many investigators realized the great research potential of intracerebral methods for the study of behavioral-cerebral correlations in awake animals. With this increased interest, a variety of technical improvements appeared. Electrodes were no longer introduced free-hand into the brain, but were inserted with geometric precision with the aid of micro-manipulators and stereotaxic coordinates. Anatomical maps of the depths of the brain were compiled for rats, cats, dogs, and monkeys. Aseptic precautions and instrumental refinements permitted long-term implantation of electrodes, which in some cases lasted for several years. The sight of experimental animals with sockets on top of their heads was exceptional in 1950 but had spread to hundreds of laboratories around the world by 1960. Electrodes were implanted not only in the usual laboratory animals, but also in other species, including crickets, roosters, chimpanzees, dolphins, and brave bulls.

Experiments were generally performed under some restraint. Rats were convenient subjects because of their behavioral simplicity, and they were not disturbed by a light coil of wires connecting their terminal head sockets with the stimulators. In this way, the brain was stimulated in fully conscious rats while they pressed levers, ran mazes, and maneuvered with considerable freedom, being limited only by the length of the leads and the size of the cage. A similar set-up was also used successfully with cats, providing they were peaceful and tame. These studies were often extended for months and were very appropriate for the investigation of autonomic, somatic, and behavioral effects evoked by electrical stimulation of the brain, and also for the analysis of electrical recordings taken during spontaneous or induced activities. The combination of intracerebral electrodes with other physiological and psychological techniques was very fruitful and showed that animals can learn to perform instrumental responses to seek or avoid stimulation of determined cerebral structures. Scientific exploitation of these techniques continues today with universal acceptance, as shown by current scientific literature.

The use of electrodes in monkeys presented a greater challenge because of their destructive skills and restless curiosity. A heavy protection of the connecting leads was necessary when the animal was observed on a testing table. In other cases, the monkey was placed in a special restraining chair where it could manipulate levers and feed itself without being able to reach the terminal sockets on its head. In these situations, conditioning and psychological testing were successfully performed, but spontaneous behavior was naturally curtailed.

The connecting leads trailing behind each animal were a serious handicap for behavioral studies and were unsuitable for use in chronic stimulations or investigations of group activities. The obvious solution was to use remote-controlled instrumentation, with a receiver carried by the animal and activated by induction or by radio. Several stimulators of this type have been proposed in the last 30 years (see bibliography in Delgado, 1963b), but solutions to many of the technical problems involved were not found until recently, when the development of transistors and electronic miniaturization permitted the construction of small, practical, and reliable cerebral radio stimulators (Delgado, 1963b). After a considerable amount of trial and error,

7

and in spite of the primates' genius for destroying any equipment within reach, monkey-proofing of instruments was achieved (figs. 3, 4, 5). The use of radio stimulators allowed the excitation of cerebral structures in completely free animals engaged in normal activities within an established colony and unaware of the scientist's manipulations. In this way, the role of specific areas of the brain in social relations was investigated. At the same time, blood pressure, body temperature, electrical activity of the heart and brain, and other physiological variables could be recorded by radio telemetry. In addition, individual and social behavior have been continuously recorded, day and night, by time-lapse photography. Radio techniques represented an important step toward physical control of the brain, providing an essential tool for behavioral studies, and it may safely be predicted that within a few years telestimulation will spread to most brain research institutes. We can also expect that new developments in micro-electronics, including integrated circuits and thin film techniques, will facilitate the construction of multichannel radio-activated stimulators reduced in size to a few millimeters. The limits of brain control do not seem to depend on electronic technology but on the biological properties of living neurons.

Among possible physiological handicaps, the presence of electrodes and repeated applications of electricity could be disrupting factors for the normality of the nerve cells. Insertion of electrodes into the brain substance is certainly a traumatic procedure which destroys neural tissue and produces local hemorrhage, followed by inflammation, foreign body reaction, and the formation of a glial capsule 0.1-0.2 mm. thick around the inserted wires. All of this reactive process is limited to a very small area measured in tenths of millimeters, and there is no evidence of functional disturbance in the neighboring neurons. Beyond the electrode tract, the brain appears histologically normal and electrodes seem to be well tolerated, as judged by the absence of abnormal electrical activity, by the reliability of effects evoked by electrical stimulation, and by the consistency of thresholds through months of experimentation (Delgado,

8

1955b). The longest reported implantation time of electrodes in the brain has been over four years, in a rhesus monkey.

From the functional point of view, two aspects should be considered in implantation experiments. The first is related to fatigability and the second to lasting functional changes. Physiological textbooks state that motor effects produced by electrical stimulation of the cerebral cortex fade away in a few seconds, and that a rest period of about one minute is necessary before the cortex recovers its excitability. If this were true throughout the brain, electricity could not be effectively used for control of cerebral function. However, experimentation has shown that the fatigability of some areas is slow or negligible. In monkeys, the putamen has been stimulated for more than 30 minutes without diminution of the elicited postural changes, and the hypothalamus has been excited for days without fatigue of the evoked pupillary constriction. Red nucleus stimulation repeated every minute for 14 days has evoked reliable and consistent sequential responses. Thus, while a few areas of the brain show quick fatigability, it should be recognized that many others can be stimulated effectively for minutes or even days. The evoked effects generally have lasted only as long as the stimulation, but in some cases enduring aftereffects have been obtained. In the cat, programmed intermittent stimulations of the amygdala for one hour daily evoked bursts of high-voltage fast activity and other signs of increased electrical activity, along with changes in spontaneous behavior which outlasted stimulation periods for many hours and occasionally for days. In other studies, excitation of the basolateral nucleus of the cat's amygdala for only 10 seconds inhibited food intake for minutes, and, in one case, the inhibitory effect persisted for three days (Fonberg and Delgado, 1961). These findings together with extensive experimentation by many authors have demonstrated that intracerebral electrodes are safe and can be tolerated for years, providing an effective tool for sending and recording electrical impulses to and from the brain of unanesthetized animals.

9

Electrodes in the Human Brain

With the background of animal experimentation, it was natural that some investigators should contemplate the implantation of electrodes inside the human brain. Neurosurgeons had already proved that the central nervous system is not so delicate as most people believe, and during therapeutic surgery parts of cerebral tissue had been cut, frozen, cauterized, or ablated with negligible adverse effects on the patient. Exploratory introduction of needles into the cerebral ventricles was a well-known and relatively safe clinical procedure, and, as electrodes are smaller in diameter than these needles, their introduction into the brain tissues should be even less traumatic. Implantation of electrodes inside the human brain offered the opportunity for prolonged electrical exploration which could be decisive for several diagnostic and therapeutic procedures. For example, when brain surgery and ablation are contemplated in patients suffering from epileptic attacks, it is essential to identify the focal areas of abnormal electrical activity. Electrodes may remain in place for days or weeks, during which spontaneous seizures may be recorded and detailed exploration repeated as many times as necessary. In other cases, intracerebral electrodes have been used to deliver intermittent stimulations for periods of days or even months (Feindel, 1961; Heath, 1954; King, 1961; Sem-Jacobsen *et al.*, 1956; Walker and Marshall, 1961). Similar procedures have also been used in patients with intractable pain, anxiety neurosis, and involuntary movement. These therapeutic possibilities should be considered rather tentative, but accumulated experience has shown that electrodes are well tolerated by the human brain for periods of at least one year and a half, and that electrical stimulations may induce a variety of responses, including changes in mental functions, as will be explained later. The prospect of leaving wires inside the thinking brain could seem barbaric, uncomfortable, and dangerous, but actually the patients who have undergone this experience have had no ill effects, and they have not been concerned about the idea of being wired or by the existence of leads in their heads. In some cases, they

10

enjoyed a normal life as out-patients, returning to the clinic for periodic stimulations. Some of the women proved the adaptability of the feminine spirit to all situations by designing pretty hats to conceal their electrical headgear.

The use of electrodes in the human brain is part of the present medical orientation toward activation of physiological mechanisms by electronic instrumentation, which already extends to several organs of the body. The clinical success of electrical driving of cardiac functions in man has been widely acclaimed. In spite of the delicacy and continuous mobility of the heart, stainless steel leads have been sutured to it, and in cases of block in the cardiac conduction system, artificial electronic pacemakers have been able to regulate heart rhythm, saving the lives of many patients. The bladder has been stimulated by implanted electrodes to induce urination in patients with permanent spinal block, and paralyzed limbs have been activated by programmed stimulators. A method has recently been described for placing leads in the auditory nerve to circumvent deafness caused by inner ear damage. Driving malfunctioning organs is simpler than attempting to direct the awake brain where millions of neurons are functioning and firing simultaneously for different purposes, but the expected results in this case are even more interesting. Exploring intracerebral physiology, we are reaching not only for the soma but also for the psyche itself. Cerebral functions are usually classified in three groups: autonomic, somatic, and psychic, and in the following pages I shall discuss present experimental evidence for their electrical control.

Electrical Control of Autonomic Functions

Several areas of the brain play important roles in the regulation of visceral activity, and extensive studies have shown that electrical stimulation of the hypothalamus and other cerebral structures can influence vasomotility, blood pressure, heart rate, respiration, thermal regulation, gastric secretion, food intake, and many other functions of the autonomic system. To illustrate

11

the artificial regulation of autonomic reactions by electrical means, I shall discuss pupillary motility because its mechanisms are relatively simple and easy to control.

The areas that participate in the regulation of pupil size are represented on the surface and in the depth of the brain. Cortical zones which have inhibitory effects upon respiration and upon spontaneous movements also produce pupillary dilatation (mydriasis). In cats, dogs, and monkeys, these areas are situated around the sylvian fissure, orbital cortex, temporal tip, cingulate gyrus, insula, rhinal fissure, and hippocampal gyrus. In the depth of the brain, pupillary dilatation may be evoked by stimulation of the basal telencephalon, hypothalamus, septum, midline group of thalamic nuclei, subthalamus, and a large part of the midbrain (Hodes and Magoun, 1942; Kaada, 1951; Showers and Crosby, 1958). Pupillary constriction (miosis) has a more limited representation, localized mainly around the genu of the corpus callosum (Hodes and Magoun, 1942; Kaada, 1951), thalamus, and hypothalamus (Hess, 1954). According to the region stimulated, pupillary responses will be unilateral or bilateral; if bilateral, each eye may respond synergically or antagonically. Most classical studies were performed under anesthesia and with the brain exposed, but recent investigations have been carried out with the use of awake animals equipped with intracerebral electrodes.

In monkeys (Delgado, 1959), electrical stimulation of the inferior part of the lateral hypothalamus produced marked ispilateral miosis, while stimulation of another point situated 6 mm. higher in the same tract evoked ipsilateral mydriasis (fig. 1). The magnitude of the effect was proportional to the electrical intensity employed. Stimulation of the inferior point with 0.8 milliampere (mA) produced slight pupillary constriction which increased progressively as the intensity was augmented to 1.5 mA. At this moment, miosis was maximum, and further increase in stimulation did not modify the effect. If the hypothalamic stimulation was slowly decreased in strength, the ipsilateral pupil gradually returned to its normal size. In these experiments, pupil diameter could be controlled precisely like the diaphragm of a camera, by turning the stimulator dials to the left or right. A similar dose-response relation was seen in the higher hypo-

TABLE OF HISTORICAL EVOLUTION
OF PHYSICAL CONTROL OF THE BRAIN

FINDINGS	IMPLICATIONS
Frog muscle contracted when stimulated by electricity. Volta, Galvani, DuBois-Reymond; 1780, 1800, 1848	"Vital spirits" are not essential for biological activities. Electrical stimuli under man's control can initiate and modify vital processes
Electrical stimulation of the brain in anesthetized dog evoked localized body and limb movements. Fritsch and Hitzig, 1870	The brain is excitable. Electrical stimuli of the cerebral cortex can produce movements
Stimulation of the diencephalon in unanesthetized cats evoked well-organized motor effects and emotional reactions. Hess, 1932	Motor and emotional manifestations may be evoked by electrical stimulation of the brain in awake animals
In single animals, learning, conditioning, instrumental responses, pain, and pleasure have been evoked or inhibited by electrical stimulation of the brain in rats, cats, and monkeys. See bibliography in Sheer, 1961	Psychological phenomena may be controlled by electrical stimulation of specific areas of the brain
In colonies of cats and monkeys, aggression, dominance, mounting, and other social interactions have been evoked, modified, or inhibited by radio stimulation of specific cerebral areas. Delgado, 1955a, 1964	Social behavior may be controlled by radio stimulation of specific areas of the brain
In patients, brain stimulations during surgical interventions or with electrodes implanted for days or months have blocked the thinking process, inhibited speech and movement, or in other cases have evoked pleasure, laughter, friendliness, verbal output, hostility, fear, hallucinations, and memories. See bibliography in Ramey and O'Doherty, 1960	Human mental functions may be influenced by electrical stimulation of specific areas of the brain

SUMMARY: Autonomic and somatic functions, individual and social behavior, emotional and mental reactions may be evoked, maintained, modified, or inhibited, both in animals and in man, by electrical stimulation of specific cerebral structures. Physical control of many brain functions is a demonstrated fact, but the possibilities and limits of this control are still little known.

FIG. 1. The diameter of the pupil may be electrically controlled as if it was the diaphragm of a photographic camera. The pictures show normal eyes in a monkey and the dilatation and constriction of the right pupil evoked by stimulation of the hypothalamus. Some of these effects are indefatigable and persist for days as long as stimulation is applied.

thalamic point where stimulation produced mydriasis. Implantation of electrodes in points with antagonistic pupillary effect
made it possible to introduce an artificial conflict by stimulating
both areas simultaneously with separate instruments. Results
showed that a dynamic equilibrium could be established at different levels of simultaneous antagonistic excitation. With 1.6
foot-candle units of illumination in the laboratory, the initial
pupillary diameter of 4 mm. was maintained when the hypothalamic points were stimulated together at similarly increasing
intensities up to 4 mA. At any level in this dynamic equilibrium,
the pupil constricted if intensity was increased in the inferior
or decreased in the higher point. The reverse was also true, and
the pupil dilated if stimulation decreased in the inferior or increased in the superior hypothalamic point. To some extent, the
effect of excitation of the inferior miotic point could be substituted for a light shone in the eye, illustrating the possibility of
algebraic summation of physiological, sensory, and electrical
stimuli within the brain. These experiments demonstrated that a
regulation of an autonomic function like pupillary size can
be effectively maintained by direct stimulation of cerebral
structures.

For how long would this regulation be effective? Would the
brain fatigue? To answer these questions, long-term experiments
were designed. Under continuous hypothalamic excitation, mydriasis lasted for about 30-40 minutes, after which stimulation was
ineffective and the pupil gradually returned to its original size,
indicating a slow fatigability of the effect. In contrast, pupillary
miosis was maintained in several monkeys for as long as stimulation was applied. Each animal was studied while free in a cage
and equipped with a portable stimulator connected by subcu-
taneous leads to the inferior hypothalamic point. Under continuous 24-hour stimulation, the size of the ipsilateral pupil was
maintained at less than 1 mm. in diameter, while the other pupil
measured a normal 4 mm. As soon as the stimulation was discontinued, a rebound effect appeared and the ipsilateral pupil dilated to about 6 mm. for several hours, and then slowly returned
to its normal size. In one monkey, the stimulation was applied
for as long as three days, during which pupil constriction was

continuous; with cessation of stimulation, a rebound effect appeared which lasted for two days.

In other experiments, when the intensity of hypothalamic stimulation was adjusted to produce only a 20-30 per cent reduction in pupillary size, the reactivity of both pupils to light was preserved, although the stimulated pupil was always smaller than the control. These results demonstrated that a lasting functional "bias" can be introduced in autonomic reactions by the artificial means of electrical stimulation of the brain. The physiological equilibrium was electrically modified, preserving the responses but changing the level of functional adjustment. These results are comparable to the modifications in autonomic reactivity (tuning) induced by injection of sympathetic or parasympathetic agents (Gellhorn, 1957).

In summary, autonomic functions can be controlled by electrical stimulation of the brain. As an example it has been shown that constriction of the pupil evoked by cerebral stimulation is reliable, precise, does not fatigue, can interplay with physiological stimuli, and may provide a functional "bias" to modify the level of physiological responses.

Motor Performance Under Electronic Command

The significant nineteenth-century discovery of central nervous system excitability was based on the fact that electrical stimulation of the cerebral cortex produced observable motor responses. Since that discovery, many investigations have been devoted to the analysis of motor representation in different areas of the brain. The evoked effects were usually described as stereotyped tetanic contractions, producing clumsy movements of the body and extremities and lacking the precision and coordination of spontaneous activities. These results were obtained under anesthesia, but it was assumed that because of the complexity of the mechanisms involved, artificial stimulation could never induce, even in awake animals, responses as skillful and well organized as voluntary movements. In spite of this assumption, when stimulation was applied through intracerebral electrodes to completely unrestrained animals, it was evident that

14

motor performance under electronic command could be as complex and precise as spontaneous behavior. Before discussing the reasons for success in the electric driving of behavior, I will describe examples of simple motor responses, complex behavior, and social interaction.

Simple Motor Responses

In the cat, electrical stimulation of the right sulcus cruciatus, in the anterior part of the brain, produced flexion of the left hind leg (fig. 2) with an amplitude of movement proportional to stimulation intensity, provided the experimental situation was constant. For example, in a cat standing on all fours, a five-second stimulation of 1.2 mA (monopolar, cathodal, square waves, 0.5 millisecond of pulse duration, 100 cycles per second) evoked a leg flexion barely off the ground. When the intensity was increased up to 1.5 mA, the hind leg rose about 4 centimeters, and when 1.8 mA were applied, the flexion of the leg was complete. The evoked movement usually began slowly, developed smoothly, reached its peak in about two seconds, and lasted until the end of the stimulation. This motor performance could be repeated as many times as desired, and it was accompanied by a postural adjustment of the whole body which included a lowering of the head, raising of the pelvis, and a slight weight shift to the left in order to maintain equilibrium on only three legs. The electrical stimulation did not produce any emotional disturbance, and the cat was as alert and friendly as usual, rubbing its head against the experimenter, seeking to be petted, and purring. However, if we tried to prevent the evoked effect by holding the left hind leg with our hands, the cat stopped purring, struggled to get free, and shook its leg. Apparently the evoked motility was not unpleasant, but attempts to prevent it were disturbing for the animal. The artificial driving of motor activities was accepted in such a natural way by the animal that often there was spontaneous initiative to cooperate with the electrical command. For example, during a moment of precarious balance when all paws were close together, stimulation produced first a postural adjustment, and the cat spread its forelegs to

15

achieve equilibrium by shifting its body weight to the right, and only after this delay did the left hind leg begin to flex. It was evident that the animal was not in a hurry and was taking its time to prepare its position for the induced movement. Preliminary adjustments were not seen if the cat's posture was already adequate for the required motor performance. In other cases, when the animal was lying down with its hind legs already flexed, the stimulation effect was greatly diminished and consisted mainly of increased muscular tension.

In cases of conflict between the free movements of the animal and those elicited by the experimenter, the final result depended on the relative strength of opposing signals. Stimulations of the cruciate sulcus at threshold level of 1.2 mA, which produced a small leg flexion, were ineffective if applied while the cat was walking. To test stronger conflicts, the cat was enticed into jumping off a table to reach food placed on the floor, and, while it was in the air, the cruciate sulcus was electrically stimulated. In this situation, intensities of up to 1.5 mA, which usually evoked a clear motor response, were completely ineffective; physiological activity seemed to override the artificial excitation and the cat landed with perfectly coordinated movements. If the intensity was increased to 2 mA, stimulation effects were prepotent over voluntary activities; leg flexion started during the jump, coordination was disrupted, and the cat landed badly.

A variety of motor effects have been evoked in different species, including cat, dog, bull, and monkey. The animals could be induced to move the legs, raise or lower the body, open or close the mouth, walk or lie still, turn around, and perform a variety of responses with predictable reliability, as if they were electronic toys under human control (see figs. 1-6). Behavior elicited by electrical stimulation was not always comparable to spontaneous activity. In a few experiments, movements beyond the animal's voluntary control were observed, such as the clockwise rotation of the eye. In other cases, abnormal responses, disorganized contractions, and loss of equilibrium have also been induced, depending on the cerebral area and parameters of stimulation.

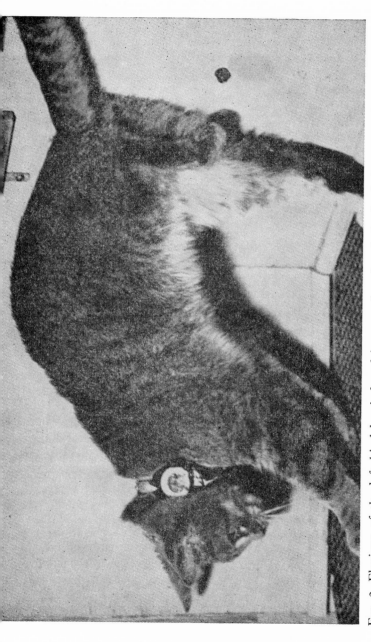

Fig. 2. Flexions of the left hind leg induced in a cat by electrical stimulation of the cruciate sulcus. This evoked effect is not unpleasant for the animal and may interact with spontaneous activities. Observe the good postural adaptations and the peaceful attitude of the cat.

Complex Behavior

Normal activities in animals are not confined to simple motor responses such as hind-leg flexion but include a succession of different acts such as body displacement and social interaction. In order to study these complex activities, which require a situation as free and normal as possible, our experimental design included (1) the establishment of a colony with four to six monkeys, (2) the continuous recording of spontaneous and evoked behavior by time-lapse photography, in order to qualify and quantify individual and social actions, and (3) stimulation of the animals by remote control. The behavior of a group of monkeys is an entertaining spectacle, and a few minutes' observation gives the impression that their playing, grooming, chasing, and comic activities are rather unpredictable. Long-term studies, however, have shown that individual and social behavior is predictable within a known range of variability. The study of group behavior is possible precisely because of the recurrence of patterns that can be identified. Every day the monkeys will eat, play, groom, pick, sit, and perform a series of acts which can be analyzed and qualified (Delgado, 1962). After the individual profiles of behavior are established, the responses evoked by electrical stimulation of the brain may be precisely evaluated.

A typical example of complex behavior was observed in a monkey named Ludi while she was forming part of a colony with two other females and two males. Ludi was an aggressive female who dominated the whole group and exercised the usual prerogatives of being the chief, enjoying greater territoriality and more food, and moving freely around the colony. After different areas of the brain had been studied under restraint, the radio stimulator was strapped to Ludi, and excitations of the rostral part of the red nucleus were started, with the monkey free in her colony. Stimulation produced the following complex sequence of responses (fig. 4): (1) immediate interruption of spontaneous activities, (2) change in facial expression, (3) head turning to the right, (4) standing on two feet, (5) circling to the right, (6) walking on two feet with perfect preservation of equilibrium by balancing the arms, touching the walls of the

17

cage, or grasping the swings, (7) climbing a pole on the back wall of the cage, (8) descending to the floor, (9) low tone vocalization, (10) threatening attitude directed toward subordinate monkeys, (11) changing of attitude and peacefully approaching some other members of the colony, and (12) resump-

FIG. 3. Yawning evoked in the monkey by radio stimulation of the pars magno cellularis of the red nucleus. Observe the spontaneous qualities of the evoked effect and also the fact that when the monkey is asleep the response diminishes.

tion of the activity interrupted by the stimulation. The whole sequence was repeated again and again, as many times as the red nucleus was stimulated. Responses 1 to 8 developed during the five seconds of stimulation and were followed, as aftereffects, by responses 9 to 12 which lasted from five to 10 seconds. The excitations were repeated every minute for one hour, and results were highly consistent on different days. The responses resembled spontaneous activities, were well organized, and always maintained the described sequence. Climbing followed but never preceded turning of the body; vocalization followed but never preceded walking on two feet; the general pattern was similar in different stimulations, but the details of motor performance varied and were adjusted to existing circumstances. For example, if the stimulation surprised the animal with one arm around the vertical pole in the cage, the first part of the evoked response was to withdraw the arm in order to make the turn possible. While walking on two feet, the monkey was well oriented and was able to avoid obstacles in its path and to react according to the social situation. In some experiments, three monkeys in the colony were simultaneously radio-stimulated in the red nucleus, and all three performed the full behavioral sequence without interfering with one another. Changes in the experimental situation could modify the evoked response, as shown in the case of external threat to the colony. Waving the catching net or a pair of leather gloves on one side of the home cage induced a precipitous escape of all monkeys to the other side. Red-nucleus stimulation applied at this moment was ineffective and did not interfere with the escape of the animals. In other experiments, after being deprived of food for 24 hours, the animals were offered bananas and oranges which they grabbed and ate voraciously. During this time, Ludi's response to radio stimulation of the red nucleus was completely absent or was reduced to only a short turn. In one long experiment, excitation of the red nucleus was repeated every minute, day and night, for two weeks, with a total of more than 20,000 stimulations. The remarkable reliability of responses was demonstrated throughout the whole period, with the following significant exception. During the day, monkeys take several naps, and during the night

Fig. 4. As mentioned in the text, a sequence of effects including walking on two feet may be evoked by radio stimulation of the red nucleus.

they have a long period of sleep which is interrupted by several periods of general activity. Time-lapse recordings showed that, as the stimulated monkey was falling asleep, the evoked responses progressively diminished until only a small head movement remained. As soon as the stimulated animal awoke, the responses reappeared with all of their complexity. This finding indicates that the effects evoked by cerebral stimulation are not inflexible and rigid, but may adapt to changes in the physiological situation. Examples of other patterns of sequential behavior have been evoked by excitation of several diencephalic and mesencephalic structures (Delgado, 1963a, 1964a, 1964b), showing that sequential activities are anatomically represented in several parts of the central nervous system.

Social Interaction

The social interaction of animals requires continuous mutual adaptation, and activities depend on a variety of factors, including sensory inputs, problem-solving capacity, emotional background, previous experience, conditioning, drives, instincts, and intelligent integration of all these processes. In spite of the extraordinary complexity of these supporting mechanisms, there is experimental evidence that electrical stimulation of specific areas of the brain may influence social interaction such as contactual relations, hierarchical situations, submissive manifestations, sexual activity, aggressive behavior, and social fear. By definition, this type of research requires at least two animals which can interact with each other, but the study of groups is naturally preferable.

In 1928 Hess demonstrated that during electrical stimulation of the periventricular gray matter, cats responded as if threatened by a dog, with dilatation of the pupils, flattening of the ears, piloerection, growling, and well-directed blows with unsheathed claws. Similar offensive-defensive reactions have been described by several authors (see bibliography in Delgado, 1964a), but it was debatable whether the apparently enraged animal was aware of its own behavior and whether the evoked reactions were purposefully oriented; in other words, if the

20

observed phenomena were true or false rage. Today it is known that both types of rage may be elicited, depending on the location of the stimulated points, and we have conclusive evidence that, in cats and monkeys, well-organized behavior may be evoked by stimulation of the amygdala, posteroventral nucleus of the thalamus, fimbria of the fornix, tectal area, central gray, and other cerebral structures. The fact that one animal can be electrically driven to fight against another has been established (Delgado, 1955a). In this experiment, stimulation of the tectal area in a male cat evoked the well-known pattern of offensive-defensive reactions. When this animal was placed on a testing stage in the company of a larger cat, they enjoyed friendly relations, lying close to each other and purring happily until the smaller cat was stimulated in the tectal area. At this moment, it started growling, unsheathed its claws, and launched a fierce attack against the larger animal which flattened its ears, withdrew a few steps, and retaliated with powerful blows. The fight continued as long as the stimulation was applied. The effect could be repeated, and the stimulated cat always took the initiative in spite of the fact that it was smaller and was always overpowered in the battle. After several stimulations, a state of mistrust was created between the two animals, and they watched each other with hostility.

Similar experiments were repeated later in a colony formed by six cats. When one of them was radio-stimulated in the tectal area, it started prowling around looking for fights with the other subordinate animals, but avoiding one of them which was the most powerful of the group. It was evident that brain stimulation had created a state of increased aggressiveness, but it was also clear that the cat directed its hostility intelligently, choosing the enemy and the moment of attack, changing tactics and adapting its motions to the motor reaction of the attacked animal. In this case, brain stimulation seemed to determine the affective state of hostility, but the behavioral performance seemed dependent on the individuality of the stimulated animal, including its learned skills and previous experiences. Stimulation that increased aggressiveness was usually tested for only five to 10 seconds, but, as it was important to determine the fatigability of

21

the effect, a longer experiment was performed by reducing the intensity to a level which did not evoke overt rage. The experimental subject was an affectionate cat which usually sought petting and purred while it was held in the experimenter's arms. When it was introduced into the colony with five other cats, a low-intensity radio stimulation of the amygdala was applied continuously for two hours during which the animal's behavior was affected. It withdrew to a corner of the cage and sat there motionless, uttering barely audible growls from time to time. If any other cat approached, the stimulated animal started hissing and threatening, and, if the experimenter tried to pet him, the growls increased in intensity and the animal often spat and hissed. This hostile attitude disappeared as soon as the stimulation was over, and the cat became as friendly as before. These experiments demonstrated that brain stimulation could modify animals' reactions toward normal sensory perceptions by a modulating of the quality of the responses. The effect was similar to the modifications of spontaneous behavior observed in normal emotional states.

Monkeys offer better opportunities than cats for the study of social interaction because of their more numerous and skillful spontaneous activities. It is well known that these animals form autocratic societies, where one establishes himself as boss of the group, claiming a large amount of the living quarters as his territory, feeding first, and being avoided by the others, which usually express their submissiveness by typical actions such as grimacing, crouching, and presenting. In several of our monkey colonies, we demonstrated that radio stimulation of the posteroventral nucleus of the thalamus and central gray increased the aggressiveness of the stimulated animal and affected the social hierarchy. Stimulation of the boss monkey induced well-directed attacks against the other members of the group, which were chased around and occasionally bitten, but it was evident that the orientation of the evoked response was influenced by previous experiences. During stimulation, the boss usually attacked and chased the male monkeys which represented a challenge to his authority, but he did not threaten the female who was his favorite partner. These results confirmed the finding in cat colonies that aggressiveness induced by cerebral stimulations was not blind and automatic, but selective and intelligently directed.

Rhesus monkeys are destructive and dangerous creatures which do not hesitate to bite anything within reach, including leads, instrumentation, and occasionally the experimenter's hands. Would it be possible to tame these ferocious animals by means of electrical stimulation? To investigate this question, a monkey was strapped to a chair where it made faces and threatened the investigator until the rostral part of the caudate nucleus was electrically stimulated. At this moment, the monkey lost its aggressive expression and did not try to grab or bite the experimenter, who could safely put a finger into its mouth! As soon as stimulation was discontinued, the monkey was as aggressive as before. Later, similar experiments were repeated with the monkeys free inside the colony, and it was evident that their autocratic social structure could be manipulated by radio stimulation. In one case in which the boss monkey was excited in the caudate nucleus with 1.5 mA for five seconds every minute, after several minutes the other monkeys started to circulate more freely around the cage, often in proximity to the boss, and from time to time they crowded him without fear. The intermittent stimulation continued for one hour, and during this time the territoriality of the boss dropped to zero, his walking time was diminished, and he performed no aggressive acts against the other members of the colony. About 12 minutes after the stimulation hour ended, the boss had reasserted his authority, and his territoriality seemed to be as well established as during the control period. In other experiments, monkeys instead of investigators controlled the activation of radio stimulation. In this situation, subordinate animals learned to press a lever in the cage which triggered stimulation of the boss monkey in the caudate nucleus, inhibiting his aggressive behavior (fig. 5; Delgado, 1963c). Inhibitory effects have been demonstrated in several species including brave bulls, as shown in figure 6 (Delgado, et al., 1964).

A different type of effect was demonstrated in another monkey colony. Radio stimulation of the nucleus medialis dorsalis of the thalamus in a female monkey produced a sequential pat-

FIG. 5. Monkeys may learn to press a lever in order to stimulate by radio the brain of another aggressive animal and in this way to avoid his attack. Heterostimulation in monkey colonies demonstrates the possibility of instrumental control of social behavior.

tern of behavior characterized by a movement of the head, walking on all fours, jumping to the back wall of the cage for two or three seconds, jumping down to the floor, and walking back to the starting point. At this moment, she was approached by the boss of the colony and she stood on all fours, raised her tail and was grasped and mounted by the boss in a manner indistinguishable from spontaneous mounting. This entire behavioral sequence was repeated once every minute following each stimulation, and a total of 81 mountings was recorded in a 90-minute period, while no other mountings were recorded on the same day. As is natural in social interaction, the evoked responses affected not only the animal with cerebral electrodes, but also other members of the colony.

Analysis of Evoked Motor Behavior

The experimental evidence presented in the previous pages clearly demonstrates that electrical stimulation of the brain can induce predictable behavioral performance similar to spontaneous activities. Understanding the significance of these findings requires analysis of the physiological mechanisms involved in voluntary movements. A simple act such as leg flexion requires the precise and progressive contraction of several muscles in which the strength, speed, and amplitude of activation of many motor units are determined by the processing of messages coming from joints and muscle spindles integrated with another vast amount of information circulating through the central nervous system. The complexity of neuronal events is even greater during performance of sequential responses, in which timing and motor correlations must be adjusted to the purpose of the movement and adapted to changes in the environment. Mechanisms responsible for the physiological excitation of spontaneous motility must be highly sophisticated. In contrast, electrical stimulation of the brain is very simple and depends on primitive techniques that apply a train of pulses without modulation, without code, without specific meaning, and without feedback to a group of neurons which by chance are situated within an artificially created field. In view of the complexity of neuronal

Fig. 6. A bull in full charge may be suddenly stopped by radio stimulation of the anterior part of the thalamus.

26

integrations, it is not surprising that a few authors have down-graded the significance of stimulation effects. How can we explain the contradiction between the crudeness of these excitations and the refinement of the responses that they can elicit?

When considering whether a simple electrical stimulus could be the cause of the many events of a behavioral response, we could ask whether a finger pushing a button to launch a man into orbit is responsible for the complicated machinery or for the sequence of operations. Evidently the finger, like a simple stimulus, is only the trigger of a programmed series of events, and consequently electrical charges applied to the brain cannot be accepted as the direct cause of leg flexion or aggression. The effect of electricity is simply to depolarize some neural membranes and to initiate a chain reaction. We must remember that even at the neuronal level, electrical excitation is not responsible for the many biochemical, enzymatic, thermal, and electrical processes which accompany the evoked action potentials. Evoked effects, like other chain reactions, depend more on the functional properties of the activated structures than on the starter. If electrical stimulation is considered as a non-specific trigger, our discussion must be focused on *what* is triggered. Why do movements start, develop, and end? Which motor mechanisms are involved within the brain? These basic neurophysiological questions are very difficult to answer because of our limited knowledge, but at least we now have some new tools to initiate their study, and experimental hypotheses to guide future research.

A tentative explanation of some of the mechanisms involved in motor activities has been proposed in the theory of fragmental representation of behavior (Delgado, 1964a) which postulates that behavior is organized as fragments which have anatomical and functional reality within the brain, where they can be the subject of experimental analysis. The different fragments may be combined in different sequences like the notes of a melody, resulting in a succession of motor acts which constitute specific behavioral categories such as licking, climbing, or walking. The theory may perhaps be clarified with one example. If I wish to take a cookie from the table, this wish may be considered as a force called *the starter* because it will determine the initiation of

27

a **series** of motor acts. The starter includes drives, **motivations,** emotional perceptions, memories, and other processes. To take the cookie it is necessary to organize a motor plan, a mechanical strategy, and to decide among several motor choices, because the cookie may be taken with the left or right hand, directly with the mouth, or even by using the feet if one has simian skills. Choice, strategies, motor planning, and adjustments depend on a set of cerebral structures, *the organizer,* which is different from the set employed by the starter, because the desire for cookies may exist in hungry people or in completely paralyzed patients, and the hands can move and reach the table for many different reasons even if there are no cookies. Finally, the actual contraction of muscles for the performance of the selected movement to reach the cookie—for example, using the right hand—depends on a cerebral set, *the performer,* different from the previous two, because motor representation of hands, mouth, and feet is situated in different areas of the brain, and the choice of muscle group to be activated is under the supervision of a given organizer. Naturally, there is a close correlation among these three basic mechanisms, and also between them and other cerebral functions. The concept of a brain center as a visible anatomical locus is unacceptable in modern physiology, but the participation of a constellation of neuronal groups (a functional set) in a specific act is more in agreement with our present knowledge. The functional set may be formed by the neurons of nuclei far from one another: for instance, in the cerebellum, motor cortex, pallidum, thalamus, and red nucleus, forming a circuit in close mutual dependence, and responsible for a determined act such as picking up a cookie with the right hand.

If we accept the existence of anatomical representation of the three functional sets: starter, organizer, and performer, it is logical that they can be activated by different types of triggers, and that the evoked results will be related to the previous experiences linked to the set. The same set, evoking a similar behavioral response, may be activated by physiological stimuli, such as sensory perceptions and ideations, or by artificial stimuli, such as electrical impulses. Depending on the location of contacts, when we stimulate the brain through implanted electrodes we can activate the starter, the organizer, or the performer of different behavioral reactions, so that natural and artificial stimuli may interplay with one another, as has been experimentally demonstrated.

These theoretical considerations may facilitate the understanding of so-called willful, free, or spontaneous activity. Obviously, the will is not responsible for the chemistry of muscle contraction, for the electrical processes of neural transmission, or even for the intimate organization of movements; these phenomena depend on spindle discharges, cerebellar activation, synaptic junctions, reciprocal inhibitions, and other subconscious mechanisms. Voluntary activity is initiated by a physiological trigger which activates a chain of preformed mechanisms which exist independently inside the brain. The uniqueness of voluntary behavior lies in its wealth of starters, each one of which depends on a vast and unknown integration of past experiences and present receptions. However, the organizers and performers are probably activated in a similar manner by the will and by electrical means, providing the possibility of investigating experimentally some of the basic mechanisms of spontaneous behavior.

One limitation of electrical activation of behavior is the anatomical variability of the brain. Just as there are external physical differences between individuals, there are variations in the shape and size of our cerebral structures which make it impossible to place an electrical contact in exactly the same location in different subjects. Another important limitation is functional variability. The organization of brain physiology depends to a great extent on individual experience which determines the establishment of many temporary or permanent associations among neuronal fields. For example, the sound of a bell is neutral for a naive animal, but will induce secretion of saliva if it has previously been paired with food, and stimulation of the auditory cortex should increase salivary secretion only in the conditioned animal. Anatomical and functional variabilities are the bases for the differences in individual personalities. When we stimulate the motor cortex, we can predict the appearance of a movement but not the details of its performance, indicating that the effects elicited by electrical stimulation of the brain have a statistical but not an individual determination.

Electrical Driving of Mental Functions in Man

Elemental psychic phenomena such as hunger and fear can be analyzed in both animal and man, but processes like ideation and imagery that are expressed verbally can be studied only in human beings. The most extensive information on this subject has been obtained by Penfield and his group (see, for instance, Penfield and Jasper, 1954) during surgical operations for epilepsy, tumors, or other illnesses. In these procedures, the brain was exposed under local anesthesia and stimulated electrically under direct visual control. More recently, as explained in a previous section, electrodes have been implanted in the brain for days or weeks, permitting repeated studies in a relaxed atmosphere, with the patient in bed or sitting comfortably in a chair. From Penfield's publications and from implanted-electrode studies, a considerable amount of information has demonstrated that brain stimulation may induce anxiety, fear, hostility, pleasure, feelings of loneliness, distortion of sensory perception, recollection of the past, hallucinations, and other psychic manifestations. From all this material, I shall select several representative examples dealing mainly with ideation, which is perhaps the most interesting and least understood of the mental processes.

Speech Increase

Patient A. F. was an 11-year-old boy committed to an institution because of his uncontrollable epileptic seizures and destructive behavior (see Higgins *et al.*, 1956). Since his response to drugs and treatment was unsatisfactory, brain surgery was decided upon. To direct the operation, four electrode assemblies were implanted in the temporal lobes for six days. During this time, intracerebral activity was recorded, and several spontaneous seizures were registered. Exploration of the patient included several tape-recorded interviews of from one and a half to two hours, behavioral observations, and 69 intracerebral stimulations.

30

Study of the collected data indicated the existence of a focus of abnormality in the left temporal tip, and this area was successfully removed. Recovery from surgery was uneventful, and in a few weeks the boy was able to enjoy a normal life and return to school. Five years later he was still seizure-free.

In our investigations, the conversations between patient and therapist were tape-recorded while the spontaneous electrical activity of the brain was also being registered, and programmed stimulations were applied to different cerebral points. The general procedure was explained to the patient, but, to avoid possible psychological influences, he was not informed of the exact moment of the stimulations. To establish behavioral and electrical correlations, the recorded interviews were transcribed, divided into periods of two minutes, and analyzed by two independent investigators who counted the number of words and identified and quantified the verbal expressions according to 39 different categories. Table 1 shows the stimulation effects on verbal production. During this interview, the patient was quiet and spoke only four to 17 words every two minutes. Whenever point RP 1-2 was stimulated, the patient's attitude changed; he became more animated, and his verbal output increased sharply to a mean of 88 words per two-minute period.

TABLE 1
(From Higgins, Mahl, Delgado, and Hamlin, 1956)

Stimulations Time interval	RP 1-2 (N-7) 2'Postim. 2'Prestim.		t-Test P-Value	All Others Stimulations (N-7) 2'Postim. 2'Prestim.		t-Test P-Value
Mean % friendly remarks	6	53	0.02	17	10	—[a]
Mean N words by patient	17	88	<0.01	4	9	0.15
Mean N words by Int.	43	46	—[a]	16	30	>0.30

[a]Insignificant by inspection.

These effects were repeated seven times, and in each stimulation the patient appeared to be especially optimistic, emphasizing the pleasant side of sensory perceptions and the happy aspects of his memories and ideas, with many of his comments affectionately directed and personally related to the therapist. Verbal expression was spontaneous in character, his usual personal style and phraseology were preserved, and conversational topics were related to the experimental situation without a preferred theme. Table 1 shows that the evoked increase of words and of friendly remarks were highly significant, as evaluated by the t-test, and also that the effect was specific because it was not produced by stimulation of other cerebral points.

Sexual Ideation

In three different patients, thoughts and expressions with sexual content were induced by electrical stimulation of the temporal lobe. The first case, S. S., was an intelligent and attractive woman, 32 years old, who had suffered from uncontrollable epileptic attacks for several years. During the interviews she was usually reserved, but the first time that point A in the second temporal convulsion was excited with 6 volts, she became visibly affected, holding the hands of the therapist to express her fondness for him and to thank him for all his efforts. Several minutes later, after another stimulation of the same point, she started to say how much she would like to be cured so that she might marry, and other stimulations of point A were also followed by flirtatious conversation. The provocative play and ideas expressed under stimulation of point A did not appear following stimulation of other cerebral points and contrasted with this woman's usually reserved spontaneous behavior.

The second patient, V. P., was a woman 36 years old who had suffered from epilepsy since childhood. Point C in the temporal lobe was excited five times at intervals of from five to 10 minutes, and after each stimulation the patient's mood became friendlier; she smiled, questioned the therapist directly about his nationality, background, and friends, and declared that he "was nice," that his country (Spain) "must be very beautiful," that "Spaniards are very attractive," and she ended with the statement "I would like to marry a Spaniard." This particular train of thought and manner of speaking seemed completely spontaneous, but it appeared only after stimulation of point C in the temporal lobe, and no such shift to a flirtatious mood was noted in her spontaneous conversations following stimulations of other cerebral points.

The third case of evoked change in sexual ideology was a young epileptic boy, A. F., who, following stimulation of point LP 5-6 in the left temporal cortex, suddenly began to discuss his desire to get married. After subsequent stimulations of the point, he elaborated on this subject, revealed doubts about his sexual identity, and voiced a thinly veiled wish to marry the male interviewer.

Experiential Hallucinations

Hallucinations evoked by electrical stimulation of the brain have been lucidly described by Roberts (1961), who wrote: "It is as though a wire recorder, or a strip of cinematographic film with sound track, had been set in motion within the brain. A previous experience—its sights and sounds and the thoughts— seems to pass through the mind of the patient on the operating table. . . . At the same time he is conscious of the present. . . . The recollection of the experiential sequence stops suddenly when the electric current ceases. But it can again be activated with reapplication of the electric current." The hallucination may develop during the stimulation, with a normal-like progression of movements and sounds, which appear more real and vivid than when the events actually happened. It is as if the patient had a double life, one in the past recalled by the electrical stimulation, and another in the present, perceiving all the sensory stimulation of the surroundings, but both with a similar quality of reality, as if the person had a "double consciousness" of subjective sensations. In some cases, components of the hallucination are completely new and do not belong to the subject's past experience, but usually, as Penfield (1952, 1958, 1960) emphasized, the responses are a detailed reenactment of previous experiences, an exact "flash-back" activation of memories.

In one of our patients with intracerebral electrodes, detailed study of the tape-recorded interviews demonstrated that the perceptual content of some experiential responses was related to the patient's thoughts at the moment of stimulation. For example, when the patient was talking about her daughter's desire for a baby sister, a stimulation was applied to the temporal lobe and the patient heard a female voice saying "I got a baby—sister." Baldwin (1960) has reported a similar observation in which the content of visual hallucinatory responses evoked in a 28-year-old man varied with the sex and identity of the observer seated before him in the operating room. In a previous article (Mahl *et al.*, 1964) we have suggested that "The patient's 'mental content' at the time of stimulation is a determinant of the content of the resulting hallucinatory experiences," and we offered the so-called "altered-state hypothesis" in which the essential effect of stimulation is to alter the state of consciousness of the patient in such a way that primary process thinking replaces secondary process thinking. (See Freud, 1900.) According to this hypothesis, the electrical stimulation of the temporal lobe would not activate memory traces in the ganglionic record, as postulated by Penfield, but would induce a state of consciousness which would increase the functional probability of primary processes.

Pleasure

The possibility that "pleasure centers" might exist in the brain was supported by the extensive work of Olds and his collaborators (1954, 1956, 1961), who demonstrated that rats prefer to stimulate some points of their brains by pressing a treadle, rather than to satisfy drives of hunger, thirst, and sex. Positive behavioral qualities of cerebral stimulation have been confirmed in other species including the cat (Sidman *et al.*, 1955) and the monkey (Bursten and Delgado, 1958). However, "pleasure" has an experiential factor which animals cannot report because they lack verbal communication. Only studies in humans could reveal whether electrical stimulation of the brain is able to induce pleasurable sensations. The study of patients with implanted electrodes yielded affirmative evidence (Delgado, 1960; Sem-Jacobsen and Torkildsen, 1960). In one of our cases, stimulation of the temporal lobe evoked "pleasant tingling sensations of the body" which were openly declared to be very enjoyable. The patient's mood changed from its usual peaceful state to one of giggling and laughing. She teased the doctor and made fun of the experimental situation with humorous comments.

In another patient, temporal-lobe stimulation evoked "statements avowing his pleasure at being 'up here' and 'subject to us' which were classified as 'passive compliance' " (Higgins *et al.*, 1956). For example, when the patient had been silent for five minutes, a point in the temporal cortex was stimulated and he immediately exclaimed, "Hey! You can keep me longer here when you give me these; I like those," and he insisted that the "brain wave" testing made him "feel O.K." Similar statements followed stimulation of other temporal points, but were never expressed spontaneously in the absence of excitations. The statistical significance of these results was P <0.001, as contrasted by X^2 analysis.

During increased pleasure, the subjects were oriented mainly toward themselves, and they often reported experiencing agreeable physical sensations, while during artificially increased speech and changes in sexual ideology they expressed friendliness for the nearby people. In both cases, there was a shift of emotional mood to a happy interpretation of reality, and this experience was interpreted by the patient as spontaneous and valid, usually without being directly related to the stimulation. A shift from pleasurable thinking to friendliness and to sexual ideas has been observed in some cases.

Consequences of Brain Control

Probably the most significant conclusion derived from electrical stimulation of the awake brain is that functions traditionally related to the psyche such as friendliness, pleasure, and verbal expression can be induced, modified, and inhibited by direct stimulation of cerebral structures. This discovery may be compared with the revolutionary finding almost two centuries ago that contraction of frog muscle may be induced by electricity without need of the soul's "animal spirits," because experimental analysis of mental functions can now proceed without implicating metaphysical entities. Research concerning the electrical driving of emotions, anatomical correlates of memory, or electrical signals related to learning does not interfere with personal ideas about the natural or supernatural destiny of man and does not involve theological questions, which should be disassociated from neurophysiological inquiry. In addition to electrical stimulation, there are now techniques for exploration of brain function which include electrical recording, chemical stimulation, intracerebral chemistry, and electron microscopy. The task that we are facing is the correlation of neuro-anatomy and physiology with mental functions; the investigation of cerebral areas involved in psychic manifestations; the analysis of their electrical and chemical background; and the development of methods to induce or inhibit specific activities of the mind.

Already we know that some structures, including the hypothalamus, amygdala, central, gray, and temporal lobe, are involved in emotional phenomena, while other areas, such as the parietal cortex, do not seem to participate in psychic experience. Brain research has expanded rapidly in recent years with the creation of institutes for multidisciplinary studies, but this field should attract even more of our intellectual and economic resources. Human behavior, happiness, good, and evil are, after all, products of cerebral physiology. In my opinion, it is necessary to shift the center of scientific research from the study and control of natural elements to the analysis and patterning of mental activities. There is a sense of urgency in this redirection because the most important problem of our present age is the reorganization of man's social relations. While the mind of future generations will be formed by pedagogic, cultural, political, and philosophical factors, it is also true that education is based on the transmission of behavioral, emotional, and intellectual patterns related to still unknown neurophysiological mechanisms. Investigators will not be able to prevent the clash of conflicting desires or ideologies, but they can discover the neuronal mechanisms of anger, hate, aggressiveness, or territoriality, providing clues for the direction of emotions and for the education of more sociable and less cruel human beings. The precarious race between intelligent brains and unchained atoms must be won if the human race is going to survive, and learning the biological mechanisms of social relations will favor the cerebral victory.

Electrical and chemical analyses of mental functions have introduced new facts into the much debated problem of mind-brain relations. In the interpretation of data, we should remember that spike potentials, neurohumors, and synaptic transmitters may represent happiness and sorrow, love and hate, war and peace, and in the near future we can expect to find answers to classical questions concerning psychological aspects of the physical brain. How can electrical stimulation of the temporal lobe be felt as pleasure, music, or fear? Why is a ferocious monkey tamed by applying a few volts of electricity to its caudate nucleus? As discussed in a previous article (Delgado, 1964b), psychophysical correlations may be related to the two elements which transmit information in the nervous system, namely, the *material carrier* and the *symbolic meaning*. In the reception of sensory inputs, there is an initial *electrical coding* which is the carrier necessary for neural circulation of impulses. When a monkey, a savage, or a civilized man looks at a pencil, the received visual stimulus is transformed into electrical signals and transmitted through optic pathways to the brain. At the levels of retina and optic nerve, the coding of the stimulus depends on the visual input, independent of its possible meaning. Symbolism is created by the association within the brain of two or more sensory receptions or of present and past experiences, but it does not depend on the material structure of the object or on the pattern of its electrical coding. For a naive monkey or for a savage, the pencil is a neutral object; for a writer, the pencil is full of associations, uses, and meaning. Symbolism is not intrinsic in the object, nor inborn in the brain: it must be learned. The most important symbolic tool of the mind, language, is not invented by each individual; it is a cultural gift of the species. The symbolic meaning may be considered an *immaterial element of mental functions* in the sense that it is related to a spatio-temporal association between two or more sensory receptions and not to the material structure of the inputs. The elements for symbolic recognition already exist in the electrical code of the transmitted signals; however, they are not determined by the pattern of the code but by spatio-temporal relations between present and past codes which cannot be deciphered by any instrument if the refer-

37

ence point of the past is not known. These temporal and spatial relations may be considered as material or immaterial, depending on the investigator's point of view. Obviously, the relations depend on the material existence of some events, but, at the same time, the relations are independent of the material organization of each event. It is a question of definition, and, if we explain the meaning of our terms, there is no conflict. I think, however, that it is more practical to consider symbolism as *non* material in order to emphasize the relativity of its existence and the fact that it does not depend on the intrinsic qualities of matter but on the previous history of the object and of the observer. In the last analysis, behavior could be reduced to movement of atoms, but if we are discussing the emotional behavior of the monkey, it would be difficult to explain it in terms of orbiting particles, and it is far more useful to employ psychological concepts. It should be clarified that, in the observer, conscious understanding of meaning is probably dependent upon progressive steps of electrical subcoding of sensory inputs with the creation of new material and symbolic elements related to the activation of a new series of chemical and electrical phenomena affecting specialized neurons. However, the distinction between material carrier and symbolic meaning simplifies the interpretation of neurophysiological data, because analysis of events in receptors and in transmitting pathways will provide information about the carrier but not about symbols. At the same time, it should be expected that electrical stimulation of neuronal groups may activate processes related to both material carriers and symbolic meaning. This working hypothesis may help in the differentiation between cerebral mechanisms responsible for transmitting inputs and for cognitive processes of received signals.

From its beginning, wiring of the human brain aroused emotional opposition even among scientists, while similar wiring of the heart or of the bladder has been received enthusiastically. The difference in attitude was no doubt related to a more or less conscious personal fear that our identity could be attacked and that our mind could be controlled. Personal traits such as friendliness, sexual inclination, or hostility have already been modified during cerebral stimulation, and we can foresee other influences on emotional tone and behavioral reactions. Electricity is only a trigger of pre-existing mechanisms which could not, for example, teach a person to speak Spanish, although it could arouse memories expressed in Spanish if they were already stored in the brain.

Entering into the field of speculation, I would like to comment on one question which has already caused widespread concern. Would it be feasible to control the behavior of a population by electrical stimulation of the brain? From the times of slavery and galleys up to the present forced-labor camps, man has certainly tried to control the behavior of other human beings. In civilized life, the intervention of governments in our private biology has become so deeply rooted that in general we are not aware of it. Many countries, including the United States, do not allow a bride and groom to marry until blood has been drawn from their veins to prove the absence of syphilis. To cross international borders, it is necessary to certify that a scarification has been made on the skin and inoculated with smallpox. In many cities, the drinking water contains fluoride to strengthen our teeth, and table salt is fortified with iodine to prevent thyroid misfunction. These intrusions into our private blood, teeth, and glands are accepted, practiced, and enforced. Naturally, they have been legally introduced, are useful for the prevention of illness, and do generally benefit society and individuals, but they have established a precedent of official manipulation of our personal biology, introducing the possibility that governments could try to control general behavior or to increase the happiness of citizens by electrically influencing their brains. Fortunately, this prospect is remote, if not impossible, not only for obvious ethical reasons, but also because of its impracticability. Theoretically it would be possible to regulate aggressiveness, productivity, or sleep by means of electrodes implanted in the brain, but this technique requires specialized knowledge, refined skills, and a detailed and complex exploration in each individual, because of the existence of anatomical and physiological variability. The feasibility of mass control of behavior by brain stimulation is very unlikely, and the application of intracerebral electrodes in man will probably remain highly individualized and

39

restricted to medical practice. Clinical usefulness of electrode implantation in epilepsy and involuntary movements has already been proved, and its therapeutical extension to behavioral disorders, anxiety, depression, and other illness is at present being explored. The increasing capacity to understand and manipulate mental functions of patients will certainly increase man's ability to influence the behavior of man.

If we discover the cerebral basis of anxiety, pleasure, aggression, and other mental functions, we shall be in a much better position to influence their development and manifestations through electrical stimulation, drugs, surgery, and especially by means of more scientifically programmed education.

These possibilities pose tremendous problems. As Skinner asked recently (1961), "Is the deliberate manipulation of a culture a threat to the very essence of man or, at the other extreme, an unfathomed source of strength for the culture which encourages it?" Scientific discoveries and technology cannot be shelved because of real or imaginary dangers, and it may certainly be predicted that the evolution of physical control of the brain and the acquisition of knowledge derived from it will continue at an accelerated pace, pointing hopefully toward the development of a more intelligent and peaceful mind of the species without loss of individual identity, and toward the exploitation of the most suitable kind of feedback mechanism: the human brain studying the human brain.

Acknowledgments

Part of the research described in this paper was supported by grants from the United States Public Health Service and the Office of Naval Research. Some of the studies were conducted during a John Simon Guggenheim fellowship. This paper is an abbreviated version of the James Arthur Lecture delivered at the American Museum of Natural History in New York, May, 1965.

Bibliography

Baldwin, M. Electrical stimulation of the mesial temporal region. Pp. 159-176 in: "Electrical Studies on the Unanesthetized Brain", E. R. Ramey and D. S. O'Doherty, (Eds.). New York: Paul B. Hoeber, 1960.

Bursten, B. and J. M. R. Delgado. Positive reinforcement induced by intracerebral stimulation in the monkey. J. comp. physiol. Psychol., 51:6-10, 1958.

Delgado, J. M. R. Prolonged stimulation of brain in awake monkeys. J. Neurophysiol., 22:458-475, 1959.

Delgado, J. M. R. Emotional behavior in animals and humans. Psychiat. Res. Rep., 12:259-271, 1960.

Delgado, J.M.R. Pharmacological modifications of social behavior. Pp. 265-292 in: "Pharmacological Analysis of Central Nervous Action," W. D. M. Paton, (Ed.), Oxford: Pergamon Press, 1962.

Delgado, J. M. R. Effect of brain stimulation on task-free situations. EEG clin. Neurophysiol., Suppl. 24, pp. 260-280, 1963a.

Delgado, J. M. R. Telemetry and telestimulation of the brain. Pp. 231-249 in: "Bio-Telemetry," L. Slater, (Ed.). New York: Pergamon Press, 1963b.

Delgado, J. M. R. Free behavior and brain stimulation. Pp. 349-449 in: "International Review of Neurobiology" Vol. VI, C. C. Pfeiffer and J. R. Smythies, (Eds.). New York: Academic Press, 1964a.

Delgado, J. M. R. Factores extracerebrales de la mente. Rev. Occidente, No. 14, pp. 131-14, 1964b.

Delgado, J. M. R., F. J. Castejón, and F. Santisteban. Radioestimation cerebral en toros de lidia. VIII Reun. Nac. Soc. Ciencias Fisiológicas. Madrid, 1964.

Ewald, J. R. Ueber künstlich erzeugte Epilepsie. Berliner klin. Wochenschr., 35: 689, 1898.

41

Fonberg, E., and J. M. R. Delgado. Avoidance and alimentary reactions during amygdala stimulation. Jour. Neurophysiol., 24:651-664, 1961.

Feindel, W. Response patterns elicited from the amygdala and deep temporo-insular cortex. Pp. 519-532 in: "Electrical Stimulation of the Brain," D. E. Sheer, (Ed.). Austin, Texas: Univ. Texas Press, 1961.

Freud, S. The interpretation of dreams. "Standard Edition of Complete Psychological Works of Sigmund Freud." Vols. 4 & 5. London: Hogarth Press, 1953.

Fritsch, G., and E. Hitzig. Ueber die elektrische Erregbarkeit des Grosshirns. Arch. Anat. Physiol., 37:300-332, 1870.

Gellhorn, E. "Autonomic Imbalance and the Hypothalamus. Implications for Physiology, Medicine, Psychology and Neuropsychiatry." Minneapolis: Univ. Minnesota Press, 1957.

Heath, R. G. "Studies in Schizophrenia. A Multidisciplinary Approach to Mind-Brain Relationships." Cambridge: Harvard Univ. Press, 1954.

Hess, W. R. Beitrage sur Physiologie d. Hirnstammes I. Die Methodik der lokalisierten Reizung und Ausschaltung subkortikalier Hirnabschnitte. Leipzig: Georg Thieme, 1932.

Hess, W. R. "Diencephalen. Autonomic and Extrapyramidal Functions." New York: Grune and Stratton, 1954.

Higgins, J. W., G. F. Mahl, J. M. R. Delgado and H. Hamlin. Behavioral changes during intracerebral electrical stimulation. Arch. Neurol. Psychiat., Chicago, 76:399-419, 1956.

Hodes, R., and H. W. Magoun. Autonomic responses to electrical stimulation of the forebrain and midbrain with special reference to the pupil. Jour. Comp. Neurol., 76:399-419, 1956.

Kaada, B. R. Somate-motor, autonomic and electrocorticographic responses to electrical stimulation of "rhinencephalic" and other structures in primates, cat and dog. Acta Physio. Scandinavica, Vol. 24, Supplement, 1961.

King, H. E. Psychological effects of excitation in the limbic system. Pp. 477-486 in: "Electrical Stimulation of the Brain," D. E. Sheer, (Ed.). Austin, Texas: Univ. Texas Press, 1961.

Mahl, G. F., A. Rothenberg, J. M. R. Delgado and H. Hamlin. Psychological responses in the human to intracerebral electric stimulation. Psychosom. Med., 26:337-368, 1964.

Olds, J. Pleasure centers in the brain. Sci. Amer., 195:105-116, 1956.

Olds, J. Differential effects of drives and drugs on self-stimulation at different brain sites. Pp. 350-356 in: "Electrical Stimulation of the Brain," D. E. Sheer, (Ed.). Austin, Texas: Univ. Texas Press, 1961.

Olds, J. and P. Milner. Positive reinforcement produced by electrical stimulation of the septal area and other regions of the rat brain. J. comp. physiol. Psychol., 47:417-428, 1954.

Penfield, W. Memory mechanisms. Arch. Neurol. Psychiat., 67:178-198, 1952.

Penfield, W. The excitable cortex in conscious man. The Sherrington Lectures V. Springfield, Illinois, C. C. Thomas, 1958.

Penfield, W. A surgeon's chance encounter with mechanisms related to consciousness. Jour. Roy. College Surgeons, 5:173, 1960.

Penfield, W. and H. Jasper. "Epilepsy and the Functional Anatomy of the Human Brain." Boston, Mass.: Little, Brown, 1954.

Roberts, L. Activation and interference of cortical functions. Pp. 533-553 in: "Electrical Stimulation of the Brain," D. E. Sheer, (Ed.). Austin, Texas: Univ. Texas Press, 1961.

Sem-Jacobsen, C. W., M. C. Petersen, H. W. Dodge, Jr., J. A. Lazarte and C. B. Holman. Electroencephalographic rhythms from the depths of the parietal, occipital and temporal lobes in man. EEG clin. Neurophysiol., 8:263-278, 1956.

Sem-Jacobsen, C. W. and A. Torkildsen. Depth recording and electrical stimulation in the human brain. Pp. 275-290 in: "Electrical Studies on the Unanesthetized Brain," E. R. Ramey and D. S. O'Doherty, (Eds.). New York: Paul B. Hoeber, 1960.

Showers, M. J. C., and E. C. Crosby. Somatic and visceral responses from the cingulate gyrus. Neurology, 8:561-565, 1958.

Sidman, M., J. V. Brady, J. J. Boren, D. G. Conrad and A. Schulman. Reward schedules and behavior maintained by intracranial self-stimulation. Science, 122:830-831, 1955.

Skinner, B. F. The design of cultures. Daedalus, pp. 534-546, 1961.

Walker, A. E. and C. Marshall. Stimulation and depth recording in man. Pp. 498-518 in: "Electrical Stimulation of the Brain." D. E. Sheer, (Ed.). Austin, Texas: Univ. Texas Press, 1961.

PSYCHOLOGY AND THE FUNCTIONAL ILLITERATE

MYRON WOOLMAN, PH.D.

The Institute of Educational Research, Washington, D.C.

Editorial Note

Few problems are more urgent than those involving the functional illiterate and his integration into the mainstream of society. One of the most promising approaches to the solution of such problems is the Progressive Choice Reading Method designed by the author of the following paper.

Dr. Myron Woolman received his B. S. (1950), M. S. (1951), and Ph. D. in Educational Psychology (1955) from Columbia University. He now serves as Director of the Institute of Educational Research, Inc., in Washington, D.C., and as Advisor to The Office of Education and The Office of Economic Opportunity.

As Chief of Proficiency Measurements at McConnell Air Force Base in Wichita, Kansas (1953-1955), Dr. Woolman developed technical training systems and designed various methods of evaluating attitudes and performance of military personnel. As Senior Scientist for The Human Resources Research Office of George Washington University (1956-1961), he investigated fundamental problems of human learning as related to organization of materials, sequence of presentation, and level of difficulty. Since 1962 he has developed a Programmed Reading Method for the Mentally Handicapped (NIMH Project No. 1010); developed and tested a reading method for urban drop-outs, pre-drop-outs and adults under the auspices of the President's Committee for Juvenile Delinquency and Youth Development; and directed a Summer Catch-Up Program in Prince Edward

County. He is the Principal Investigator in the Literacy Instructor, an OEO project designed to develop reading skills for functional illiterates and to train supervisory and teaching personnel. Dr. Woolman is active in professional societies and has written numerous articles and reports on technical subjects.

A family crisis prevented Dr. Woolman from completing his paper, but he has kindly indicated his willingness to have us publish this partial statement of his findings.

•

PSYCHOLOGY AND THE FUNCTIONAL ILLITERATE

Illiteracy denies approximately eleven percent (11%) of Americans their right to fully participate in our democratic society. The adult illiterate has a low income, unstable family relationships, and a higher probability for commitment to institutions. As has been repeatedly demonstrated, an impoverished environment results in a paucity of social and intellectual inputs and can result in spuriously low intellectual measures and personal and social inadequacies. These in turn combine to limit the development of job skills and the ultimate result is a dependent and inadequate adult who requires support through public agencies such as prisons or other institutions and/or survives as a chronic welfare client. Further, the force of moral and legal mechanisms for control over behavior is reduced on the basis of the lack of awareness and a resulting insensitivity to societal demands. Enrichment of the social environment has repeatedly produced positive changes on standardized measures. Some of the changes, as in the studies of Cooper (1960), Gault (1914), Slawson (1926), Miner (1918), Merrill (1926), Kvareceus (1945), Shulman (1938), Maller (1937), Healy and Bronner (1936), Shaw (1929, 1930, 1938), E. Glueck and S. Glueck (1950, 1952), Terman (1925), and Wechsler (1944), have been quite dramatic.

The illiterate mother has a greater number of illegitimate children than her literate peer. The illiterate inmate of a criminal institution has a greater probability of recidivism (Shaw, 1929,

46

1930, 1938; Glueck, 1935). Likewise, the school dropout is often a frustrated adolescent at the peak of his energy levels, who faces low employability and a future ridden with social parasitism (Terman, 1925; Wechsler, 1944; E. Glueck and S. Glueck, 1950, 1952). Their impulsive societal activities are largely limited to nonproductive and even destructive behavior as a consequence of low literacy levels and consequent low job skills. A report of the Subcommittee to Investigate Juvenile Delinquency of the Senate Judiciary Committee (E. Brice, 1959) stated:

> Today in many communities youth unemployment is a serious social and economic problem. Unless remedial measures are found and applied, this problem may soon reach critical proportions all over the country with a direct bearing on the youth crime rate which has risen sharply each year for the last decade. Teenagers in the labor market have the highest rate of unemployment for any age group, generally about double the national average.[1]

The questions inevitably arise as to whether these emotional castoffs are set adrift because of personal inadequacy, or whether they are unable to learn under conventional classroom methods. Conversely, if training methods were designed to provide goals perceived as more realistic in a context consistent with the needs and values of these learners, could we not anticipate a considerable educational resurgence in these resilient young people?

The Bureau of Labor Standards of the United States Department of Labor has stated:

> The teenage dropout, whether a delinquent or a nondelinquent, begins his adult life economically and socially handicapped. Since more than two-thirds of these youngsters, according to National Education Association figures, have average or above average ability, the high dropout rate is not only tragically limiting to the individuals in-

1. Edward W. Brice, "Illiteracy in a Changing America." U.S. Department of Health, Education and Welfare. Office of Education Publication OE-13605, 1959.

volved, but also is a costly waste of potential to American Society as a whole.[2]

Cultural Asynchrony

To properly understand the problem of the functionally illiterate drop-out, it is imperative to consider him in a cultural context. A term commonly used to characterize his societal condition—"cultural deprivation"—connotes a defect, or lack, or insufficiency in his cultural condition. The remedy that then follows is to bring into the functionally illiterate drop-out's world the "missing" materials.

Experience with the functionally illiterate drop-out strongly suggests that such thinking in terms of "cultural deprivation" is inaccurate and inimical to constructive solutions of the problem. The functionally illiterate drop-out is not culturally deprived, but culturally different; the problem is not one of cultural *deprivation*, but of cultural *asynchrony*.

When an individual in one sub-cultural stage lacks the behavioral repertoire necessary to transfer to the next stage, he tends to remain at the earlier stage. Thus a child who learned to obtain gratification through the use of anti-social behavior such as tantrums, crying, banging, etc., could be rejected by his Community Level age-mates as he fails to adapt to their behavioral requirements and to obtain need satisfactions outside the home and continues with the skills he learned within his Primary Home Level environment. If he continued to persist in those behavioral patterns which were successful within the Primary Home Level environment within the new Community Level sub-culture, he would be culturally asynchronous. His great success in adjusting to his home environment would operate as a barrier to meeting the requirements of the new sub-cultural system.

Thus the problem of adaptation to a modern technological society has little to do with cultural deprivation. It would appear

2. *Design for Community Action*. Bureau of Labor Standards, U.S. Department of Labor, Government Printing Office, Bulletin No. 248, 1962, p. 5.

SUCCESSIVE SUB-CULTURAL STAGES

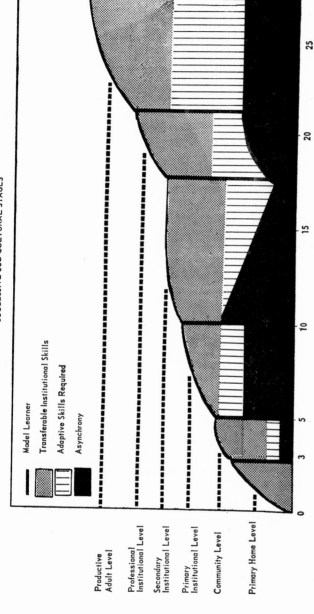

FIGURE I

49

that a rich and emotionally satisfying sub-culture exists; there is no problem of cultural deprivation. Rather, the Community Level sub-culture tends to perseverate because (1) it represents an emotionally satisfying milieu and (2) the language base, relationship to authority and the behavior norms in the Community Level sub-culture are largely asynchronous with the Institutional Level requirements. Thus the children from the urban and rural ghettoes have an enormously greater amount to learn in their first months of school than those from homes and communities which provide those aspects of the spectrum of behavior which are called for within the Institutional Level setting. Therefore, the probability of success under these conditions is so much lower for the slum dwelling child that many are so frustrated in their inability to satisfy the Institutional Level requirements that they fail to maintain involvement at the Primary Institutional Level. This in turn produces the inadequate and/or troublesome adolescent at the Secondary Institutional Level who drops out of school at his first opportunity to end ten or eleven years of a self-perception of inadequacy. The problem thus reduces to one of motivational thrust which can be employed to help those who are caught in an emotionally unsatisfying sub-culture which operates as a barrier to the achievement of their own life goals.

More formally, we may consider that to survive in our complex society, an individual must be capable of accommodating to a series of changes which are so profound that they require him to adapt to successive sub-cultural stages. He must flexibly modify his interests, values, language and overt behaviors in accordance with the requirements existing in each sub-cultural milieu.

The fact is that the functionally illiterate drop-out who is well adjusted to an earlier sub-cultural stage tends to maintain these behaviors as he gets older; his behavioral continuity (continuing Community Level behaviors in an Institutional Level setting) makes him culturally asynchronous in the school situation. Thus, it is the more fully integrated members of the ghetto community who tend to maintain their Community Level behaviors in a later phase and come into conflict with institutional authorities.

Those who are arrested in their sub-cultural development can be expected to display the following in-group reactions to the alternative sub-cultures to which they could not or would not adjust:

1. Preference for use of the parochial and restricted language of the community.
2. Interests and values directed to personal and Community Level goals. These tend to emphasize youthful activities such as athletic contests, personal dress, relative physical prowess, etc., rather than productive performance related to job skills.
3. In-group attitudes such that the external society is perceived with suspicion, hostility and fear.
4. Deep feelings of frustration and hostility based on inability to obtain either the status or the material goals possessed by those who succeeded in adapting to successive sub-cultures.

The well adjusted American adult has successfully moved through a number of complex life stages. His language, attitudes, interactions with others, and overt behaviors have shifted radically in the course of meeting the requirements of differing life contexts as he has moved from infancy to adulthood. First he learns the language and adjusts to behaviors required to obtain need satisfactions in the home. Then he must learn to conform to the language and behaviors expected from him in the immediate neighborhood. Following this he must adapt to the school society which imposes requirements to use certain kinds of language, to control impulsive behavior, and to conform to rules and authority. Finally the successful young man or woman progresses to an adult stage where the emphasis is on work skills, social interaction skills, ability to adapt to the attitudes of others, control over impulsivity and decision making skills.

The functionally illiterate drop-out may be viewed as an

individual who has failed to meet the requirements of the institutional (school) stage. In a deep sense, he has adjusted too well to the language, attitudes and behaviors of his immediate community and is unable to learn the new skills required for adaptation at the next higher life stage.

Figure I presents graphically a view of the successive subcultural stages through which an individual must adapt to successfully meet the demands of American adult life. Note that in the first three years of life the human infant learns at a phenomenal rate even though at the outset he faced a period of accommodation to an air breathing environment, recuperation from the birth ordeal, and an immense increase in the complexity of his environment. Soon after birth he adapts sufficiently to respond with those behaviors necessary to satisfy body needs and quickly evolves behaviors neatly attuned to his environmental social capsule.

During these first three years, he adapts to his primary life environment. In this vital, initial life phase he learns to generate those responses which will satisfy his existing needs. One fundamental assumption underlying this analysis is that the infant is a highly efficient organism and will therefore learn the *least* number of responses necessary to satisfy existing needs. A second learning efficiency assumption is that existing infantile response patterns will be retained until they fail to satisfy existing needs.

To make the same statement in complementary form: The human infant tends to learn new responses at a minimum rate where existing responses are sufficient to achieve those goal objects and events associated with need satisfaction. Finally, it is assumed that he modifies or shifts responses on the basis of the relationship between learning difficulty and reinforcement value.

At the first Level of Figure I the shaded pattern represents the constellation of behavioral and language skills which the infant learns in order to obtain need gratifications within the family group. By the time the child is three years of age he has developed a fairly well integrated set of values, interests, needs, language and overt behaviors which operate to minimize the amount of energy he must expend in order to maximize the number of satisfactions he receives. This body of skills represents the behavioral repertoire which he has available in moving from the home to the immediate neighborhood (Community Level). The transfer of the Primary Level skills to the Community Level is represented by the lined area within the Community Level. However, at the Community Level certain new adaptive behaviors are required involving new language terms, forms of social interaction such as games, methods of reacting to aggression, methods of aggressing, etc. These new life skills are indicated by the shaded portion over the lined portion within the Community Level area. From the Community Level the child must transition to the Institutional Subcultural Level. At the Institutional Level, the child has available to him only his Primary and Community Level skills (indicated by lined portion) and must, in addition, learn how to adapt to the institutional rules, classroom behavior, teacher authority and the complex performance demands indigenous to this institutional culture.

At the Primary Institutional Level (5-9 years of age), the child must demonstrate his ability to master the requirements of the school sub-culture. He must show that he can comprehend the language, read printed materials, perform simple computations with numbers, obey institutional rules and be sensitive to the complex authority structure as well as to the mores of his own peer group society.

The Secondary Institutional Level is considered to embrace the period from approximately 9 years of age through 18 (completion of secondary schooling). It should be noted that at the Secondary Level, the amount of information and skills which must be learned by the individual require him to flexibly adapt to a great number and variety of institutional demands. (See Figure I). In addition there is a sharp increase in the number of additional life skills which must be mastered, particularly during the early adolescent years. Drop-out takes place at the Secondary Institutional Level for one of two reasons: either the Primary Institutional skills are not available or the individual is unable to meet the continually increasing demands of the Secondary Institutional Level environment.

At the Professional Institutional Level, starting at approximately 18 years of age, the transferability of Level Two Institutional life skills is quite high. It should be noted, however, that the requirement in adaptation to the Professional Level environment is greatest in the first year or two.

Finally, at the Productive Adult Level, the life skills which transfer from the Professional Institutional Level have relatively minor importance, but there is a substantial requirement for developing a large repertoire of additional skills unrelated to the institutional setting.

The Motivational Problem

The dropout adolescent typically has a history of academic defeats accompanied by feelings of inadequacy. These combine to produce feelings of apprehension and even anxiety in any setting which is at all reminiscent of the school classroom. (See Abrahamson, 1952; Child, 1954; Havighurst and Taba, 1949; Hess and Goldblatt, 1957; Mead, 1951; Sears, 1940; and Taba, 1955a.)

It is anticipated that, if faced with a typical classroom setting, the functionally illiterate drop-out would (1) quickly pass his tolerance threshold and drop out of the situation; (2) respond so as to transform the situation (by digression, aggression, inattention, clowning, poor attendance, etc.) to minimize its threat value; or (3) reject his own group by attempting to mimic the instructor and interject his system of values. The reinstitution of a typical classroom situation is viewed as a highly inefficient procedure which would tend to lose trainees, and/or become a travesty and/or form strong antagonisms between those who are "serious" and those whose anxieties were too strong to permit involvement. Thus, it is necessary to develop a new kind of classroom setting which reduces anxieties to a minimum, produces a high proportion of work-time, and results in the retention of a high proportion of literacy trainees.

Successive failures have crystallized the suspicion of personal inadequacy into deep-felt conviction; effort has so often been a prelude to defeat that even the prospect of effort produces anxieties, conflicts and frustrations inherent in failure. Where responses tend to be made to satisfy immediate needs and where the individual feels himself inadequate to attain upward social mobility we have the conditions necessary for low self-image. It is assumed that a poor self-image results when:

1. An individual perceives himself as deficient in a "core" life area.
2. The individual attributes his low status to the existence of the perceived defect.
3. This defect has been perceived over a number of years and the individual has found himself powerless to change it.

His history of failure builds a perceived self-image of a loser. (See Atkinson, 1957; and Steiner, 1957). That is, the energies and frustrations involved in an effort to attain meaningful life goals so far outweigh the probabilities of goal attainment, that there is a perceived advantage in avoiding goal seeking activity. The individual with a "loser self-image" may seek his immediate no-risk gratifications in many ways, but he cannot break out of the emotional consequences of his defeat-filled life history. His self-image requires him to substitute fantasy for aspiration and immediate need-gratification for long-range goals. For example, a perceived core area of defect may be sports and/or dancing for the person crippled by polio. He feels generally inadequate and experiences genuine feelings of success only in the process of overcoming the defect. This feeling of success takes place only when there is a perceptible bit of evidence that the core defect is being overcome. Analogously, the functionally illiterate jobless drop-out is assumed to view his deficit in literacy and language skills as a core area of defect. Further, it is assumed that, for precisely this reason, he can experience deep feelings of success if he can perceive himself as improving his literacy and language skills.

Our previous research has convinced us that many functionally illiterate drop-outs would be quite willing to enter literacy training. Apparently there is a general recognition of the sober fact that, in the absence of a diploma, there is a requirement for

(1) the possession of some job skill; (2) some type of credential in lieu of the diploma; and (3) some means of passage into the job market.

Although the functional illiterate makes every effort to hide this defect, it is a core area of defect of which he is profoundly aware; the attainment of adequate literacy skills by this definition is a major life goal which is generally repressed because of the history of failure and its unattainability at such a late life stage.

The motivational patterns of drop-outs have been discussed *ad nauseam*. (See Longstreth, Shanley and Rive, 1964; Graves and Peagler, 1961; Kansas City Public Schools, 1964; National Education Association, American Association of School Administrators and Research Division, 1965; Riessman, 1963; and Sewel, Haller, and Straus, 1957.) However, the centrality of motivation to this statement makes it mandatory that my position on motivation be explicitly presented here.

Briefly, motivation is viewed as having three fundamental aspects:

1. *The Drive or Tension Component*: First, there is a requirement for drive or emotional tension which generates a requirement for some immediate action on the part of the motivated individual.
2. *The Goal Stimulus or Tension Reducer*: The motivated individual must have some type of goal which is necessary for reduction of the intensity of the tension or drive which he feels.
3. *The Directional Component*: The motivated individual moves in that direction which he perceives as providing maximal tension reduction.

The Behavioral Carom

Where the tension or drive is largely based on apprehension, anxiety, or fear, the individual finds it necessary to move simply from where he is to somewhere else, so that his immediate goal is the avoidance of the tensions produced within the locality in which he happens to be. For example, if an adolescent boy has a requirement to do homework and becomes anxious because he feels inadequate, he may avoid the situation by such avoidance activities as turning on the television, calling a friend on the telephone, getting a snack, etc. In his new situation, for example, in watching television, he can feel guilty about not performing his homework and apprehensive about the possibility of parental criticism which may combine to move him back into his own room where he reads a comic book under conditions free from the possible surveillance of his parents. And so it goes. The individual whose fundamental motivational pattern involves the constant requirements for anxiety reduction bounces or caroms from one situation to the next. Each new situation in turn produces its own anxiety components which, as soon as they reach his rather low frustration threshold, move him into a new situation where the cycle again begins.

Thus, in Paradigm 1(a), following, we have the behavioral carom where the individual starts in the upper lefthand corner. The two lines indicate tension vectors which combine to force him to move to "B" (upper right corner), away from the direction of goal achievement (indicated by a dotted line). At "B" he moves to point "C" which happens to be a goal related activity, but at this point, he moves away from the goal to "D" because the immediate tension vectors propel him in this direction.

This continues as the individual captured by the requirement for immediate tension reduction never approaches his real goal, but rather moves from situation to situation on the basis of the tensions produced within the situational context. He thus responds impulsively and spontaneously without necessary reference to real objectives or values and, by the same token, tends to operate against his own long range interest because he must necessarily satisfy the demand for immediate reduction of his anxieties. The individual characterized by a low frustration threshold tends to carom, like a billiard ball, from situation to situation on the basis of impulses unrelated to his rational life needs.

Paradigm 1(b) represents the pattern of the efficient Goal

TWO MOTIVATIONAL PARADIGMS

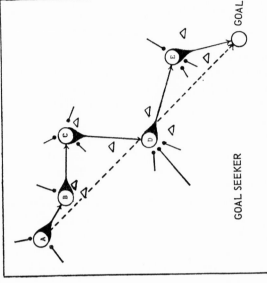

1A: The Behavioral Carom - paradigm presents an individual in process of performing a task and changing his mode of response in reaction to immediate situational tensions.

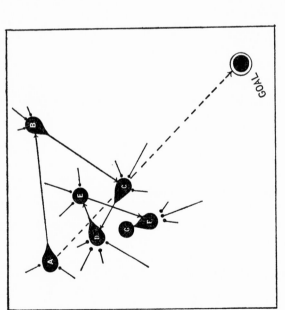

1B: Goal Directed Behavior-individual shown in process of goal directed behavior. Changes in direction are made to adapt to obstacles (△'s) between successive sub-goals.

58

Seeker. Again, the individual is located at "A" (in the upper left-hand corner) and has immediate tension vectors operating to push him away from attainment of his goal requirement. However, the Goal Seeker maintains a consistent pattern of movement in the direction of the goal (in lower right-hand corner). He shifts his position only to by-pass obstructions to the achievement of his successive sub-goals. His level of frustration tolerance is sufficiently high that he can disregard the immediate tension vector forces. He is capable of moving in the direction of goal achievement even when his personal preferences, feelings of discomfort and apprehension would be reduced by situational avoidance. For example, the student faced with the requirement to do homework in order to satisfy the goal of achieving high grades to enable acceptance at a good college would tolerate tensions generating within the situation, or would resolve them in such way as not to be deflected from his goal. He would be able to simply forego some favorite TV program; arrange a convenient snack at his study desk; solicit his parents' help to answer the phone; etc. Put another way, the Goal Seeker has so great a drive for goal attainment that the value of immediate tension reduction is always subordinate to the gratifications and satisfactions felt by achievement of the goal.

For the Goal Seeker, then, there is a net motivational gain in maintaining responses towards a goal rather than succumbing to the temptation to reduce immediate situational tensions; the attainment of the satisfaction of the sub-goal fails to diminish the necessity for attaining the satisfactions inherent in reaching the ultimate goal. Avoidance responses to immediate tension generating situations delay the gratifications anticipated in goal attainment; therefore, for the Goal Seeker, the tension reductions which take place through situational avoidance are not worthwhile. It should be noted, however, that even if the drive intensity levels are the same, in the "A" case the drive occurs at the instant the individual bolts out of the tension producing situation (the direction being largely irrelevant). In the "B" case, on the other hand, the tension reduction is delayed. It is partially and temporarily reduced when sub-goals are achieved and more fully reduced only when the ultimate goal is attained.

For the Goal Seeker, tensions are reduced by the satisfactions received in reaching the mileposts and completing some pre-existing set of requirements. The Goal Seeker tends to be dominated by more remote "future" goals and is resistant to the tensions which occur in other courses of action required to attain these anticipated goal achieving situations. Finally, the Goal Seeker tends to have a much simpler rationale for movement. He can limit his choices to those which are consistent with the attainment of his goals and sub-goals.

An individual in a situation with intolerable situational anxiety has an almost infinite range of choices, as anything else will presumably produce an initial diminution of the tension he is now experiencing.

Thus, in motivational terms, goal seeking based on anxiety reduction is irrational, diffuse, and has little relation to the life interests of the individual. Where those individuals who possess goal seeking motivational patterns possess some rational goal and sub-goal structure, then there is a consistent direction of motion, and the attainment of goals tends to be consistent with the individual's overall life needs, interests and values.

It is assumed that the functionally illiterate drop-out will tend to exhibit the pattern of behavior as illustrated and described in Paradigm 1(a); that for the most part there will be strong tendencies to impulsively avoid situations where there are feelings of apprehension, tension or anxiety. Further, it is assumed that these impulsive acts will be unrelated to their longer range goals and life values.

At a macroscopic social level, these paradigms argue strongly that programs must be designed to develop long-range goal-related behaviors rather than to reduce immediate situational or community tensions. In fact, these tensions are, on the basis of this analysis, a necessity for obtaining the movement toward a goal. This dynamic force becomes instrumental for goal attainment. However, unless there is a perceived goal, impulsive activities will occur with more or less frequency in response to situational tensions. Paradigm 1(b) suggests that incidence of impulsivity would be reduced if communities would systematically involve ghetto members in shared and clearly perceived goals which would be associated with a clear-cut plan of action for goal attainment. Under these circumstances Paradigm 1(b) argues further that a community tension is not necessarily destructive but is the dynamic prerequisite necessary to sustain the community through the many activities and problems involved in goal achievement.

Progressive Choice Reading Method

One of the most promising techniques developed in response to widespread recognition of the problems associated with the functional illiterate and related motivational problems is the Progressive Choice Reading Method. This technique was designed by Woolman in 1950 and is based on theoretical considerations involved in the learning process. It embodies the following characteristics:

1. Programmed material is presented in small, readily digestible units.
2. A rigorous sequence of reading skill development is imposed following the principles of the Progressive Choice Reading Method.
3. Learner response rate is high.
4. There is continuous feed-back of the adequacy and relevancy of learner responses.
5. Learners progress only on the basis of demonstrated proficiency using built-in evaluation methods.
6. Learners are required to achieve specified goals and sub-goals.
7. Both extrinsic and intrinsic motivational devices are used.

The instructor is thus a human vehicle through which the program moves to the learner. However, in contrast to the teaching machine, the instructor can be sensitive to areas of learner difficulty, offer support and encouragement, and correct special student learning problems on the basis of new insight and skill. To facilitate this process, and to avoid mechanistic classroom behaviors, a Program Rationale is included in the Teacher Manual. This is an independent self-instructional program, designed to provide conceptual understanding of the principles and techniques underlying the Progressive Choice Reading Method. The teacher (or unskilled literate instructor) is therefore systematically provided with a course of study in the Progressive Choice Reading Method while using it in a realistic training situation. Thus, the underlying rationale and implications of the teaching procedure are exposed at a more fundamental level. The function of the conceptual program is four-fold:

1. Eliminate the necessity of special training for program instructors.
2. Increase motivation and involvement of program instructors.
3. Increase the precision of their diagnosis of reading problems.
4. Increase their adaptability in the use of the program in the classroom situation.

This self-instructional feature has been received very positively by teachers of the mentally retarded.

A National Institute of Mental Health grant involving the use of a Progressive Choice Reading Program was used to teach reading skills to mental retardates, and succeeded in upgrading reading skills for most retardates. Excerpts from the Summary and Conclusions follow:

> The study was designed to obtain a "minimal yield" estimate and therefore no assistance or training was given to teachers in the form of workshops, evaluations, critiques or supervision. E and C teachers were regular public school teachers and were oriented to the experimental situation in two after-school sessions totalling approximately three hours. There were 23 classes in 19 schools covering the Fairfax County, Baltimore City and Baltimore County systems. In addition, some private schools used the Basal Progressive Choice Reading Program under

less rigorously controlled conditions. All classes were pre-tested (Fall, 1962) using the Metropolitan Achievement Test (MAT), Primary I Level, Form A; the Progressive Choice Marginal Diagnostic Reading Test ($r = .95$ applying the Spearman-Brown correction for $N - 170$) and post-tested with alternate forms of the same tests on completion of the school year. Differences in performance on the Progressive Choice Diagnostic Reading Test were used as the basis for evaluation, as the MAT used lower case letters which had not yet been taught to the E children.

The results, as measured by difference scores on the Progressive Choice Marginal Diagnostic Reading Test, favored E subjects at significant levels of confidence; Trainable E subjects were superior to Trainable C subjects; Educable E subjects were superior to Educable C subjects. The gain in reading scores by Trainables was almost as great as the gain obtained by Educables.[3]

One conclusion of the study was that teachers can use the Basal Progressive Choice Reading Program effectively without prior instruction or supervision.

The Progressive Choice Reading Method has been subjected by Bloomer (1961) to six experimental tests with first grade children (these studies employed teachers trained in the principles and techniques of the method). Each of the six studies by Bloomer established a significant difference favoring Progressive Choice trained children at the end of the first grade when compared with various conventional methods using standard tests of reading proficiency such as the Gates and Metropolitan tests. (See Table 1 below.)

Table 1 represents a summary of six studies and shows that at the end of the first grade Progressive Choice trained children obtained superior reading post-test scores ($P < .001$) when compared with children trained by other methods. Briefly, at

3. M. Woolman and Ruth A. Davy, *Developing Symbolic Skills in The Mentally Retarded*. Washington, D.C.: Institute of Educational Research, Inc., 1963.

the end of first grade, only six per cent of Progressive Choice children failed to achieve second grade level as compared with 29% for conventional reading methods. Progressive Choice and conventional reading methods were about equal in the proportion of children reading at second grade level, but only 18% of the control children obtained reading scores at the third grade level, while 42% of Progressive Choice trained children scored at the third grade level. Davy (1961, 1962) adapted the Progressive Choice Reading Method and demonstrated that retarded children could learn to read by this means.

Table 1

Summary of Six Experimental Studies
Comparing PC and Conventional Reading Methcds

Achievement Level of First Grade Pupils by Percent

Teaching Method	Number of Classes	Number of Pupils	Reading Achievement Grade		
			1.0-1.9	2.0-2.9	3.0-3.9 %
Progressive Choice	7	178	6	52	42	100
Combined other Methods	15	383	29	53	18	100

Chi-Square - 138.21 using actual frequencies (P less than .001)

The mean achievement level of normal first grade children in the six Bloomer studies was 2.88, i.e., mean achievement was almost at third grade level at completion of first grade. Work with problem-reader adolescents over the last ten years indicates that they can increase their reading achievement level at far greater rates than first grade children. Although it is not possible to predict with certainty, it is our expectancy that a mean sixth grade achievement level is a reasonable goal for illiterate normal adolescents and adults over the same time period using programmed Progressive Choice materials. Using these programs, illiterates could be taught by certified teachers, literate adults and adolescents at higher levels in the program.

The Progressive Choice Reading Program has also been evaluated in other contexts. Some of the findings follow:

1. Bank Street College Study[4]: Job Opportunities in Neigh-

4. E. Terry Schwarz, *An Evaluation of the Accelerated Progressive Choice Reading Program.* Bank Street College, New York, N.Y., 1964.

64

borhoods and The Police Athletic League of New York City supplied the subjects (approximately 200). Instruction was given by volunteer, unpaid adults. Literacy trainees were unpaid. Pre- and post-test scores were not obtained for most subjects. Those on whom tests were obtained gained about a year on the Gates Reading Survey Test. Recorded interviews were given to 22 literacy trainees on completion. Ninety-two percent stated that they believed that they had improved and one hundred percent stated that the reading program should be given to all urban drop-outs.

2. Morgan State College Study [5]: This was a three-week intensive reading program given in a camp setting to 80 children who demonstrated a minimum of one year reading deficiency. The total instruction and reading practice time was 45 hours. The mean gain on the Gates Reading Survey Test was six months or a decrease in retardation of 23.2 percent. Harvey Block concluded:

> Eighty students from Baltimore City's poverty target area were provided a camp experience which included a reading improvement program. Children demonstrate (sic) an average gain of six months after forty hours of instruction. The data demonstrated the effectiveness of the particular tool used and in addition, methods for further improvement are discussed. It was concluded that these programs are of value but require additional examination.[6]

3. Washington, D.C. Study:[7] This was an intensive six-week summer school evaluation with 45 hours of instruction to 66

5. Harvey A. Block, *An Examination of the APC Reading Method As a Tool for Decreasing Reading Deficiencies of Children From Low Socio-Economic Backgrounds.* Morgan State College, Baltimore, Md., 1965.

6. *Ibid.*

7. Anne W. Pitts and Frances C. Payne, *The Effectiveness of Programmed Instruction.* Public Schools of the District of Columbia, Washington, D.C. 1964.

pupils of the 7th, 8th, and 9th grades. The reported mean gain was 1½ years on the Gates Reading Survey Test.

4. Galena Park Study [8]: Galena Park has used this method over a longer period of time and with a greater number of students than any other group. They report gains of 1.8 grades in reading skill and a sharp reduction in drop-out rate.

Other data received from such organizations as the Systematic Training and Redevelopment (STAR) Program in Mississippi, and the New Albany-Floyd County School System [9] give at least comparable results. Also, Arthur Greenleigh Associates [10] compared various adult literacy training systems in a study which is difficult to summarize, as results vary in the different localities used. They do conclude that literacy systems such as *Reading in High Gear* (one published version of the Progressive Choice Reading Method) tested in their study can be used effectively by persons lacking teacher credentials.

More important than any of the studies showing literacy gain was *The Summer Catch-Up Project in Prince Edward County*.[11] This study, performed during the summer of 1965, was undertaken at the request of community leaders to avert a threatened mass drop-out of approximately 500 adolescents, most of whom had a four or five year schooling gap in their histories. Instructors were vacationing college students recruited by various church organizations who worked for a nominal stipend plus subsistence. Literacy trainees were unpaid and usually worked in the fields before or after their instruction. Literacy training was given in primitive facilities (poor lighting, and often no drinkable water) but attendance remained high and practically

8. F. E. McGahan, *Nine Years of Public School Education for Children With Learning Disabilities*. A paper presented at the First Annual Convention of the Texas Association for Children with Learning Difficulties. Houston, Texas, 1965.

9. Duplicates of data submitted from these two studies can be supplied upon request.

10. Greenleigh Associates, Inc., *Field Test and Evaluation of Selected Adult Basic Education Systems*. Greenleigh Associates, Inc., New York, N.Y. 1966.

11. Myron Woolman, *The Summer Catch-Up Project in Prince Edward County*. Institute of Educational Research, Washington, D.C. 1965.

all trainees returned to the public school situation on the resumption of formal schooling in the fall.

Summary and Conclusions

The motivational problem ultimately reduces to shifting an individual's response tendencies away from the reduction of apprehension and anxieties and toward goal attainment. Of primary importance here is the concept of a "core" area where a successful response is *important* to the trainee. Since functionally illiterate drop-outs seem to have almost no tolerance for failure in the core area of literacy skill development, the probabilities of making an error should approximate zero at the outset. Further, as the functionally illiterate drop-out is assumed to be convinced that he is probably involved in a vain effort, his evidence of progress should (1) be unambiguous, (2) occur without help from others, and (3) take place at a sufficiently high rate to provide a cumulative build-up of feelings of achievement. The Progressive Choice Reading Method meets these requirements and can be effectively used to help large numbers of functionally illiterate Americans to assume their rightful place in our democratic society.

Partial Bibliography

1. Cooper, C. H. "Comparative Study of Delinquents and Non-Delinquents." *Psychological Service Center Journal.* 1960, X, 117-194.
2. Gault, R. H. "Preventives of Delinquency." *Journal of Educational Psychology*, 1914, V, 32-36.
3. Slawson, J. *The Delinquent Boy.* Boston: Badger, 1926, pp. viii, 477.
4. Miner, J. B. *Deficiency and Delinquency*, Educational Psychology Monographs, No. 21. Baltimore: Warwick & York, 1918. Pp. xiv, 355.
5. Merrill, M. A. "Mental Differences Among Juvenile Delinquents." *Journal on Delinquency*, 1926, X, 312-323.
6. Kvareceus, W. C. *Juvenile Delinquency and the School.*

Yonkers, N. Y.: World Book Company, 1945, pp. 122-123.

7. Shulman, H. M. *Slums of New York*. New York: Bonie Brothers, 1938, p. 107.

8. Maller, J. "Juvenile Delinquency in New York City," *Journal of Psychology*. 1937, pp. 3, 1-25.

9. Healy, W. and Bronner, A. *New Light on Delinquency and Its Treatment*. New Haven: Yale University Press, 1936, p. 75.

10. Shaw, C. R. *Delinquency Areas*, Chicago: University of Chicago Press, 1929.

11. Shaw, C. R. *The Jack-Roller*, Chicago: University of Chicago Press, 1930.

12. Shaw, C. R. *Brothers In Crime*. Chicago: University of Chicago Press, 1938.

13. Glueck, E. "Mental Retardation and Juvenile Delinquency." *Mental Hygiene*, 1935, pp. 549-572.

14. Terman, L. M. "Research on the Diagnosis of Pre-Delinquent Tendencies," *Journal on Delinquency*. 1925, p. 6.

15. Wechsler, D. *Measurement of Adult Intelligence*. Baltimore: Williams & Wilkins, 1944, p. 53.

16. Glueck, S. and E. *Unraveling Juvenile Delinquency*, Cambridge, Mass.: Harvard University Press, 1950.

17. Glueck, S. and E. *Delinquents in the Making*, New York: Harper & Brothers, 1952.

18. Brice, Edward W. "Illiteracy in a Changing America." U.S. Department of Health, Education and Welfare. Office of Education Publication OE-13605, 1959.

PSYCHOLOGY AND INSTRUCTIONAL TECHNOLOGY

WILLIAM A. DETERLINE, PH.D.

President of the General Programmed Teaching Corporation

Editorial Note

One of the most revolutionary concepts of our age is the human engineering approach to the shaping of behavior. The population explosion, the teacher shortage, the expansion of knowledge, and elimination of jobs for the unskilled have made new demands on psychologists concerned with the process of learning and generated a rapidly growing field of instructional technology. In addition to surveying the present and future prospects of applied instructional technology, the author stresses a particular approach to the development of competence through continuing self-reinforcement, with learning for its own sake serving as the ultimate reinforcer.

Dr. William A. Deterline is President of General Programmed Teaching, a division of Commerce Clearing House, Inc. General Programmed Teaching is a research and development organization specializing in programmed instruction and instructional systems. Dr. Deterline has been President of General Programmed Teaching since 1964.

He received his B.S., M.S., and Ph.D. degrees from the University of Pittsburgh in 1953, 1955, and 1957 respectively. He has been a member of the faculty of the University of Pittsburgh, Alma College (Michigan), Trinity University (Texas), and San Francisco State College. From 1960 to 1963 he was Research Scientist with the American Institute of Research.

Dr. Deterline is a member of the American Psychological Association, The American Association for the Advancement of Science, the American Educational Research Association, and is a past President of the National Society for Programmed Instruction. His professional interests center on learning theory, behavioral technology, and instructional technology.

•

PSYCHOLOGY AND INSTRUCTIONAL TECHNOLOGY

> "The universal requirements of teaching and of learning; that is to say, a method of teaching and of learning with such certainty that the desired result must of necessity follow . . . Hitherto the method of instruction has been so uncertain that scarcely anyone would dare to say: In so many years I will bring this youth to such and such a point, I will educate him in such and such a way. We must therefore see if it be possible to place the art of intellectual discipline on such a firm basis that sure and certain progress may be made."
>
> Comenius, *The Great Didactic*, c. 1650

Historical Overview

More than a dozen years have passed since B. F. Skinner first reported on the work in progress at Harvard in the design of teaching devices and teaching materials, a project concerned with applying certain behavior-shaping procedures to the systematic development of human conceptual learning (Skinner, 1954). The assumptions upon which that original research and developmental work was based were elegant in their simplicity; and because of the types of educational applications for which the approach was said to be most promising, it appeared that at last a direct link was to be forged between psychological learning theories and educational practice. In essence, the rationale was this: learning is basically an individual process, affected by individual differences of various kinds; learning is also an active process, apparently most effective when the student interacts, responding to the instructional stimulus inputs;

students learn by doing, and they also learn what they practice, so practicing of incorrect or undesirable responses should be avoided as much as possible; learning requires some form of feedback, whether reinforcement in the functional sense, or knowledge of results in the differential reinforcement or correction sense; and feedback needs to be as immediate as possible.[1]

At least two "instructional" models immediately suggest themselves: the tutorial interaction between tutor and student, and the behavior-shaping techniques used in the animal laboratory. Both lead to the same general form of instruction, although from different directions (Klaus, 1965). Both models point to individualization, since students learn at different rates and because each student should respond throughout the course of instruction. Textbooks, of course, do provide for individualized study, while classroom lectures, films, and demonstrations are externally paced. But textbooks do not systematically specify active responding throughout, nor do they provide any basis for knowledge of progress. How might the student-paced textbook be designed to provide for more effective learning? Thorndike, more than half a century ago, suggested an answer:

"If by a miracle of mechanical ingenuity, a book could be arranged so that only to him who had done what was directed on page one would page two become visible, and so on, much that now requires personal instruction could be managed by print." (Thorndike, 1912.)

Finn and Perrin (1962), in a survey of the field of programmed instruction, comment, "Here are the insights of a genius. History can very often teach us a lesson in humility—and it does here. The interesting question is: why couldn't we see it then?" Skinner, noting their comment, adds, "It might also be asked, why didn't Thorndike see it then? He remained active in education for at least thirty years . . ." (Skinner, 1965).

1. The initial response to Skinner's 1954 paper, *The Art of Teaching and the Science of Learning,* was not uniformly enthusiastic. As a graduate student at the University of Pittsburgh, where Skinner presented that paper, I overheard an informal critique of Skinner's views. A visiting academic dean commented "He's talking about *training*, not *teaching*"! and a noted educator asked, "Is he kidding?"

When one considers the creativity and productivity of Thorndike, it is apparent that he did not become intrigued with his own idea since it would have been a relatively simple matter to devise exactly the kind of book he suggested. The behavioral technology employed later by Skinner was not available to Thorndike, but Thorndike's own "Laws of learning" would have guided him into active responding, overt practice, and immediate feedback or "reward," *if* he had decided to implement his own idea. Instead, the idea lay dormant for forty years, until the inefficiencies and inadequacies of group classroom procedures led Skinner to the same problem.

The material to be read in a textbook *can*, "by a miracle of mechanical ingenuity," be presented on pretty much the basis described by Thorndike, for in 1954 Skinner described a device that *replaced* the textbook but conformed to Thorndike's specifications. The device was designed for individual use by one student, at his own pace. Information and response requirements were presented in small amounts by the device; overt responses were required; and the correct answer was then shown, presumably reinforcing the response if correct, and correcting any errors. Skinner's device, inevitably called a "teaching machine," presented one or two short statements at a time, visible through a small window. The student read each sentence, which had one or more critical words left blank, and wrote the missing words on a special paper tape. Only after he had committed himself to a response was the student shown the correct answer. The features of that device—there were other devices designed for specific purposes or subject matter areas—have often been summarized as *the* characteristics of the methodology:

1. Information, logically sequenced, is presented in small steps.
2. Each step requires an active (overt) response.[2]

2. Early Skinnerian programs, and hundreds developed subsequently utilizing similar programming procedures, have been criticized as consisting of too many, too small steps; and data from some studies indicate that the "small step" approach can be overdone, making some programs dull, tedious, and quite aversive to the student. Unfortunately, this has often been interpreted as refuting Skinner, his views, his contributions, and pro-

3. Each response is immediately confirmed or corrected.
4. The instructional material must be tested on students and revised until it accomplishes the objectives specified for it.
5. Each student proceeds at his own pace.

The Tutorial Model and the Laboratory Model

These characteristics describe programmed instruction and tutorial instruction; they are also extrapolations from the techniques used to shape the behavior of laboratory animals—a process carried out as a matter of course in a predictable, systematic, and highly efficient manner. The difference between behavior-shaping in the laboratory and college teaching in the classroom is very striking, not only in the obvious ways but in the effectiveness with which learning is produced. The research psychologist proficient in the techniques of successive approximations, differential reinforcement, and chaining (Keller and Schoenfeld, 1950; Homme and Klaus, 1957), is aware of a striking difference between the effectiveness of his classroom activities and that of his laboratory activities, for his experimental organisms respond more reliably, predictably, and under far more effective control than most of his students.

Consider what is done in the laboratory. An experimenter (E) plans to study some aspect of a repetitive, measurable response (R), say, lever pressing, by one or more subjects (S), say, rats. The dependent variable might be the rate of occurrence of R and the independent variable may be some manipulation of S or S's environment.

The preliminary preparations include handling, adaptation to the equipment and to the deprivation schedule, and, finally, the acquisition of the required response. Each S may have to learn

---

grammed instruction itself! A more justifiable conclusion is that the small-step concept requires more refinement and revision to match the requirements of subject-matter goals and student characteristics. The basic methodology has evolved, but it is still based on Skinner's ingenious and insightful approach to the modification of behavior. Progress does not refute its originator: lack of progress does.

to press the bar only when a specific stimulus is present, while all responses that occur in the absence of that stimulus are extinguished. A chain of responses might be involved, in which S must carry out a sequence of responses, each, in turn, producing the stimulus for the next response. This instruction (manipulation of conditions in such a way that the necessary learning occurs) is not even generally considered to be a part of the experiment itself; the consequences are predictable and are only part of preparing S for the experimental manipulations. Occasionally E encounters an S that does not acquire the desired behavior pattern. When he does so, it would not occur to him to say, as he does in his other role as classroom teacher, "This organism did not learn because of inadequate intelligence, inadequate motivation, a poor attitude, or lack of interest." Relative grading of subjects would not be appropriate because the standard is an absolute one: each S either does or does not learn to specification. As Bugelski (1964) points out, a human engineering approach to instruction or to any other problem has a practical, no nonsense, "go-no go" criterion. A system meets specifications or it does not; and if it does not, the producers of the system are at fault. This is the approach needed in education; success or failure is the responsibility of the system, and failures cannot be shrugged off by assigning them to the students.

The shaping of behavior in the laboratory can be done with a precision that is not characteristic of classroom instruction: E would not put all of his S's into one experimental space, talk to them, test them, and then grade them on a curve! E's concern is that each individual S learn a specified response pattern within certain limits, and to do this he provides individualized "instruction," systematically manipulating stimuli and conditions, and making certain events contingent upon the behavior of S. As a result, S and the environment interact, and the desired behavior develops. In the laboratory, S does all of the "performing." In the classroom, E, as the teacher, does most of the performing, and only some of his students learn only some of the things they have heard and read about during the course.

Obviously the comparison between laboratory and classroom in the preceding paragraph is over-simplified and drawn in this

74

fashion only to make a point: behavioral technology—a set of procedures for shaping behavior—does exist in a form that can be and has been applied to animal and human S's of many descriptions under a wide range of circumstances, producing specified changes in behavior with a high degree of reliability. Education—from nursery school through college and professional schools—needs such reliability and effectiveness, but does not have it.

The population explosion, the knowledge explosion, the teacher shortage—all are conditions that require increased effectiveness, increased efficiency, and a high degree of automation of instruction. The answers do not lie in the development of audiovisual devices *per se*, regardless of their sophistication, but in the technology of instructional design and the combination of devices (hardware) with materials (software) produced by that technology. The work of Skinner and his associates and the developments generated by the rapidly growing field of instructional technology have come at a time when a technology and empirical approach to education are critically needed.

Pressey and Remedial Feedback

The role of immediate feedback, which is an essential element in both our models, has been studied by S. L. Pressey from another position over many years, dating back to the 1920's. Pressey's work is related to the field of instructional technology, but from a very different point of view than that of either the tutorial or Skinnerian model. Pressey originally became concerned with the problem of providing immediate correction of test questions as a student takes a test. This problem is a real one because the process of taking a test is also a learning experience. The student who studies a question, thinks about it, and applies what he can to the identification of the correct answer, is engaging in a type of behavior similar to that involved in studying. When he arrives at an answer (unless he has simply given up and admitted that he doesn't know, hoping that his guess is going to be correct), he more or less convinces himself that the answer that he has selected is correct. There can, of course, be varying degrees of analysis, reasoning, and certainty concerning the final answer. Students can learn and remember answers— correct or incorrect—through the active process of taking tests.

Pressey developed a number of techniques for providing immediate feedback to the student as he answers each question. These included self-scoring mechanical devices and punchboards, and there are presently available a variety of special self-scoring, answer sheets and tab cards used as answer records by each student. Pressey was concerned, not so much with the effectiveness of the learning that preceded the test during classroom instruction, textbook study, and so on, but with the learning that might occur as the student answers test questions. Skinner's design is more concerned with programming the learning itself, rather than only with correcting errors and confirming correct responses on examinations that follow the original learning. Somewhere between Pressey's approach and Skinner's was a third, developed primarily in the military, and generally associated with the name of N. A. Crowder (1962). This approach consists of presenting small amounts of textual materials, perhaps a page or a few paragraphs, and then asking a multiple-choice question about the main point or principle covered by that material. After the student has read the material and selected one of the possible answers, he turns to a page indicated beside his answer choice. If his answer is incorrect, the page on which he finds himself tells why that choice was not correct, and he might then be sent back to choose another answer to the question. If his choice is correct, he is sent to a page that tells him that he is correct, and then the next unit of information is presented. This approach was called "branching," and the sequencing was described as "intrinsically" determined, because at each diagnostic question the student was routed to a next step depending on his correct interpretation of the material or various types of incorrect interpretations. This approach has the test-taking correction feature of Pressey, but it also has one feature of Skinner's approach, that of concern for original learning, in that the course material is broken down into steps. In the main, however, Crowder's approach, like Pressey's, has a remedial emphasis: when the student doesn't learn correctly, then corrective feedback is provided.

Skinner, Controlled Learning, and Evolving Technology

Skinner might well ask, why allow the student to waste time, possibly practicing errors, misinterpreting—in effect, failing—and then attempt to repair the damage? A philosophy of remediation is an acceptance of failure by the student and a plan to provide remedial instruction in some form after failure has occurred. Why not program the instruction and the learning itself, and eliminate the need for later remedial training?

Skinner has recently commented on both the remedial approach and the related view of organization of materials:

> "Proposals for improving education by reorganizing what is to be learned usually contains an implicit assumption that students will automatically perceive and remember anything that has 'good form'—a doctrine probably traceable to Gestalt psychology. Current revisions of high school curricula seem to lean heavily on the belief that if what the student is to be taught has been 'structured,' he cannot help understanding and remembering it" (1965, p. 9).
>
> "In [the] 'tell-and-test' pattern, the test is not given to measure what he has learned, but to show him what he has not learned and thus induce him to listen and read more carefully in the future. . . . The student may learn to read carefully, to make notes, to discover for himself how to study, and so on, because in doing so, he avoids aversive consequences, but he has not necessarily been taught. Assigning and testing is not teaching" (1965, p. 14).

Active controversies developed between the proponents of "branching" programs and "linear" programs (Skinner's programs did not include adaptive sequencing; each student followed the same "straight line" sequence, hence, "linear"), but unfortunately most of the controversies *dealt* with superficial differences. The important difference between the position of Skinner, on the one hand, and Pressey and Crowder on the other, is a difference in philosophy of instruction and in the technology used to implement their respective approaches. Pressey (1964) now uses the term "auto-elucidation" to refer to his approach, which is, in effect, the "structure plus remedial" philosophy commented on by Skinner, above, and the branching method is based on that same philosophy. But Skinner—and the main stream of programmed instruction follows him in this—wants to design and control the effectiveness of learning, but not on a remedial basis. Klaus (1965) distinguished between "response-centered" and "stimulus-centered" programs: Skinner's response-centered programs are designed around the student's responses and *minimization* of errors; Pressey's and Crowder's stimulus-centered programs are designed around stimulus structure and *correction* of errors.

Because programmed instruction is an empirically-based technology, it is self-correcting and evolutionary. As it has evolved, many of the surface characteristics have changed, and the more superficial, linear-branching controversies have all but disappeared, although the philosophical differences remain. At one time a response-centered program had to consist of very small steps, while a stimulus-centered program was made up of very large steps, and this difference was a basis for controversy. It has turned out that rigid adherence to *either* extreme is inappropriate since step size can and should vary depending on both student and subject matter characteristics. Gilbert, whose view of behavioral technology is basically Skinnerian, has developed a set of design techniques and principles which he calls "mathetics" (Gilbert, 1962). Gilbert's concept of "operant span," as it applies to step size, specifies that each step should be as large as the student can handle, as determined by actual student testing. This is in contrast to the steps in a branching program, which are larger, but whose length is an *a priori* determination. It is also in contrast to the step in a linear program. Most early linear programs were made up of steps that were all approximately the same size, in terms of both the physical space occupied on a page and the approximate maximum number of words that could be used. The working principle seemed to be that "small steps are good things, and therefore the greater the number of steps, the better the program!"

The concept of operant span, on the other hand (similar in some respects to the concept of memory span), recognizes that students of different capabilities and past histories, studying different subject matters, react in such a way that the operant span—the amount of material that the student can read and respond to at a given point in an instruction sequence—varies; therefore, the size of the steps should also vary. In practice, it means that for maximum efficiency each step should be as large as possible without reducing the probability that all appropriate responding will occur.

In addition to a reevaluation of the concept of step size, there has also been increasing concern with the use of adaptive sequencing in all types of programs (Stolurow, 1961; Lewis & Pask, 1965). A variety of adaptive techniques, including branching, are sometimes required and presently play an important role in computer-assisted instruction, as we shall see later in this chapter. The concept of adaptive sequencing is a very attractive one, since it provides for sending each student through a course of instruction, not only at his own pace, but through a sequence that is especially suited to his needs and characteristics. Individual differences are certainly real, and it is highly unlikely that a single program will adequately teach all students who use it. Some students will require review or individual remedial instruction on specific objectives. Some of them will encounter difficulty with certain concepts requiring additional elaboration, discussion, and explanation beyond that needed for other students. For example, consider a programmed sequence that might proceed in this fashion—active responding, of course, being required throughout: a given principle is introduced, explained briefly, perhaps with some examples and analogies, and then the student is given a criterion question or set of complex application questions to answer. Some students will require no further instruction, some may be able to respond appropriately to only

79

some of the questions, and others will be hopelessly confused because the jump to the criterion question is too large. At this point, some form of adaptive sequencing is highly desirable. One possibility is the by-pass technique in which the student is allowed to by-pass any redundant elaboration and explanation that he does not need, while other students are given all the additional instruction they need, perhaps including going back through the original presentation or through diagnostic and remedial branches.

A multi-track arrangement is a more elaborate possibility, based on some form of cumulative and continuous progress evaluation. One problem with this approach is the storage requirement. If the program were printed in the form of a book, the book would have to include all of the content, branches, and tracks, even though the faster student may actually use only twenty or thirty percent of it. Because of this, the storage problem can be a very serious one. Another complexity is the diagnostic questioning involved, since this adds to the storage problem. An ideal solution to the problems of adaptive sequencing seems to be provided by the computer, and computer-assisted instruction has attracted a great deal of attention in recent years (Stolurow, 1965). The storage problem becomes less severe since all of the necessary instructional content can be stored in the computer, which can also be programmed to perform the necessary diagnostic evaluations and the assignment of sequences following each progress evaluation. A computer can communicate with a number of students at the same time. At present, most of the research and development projects involving computer-assisted instruction involve only a small number of student stations, generally between ten and thirty; but theoretically, at least, a computer could provide tutorial instruction for hundreds—possibly thousands of students at the same time. Adaptive sequencing is possible on a large scale through use of a computer; however, most present computer-assisted instruction is not programmed instruction, but programmed diagnosis and remediation. Adaptive sequencing ideally should involve both.

Consider what all of these things mean for the instructional setting of the future. Students could be assigned to courses on the basis of their present level of competence and achievement rather than to grade levels on the basis of their age. A student nine years of age might be at work on a course equivalent to our present seventh-grade mathematics, while at the same time studying what we would now call eleventh-grade history and third-grade grammar. The length of the course, rather than being from September to June, would depend upon his own rate of progress through the course. Instead of instruction aimed at the "average" student, which does a disservice to both the slower students and the more able students, instruction could be provided at a pace, level, and time that more ideally meets the needs and fits the capabilities of every single student. How might we visualize a school functioning along these lines? Certainly the students would encounter some form of computer-assisted instruction. They would use programmed textbooks on an individual basis. They would also use conventional texts and reference books, as well as audiovisual teaching devices, both responsive teaching machines and presentation devices. They might attend occasional large-group lectures and demonstrations; they would also attend small group lectures, seminars, discussion periods, and demonstrations; and they would take part in field trips, applied projects, and laboratory exercises. Students would still meet for purposes of interacting with each other or with special instructors or advisers, and they would probably also be scheduled to meet for certain types of presentations that are more conveniently presented to groups: presentations by visiting specialists, videotape, live TV, motion pictures, audiotape, or other audiovisual presentations that might be more conveniently presented on a group basis.

The library would certainly become more than a storage area for books and a place where students go to get books and occasionally read them. The library or other study centers would include individual study carrels, some of which would include access to the computer-assisted instruction materials. They would also include dial access to other stored instruction such as audiovisual presentations of various kinds; a student could simply dial the videotape, motion picture, audiotape, or other presentation, which would be presented on a screen and speaker in the study carrel. All of these presentation features and capabilities presently exist. Some school and college operations of this sort are being conducted as research and development projects, but some of them have been established and are in use as part of the ongoing instructional system at several sizes and types of institutions.

Not everyone has welcomed either the advent of the individualized instructional device and study center or the idea of systematically designing instruction and learning. To many people, the unreliability, inadequacy and inefficiency of the group lecture method are somehow "dignified," and "democratic." The idea of a technology of education is somehow appalling, as is the idea of automating instruction, or having devices perform instructional functions. Here, too, Thorndike anticipated our current developments and had this to say:

"From the point of view of interest in work, personal teaching is usually more sociable, but the difference between it and textbook training in this particular could be reduced by skill in organizing the latter . . . Great economies are possible by printed aids, and personal comment and question should be saved to do what only it can do. A human being should not be wasted in doing what forty sheets of paper or two phonographs can do. Just because personal teaching is precious and can do what books and apparatus cannot, it should be saved for its peculiar work. The best teacher uses books and appliances as well as his own insight, sympathy, and magnetism." (Thorndike, 1912)

The developments described above are exciting in some ways and depressing in others. They are exciting because the hardware capabilities exist; they are depressing because the software does not, and because hardware is too often designed with little or no consideration for software, what its physical specifications should be, where or how it is to be produced, what types of quality should be specified, or what results it should produce. A classic example of this is in the use that some educators have made of closed circuit television and videotape recording equipment. The easiest thing to do with a school television system is to broadcast lectures by subject-matter specialists who (sometimes) have some skill in public speaking and in platform procedures. This is a waste of the potential of the medium. The same kind of waste has and will continue to occur in the use of other media of instruction until such time as behavior-based design techniques are systematically applied to the development of all materials. Education is more advanced in the design of the hardware systems than in the design of instructional materials not because the technology does not exist, but because it is not used.

Behavioral Objectives

The developmental technology that has been developed and refined out of the early work of Skinner and his group can provide the basis for the design of the total instructional systems of the present as well as the future, including the design and development of all instructional materials, the selection of relevant presentation media and equipment, and specification of all student participation. The basis for this sweeping statement is best defined in terms of the techniques and procedures that have become a part of instructional technology.

The objectives of any activity requiring precision should be specified in advance in order to insure the maximum effectiveness and efficiency of those actions taken as part of the activity. This is as true of instructional design as it is of an automobile trip; in fact, it is far more critical since an aimless trip by car can still be enjoyable even though nothing is accomplished. Instruction that does not reach a specific destination, however, is a waste that we can ill afford, and the first step should always consist of a precise analysis of objectives. The definition of instructional objectives has always been a serious problem, both theoretically and practically (Bloom, 1956; Melton, 1964). Objectives have too often been defined in vague terms such as "understanding," "appreciating," "knowing," "developing a feel for," and so on. For many purposes, vague terminology of this sort is adequate, and occasionally even different levels of vagueness are resorted to—for instance, in differentiating, or attempting to differentiate, between "understanding," "really understanding," and "understanding in depth"! To a person preparing an instructional program, statements like this are worse than useless. What does it mean to "understand" the concept of *intelligence quotient*, or "really understand" it, or "understand it in depth"? What *is* required in preparing a program is a behavioral definition of this knowledge: what demonstrable and measurable behavior indicates "understanding," and what behavioral differences are there between "understanding," "really understanding," or "understanding in depth"? (Mager, 1961). It has always been appallingly clear to students that they usually cannot identify course objectives by reading the assigned textbook. Much of the content is illustrative only, much is irrelevant, and much will be ignored by the instructor. Nor is it usually possible to identify course objectives by attending carefully to a lecture presented by a teacher. What is even worse, there is often little relationship between the course objectives and the course examinations.

Programmed instruction was certainly not the first field to become concerned with instructional objectives, but it was the first to be helpless without them. This dependence resulted in the development of techniques for defining, classifying, and preparing specifications of course objectives, and in increased interest in already available methods of task analysis (Stolurow, 1961; Gagné, 1965). One direct approach to the problem of objectives is the preparation of every question that the student should be able to answer, every problem he should be able to solve, every direction that he should be able to follow, and every action he should be able to take upon completion of a given course. At the next level of detail, this involves breaking down each question, problem, or direction into precise definitions of the range of stimuli and of the responses that must be made to those stimuli (Gilbert, 1962). This "behavioral blueprint" identifies the relevant contents and behavioral objectives in a way that no other course description has ever done. The development of such a document requires many skills, including behavioral analysis, subject matter expertise, and skill and experience in teaching a given course to a given target audience. And even then, there is no guarantee that all subject matter specialists will agree on the validity of the content of the behavioral blueprint. Few, if any, instructors have ever defined their courses in such a precise way. Nor was it ever defined in that way for them. As a result, teachers who are supposedly teaching the same course talk about different things, and emphasize different things, and test for different things. Curriculum specialists and educators concerned with instructional design and curriculum design must also become involved, since course validity also requires standardization of objectives.

In some cases the sequence of course content is specifiable and justifiable without a great deal of difficulty; for example, in a sequence of mathematics courses in which certain topics are successively built on prerequisite topics. On the other hand, consider a course in "introductory psychology" or some other typical survey course. Of what should the content of such a course consist? Why are most introductory courses constituted as they are? Probably because that is the way that the available textbooks are structured and sequenced, but then we must ask why the textbooks are structured as they are. And the answer is apparently that, like Topsy, most courses and textbooks "just growed." The content and structure of courses have solidified over the years and for most courses complete objectives have never been specified.

The question is often asked, "What subjects can be programmed?" And the answer usually given is, "Anything can be programmed if objectives can be stated in behavioral terms." Most courses, even those given labels like "music appreciation" or "creative writing," have *some* specifiable objectives, even though it may be impossible to define all of the course goals in adequate terms. It might even be difficult to determine exactly what is meant by the *terms* "music appreciation," or "creative writing." We would need to determine exactly what constitutes the behavior of appreciating music, and how it differs from the behavior of not appreciating music. And we would need to define behaviorally the performance called creative writing, and be able to show how it differs from writing that is not to be so labelled (Miller, 1962). Only after the objectives have been analyzed and defined in precise and measurable form can there be any precise and measurable specifications of the purpose and goals of a course of instruction. Examination of a textbook does *not* reveal what a student will learn from the textbook; examination of the behavioral objectives of a program *should* reveal what a student will learn since the program is designed specifically to produce those behaviors.

A programmed textbook, or a program presented by a teaching machine, can produce a tutorial interaction, but the point of view offered here is that *all* instruction should be based on behavioral objectives and should be designed in such a way as to produce an interaction of this sort. But this is certainly not a recommendation that all instruction should be reduced to the form of a programmed text. The earlier description of instructional systems of the future included many different kinds of instructional presentations; ideally all of them should be devised in such a way as to insure student participation and relevant and correct responding (Kersh, 1965).

Individualized instruction does not necessarily imply self-pacing, adaptive sequencing, or one student learning at a time. Instruction presented to a group can be considered to be individualized instruction if each student interacts with the instruction, responding actively throughout, and receiving evaluation feedback. This is individualized instruction in the sense that it is specifically designed to provide a tutorial interaction and is as effective with fifty students together as it is with a single student.

Controlled Interaction versus Information Presentation

A tutorial interaction, whether the student interacts with a teaching machine, a programmed text, a tutor, or some other programmed medium, includes the necessary active responding

86

and feedback. An unprogrammed presentation neither specifies active participation nor provides evaluation feedback. Most presentations of the latter variety could proceed without a single student being present, and the lecturer or film or other medium could continue without being affected in any way.

It is possible and often practical to convert a conventional presentation to a programmed presentation. The first step in making a tutorial interaction out of a group presentation, regardless of the medium employed, is to prepare the statement of behavioral objectives. If a new presentation were to be developed, the objectives would be used as the basis for the design of the presentation. If existing materials are to be used, then the objectives can be matched to that existing presentation, and any objectives not covered can be specified for inclusion in some other part of the course of instruction. Once the objectives have been established, then a special workbook or booklet of response notes, or applicable questions can be prepared. These are given to each student with instructions regarding their use during the presentation. In a school system in which an extensive tape and film library already exists, this kind of modification can, at minimal expense, greatly increase the effectiveness of the existing materials.

The same kind of thing needs to be done for all teacher classroom presentations, excepting possibly that content which is considered only motivational or situations in which the instructor is to respond almost exclusively to questions or other inputs from the students. This method, referred to as the "programmed lesson plan" (Deterline, 1967), is not likely to come into wide use, however, unless textbook publishers or education agencies begin to provide the lesson plans in the form of special teacher's manuals. For one thing, a great deal of work is required in the analysis of objectives, the design of the response requirements, student notes, and visual materials, and few teachers have the necessary time available. Also, many teachers would feel that any required lesson plan or teaching sequence, even if they prepared it themselves, would infringe on their "academic freedom," a term too often misused as an excuse for inadequate and ineffectual instructional performance.

There is also the problem of who should legitimately have the responsibility for the instructional design and preparation of such materials. To require teachers to do these things, even if they are given adequate training in the necessary skills, seems very much like requiring each pilot to design and build his own plane as well as fly it.

The Concept of Validity Applied to Instruction

The concept of validity is as relevant in programmed instruction and any kind of instruction as it is in psychological testing. Instruction that is valid is instruction that accomplishes what it is designed to accomplish. The criterion—and there must always be some criterion for validation purposes—must itself be valid; that is, valid instruction achieves specified objectives, but if the objectives are invalid, the instruction will obviously be irrelevant to the required course goals. A program is tested on students, and achievement data are compared with the objectives. If the students do not successfully achieve the objectives, that fact is not taken as evidence that they should be given failing grades; rather, it is an indication that the program is inadequate and needs to be revised. Programs, regardless of their format, undergo a process generally referred to as developmental testing (Horn, 1965). This is part of an empirical process of building a program that will effectively achieve the objectives specified for it. Programs are tested on individual students, revised and retested; and program effectiveness increases as the program goes through the test and revision cycle, until finally it is field tested in the actual instructional setting for which it is designed. Programs are not tested to see if they work, but to make them work (Markle, 1966). Validation is not a measure of effectiveness of instruction; it is a *process* for insuring that effectiveness.

Conventional textbooks and lectures can almost be considered theoretical in their development; they are carefully designed but generally do not go through a series of revisions on the basis of data regarding their item-by-item effectiveness. The teacher, the textbook author, or the audiovisual designer—each assumes that his presentation will be adequate and will allow the student to learn from it. But this is a stimulus-centered approach, since their concern is not with specifying the student behavior that is to be produced, but with the presentation of stimulus material, without specification of what the presentation is to achieve. It would be difficult to test a conventional textbook, then revise it on the basis of its effectiveness, because of the difficulty in identifying exactly what is wrong and what needs to be revised. Revision of a program is quite simple, however, because the required student responses are tabulated, compared to those desired, and the entire program can be revised on a step-by-step basis. This concept—validating instruction—is an exciting and promising one for education because it puts the primary responsibility for effective instruction where it belongs —with the teacher, textbook writer, curriculum specialist, and others concerned with the development of instruction. The use of individualized instruction, whether self-paced or group inter-active in form, provides the access to student responses that is needed in order to determine what and how to revise. The more usual approach, of course, is to concentrate on the design of stimuli, not responses, and then hope for the best. It is the student who is given any failing grade, and it is the student who has to contend with the problem of his own cumulative incompetence as he progresses through a course, or through his entire academic career. Validation of instruction clarifies the objectives, and it also clarifies the responsibilities and the effectiveness of all of the instructional inputs and their components (Lumsdaine, 1965). The developmental testing approach makes program development largely an empirical process; this is one feature that instructional design has always lacked and has always needed.

Many research projects designed to evaluate the effectiveness and efficiency of programmed instruction have overlooked this empirical, developmental procedure (Holland, 1965). One might find, for example, that the post tests for an experimental group which used a program indicated average achievement of 80%. Regardless of how well this group compares with the control group, subjected to a more conventional method of instruction, the post test scores for the experimental group indicate that the program was not adequately developed. Because it is possible to measure the effectiveness of every step in a program, to revise when necessary and to design and include practice and review on either a systematic or an empirically developed spaced schedule, or both, there is no reason why a program should achieve only 80% average performance. A comparison between programmed instruction and conventional instruction is almost a meaningless question (Skinner, 1965). No matter how effective conventional instruction might be, a program can always be modified and revised to produce better results as long as the objectives to be measured are specifiable in behavioral terms. Once the desired level of effectiveness of a program has been achieved, then other comparisons between programmed instruction and conventional instruction can be made. For example, data might indicate that although the program is extremely *effective*, it is much less *efficient*, requiring considerably more time than conventional instruction. This again, however, should not be interpreted to mean that *programmed instruction* takes longer, only that that *version* of the program took longer. And again, the need for revision is indicated. If conventional instruction can achieve certain objectives in a certain amount of time, then the programmed version should incorporate all of the most efficient and effective characteristics of the conventional presentation in order to make the programmed version at least as efficient. These characteristics, effectiveness and efficiency, should be the goals for any program, but only empirical design and development procedures can maximize both.

Educational Psychology: Theoretical versus Applied

Programmed instruction, it has been said, has the potential of becoming the second most widely used product of psychological theory and research, the other being psychological testing. Educational technology will very likely become the new educational psychology, requiring evaluation specialists, behavior analysts, researchers in the applied areas of concept formation, creativity, communication and information, and others—all con-

90

cerned with the processes of learning and teaching, and with objectives and validation of instruction. A student who completes a typical college course in "Educational Psychology" as part of his preparation for becoming a teacher does presently not learn specific skills related to objectives, tutorial presentations, behavioral analysis, or other elements of instructional technology. In most of its topics, the course is theoretical, rather than applied, particularly in its coverage of learning. The discussion of theories of learning and learning research is worlds removed from classroom events. The teacher-to-be is told about Pavlov's salivating dogs, Skinner's bar-pressing rats, Thorndike's box-escaping cats, and about abstract and often incomprehensible theoretical controversies. He is also confronted with data regarding massed and spaced trials, nonsense syllables and memory drums, learning and retention curves, and so on. What, from this *potpourri*, can he take into the classroom? Very little. Educational psychology courses teach very little about learning, how it occurs, or what can be done to facilitate and insure its occurrence; and education departments may teach teaching, but they do not teach learning. As a result, most teachers work without practical assistance from the field of psychology in the area of teaching and learning.

Learning Theories and Education

There are many excellent textbooks about learning theory. Some have been especially developed for teachers. Unfortunately, the discussion of learning theories often leaves the teacher more confused than helped, since the present state of all learning theories provides very little exact guidance in the application of theoretical concepts to actual instructional design or implementation. The teacher learns that he should do something to produce and maintain motivation and that he should provide reinforcement, but recommendations for this are too much like the general advice of "think positively," "try harder," and similar statements that do not define exactly what is to be done or what actions are to be taken. The relationship between learning theories and educational practices has been described by many theorists as being practically nonexistent (e.g. Bugelski, 1964; Estes, 1960), primarily because learning theorists have not turned their attention, their research, and their analyses of learning to applied, educational problems. There are certain constructs, however, that are useful in the design and implementation of instruction, dependent upon the degree of specificity possible and the extent to which they can be expressed in terms of manipulable variables.

Motivation and Reinforcement

Up to this point nothing has been said about motivation, in spite of its theoretical as well as "common sense" importance to learning. Nor has there been any discussion of reinforcement, even though these two topics, motivation and reinforcement, are central to almost all learning theories in some form or other. In fact, Skinner's initial work in programmed instruction emphasized not only the lack of active responding in the classroom, but also the absence of continuous and systematic reinforcement, for correct, relevant, responses. During the first few years of research and development, the evaluation feedback given by the program was glibly referred to as reinforcement, but the analysis of learning and programmed instruction in terms of reinforcement has proved to be much more complex than it had originally appeared. For example, consider a student proceeding through a program in textbook form. After reading a single frame or step, the student responds and then reads the confirmation information. If he is correct, this information presumably provides reinforcement; if the response is incorrect, the information provides a basis for discriminating between the correct answer and the incorrect answer that was given. But is the confirmation information the reinforcer? In a well-designed program, the students do not always read the confirmation; the more certain they are of the correctness of the response, the less likely they are to read the confirmation. In that case, what is the reinforcement? The better the program, the less frequently the student has to read the confirmation information. Does that mean that he receives no reinforcement, so that the better the program, the fewer the reinforcers?

Several views have been expressed regarding the question of exactly what constitutes the reinforcer in programmed instruction. Some of these have begun with the assumption that *since* reinforcement is required, the only problem is to identify the reinforcer. Klaus (1965), in an especially cogent discussion of "feedback or reinforcement" and the question of identification of the reinforcement in programs, describes a variety of points of view. It has been suggested that in a well-designed program the student does not have to refer to the evaluation feedback information to learn that his response is correct; he knows that it is correct when he arrives at that response so that his own evaluation of correctness is reinforcing (Deterline, 1962; Goldberg, 1962). According to this view it is not the final, overt response (e.g. completing a sentence, or answering a question) that is reinforced, but the covert responding that had to proceed the overt response. In other words, the thinking that led up to the final answer, or conclusion, or response determination, is reinforced by completion of that activity and arriving at an answer that the student knows to be correct. Writing it down, or whatever overt response mode may be required, is far less important since it follows the critical events.

Evans, in an early study of the role of confirmation in programs, commented on the relationship between correct responses and the need for feedback:

> "The relevance of variables such as response mode and immediacy of confirmation is inversely related to the probability of correct responding. That is, in situations in which correct responses have low probability, factors such as overt responding and immediate feedback are more critical than in situations in which probabilities of correct responding are high" (Evans, 1960, p. 76).

Interestingly enough, the design of programmed materials makes it almost impossible to manipulate and study the reinforcement variable itself. The consequences of correct responses are a built-in characteristic of the materials. The reinforcing event, if it is indeed the student's immediate knowledge that his response is correct before any external feedback is provided, cannot, therefore, be withheld for purposes of providing intermittent reinforcement. Research on schedules of reinforcement has shown that for certain purposes reinforcement is more effective for maintaining high rates of responding if presented only intermittently. In programmed instruction this effect may not be relevant, at least not on a response-by-response basis, since intermittent reinforcement effects have usually been shown with recurring, similar responses rather than with the sequential development of a cumulative response repertoire. Another complication is that if reinforcement is student-mediated, then the only time that reinforcement could be withheld would be when an error is made, as it should be anyway. While there is concern with the lack of a testable explanation of the role of corrective feedback when a response is wrong (Klaus, 1965), it is possible, as intimated by Evans (quoted above), that in the case of programs with a high probability of error, the corrective function is not only more important, but may be a different phenomenon, the characteristics of which remain to be identified. Programmed instruction grew out of a reinforcement orientation, but there is certainly no one-to-one relationship between the two; and perhaps the greatest contribution of research regarding the use of programs will be its effect on reinforcement theories in their application to verbal, conceptual learning.

Motivation and reinforcement are hopelessly confounded in programmed instruction—as indeed they are in most cases—since the constant feedback (reinforcement) and the state of being correct most of the time generally "motivates" the student to remain in contact with the rest of the material. In programmed instruction it is difficult to talk about motivation without talking about reinforcement, because reinforcement is probably the only operational event we have that makes motivation manipulable. If we have reinforcers available in a situation, we are also providing for motivation; if there are no reinforcers available there is very little we can do to motivate students.

Contingency management, as a reinforcing technique, is a highly effective method of controlling motivation. Contingency management grew out of an empirical analysis of reinforcers first described by Premack (1959), and since extended both theoretically and practically into instructional technology by Homme and his associates (1963, 1966). This analysis of reinforcement assumes that of any two responses, the more probable or frequent response can be used to reinforce the less probable response. For example, a given child is more likely to engage in some types of play activities than in others, and is probably much less likely to engage in certain types of behaviors that he would generally consider as dull, uninteresting, or otherwise aversive. For this child, being allowed to play could be made contingent upon the performance of some lower-probability activity desired by teacher or parent. The more probable behavior would reinforce the less probable behavior, and the contingency arrangement is operationally motivational. For another child, social play might be less probable than isolated play, so isolated play could be used as a reinforcer for social play. Here it should be noted that the emphasis is not on identifying reinforcing stimuli or events, but on *behavior* that is reinforcing (Glaser, 1965).

Homme has reported using contingency management effectively to keep students, particularly "problem students" and school dropouts, in contact with instruction, programmed as well as conventional; after completing a specified amount of study or performance, the students were allowed to engage in, and sometimes select from options offered, a higher probability activity (Homme, 1966). The systematic management of contingencies in this fashion holds great promise for the age-old problems of motivating students to perform as required, and then providing an appropriate reinforcement when the required behavior does occur.

The view that behavior as well as stimuli can be reinforcers (e.g. allowing a higher probability behavior to occur) is related to another view of reinforcement in programs. When a student completes a step or frame, the completion of that frame is marked by his response as a signal to go to the next frame.

Being allowed to proceed or completing a frame might be reinforcing, and so might the higher probability behavior of proceeding on to the next frame.

So far we have talked only about *positive* reinforcement, in the sense of rewards. The opposite side of the reinforcement coin is negative reinforcement, the termination of an aversive stimulus, condition, or activity. A student who cannot understand a teacher during an explanation or discussion is likely to find the session increasingly aversive (frustrating), and he can terminate that aversive state of affairs by doing something else, by talking, looking at a book, or by day-dreaming. Remaining in an aversive condition is a low probability behavior. Termination of that condition is reinforcing, and the response that terminates the aversive state of affairs is reinforced and is, therefore, more likely to occur again. If in this kind of situation, contingency management is not possible, if the teacher cannot control the occurrence of undesirable, highly probable behaviors, the student will almost certainly terminate his contact with the aversive situation. On a small scale, this means day-dreaming or shifting attention; on a larger scale, it means dropping out of school.

Skill in contingency management, it appears, should be a powerful tool for teachers, both in the positive and motivating aspect, and for identifying and effectively handling student reactions to aversive situations.

Controlled interactions—tutorial interactions required by programmed lesson plans that call for frequent responding by all students in a group, or required by each of the steps in a programmed text or other programmed presentation—also provide important, motivational effects. During a conventional teacher-centered lecture, students often lose contact with a teacher only briefly, by becoming momentarily distracted or by becoming bored while the teacher reviews or provides additional explanation for slower students. This brief loss of contact can sometimes result in a student finding himself left behind, having missed a critical step or two in the sequence. Unless he asks for assistance, he can remain lost and the session becomes increasingly aversive, as a result of which he terminates contact and gets further behind. It sounds like a "vicious circle," and it is. But students are more likely to remain in constant contact with programmed materials and programmed presentations because responses are required of them, as well as because of the continuous success and progress and the related reinforcement received.

Reinforcement, from a number of points of view and from a number of directions centering around instructional technology, is becoming more than a theoretical construct or a laboratory operation; it is becoming, especially in the sense of positive knowledge of results, identifiable and manipulable, not only as an applied instruction procedure, but for purposes of basic research in an applied setting.

Programmed Instruction as a Research Tool

Theories of learning and theories of education have rarely concerned themselves with the same problems or contributed much to each other (Estes, 1960; Gage, 1963). Instructional technology, however, even in its present rudimentary form, is a meeting ground for the psychology of learning and the practice of education (Deterline, 1965).

Most of the research that has been done using programmed materials has centered around programming techniques, or comparisons with conventional instruction, or with feasibility studies, to determine what can be programmed, in what form, and for what students (Schramm, 1964; Holland, 1965).

There are many effective features of programmed instruction that account for the research evidence that, in general, most academic and skill training areas can be more effectively and efficiently taught by programmed instruction than by any other means. Validation, of course, practically insures that this has to be the case, but the analysis and specification of objectives is the single most valuable technique even if the next step, the systematic design of materials, is not done. Mager and McCann (1961) found, for example, that students given detailed descriptions of objectives, and access to a variety of instructional materials and sources of information, achieved the objectives, without a reduction in effectiveness, in far less time when they were permitted to determine their own sequence, select their own materials, and devote time to each topic as they saw fit. Without the detailed objectives, however, the students would not have had any basis for discriminating their own progress and their own achievement; they would have had no choice but to do what all students have always had to do: attempt to learn everything presented to them. Every study of programmed instruction has, by definition, incorporated the specification of objectives so that this feature alone, even when the programming techniques might have been crude or less than appropriate, probably accounted for the effectiveness of the programmed materials. Studies of this sort have advanced the technology, have settled some controversies, and have produced new and more powerful techniques. In some cases favorite biases have had to be discarded; for example, most linear programmers at one time tended to believe, with Skinner, that constructed (completion) responses were desirable, while multiple-choice (selected) responses were inappropriate. Among the reasons for rejecting multiple-choice was the idea that letting the student even wrong answers was bad, and that multiple-choice responding did not prepare the student to respond correctly in the absence of a list from which to choose the right answer.[3] Studies by Evans (1961) and Holland and Matthews (1963) have shown that discrimination training by means of multiple-choice programs can effectively prepare the student for at least some types of performance without overt practice of the performance responses themselves. Obviously, when objectives consist of discriminative behavior, discrimination training is required; where other kinds of objectives are involved, the requirements are not so clear. This area of research —now a question rather than a controversy—is related to the whole spectrum of performance, performance evaluation, and self-evaluation. If a student cannot discriminate adequate from inadequate responses, correct from incorrect answers, appropriate from inappropriate action, he is not likely to show much

3. In 1961 I wrote a brief paper on these points. The argument in that paper was clear, detailed, and wrong (Deterline, 1961).

improvement unless some external source of evaluation is always present. Discrimination training, systematically accomplished, should become a significant part of standard instructional practices, which at present it is not. Considerable research will be required to specify where and when discrimination training is essential, or helpful, or unnecessary, or irrelevant.

The theoretical problems of learning and retention can be studied in detail, and relevant variables can be manipulated in programmed instruction at various molar and molecular levels. The frequency of overt responding in programs can be manipulated along many dimensions, related to stimulus characteristics, response characteristics, redundancy, type of objectives, student characteristics, and so on, through an almost unlimited list of relevant problem areas. Each student, responding overtly, produces a cumulative record of his interaction with every rule, example, question, problem, and explanation, and other stimulus components. Not only can learning theory variables be manipulated and studied within this immediate stimulus-response network, but other topics and research areas also lend themselves to data collection and analysis with considerable clarity: information theory; communication theory; verbal concept learning and creativity learning as a function of numerous possible manipulations; test and measurement concepts; subject matter composition; hierarchies and taxonomies of response and stimulus characteristics; and certainly many aspects of behavior and learning still to be identified.

The memory drum and the Skinner box have been favorite devices for the experimental study of learning, at least in part because each provides for subject responses in such a way that detailed records of performance can be taken throughout an experimental session. Reams of data can be collected on individual subjects or groups of subjects and horizontal comparisons and vertical (sequential) analyses can be made. Programs provide the same wealth of data with considerable sensitivity and in a wide range of categories.

In what is probably the most definitive recent progress statement, Glaser has discussed the present and future of applied instructional technology, its research requirements, and a position he labels "Toward a behavioral science base for instructional design" (Glaser, 1965, ch. 17). There is little that is abstract or theoretical about the topics, the questions, the implementation procedures and problems, the design and development techniques, or any of the other variables that Glaser discusses. Programmed instruction is not only a method of instruction; it is a philosophy of education, a set of principles, and a technology which, like all technologies, is empirically based, self-correcting, and performance-oriented. Programmed instruction serves as its own research tool for its improvement and refinement, as well as for the expansion of behavioral technology and our understanding of human learning.

Implications for Instruction, Theory and Practice

". . . we enunciate two educational commandments, 'Do not teach too many subjects,' and again, 'What you teach, teach thoroughly.' The result of teaching small parts of a large number of subjects is the passive reception of disconnected ideas, not illumined with any spark of validity. . . . Pedants sneer at an education that is useful. But if education is not useful, what is it? Is it a talent to be hidden away in a napkin? Of course education should be useful, whatever your aim in life. It was useful to Saint Augustine and it was useful to Napoleon" (Whitehead, 1929).

Theories are not right or wrong; they are useful or they are not useful, and to varying degrees. In the simplest sense, a theory is first an attempt to order and explain phenomena. To that extent, and to that extent only, part of what follows is theoretical, and part is an extrapolation from what has come before. In the main, this section is an attempt to summarize and integrate instructional technology and instructional practice, and to recommend some actions that can be taken to apply the former to the latter. The assumption is maintained throughout that the key element on which present educational effectiveness hinges is the teacher. For that reason, this section might be labeled "teacher-implemented instructional technology, and a theoretical analysis of instruction."

This analysis draws heavily on Skinner, who, although he occupies a prominent position among learning theorists, is not in the strictest sense a theorist at all; and Skinner himself has emphasized that fact (Skinner, 1950). Skinner's "descriptive behaviorism" is a search for functional relationships between environmental and behavioral events, and his experimental analysis of behavior is relatively free of theoretical constructs beyond the level of objective data. This is the primary reason why programmed instruction was possible as a direct application and outgrowth of Skinner's system, rather than any of the more abstract and construct-laden theories of learning. Programmed instruction is of necessity behavioristic.

Learning, a modification of behavior, is a function of stimulus events that both precede and follow responses. To the extent that the relationships between the stimuli and responses are specifiable and manipulable, learning can be designed, engineered, and controlled with a high degree of effectiveness and reliability. Skinner and his followers have been concerned with precisely those activities since the 1930's; little wonder that Skinner's behavioral technology lends itself so well to instructional technology.[4]

The Evaluation of Instruction

Students "take" tests and are given test scores and course grades, all of which are, to some degree or other, "inadequacy scores." Even the "A" students rarely achieve all course objectives, assuming—and this is a dangerous assumption— that examinations test all of the course objectives and only those objectives. Test scores, obviously, identify student deficiencies.

4. Evans, in a strong advocation of the behavioral psychologist's viewpoint, notes in passing that, "Psychology, as a science of the behavior of organisms, is derivative from behaviorism, which is a *philosophy of science*. Unfortunately, behaviorism is an 11-letter word to many students of education. As a result, studies which are too behavioristic tend to be avoided or ignored."

That they at the same time identify weaknesses in instruction is too often overlooked or ignored, possibly because nothing usually can be done about it anyway. Public education is one of the very few fields in which the responsibility for failure to perform to specification is delegated to the victims of that failure; the students who are not effectively instructed not only carry that deficiency with them, but are made to feel that the failure was theirs.

The concept of validation of instruction is based on the view that students cannot be considered failures if there is any possibility that the instruction itself is at fault. Until evidence to the contrary is available, we should assume that failure to learn is actually failure to instruct.

Test theory is also at fault, since tests are usually designed to discriminate between students, to be sensitive to measurement of individual differences rather than to curriculum evaluation (Glaser, 1965, p. 801). Grading "on a curve" is a part of the emphasis on individual differences. Relative grading systems tend to ignore objectives and de-emphasize the problem of whether or not objectives have been achieved. Absolute standards, "go—no go" criteria, make more sense in evaluating achievement of any kind of minimum performance standards (Deterline, 1967). Until educational practice is based on valid objectives, validated instruction, and absolute evaluation systems, both students and teachers will continue to function under conditions in which only limited success is possible for either of them.

One basic principle of instructional technology is quite simple and straightforward: the evaluation of students is primarily, although indirectly, an evaluation of instruction; deficiencies detected should serve as a basis for both student remediation *and* corrective revision and improvement of instruction. The grossest violation of this principle involves providing instruction, testing students, assigning grades, and then doing nothing on the basis of test scores to revise and improve instruction in order to reduce student failure.

A teacher must be more than a subject matter specialist. The World's Greatest Authority in any field is not, by virtue of that characteristic, necessarily even a mediocre teacher. If a teacher concerns himself primarily with the technical accuracy of his own performance in the classroom he might, as a result, neglect the far more important consideration of student responses during that performance. Too often, if a teacher becomes concerned with behavior at all, it is his own behavior—not the students'—to which he directs his attention.

This may appear to be the beginning of a diatribe aimed at teachers, or at schools of education. It is not. It *is* a criticism of the *status quo*, but the lack of adequate tools is not necessarily the fault of the artisan; the criticism is directed at teaching, not teachers. If teaching does not become more behavioral science-based during the next decade, accusing fingers will be pointed, but if we follow the practice of the past, we will point them at our students.

Courses in learning theory are of little help to teachers, but courses in instructional technology and in the techniques of program development can be useful if they deal with behavioral analysis and specific courses of action. A course *about* programmed instruction is of no more value than a course about thinking, or about instructional television. But a course in which a teacher has to design, develop, and validate an instructional program can have a significant effect on his classroom teaching activities in the future (Deterline, 1963; Kersh, 1965; Lysaught, 1965).

If a curriculum committee were to develop a valid set of course objectives defined in measurable and behavioral terms, if all teachers who were to teach the course first had to demonstrate that they could prepare and implement a valid presentation to a group or to an individual, if valid selection standards were developed and used to screen all entering students, these elements alone would produce startling results. If, in addition, behavior analysts and instructional design specialists prepared materials requiring tutorial interactions (e.g. programmed lesson

103

plans, programmed textbooks, and audiovisual presentations) the results would be even more impressive. But teachers are not taught the kinds of skills required for this role as a matter of course, although increasing numbers of teachers are attending workshops and special courses that cover at least some technology of instruction. The teacher needs to become more student-performance oriented, to learn to observe and attend to relevant activities of students, to evaluate and diagnose student performance, and to learn how to teach by helping students practice relevant responses that lead to the development of criterion performance. No small requirement this!

A teacher preparing an instruction program can see firsthand that each step in instruction is really an experiment. Some experiments are successful and some are failures, and the student responses make up the data that indicate whether or not each step is successful in achieving its objectives. In more conventional instruction the teacher is also experimenting, but without the data regarding the outcome of the experimentation. The teacher who develops and tests and revises an original program is often startled to see how many predictions of successful communication prove to be wrong. Fortunately, the increased effectiveness of subsequent revisions is massively reinforcing for all of the test and revision activities. Successful programs are, perhaps, even more reinforcing to the programmer than to the student.

The question of how to evaluate teaching has always posed a serious problem, primarily because there is little agreement on what constitutes "appropriate teacher performance." Observers—whether experienced teachers, administrators, or evaluation specialists—watching the same teacher perform, will not arrive at equivalent evaluations of that teacher (Barr, 1961). An evaluation of that same teacher's performance, if related to student success in achieving specified objectives, would be more meaningful and would produce greater agreement among the evaluators. If two teachers, performing in different ways, both achieve the same measurable high level of success with their students, what basis exists for saying that one teacher is better or worse than the other? The proof of a teacher's effectiveness is in the performance of the students.

Teaching is one of the few professions that does not require a qualifying, licensing examination, but bases certification almost entirely on a record of completion of required course work. If and when teacher training has objectives of its own, objectives that relate to student achievement, and teachers are taught to achieve those objectives, then teacher certification and evaluation will be practical, and teaching, like learning, will be far more self-reinforcing.

Motivating and Reinforcing Students

It has already been commented on above that while most books about learning theories and teaching tell teachers to motivate students and provide reinforcement, in practice much of this advice is difficult to follow. Contingency management, discussed earlier, is one effective method of providing for both motivation and reinforcement. In addition to a course in the design and development of validated instruction, teacher training might also fruitfully include a course in contingency management—both courses, obviously, to be practicum or workshop courses, providing actual field practice.

Certain operations more readily identifiable as reinforcing are also part of producing and sustaining motivation, or rather, producing and sustaining motivated behavior which is directed toward the available reinforcements. Aversive control is one traditional method of motivating and reinforcing—permitting students to avoid aversive consequences only by performing the required behavior—but aversive control has too many undesirable aspects and by-products (Skinner, 1953, 1965).

What reinforcers are available to the teacher? Contingency management is one method of identifying and utilizing reinforcers. The continuous successful progress through a program is another source of reinforcement, a source that has many ramifications. Successful control of the learning environment is assumed to be reinforcing in that the general activities involved in study and interaction become reinforcing for their own sake (Moore, 1964).

A question might reasonably be asked concerning possible "satiation" effects if the student experiences only success. What might happen to the capable student to whom continued success begins to pall and for whom success and progress are no longer reinforcing? We might expect him to search for more challenging experiences, and this is not an insignificant consequence.

It has become a truism that brighter students are more curious, more apt to participate actively and to interact with confidence and perseverance. But is this a function more of intelligence or of past experience? Curiosity, exploratory behavior and attention, as behaviors, have been studied in the animal laboratory and shaped up by reinforcement or eliminated by extinction techniques (e.g. Wyckoff, 1952; Miller, 1957). Certainly, "brighter" students are more apt to be successful (i.e. be reinforced) when showing curiosity or when participating actively, and self-confidence can result when a student can discriminate a high probability of obtaining reinforcers. The individual response tendencies that a student brings with him on the first day of formal schooling are partly built-in, already affected by his past history of reinforcement, non-reinforcement, and punishment. The further accumulation of such history over years of classroom experiences is bound to reflect itself in his classroom performance.

The student with a past history of failure (non-reinforcement) expects failure, and this is part of "being unmotivated." The student with a past history of success (reinforcement) expects success, and this is part of "being motivated." White (1959), from a clincal standpoint, has discussed the concept of "competence," a cumulative motivation resulting from successful experiences in gaining control over the environment or some aspect of the environment. The "problem student" is one who, contrary to popular usage of the term, finds himself in an environment in which he has more problems than competencies.

Markle (1965) has commented that the entering behavior of students, that repertoire upon which a course of instruction must build, ranges from no information to misinformation.

Glaser (1965) adds the comment that previous learning can provide for positive or negative transfer, and Evans (1965) suggests that although certainly it is of value to know both the entering behaviors and the student's aptitudes (e.g. I.Q.), it is probably more important to know the entering behaviors. All of these emphases on knowing the existing behavior repertoires of students are based on the requirements of program development rather than traditional educational practice. The teacher and the instructional designer need to know, in a fairly precise way, the behaviors the students bring with them to the course, in terms of the course objectives and prerequisites, and also in terms of individual performance histories. Too often course presentations are based on faulty assumptions, unnecessarily, since assumptions about entering behavior can be tested. A presentation that assumes entering behaviors that do not exist is at least as far off target as a presentation that assumes no relevant entering behavior at all, either of a facilitative or interfering nature.

There are many reasons why students should be pretested on the objectives of a course or presentation, both as part of instructional design and as part of course implementation (Lumsdaine, 1965; Deterline, 1967). The students, as well as the teacher, find it advantageous to have some information pertaining to the behavioral objectives and the match or mismatch between those behaviors and their own repertoires. It is also reinforcing to be able to discriminate the progressive narrowing of any existing gap.

A Functional Concept of Ambiguity

If a student cannot discriminate any relationship between new information and already familiar information, cannot "see the point" of new information, and is, as a result, unable to respond in any relevant fashion to information, an effective interaction is impossible. When the student cannot identify objectives or direction, cannot use the new information or relate it to his existing repertoire, then we can define the information or instruction, and the situation itself, as "ambiguous." Obvi-

107

ously ambiguity would be related to a high probability of error where responses do occur.

If success, progress, control over the environment, and competence are considered to be reinforcing, then continuing ambiguity may be considered to be aversive. The very events that are already identified as being reinforcing result from the same processes and activities that remove ambiguity: clarification of objectives, and validated achievement of the objectives as a function of frequent and correct responding and reinforcement. Instructional design and implementation, utilizing the principles of positive reinforcement, can also make use of the concept of ambiguity and negative reinforcement. Each step, explanation, example, definition, and demonstration—each of these can be more effectively designed if possible sources of ambiguity are identified, their elimination specified and all content written toward that end.

The introductory description of the objectives, in a pretest or simple listing of objectives, both reduces general ambiguity and also identifies specific topics which are initially ambiguous. Each step must reduce some aspect of that ambiguity. From the student's point of view, each correct response is unambiguous, either because the step itself had removed all of the ambiguity related to that response, or because any remaining ambiguity was finally removed by the evaluation feedback.

Instruction is said to be more effective when it proceeds from the simple to the complex, from the known to the unknown, and from the concrete to the abstract. Consider the rule "proceed from the known to the unknown," sometimes described as "proceeding from the familiar to the unfamiliar." This is closely related to the concept of ambiguity, since ambiguity is more likely to develop in unfamiliar than familiar contexts. ("Familiarity" as used here is not considered to be a function of past exposure alone, but the number of related responses available).

If the explanatory examples, contexts, analogies, terminology, and frames of reference are not familiar to the student, the situation is already ambiguous. Examples used in instruction should be simple and familiar, and analogies should be obvious, since these supporting explanatory statements of relationships must serve as a context in which there are many existing associations and many available responses. In this way, the student's interaction with the instruction consists of extensive, covert responding to many relationships. The extent of responding is restricted by any ambiguity present and by contextual material that is unfamiliar. The analysis of entering behavior should also specify the associative repertoires of the students for this purpose.

Effective teachers, through years of experience, acquire first-hand knowledge of the associate repertoires of their students and learn to utilize that knowledge in providing familiar, meaningful contexts. Any teacher, regardless of his skill in this area, can obtain considerable useful information by designing presentations in advance, specifying the contexts, analogies, and examples to be used, and then developing and using a simple pretest to be sure that the assumed familiar material is in fact familiar.

In summary, all of the topics discussed in this section lead to the same conclusion: that a student's past history of success and failure (reinforcement and non-reinforcement) and aversive experiences (negative reinforcement and punishment) are the primary determinants, along with aptitude characteristics, of a student's motivation, his performance and associative repertoires, and the type and frequency of reinforcers required to modify his behavior. An approach is suggested requiring extensive and continuing pretesting of students, not as aversive events to punish failure, but to identify existing repertoires in order to build on them, provide opportunities for extensive successful practice, eliminate ambiguity, and to provide the necessary reinforcement and its related motivation. To what end? The development of competence and continuing self-reinforcement. Physical perpetual motion may be impossible, but psychological perpetual motion is characteristic of the individual whose past history of reinforcement has let him become capable of generating and obtaining his own reinforcers, so that learning for its own sake is the ultimate reinforcer.

Barr, A. S. et al. Wisconsin studies of the measurement and predication of teacher effectiveness, Journal of Experimental Education, 1961, 30, 5-156.

Bloom, B. S., editor. *Taxonomy of educational objectives.* New York: Longmans, Green, 1956.

Bugelski, B. R. *The Psychology of learning applied to teaching.* New York: Bobbs-Merrill, 1964.

Comenius, J. A. *The Great Didactic.* London: Adam and Charles Black, 1896.

Crowder, N. A. The rationale of intrinsic programming. *Programmed Instruction,* 1962, 1, (4), 3-6.

Deterline, W. A. Response mode: different effect or different purpose? *AID,* 1961, 1 (9) 47-48.

Deterline, W. A. *An introduction to programmed instruction.* Englewood Cliffs, N. J.: Prentice-Hall, 1962.

Deterline, W. A. A practical course in educational psychology based on programmed instruction. Paper read at American Psychological Association Convention, New York, September, 1963.

Deterline, W. A., Learning theory, teaching, and instructional technology. *AV Communications Review,* 1965, 405-411.

Deterline, W. A., Practical problems in program production. In P. C. Lange (Ed.) *Programed instruction* 66th Yearbook, National Society for the Study of Education, 1967, 66. Part II.

Estes, W. K. Learning. In C. W. Harris (Ed.) *Encyclopedia of educational research.* New York: Macmillan Company, 1960.

Evans, J. L. *An investigation of 'teaching machine' variables using learning programs in symbolic logic.* Doctor's thesis. Pittsburgh: University of Pittsburgh, 1960.

Evans, J. L. *Multiple choice discrimination programming.* Paper presented at the American Psychological Association Convention, New York, September, 1961.

Evans, J. L. A potpourri of programming technology. In G. D. Ofiesh and W. C. Meierhenry (Eds.) *Trends in programmed instruction.* Washington, D.C.: National Education Association and National Society for Programmed Instruction, 1964.

Evans, J. L. Programming in mathematics and logic. In R. Glaser (Ed.) *Teaching Machines and Programed Learning,* II. Washington, D.C.: National Education Association, 1965. Pp. 371-440.

Gage, N. L. Paradigms for research on teaching. *Handbook of Research on Teaching.* Chicago: Rand McNally & Co., 1963. Pp. 94-141.

Gagné, R. M. The analysis of instructional objectives for the design of instruction. In R. Glaser (Ed.) *Teaching Machines and Programed Learning,* II. Washington, D.C.: National Education Association, 1965. Pp. 21-65.

Gilbert, T. F. Mathetics: the technology of education. *Journal of Mathetics,* 1962, 1, (2), 7-56.

Glaser, R. Toward a behavioral science base for instructional design. In R. Glaser (Ed.) *Teaching Machines and Programed Learning,* II. Washington, D.C.: National Education Association, 1965, Pp. 771-809.

Goldberg, I. A. An introduction to programed instruction. In S. Margulies and L. D. Eigen (Eds.) *Applied programed instruction.* New York: John Wiley & Sons, 1962. Pp. 15-20.

Holland, A. L., and Matthews, J. Application of teaching machine concepts to speech pathology and audiology. *Asha,* 1963, 5, 474-482.

Holland, J. G. Research programming variables. In R. Glaser (Ed.) *Teaching Machines and Programmed Learning,* II. Washington, D.C.: National Education Association, 1965. Pp. 66-117.

Homme, L. E. et al. Use of Premack principle in controlling the behavior of nursery school children. *Journal of the experimental analysis of behavior,* 1963, 6 (4), 542.

Homme, L. E. and Addison. The reinforcing event (RE) menu. *NSPI Journal,* 1966, 5 (4), 8-9.

Homme, L. E. and Klaus, D. J. *Laboratory studies in the analysis of behavior.* Pittsburgh, Pa.: Lever Press. 1959.

Horn, R. E. *Developmental testing*. Unpublished program. 1965.

Keller, F. S. and Schoenfeld, W. N. *Principles of psychology*. New York: Appleton-Century-Crofts, 1950.

Kersh, B. Y. Programming classroom instruction. In R. Glaser (Ed.) *Teaching Machines and Programed Learning, II*. Washington, D.C.: National Education Association, 1965. Pp. 321-368.

Klaus, D. J. An analysis of programming techniques. In R. Glaser (Ed.) *Teaching Machines and Programed Learning, II*. Washington, D.C.: National Education Association, 1965. Pp. 118-161.

Lewis, B. N. and Pask, G. The theory and practice of adaptive teaching systems. In R. Glaser (Ed.) *Teaching Machines and Programed Learning, II*. Washington, D.C.: National Education Association, 1965. Pp. 213-266.

Lumsdaine, A. A. Assessing the effectiveness of instructional programs. In R. Glaser (Ed.) *Teaching Machines and Programed Learning, II*. Washington, D.C.: National Education Association, 1965. Pp. 267-320.

Lysaught, J. P. Programming auto-instructional material: some observed effects upon the teacher, *NSPI Journal*, 1966, 5 (4), 3-5.

Mager, R. F. *Preparing objectives for programed instruction*. San Francisco: Fearon Publishers, 1961.

Mager, R. F. and McCann, J. Learner-controlled instruction. Palo Alto, California: Varian Associates, 1961.

Markle, S. M. Programed instruction in English. In R. Glaser (Ed.) *Teaching Machines and Programed Learning, II*. Washington, D.C.: National Education Association, 1965. Pp. 546-583.

Markle, S. M. President's page. *NSPI Journal*, 1966, 5 (6), 2.

Melton, A. W. editor. *Categories of human learning*. New York: Academic Press, 1964.

Miller, N. E. Liberalization of basic S-R concepts: extensions to conflict behavior, motivation and social learning. In S. Koch (Ed.) *Psychology: a study of a science*, Vol. 2. New York: McGraw-Hill Book Company, 1959.

Miller, R. B. Task description and analysis. In R. M. Gagné

(Ed.) *Psychological principles in systems development.* New York: Holt, Rinehart & Winston, 1962. Pp. 187-228.

Moore, O. K. Autotelic responsive environments and exceptional children. *The special child in century* 21. Seattle, Wash.: Special Child Publications, 1964.

Premack, D. Toward empirical behavior laws: I. Positive reinforcement. *Psychological review,* 1959, 66, 219-33.

Pressey, S. L. Auto-elucidation without programming. *NSPI Journal,* 1964, 3 (6), 12-13.

Schramm, W. *The research on programed instruction: an annotated bibliography.* Stanford, Calif.: Institute for Communication Research, Stanford University, 1962.

Skinner, B. F. Are theories of learning necessary? *Psychological review,* 1950, 57, 193-216.

Skinner, B. F. *Science and human behavior.* New York: Macmillan Co., 1953.

Skinner, B. F. The science of learning and the art of teaching. *Harvard Educational Review,* 1954, 24, 86-97.

Skinner, B. F. Reflections on a decade of teaching machines. In R. Glaser (Ed.) *Teaching Machines and Programed Learning,* II. Washington, D.C.: National Education Association, 1965. Pp. 5-20.

Stolurow, L. M. *Teaching by machine.* Cooperative research monograph No. 6. Washington, D.C.: U.S. Office of Education, 1961.

Stolurow, L. M. and Davis, D. Teaching machines and computer-based systems. In R. Glaser (Ed.) *Teaching Machines and Programed Learning,* II. Washington, D.C.: National Education Association, 1965. Pp. 162-212.

Thorndike, E. L. *Education.* New York: Macmillan Company, 1912.

White, R. W. Motivation reconsidered: the concept of competence. *Psychological Review,* 1959, 66, 297-333.

Whitehead, A. N. *The aims of education.* New York: Macmillan Company, 1929.

Wyckoff, L. B. Jr. The role of observing responses in discrimination learning. Part I. *Psychological Review,* 1952, 59, 431-442.

DELINQUENCY AND CRIME

SEYMOUR RUBENFELD, PH.D.
Program Development Consultant,
National Institute of Mental Health

Editorial Note

Nowhere are new approaches to persistent problems more urgently needed than in the area of delinquency and crime. Here psychology has lagged behind the other behavorial disciplines in investigating the causes of antisocial behavior and in proposing intervention techniques. Dr. Rubenfeld calls attention to a number of promising experiments and developments. "Possibly the most significant psychological developments in delinquency intervention," he writes, "are the behavior-change studies based on experimental psychological knowledge regarding learning and behavior."

Dr. Seymour Rubenfeld has been in the private practice of clinical psychology in the metropolitan area of Washington, D.C., since 1957. He has maintained an active scientific and professional interest in delinquency and youth problems.

Doctor Rubenfeld was born in Scranton, Pennsylvania. He received both his M.S. and Ph.D. degrees from the Pennsylvania State University in 1952 and 1954. He was Chief of Psychological Services at The National Training School for Boys in Washington, D.C., from 1954 to 1957, when his work in delinquency began. During the following two years he directed a social-psychological study of an inmate community in that institution.

Doctor Rubenfeld has consulted with several Federal agencies and with community action programs in the study of adolescent behavior and in provision of treatment services for offenders. He has recently taken part in the program development efforts of the Center for the Studies of Crime and Delinquency of the National Institute of Mental Health. His recent book, Family of Outcasts: A New Theory of Delinquency, represents a major theoretical effort to synthesize psychological and social-scientific conceptions of delinquency.

•

DELINQUENCY AND CRIME

It would be difficult to find another area of behavior in which there is a greater gap between sure psychological knowledge and the complexity of the problem than is true of delinquency and crime. The size and gravity of the delinquency and crime problem lends urgency to the search for understanding and intervention techniques. The psychological disciplines lag far behind the social sciences in investigations and conceptualizations of antisocial behavior at the level of society and the community, for example, while recent community action programs have been open invitations to social-psychological approaches.

Despite these qualifications, research and treatment bridgeheads of a psychological nature are impressive and enlarging. An effort such as this, to highlight significant findings and promising methods, must be selective in ways that may reflect arbitrariness or neglect of efforts that others may consider quite important. This paper attempts to summarize developments in psychological explanations of law-and norm-violators; in research and programs related to offender typologies; in behavior-change research with offenders, and in psychological contributions to control and treatment of offenders. Studies relevant to individual behavior are cited here although some of them may have originated in the context of other behavioral sciences and helping professions besides psychology.

Etiology

Two ground shifts in the direction of psychological explanations are noted. Personality formulations primarily in terms of

115

libidinal needs or other primary drives are falling into disuse. They are in an obsolescent tradition of bio-psychological theories of criminality (see Shore). An increasing current emphasis is on deficiencies in learning and thinking skills and on configurations of coping and defensive processes in offenders—on ego characteristics, in short. Behavior-theory approaches have also brought a renewed interest in habit formation and maintenance.

A second shift, important though less evident than the first, is toward social-psychological conceptions. Martin Deutsch's and Strodtbeck's (Short and Strodtbeck) investigations of cognitive deficits indicate that deficiencies in learning and interpersonal skills mediate the early onset of school underachievement in deprived children, probably the first link in the correlation of the school dropout and delinquency. Erikson's conceptions of psychosocial development are the basis of Rubenfeld's (1965) psychocultural theory of delinquency.

Psychodynamic Theories

Traditional psychoanalytic formulations viewed delinquent and criminal behavior as an expression of improperly socialized primary drives. Aichhorn, Alexander, Friedlander, Karpman, and the Healys are in the forefront in pioneering this line of investigation. These explanations also stressed the importance of distortions in character development as a result of disruptive socialization.

We owe a number of contributions of great current value to these and other original psychoanalytic developments. Insight-oriented therapists especially are indebted for their working knowledge of the unconscious, for most of the techniques and principles of exploratory psychotherapy, and for the ongoing study of treatment approaches to antisocial character disorders in adults and children as well as a continuing elaboration of these syndromes (Greenacre, Lindner, Rabinovitch, Newton Baker Project). Researchers and theorists may utilize leads as to the general symbolic significance of some anti-social acts, especially those of a compulsive nature.

Relatively recent psychodynamic explanations show as much interest in how the offender copes with and defends against reality, given certain needs and anxieties, as in how the latter came about. Redl details ego defenses and deficiencies of conduct-disordered children (Redl and Wineman). Warren's typological work, to be considered later, relies on a dynamic theory of stages of interpersonal skill formation (Sullivan, et al). D. Bloch and Kaufman have independently advanced ideas about ways in which delinquents provoke animosity from a fear of intimacy associated with a profound sense of loss.

Theoretical and empirical investigations of conscience, impulse control, and skills essential to conforming achievement—mediating functions between personal needs and environmental pressures—deserve further consideration because of their relevance to offenders.

Mediating Processes

It was suggested earlier that the relationships among educational retardation, the dropout phenomenon, and delinquency have long been a matter of study and concern (H. Bloch and Flynn, pp. 198-202). The study of cognitive deficits—in numbers concepts, preparedness, language skills, etc.—by M. Deutsch and Strodtbeck among others, is highly significant in this regard because of their findings that such deficiencies occur extremely often among very deprived preschoolers, many of whom come from high-delinquency groups. M. Deutsch's demonstrational work in remediating these deficits has given a strong impetus to subsequent Head Start programs (though there is reason to believe that the latter have often fallen disappointingly short of the remedial hopes originally raised regarding them; see Kraft).

Erikson's theory of ego development is an attempt to inventory a progression of personal-social skills a growing person must master, such as the acquisition of trust, separateness and initiative. His is a general theory of man-in-culture but it is relevant to delinquency in at least three ways. It provides a theoretical framework for the dimensions of ego functioning, a focal area, as already indicated, for much action research in delinquency intervention. Perhaps more important, his formulations relate the potentials for personal self-realization and competence to the social conditions under which an individual is reared; the significance of socio-economic deprivation in delinquency has received greatly renewed emphasis in social-scientific explanations (Cohen, Cloward and Ohlin, W. B. Miller) and in recent opportunity and community action programs. Finally, Erikson's concepts of the adolescent identity crisis, identity foreclosure and negative identity provide theoretical tools for psychological analyses of the social protest and repudiation components in delinquent value- and norm-systems.

Kohlberg's sophisticated research and theory regarding the development of moral judgment indicates how much conscience, as a mediating process, is shaped by social realities. He has proposed a genetic, developmental model of moral judgment. Kohlberg asserts that the low level of moral judgment among delinquents results from growing up in social worlds with low development of moral thought. He has found several stages of moral development, in addition to corroborating Piaget's identification of an early moral absolutism. Also, he finds that moral conduct is not solely determined by moral judgment, and that the latter cannot be taught didactically but only through interaction.

Redl and his associates have described crucial disabilities on the part of aggressive children in coping with their needs and with external reality. He and Wineman have also indicated various skills peculiar to such behavior-disordered children, techniques of provocation, manipulation and disruption in the service of gratifying their impulses.

Environmental Factors

Relatively recent investigations of family and community influences predisposing to anti-social behavior are worth noting. Some of the more basic findings of several family studies (Andry, Bandura and Walters, Bender, Bowlby, the Gluecks, Gold, the McCords and Zola) might be summarized.

The likelihood of anti-social attitudes occurring later is

heightened when there is an early deprivation of love or when parents separate early in a child's life. Psychological damages which may later find expression in delinquent acting-out may be caused not by the physical disruption of a family alone, but by chronic conflict and emotional neglect.

The importance of maternal deprivation or neglect has been established in clinical investigation. Maternal affection and her mature control may, on the other hand, counteract the ill effects of a negligent or criminal father. Recent studies have, however, underlined the importance of paternal stability and responsibility. It has been found that father's effective control over deviant impulses in his child is related to his status in and value to his family and community. The obverse seems also true; fathers who are absent, irresponsible and disparaged by the family figure often in the histories of delinquents.

Several investigations suggest that discipline which is consistent, based on the affectional bond between parent and child rather than on the power relation between them, and directed toward the development of competence in the child, will forestall delinquent behavior. Punishment of a harsh or intimidating sort accomplishes immediate conformity but is ineffective in creating enduring internalization. It leads to an identification, not with the moral attitudes of the parent, but with his aggressiveness.

Certain community-based studies have pointed up factors of a social-psychological nature which may be of considerable importance in the production of subcultural delinquency. Their existence casts doubt on the adequacy of social-scientific accounts which rely solely or chiefly on aspects of social structure and process to explain delinquency.

Certain very pervasive sentiments seem to be psychosocial accompaniments of the anomic states which may exist in deprived subcultures. These sentiments are highly valued manners and relationship attitudes which probably color self-awareness and interpersonal behavior, though they may be less evident in the more formal institutions and norms of the group. Such sentiments are attitudes typifying estrangement, antagonism, misanthropic feelings, toughness, pessimism—a dyssocial breeding ground, in other words, for delinquent and criminal values and practices (Cohen and Hodges, W. B. Miller, Hughes, et al.).

A second feature of deprived, high-delinquency groups is the high rate of psychological disorders, very often of a behavior-problem nature, to which young and adult seem susceptible (Hughes, et al., Kerr, Spinley, Stott).

Rubenfeld utilized such data and Erikson's concepts in trying to develop a psychocultural view of delinquency (1965). It was suggested there that cultural and historical deprivations imposed on some subcultures have not been solely socio-economic, as sociological theories contend. Psychologically, these were restrictions also on ego functioning, since the economic exploitation of Negroes, for example, also subjected them to racial ostracism, subordination and mistrust. Repudiation of conforming values and norms by groups treated invidiously has not been a simple function of rebellion against socio-economic constraints, therefore. Such states of anomie have also been reflections of dyssocial sentiments generated within the group by the loss of ego capacities to function collaboratively toward self-realizing ends. These psychological damages are evident in the high reported rates of personal disorder just cited for such groups. Subcultural delinquency is an adolescent version of anti-social values and norms resulting partly from disabilities to exert effort competently and to relate resourcefully and flexibly. Acting-out in delinquency is aggravated by the desperation of identity crises in which deprived adolescents abhor the prospect of the adult lives about them and do not have the ego skills to move out by whatever legitimate avenues might be available, such as through further education.

Typological Research

New approaches to defining and treating offenders are being made in recent typological researches. Modern psychological typing efforts are attempts to classify a general population of offenders (almost always youth) into a few definite categories. These are behavior categories, subject to empirical test and based on theoretical models open to revision on the basis of new data.

120

Modern psychological typologies are not based on biophysical characteristics or on offense categories.

Some sub-populations for which typological systems have been or are being constructed are pre-adolescent committed delinquents (Jesness), the intake of a medium-size city's juvenile court (Hurwitz), middle-class adjudicated delinquents (MacGregor, et al.), young adult and adolescent offenders (Sullivan, et al., Warren), pre-adolescent anti-social character disorders (Newton Baker Project). A rather remarkable consideration, in view of differences in subjects, research methods used, type names and theoretical models, is the similarities among the types being identified. All the psychological typologies seem to be describing certain general types common to them. These parallels will be discussed later.

Some Results

Warren, along with Grant and Sullivan, originally devised a nine-subtype system based on a developmental theory of stages in interpersonal maturity, in order to organize differential treatment approaches to Navy disciplinary problems at Camp Elliott. Warren and other collaborators have been applying the typology from this interpersonal maturity theory in the Community Treatment Project (CTP) of the California Youth Authority. The CTP is, to the present, the largest, most systematic application of a typological approach to diagnosing and treating delinquents. The CTP is a test of community-based probationary treatment as a substitute for institutional commitment; all CTP subjects were impartially selected from among adjudicated youths who were slated for institutional commitment. Different treatment strategies have been designed according to the diagnosed type of each subject-client.

Practically all treatment results which are statistically significant or tending toward significance are in favor of CTP subjects when compared with matched controls undergoing regular institutional treatment. The cost per capita of CTP treatment is also lower than the costs of institutionalization. The interpersonal maturity levels typology thus appears to be an advance

121

over undifferentiated explanations and rehabilitation approaches for delinquents.

Hunt and his co-workers have been constructing a theory of cognitive development; the model defines a progression of stages in refinement of concept formation. Their interest is primarily pedagogic. They are trying to identify optimal learning conditions for different conceptual types. However, since they also view treatment as a learning situation, they are also involved in developing differential treatment strategies and in treator training. The model opens new avenues for educating delinquents who are arrested in their cognitive development. The need to find effective psychoeducational approaches to the remediation of learning deficiencies in deprived offenders makes the work of Hunt and his colleagues highly relevant to delinquency intervention. The theory has been shown to have good construct validity. Also, classroom situations were devised to conform to the level of thinking of students grouped according to their conceptual level. Improvements were obtained by these means in personal development, learning, and class participation.

MacGregor and his colleagues have developed short-term, team approaches to family treatment which deserve cross-validation because initial results compare favorably with outcomes of more conventional treatment of longer duration. Working with middle-class delinquents and their families, they constructed a typology in the framework of a model of ego development. In addition, their clinical evidence led them to associate each delinquent type with a particular configuration of family interactions and dynamics. This family classification scheme is virtually unique in the psychological typology literature. This family typology, considered together with other family data from typological research, lends encouragement to the hope that differential strategies may eventually be provided for deprived as well as relatively privileged delinquents' families presuming that linkages may be established between delinquent and family types.

Rubenfeld (1966) compared the reported results from the psychological type studies of Jesness, Hunt, Hurwitz, Mac-Gregor, Makkay (Newton Baker Project), Quay, Reiss and Warren. An inspection of their published data gave the traits each author associates with each of his subtypes. These subtype traits were collated on the basis of their verbal and semantic similarity.

The classification which resulted is an armchair scheme and not based on empirical comparisons. The composite types suggested by inspection are therefore heuristic hypotheses, not confirmed concepts. Nevertheless, it seemed that almost all the subtype descriptions could be sorted into five composite categories. Enough repetitions of the same traits, and enough seeming consistency among findings relevant to each category were found to appear to warrant viewing the categories as composite or general types. Short summaries of the composites follow. Their names are this writer's.

1. Some of the studies identify a *Mentally Ill* delinquent. Relatively little close attention is paid this type, however; in general, the typologies which note his existence apparently consider him to be adequately described in the clinical literature dealing with juvenile and youth psychoses.

2. An *Impulse-Oriented* delinquent, on the other hand, is identified by almost all the typologies. He is portrayed, in all descriptions, as the most clearly infantile in his behavior of all the general types. The Impulsive delinquent is dominated by his wishes, and his fears that they might be frustrated, in his thinking, his affect life and his behavior. He is an ideal type of much, if not most psychiatric writing on delinquents-in-general; many clinical descriptions and discussions of dynamics seem to accord with characteristics attributed to his type. He relates to limits and to authority figures who represent them, as frustrations and causes of deprivation. He seems to perceive his social reality quite inadequately and has little tolerance for delay. Family data suggest that he comes from very deprived

families which are disorganized and malfunctioning; the parents are often inadequate, psychologically disordered or deviant.

3. There is also a heavy convergence of descriptions on a *Power-Oriented* type. Two variations on this type seem to be indicated. Both have much in common with the authoritarian personality; they apparently operate under the assumption that power is the most decisive factor in interpersonal relations, and that rules are to be respected primarily because, and to the extent that, they represent power. Right and wrong have pragmatic meaning but little or no moral significance. Only control seems to be respected and believed; others are perceived in terms of their relative power or as means for furthering the actor's own purposes.

One variant, the *Conformist*, submits to this way of conceiving reality rather more than he tries actively to manage it. His peers do not trust him to any great extent, and he is as easily lost to as won over by adult treators, apparently because he aligns himself to whomever seems more powerful at the moment. *Controllers* represent the active side of Power Orientation. They are manipulative, sometimes to a highly skilled degree, always seeking to control others. For this reason they may become the leaders of institution and street gang groups, when they have sufficient talent. The literature suggests that Power-Oriented delinquents come from deprived families, in which there may be chronic power struggles between the parents, who may use control against the children or enlist them against the other parent. There are other suggestions that the fathers may be the less adequate and dependable parent. Often siblings are also delinquent.

4. *Neurotic* delinquents seem dominated by intrapsychic conflicts, especially in relation to authority. In some important respects, this type represents a higher level of maturation than those previously described, since the conflicts suggest degrees of internalization that previous types do not evince. Nevertheless, they are described as guilt-ridden, fearful, socially inept and withdrawn, timorous, and anxious. Their peers often ostracize or scapegoat them. Neurotic delinquents tend to come from economically somewhat more advantaged families. The parents'

marriage may be physically intact but deeply estranged and conflicted. The fathers may be unavailable to the youths' needs or harshly punitive, although, more often than in the two previous types, they may be present and are adequate economic providers.

5. The most psychologically mature of the composite types is the last; he shows benchmark features of the adolescent identity crisis, in his attempts to separate himself from his family or from what he may seem to consider a conformity that is unrewarding and depriving. He seems drawn to peer groups with deviant values and through them to delinquency; he has therefore been labelled a *Normative Outsider*. Again, empirical findings seem to be differentiating two variants of this composite type, one economically *Privileged*, the other from *Deprived* economic circumstances.

The privileged Outsider often has a father with a valued, sometimes even a prominent position in the community, but whose status and respect in private, family life seems discounted (MacGregor, et al.). The deprived Outsider is an ideal type of sociological theory; he bears many resemblances to the "normal," "subcultural," "integrated" young offender in many social-scientific accounts. He is personally stable and relatively self-sufficient and competent. His repudiation of conventional values and norms seems rational and is subculturally supported. He is open to meaningful relationships with treators, but often consciously rejects their purposes as contrary to his best interests. His family background is often very deprived, of ethnic minority origins, but may also show considerable cohesiveness and stability. The mothers may be quite strong and resourceful people.

The collations above raise important theoretical and practical considerations. In the first place they indicate a possible resolution of some vexing differences between psychological and sociological explanations of delinquency. The fact that Impulsive delinquents and deprived Outsiders look like the favored versions of clinicians and social scientists respectively, suggests that most current etiologies may be partial theories, of separate causative processes. A careful study, of relative incidence of types, on a sample from a very large delinquent population, seems indicated.

Such a study might also be a guide to strategy decisions regarding large-scale intervention efforts: The Power-Oriented type, especially the Controller, evinces clear limitations in his ego development. Intervention for him seems to call for psycho-educational techniques of remediation (Hobbs, Hunt, Gunon). The deprived Outsider, on the other hand, might best be reached by better controls through law enforcement, and by opportunity programs. The Controller can be confused with the deprived Outsider, at least on superficial acquaintance, as a result of his "conning" the interviewer, his "cool," and the absence oftentime of anxiety indicators. Some typological studies did, in fact, seem to mis-classify subjects in one or both of these types. Since the relative incidence of the two types in deprived populations is unknown, there is no present basis to make a judgment regarding action research and program priorities.

Behavior-Change Methodology

Possibly the most significant psychological developments in delinquency intervention are the behavior-change studies based on experimental psychological knowledge regarding learning and behavior. These applications to delinquency are so new that the oldest of them was undertaken no more than seven years ago, to the writer's knowledge. Behavior-change procedures involve the manipulation of the parameters of learning and conditioning. These procedures offer the prospect of a highly effective behavior control technology. Because behavior-change methodology is highly operational, it is also highly verifiable and teachable.

On the basis of a functional analysis of the contingencies supporting the behavior to be modified, the designer of a change study devises procedures for extinguishing problem behavior; he may also plan out the nature, rates, and schedules of reinforcements to be employed in establishing alternative patterns. Change criteria are kept strictly behavioral and as measurable as possible. Subjects' responses also affect the experimenters' provision of reinforcements; in other words, operant approaches dominate conditioning procedures.

126

Behavior therapy and programmed instruction procedures are two principal expressions, clinical and educational, of behavior-change methodology. Programmed instruction is widely used in a variety of settings; behavior therapies seem clearly superior to other forms of treatment with respect to the clarity with which procedures and predicted effects may be shown. (See Shah for references to the general behavior-change literature.)

In a pioneering study Slack attracted several tough, resistive delinquents in the community into an informational interview situation which was gradually shaped into individual therapy, through the programmed use of material reinforcements, mainly payment for interviews. Positive results which persisted were obtained. The treatment effects are no less significant than the successful recruitment, in view of the notorious resistance of hardened street delinquents to any kind of treatment where no coercion is involved.

Slack replicated these findings in an extension of his first study. Each delinquent is recruited into a relationship with an ex-offender and a young businessman in the community. Their mutual relationships provide the delinquent with social reinforcements and deterrents. This study also obtained conscientious participation in psychotherapy by operant conditioning procedures. It is interesting also that delinquency in the localities from which subjects were enlisted reportedly dropped significantly; many of the successful subjects in this experiment have been gang leaders.

Schwitzgebel also obtained markedly good results with confirmed delinquents, using methods and approaches similar to Slack's. A three-year follow-up, employing controls, showed significantly reduced delinquency rates for his subjects.

At Draper Prison in Alabama, McKee employed a programmed instruction approach with the prisoners and obtained dramatic results. Many inmates made very great educational progress; some ex-inmates stayed on as programmers and instructional assistants. Draper's institutional climate also underwent notable changes. Disciplinary charges dropped off by almost one half, for example.

At the National Training School for Boys, another programmed instruction project, working with a sample of inmates, was highly successful. Rewards and privileges were made strictly contingent on academic effort, by using a token economy for scholastic work accomplished. Cohen extended this approach to a second, larger study at the same institution, with an entire dormitory unit. The project purposes involve not only academic goals but also increased social conformity within the unit and in a work-release program. Initial results look very promising.

The uniformity of positive results with several applications of the same methodology, and evaluated against relatively rigorous scientific criteria, are a signal achievement in psychological interventions with delinquents. Behavior-change methods seem to promise a technology for establishing an influence with sometimes quite recalcitrant delinquents, where before this kind of accomplishment lay in the realm of therapeutic art—a commodity by no means readily available. This consideration suggests that people without special knowledge and training may be taught behavior-change techniques. The availability of manpower has always been a sore problem in crime and delinquency intervention. As previously suggested, this general line of action research is relatively new; its further extension may be anticipated.

Other Developments in Intervention

In general, certain trends may be noted in recent developments in psychological remediation. Rehabilitation efforts with adjudicated offenders are being based increasingly in the community. The California Youth Authority CTP (Warren) is an example. Adults in the community who fulfill a socializing role are being recruited into a treatment function, such as teachers, employers and parents. Adult parolees and probationers are being rehabilitated by absorption into new careers in poverty

128

and welfare programs for the poor (Pearl and Riessman). The "new careers" approach to rehabilitation has led to a sub-professionalization in mental health, with mental health aides trained to handle some of the treatment directly, freeing the mental health professional to function as trainer, consultant, and program developer.

Treatment emphases have also been shifting. There is a lessening of interest in the uncovering and resolution of defenses and conflicts. Riessman (in Riessman and Pearl) has suggested that traditional approaches in the vein of exploratory therapy have in essence screened out those deprived clients who could or would not conform to middle-class therapists' restrictions on the conditions under which the latter were willing to dispense help. Current efforts try more to emphasize existing personal skills, aptitudes and ego strengths in order to solve immediate living problems.

Finally, there are trends toward preventive mental health programming. The Office of Economic Opportunity's and the Office of Juvenile Delinquency's controversial community action programs have been widely defended as having a primary-prevention relation to juvenile delinquency. To the extent that delinquency and crime represent psychosocial disorder, a major trend in treatment generally has been toward involvement of the significant environment, from the field of family forces (MacGregor, et al., Newton-Baker Project) to such primary socializing institutions as the school, in relation to children and youth.

In connection with the latter, OEO's Operation Head Start, its program for preschool enrichment of deprived children, might be considered a preventive delinquency effort. Kraft has indicated that, as they are now functioning, many Head Start efforts are not working out well. In many instances, they are being run in poor facilities with an inadequately qualified and trained staff. In these cases, a new careers approach seems to have operated injuriously against other program interests; some of the deprived adults recruited as instructors have lacked the personal competence, job skills and motivations to perform adequately as preschool teachers.

Sometimes, the content of the programs has meant primarily or solely, providing the children training in being a part of a group under adult guidance. Though this may be valuable, it has little to do with the goals of stimulating perceptual and learning maturation with which the original studies of cognitive deficits were basically concerned. Kraft suggests a much stronger action-research emphasis, premised on considerably greater respect for the complex educational needs involved, for the educative skills and knowledge the task requires, and for recognition of our relative ignorance concerning both.

The concept of a walk-in, neighborhood, "storefront" mental health clinic is being implemented in some community programs for deprived urban groups, notably New York City's Mobilization for Youth. This conception has been in part a response to the structure of many traditional mental health clinics, with their lengthy intake procedures and traditional long-term, insight-oriented, therapeutic approaches. Such clinics have been marketing their services to more responsive middle-class groups for years.

The structure of the storefront clinics, on the other hand, emphasizes immediate help for the client's emergent living problems, as he defines them. There is consequently a heavier casework orientation and probably a greater reliance on relationship work, without the usual preliminary negotiation of a "treatment contract" that characterizes the opening sessions of traditional approaches. An important function being evolved for the sub-professional mental health aides is to act as intermediary and representative, for deprived families, with welfare bureaucracies. He may make direct contacts for them with appropriate personnel and expedite the handling of their cases. The relative powerlessness and naivete of some deprived, needy people is often a serious stumbling block to their receiving help.

Making casework contact initially valuable by providing direct services has proved useful in recruiting resistant, delinquency-producing families into treatment. A number of techniques have been developed for channeling such families to the treatment agency when need is maximal, during crises (Bunch, et al.).

Massimo and Shore produced markedly good results by adopting a vocationally-oriented psychotherapy approach to male delinquent dropouts. Pre-employment and job counseling, remedial education and psychotherapy resulted in enduring gains in terms of academic learning, personality function, job stability and conformity in clients (see also Shore and Massimo).

Correctional Treatment

The past decade has witnessed vigorous innovating in correctional and institutional interventions, some with considerable psychological relevance. Among these are trends toward differential treatment; a proliferation of types of treatment institutions, and developments in milieu treatment for institutionalized offenders.

A fundamental advantage of typological researches is the prospect they present for differential treatment strategies. The lack of ways to make meaningful psychosocial distinctions with the legal-sociological definitions of "delinquent" and "felon" has had an unfortunate consequence. Planning treatment for individual differences has depended almost entirely on the treator's judgment, training and predilections. Typologies may change this situation. Warren's offender classification system, the most advanced in its application, is providing a basis for on-going efforts to generate several distinctive treatment strategies based on the characteristics of subtypes. Not only is treatment made relevant to type, but the treator characteristics indicated for each strategy are also undergoing definition.

The other major innovation of the California CTP, recruitment by the probation agent of a community network of influence into the treatment effort, also marks off another variation in a broadening spectrum of alternative corrections procedures. Institution classification procedures have often been determined more by custodial considerations than by treatment needs; this state of affairs sometimes resulted in a warehousing of offenders comparable to the indiscriminate lumping-together of criminals, psychotics and retardates before nineteenth century reforms. A considerable sociological literature has accumulated on the kinds of anti-social communities that come into being under such custodial conditions; these studies are outside the province of this review (Sykes and Messinger). In addition there have been some social-psychological investigations of the effects on individual behavior, attitudes and sentiments, and personality of participation in such anti-social inmate social systems (Polsky; Rubenfeld and Stafford). The most general conclusions are those of Street, Vinter and Perrow, that inmate values and behaviors tend toward legitimacy in institutions that are truly oriented toward their rehabilitation, and are more often illegitimate in institutions where they are managed coercively and restrictively.

These research findings lend scientific support to a conclusion that some correctional planners have reached, that institutional structure in large part determines inmate response. The now-famous Highfields experiment of the mid-fifties, combining intensive group and milieu treatment in a small institutional setting (McCorkle, et al.), marked a turning point in the search for alternatives to the by-then traditional correctional warehouse for adolescent and young adult offenders. Today, there is a continuum of program possibilities from the beginning to the end of the legal-correctional process, all with either individual, group, or milieu treatment emphases, or a combination of these, as primary instrumentalities of rehabilitation.

There is, first of all, the community-based probationary treatment exemplified by the CTP. The Provo experiment (Empey and Rabow) provides a model for a day-care facility using group treatment, vocational and educational training, planned group activities and job placement. The Federal Bureau of Prisons is currently planning a number of live-in treatment centers, sometimes referred to as "halfway-in" centers. These would still be in limited relation to communities in which they are to be based, in contrast with the Highfields type of small correctional institution removed from any community context. Inmates in conventional correctional institutions might enter Pre-Release Guidance Centers (Federal Bureau of Prisons, 1966), a type of community-based facility analogous to the halfway-in center. In addition, the Cottage Life Intervention Program of

132

the National Training School for Boys (Federal Bureau of Prisons, 1964) is a highly innovative model for a rehabilitation program which may be applied throughout a large conventional institution for delinquents. It combines staff-administered individual and group counseling with milieu treatment in ways which try to alter the character of the inmate social system and turn it to therapeutic advantage.

Bibliography

Aichhorn, August, *Wayward Youth*. New York: Viking, 1935.

Alexander, F., and Healy, W. *Roots of Crime: Psychoanalytic Studies*. New York: Knopf, 1935.

Bandura, A., and Walters, R. H. *Adolescent Aggression*. New York: Ronald Press, 1959.

Bandura, A., and Walters, R. H. *Social Learning and Personality Development*. New York: Holt, Rinehart, and Winston, 1963.

Bender, L. *Aggression, Hostility and Anxiety in Children*. Springfield (Ill.): C. C. Thomas, 1953.

Block, D. The delinquent integration. *Psychiatry*, 15, 1952, 297-303.

Block, H. A., and Flynn, F. T. *Delinquency: The Juvenile Offender in America Today*. New York: Random House, 1956.

Bowlby, J. *Forty-Four Juvenile Thieves: Their Characters and Home Life*. London: Boldiere, 1947.

Bunch, J., et al. Development of reaching-out techniques in the initial phase of casework treatment, in *Newton-Baker Project: Juvenile Delinquency Field Demonstration and training Project*, Interim Report, Spring, 1966, Part III. Boston: Judge Baker Guidance Center, pp. 17-37.

Cloward, Richard A., and Ohlin, Lloyd E. *Delinquency and Opportunity: A Theory of Delinquent Gangs*. New York: Free Press, 1960.

Cohen, Albert K. *Delinquent Boys: The Culture of the Gang*. New York: Free Press, 1955.

Cohen, A. K., and Hodges, H. M., Jr. Characteristics of the lower-blue-collar class. *Soc. Problems*, 10, 1963, 303-34.

Cohen, H. L., Filipczak, J. A., and Bis, J. S. CASE Project: Contingencies applicable for special education. Progress Report, August, 1965 (mimeographed).

Cohen, H. L. CASE II—MODEL. Jefferson Hall, The National Training School for Boys, Washington, D.C. (mimeographed).

Deutsch, M. The disadvantaged child and the learning process, in Riessman, F., Cohen, J., and Pearl, A. (eds.), *Mental Health of the Poor*, New York: Free Press-Macmillan, 1964, pp. 172-187.

Deutsch, M. Facilitating development in the pre-school child: social and psychological perspectives. *Merrill-Palmer Quarterly of Behavior and Development*, 10, 1964, 249-264.

Empey, L. T., and Rabow, J. The Provo experiment in delinquency rehabilitation, in Riessman, F., Cohen, J., and Pearl, A. (eds.) *Mental Health of the Poor*, New York: Free Press-Macmillan, 1964, pp. 509-531.

Erikson, Erik H. *Childhood and Society*. New York: Norton, 1950.

Erikson, Erik H. Identity and the life cycle: selected papers, *Psychological Issues*, 1, No. 1, 1959.

Federal Bureau of Prisons, *Rational Innovation: The Cottage Life Intervention Program*, Dept. of Justice, Washington, D.C., 1964.

Federal Bureau of Prisons, *Treating Youth Offenders in the Community*, Dept. of Justice, Washington, D.C., 1966.

Glueck, S. and Glueck, E. *Unravelling Juvenile Delinquency*. Cambridge: Harvard University Press, 1950.

Gold, M. *Status Forces in Delinquent Boys*. Ann Arbor: University of Michigan Press, 1963.

Greenacre, Phyllis. Conscience in the psychopath. *Am. J. Orthopsychiat.*, 15, 1945, 405-509.

Guindon, Jeannine. The concept of total reduction applied to juvenile delinquency: A group of interactions of influence. Mimeographed (French) Le Centre de Formation D'Educateurs Spécialisés, 39 Ouest, Boulevard Govin, Montreal 12, Canada.

134

Healy, W., and Bronner, A. *New Light on Delinquency and Its Treatment*. New Haven: Yale University Press, 1936.

Hughes, C. C., Tremblay, M., Rapoport, R. N., and Leighton, A. H. *People of Cove and Woodlot*, Vol. 2, *The Stirling County Study of Psychiatric Disorder and Sociocultural Environment*. New York: Basic Books, 1960.

Hunt, David E., and Dopyera, John. Indicators of developmental change in lower-class children. Interim Report, June 1963, Syracuse University Youth Development Center.

Hunt, D. E., and Hardt, R. H. Developmental stage, delinquency, and differential treatment. *J. Research Crime and Delinquency*, January 1965, 20-31.

Hurwitz, J. I. Three delinquent types: a multivareate analysis. *J. Crim. Law, Criminol., and Pol. Sci.*, 56, 1965, 328-334.

Jesness, Carl F. The Fricot Ranch Study: Outcomes with Small versus Large Living Groups in the Rehabilitation of Delinquents. Research Report No. 47, Department of the Youth Authority, State of California, October, 1965.

Karpman, B. *The Sexual Offender and his Offenses*. New York: Julian, 1954.

Kaufman, I. Three basic sources for pre-delinquent character. *Nervous Child*, 11, 1955, 12-15.

Kerr, M. *The People of Ship Street*. New York: Humanities, 1958.

Kohlberg, L. Development of moral character and moral ideology, in Hoffman, L., and Hoffman, M. (eds.) *Review of Child Development Research*. New York: Russell Sage, 1964, pp. 383-433.

Kraft, I. Head Start to What? *The Nation*, Sept. 5, 1966, 179-82.

Lander, B. *Towards an Understanding of Juvenile Delinquency*. New York: Columbia University Press, 1954.

Leighton, A. H. *My Name is Legion*. Vol. 1, *The Stirling County Study of Psychiatric Disorder and Sociocultural Environment*. New York: Basic Books, 1959.

Lindner, R. M. *Rebel Without a Cause*. New York: 1944.

MacGregor, R., Ritchie, A., and Serrano, A. C., et al. *Multiple Impact Therapy with Families*. New York: McGraw-Hill, 1964.

135

Maccoby, E. E., Johnson, J. P., and Church, R. M. Community integration and the social control of juvenile delinquency. *J. Social Issues*, 1958, 14, 38-51.

McCord, J., and McCord, W. The effects of parental role model on criminality. *J. social Issues*, 14, 1958, 61-75.

McCord, W., McCord, J., and Zola, I. *Origins of Crime*. New York: Columbia University Press, 1959.

McKee, J. M. The Draper Experiment: a programmed learning project. In Ofiesh, G. D., and Meierhenry, W. C. (eds.) *Trends in Programmed Instruction*. National Education Association, 1964.

McCorkle, L. W., Elias, A., and Bixby, F. L. *The Highfields Story*, New York: Henry Holt, 1958.

Massimo, J. L., and Shore, M. F. The effectiveness of a comprehensive vocationally oriented psychotherapeutic program for adolescent delinquent boys. *Am. J. Orthopsychiatry*, 63, 1963, 631-42.

Miller, W. B. Lower class culture as a generating milieu of gang delinquency. *J. social Issues*, 14, 1958, 3-19.

The Newton-Baker Project: Juvenile Delinquency Field Demonstration and Training Project. Interim Report—Spring, 1966. Boston: Judge Baker Guidance Center.

Pearl, A., and Riessman, F. *New Careers for the Poor: The Nonprofessional in Human Service*. New York: Free-Press-Macmillan, 1965.

Piaget, J. *The Moral Judgment of the Child*. Glencoe: Free Press, 1948.

Polk, K. Juvenile delinquency and social areas. *Soc. Problems*, 5, 1957-1958, 214-17.

Polsky, H. *Cottage Six*. New York: Russell Sage, 1963.

Rabinovitch, R. The concept of primary psychogenic acathexis. *Am. J. Orthopsychiat.*, 21, 1951, 231-37.

Redl, F., and Wineman, D., *Children Who Hate*. Glencoe: Free Press, 1951.

Redl, F., and Wineman, D., *Controls From Within*. Glencoe: Free Press, 1952.

Reiss, A. J. Social correlates of psychological types of delinquency. *Am. Sociol. Rev.*, 17, 1952, 710-718.

Riessman, F., Cohen, J., and Pearl, A. (eds.) *Mental Health of the Poor: New Treatment Approaches for Low Income People*. New York: Free Press-Macmillan, 1964.

Rubenfeld, S., and Stafford, J. W. An adolescent inmate social system: A psychosocial account, *Psychiatry*, 26, 1963, 241-256.

Rubenfeld, Seymour. *Family of Outcasts: A New Theory of Delinquency*. New York: Free Press-Macmillan, 1965.

Rubenfeld, S. Typological Approaches and Delinquency Control: A Status Report. Center for the Studies of Crime and Delinquency, NIMH (NIH, DHEW), Chevy Chase, Maryland, 1966.

Schwitzgebel, R., and Kolb, D. A. Inducing Change in adolescent delinquents. *Behav. Res. Ther.*, 1, March, 1964.

Schwitzgebel, R. *Streetcorner Research: An Experimental Approach to Juvenile Delinquency*. Cambridge: Harvard University Press, 1964.

Shah, Saleem A. A Behavioral Conceptualization of the Development of Criminal Behavior, Therapeutic Principles, and Applications. Paper prepared for the President's Commission on Law Enforcement and the Administration of Justice, Washington, D.C., August, 1966.

Shore, M. F. Psychological theories on the etiology of criminal and delinquent behavior: their relevance to program planning on national, state, and local levels. A report to the President's Commission on Law Enforcement and the Administration of Justice, Washington, D.C., August, 1966.

Shore, M. F., and Massimo, J. L. Comprehensive vocationally oriented psychotherapy for adolescent delinquent boys: A follow-up study, *Am. J. Orthopsychiat.*, 36, 1966, 609-15.

Short, J. F., and Strodtbeck, F. L. *Group Process and Gang Delinquency*. Chicago: University of Chicago Press, 1965.

Slack, C. W. Experimenter-subject psychotherapy. *Mental Hygiene*, 44, 1960, 238-256.

Spinley, B. M. *The Deprived and the Privileged*. London: Routledge, Kegan Paul, 1953.

Stott, D. H. Delinquency, maladjustment and unfavorable ecology, *Brit. J. Psychol.*, 51, 1960, 157-70.

Sullivan, Clyde, Grant, Marguerite Q., and Grant, J. Douglas. The development of interpersonal maturity: applications to delinquency, *Psychiatry*, 1957, 20, 170-4.

Street, D., Vinter, R. D., and Perrow, *Organization for Treatment: A Comparative Study of Institutions for Delinquents*. New York: Free Press-Macmillan, 1966.

Sykes, G. L., and Messinger, S. L., The inmate social system, in *Theoretical Studies on Social Organization of the Prison*. Social Science Research Pamphlet 15, March, 1960.

Warren, Marguerite Q., and Palmer, Theodore B. Community Treatment Project: Fourth Progress Report. CTP Research Report No. 6, Sacramento, Calif., October, 1965.

PSYCHOLOGY AND PUNITIVE JUSTICE

DAGOBERT D. RUNES, PH.D.
New York City

Editorial Note

Psychologists today realize that while laws and the philosophical theories behind them are noble and edifying concepts, our procedures of punishment are sometimes absurd, sometimes ineffective, and often brutal. The need for immediate reforms and measures of improvement is everywhere apparent.

Albert Schweitzer once wrote these words concerning the writings of Dr. Dagobert D. Runes: "We both travel on the same path, to bring to mankind a deeply ethical, deeply spiritual consciousness, with the purpose of leading the people back from the mentality of indifference in which they are living, to a new and higher manner of thinking."

Dr. Runes received his Ph.D. from the University of Vienna and is the former director of the Institute for Advanced Education. The following essay incorporates materials from his recent book, *The Disinherited and the Law*.

Dr. Runes' many publications include *On the Nature of Man, Twentieth Century Philosophy, The Art of Thinking, Despotism, A Book of Contemplation, Treasury of Philosophy,* and *Spinoza Dictionary* (with Albert Einstein). Among the many scientific and technical journals he has edited are *Journal of Aesthetics* and *Philosophical Abstracts*.

•

PSYCHOLOGY AND PUNITIVE JUSTICE

On Caging Man

"Imprisonment as it exists today is a worse crime than any of those committed by its victims," wrote George Bernard Shaw. It is easy to recognize the brutality and stupidity of past centuries; it is difficult to detect similar aspects of one's own time and generation. We read with indignation that in the most enlightened state of seventh-century Europe, a man might have his tongue cut off by the legal authorities because of alleged blasphemy. But we know that today in many states, Spain, Germany and other Western countries, a man can be caged in solitary confinement for up to ten years for similar utterances. By what measure is the pain of having a tongue removed worse or milder than imprisonment?

From distant antiquity up to the humanistic era in Europe, imprisonment was primarily used as a temporary means of holding the accused for final punishment, which consisted of mutilation, pillorying, bone-crushing, blinding, flogging, burning, hanging or decapitation. During the centuries-long era of the Inquisition, it is true, there was a cooperative venture between the Vatican and the royal house of Spain to expropriate nobles of Jewish, Moorish and other heretical descents. People were kept for as long as two and three years, chained to blocks in dungeons and living in their own excrement, many of them perishing of disease and malnutrition, before they had their day in the canonical court. Ostensibly, the purpose of such confinement was to break their will and make them fit for re-acceptance in the true church. Their properties, of course, had already been sequestered by the Inquisition corporation, as there is scarcely a record of anyone indicted under the Inquisition having been found innocent.

Occasionally, vagrants, drunks, prostitutes, insane and juvenile offenders were put in irons and lumped together in indiscriminate confinement. There was no separation of men from women, and boorish guards had the brutal run of those institutions. Alongside such houses of correction, which were basically the only prisons well into the eighteenth century, there existed, of course, servitude in the galleys, another form of penal confinement still prevalent at the time of the American Revolution. Some of the European countries, such as England, practiced deportation of convicts to America and Australia. This type of bondage, which continued in England until the middle of the nineteenth century, is reminiscent of the Roman deportations to remote slave-operated mines, as, of course, is the whole system of galley imprisonment.

The establishment of workhouses and prisons was regarded at the time by many reformers, such as John Howard, William Blackstone, Jeremy Bentham, Benjamin Rush and others, as a great improvement over punitive mutilations. Perhaps they really were, but are they today? Are these houses of correction—from the Hospice of San Filipo Nero in seventeenth-century Florence to the workhouses in Hamburg and Ghent, to the Pennsylvania system of silent and solitary confinement and the Auburn technique of incarceration with limited communications—the answer? Are they the answer to the multiple questions of reform? The Pennsylvania system, which held its prisoners incommunicado for the duration of the term in order to avoid mutual corruption? The Pennsylvania system, which prohibited any reading but the Bible, which cut off the prisoner from all written and oral contact with relatives and friends? This system, incidentally, became and still is dominant on the European Continent. In some prisons there the convicts had to wear face masks—mark this—to avoid their being recognized after their release by any of the other prisoners. Even the Irish system, with its grading of inmates, its introduction of indeterminate sentences and parole after progressive improvement, indicates little change from the harsh disciplinary structure which has proved, from Sing Sing to Ljubljanka, that the prison system as an institution of reform does *not* reform.

Even those among our inmates who have truly failed will not be helped by incarceration. That has been proven time and time again. Even the most traditional-minded penologists admit that prisons do not reform and that reforms must come from other directions.

141

I say reform must come through adjustment and understanding, but never through punishment.

Whatever reform does occur in prisoners is not because of their being in jail but rather in spite of their being jailed. The attitude of the prisoner, who is still, in Vienna or in Copenhagen, in Moscow or Madrid, kept barred in a cage like a wild animal, the attitude of those men, who in most cases have done little worse than most of their fellow citizens on the outside, is one of frustration, bitterness and dejection, regardless of the food and drink shoved to them through a hole in the door or dished out at the common eating place, where, when they speak, they have to do it from the side of their mouths.

Perhaps this type of torture—to which may be added a hundred petty humiliating prison regulations and customs, such as perpetual silence, the wearing of clothes of degradation, deprivation of all privacy, etc., etc.—is less offensive to our conscience than the blinding, flogging and pillorying of old, but it is hardly likely to teach the prisoner any new or reserved confidence in his own potential goodness or that of his fellow men.

Detention and Disease

To deal with the alleged criminal properly, one must understand the motivating force and the milieu of the criminal act. Without knowledge of felonious etiology, the judicial as well as sociological response will necessarily be inadequate.

Offenders against the judicial shield of social protection may be classified as either emotionally ill; mentally ill; permanently retarded; inflamed by an outsider in the fore or background; economically crushed; inebriated; in the grip of narcotics; temporarily delinquent; incorrigibly vicious; incorrigibly fraudulent; incorrigibly sexually aggressive.

During the many centuries when religious interpretations directly affected the status of the mentally ill, only those who were raving mad were exempt from the full penalty of the law. On the other hand, their status differed little from that of convicts, since they were kept chained to a block in their cell in

142

a lunatic asylum or in a yard or, as often happened, simply burnt.

It was in the early part of the eighteenth century that Justice Tracy formulated a rather important rule regarding the determination of criminal responsibility by declaring that those may escape punishment who cannot distinguish between good and evil. About a hundred years later in the famous McNaghten case, we find the ruling by fifteen English justices (with one dissent) which dominated the American scene for a long time, namely, that every person should be considered sane who possesses a sufficient degree of understanding to distinguish right from wrong. This McNaghten definition is essentially dominant in most parts of the civilized world.

It is less than a decade since the decision on the Durham case was rendered by the Court of Appeals for the District of Columbia Circuit, according to which trial judges are directed to instruct juries that where there is evidence of mental defect the jury must ascertain prior to conviction (1) that the accused was not suffering from a mental disease, and (2) that even if he was, the criminal act was not the direct product of that condition. The Durham decision, of course, leaves the degree of mental defect or disease to be determined by expert witnesses, namely, psychiatrists. As psychiatrists hardly ever agree on the mental status of any patient, the jury will invariably find itself faced, in cases where mental illness is claimed, with two or more opposing opinions, one by the prosecution, one by the defense, and perhaps one by an interested party. And as the jury is constituted of laymen, even a most discerning analytic faculty would find it difficult to reach an objective conclusion from these divergent points of view.

Moreover to this very day the origin of most mental illnesses is completely unknown and all psychiatric evidence is, generally speaking, at best highly opinionated and with little scientific foundation. While a physician or psychiatrist can clearly and indisputably testify that a patient suffers from delirium tremens or paresis or cretinism, in most other mental illnesses, such as those commonly and superficially classified as paranoia, schizophrenia, depressive mania, etc., etc., there is no true knowledge of either their origin, depth, or prognosis. In fact, it is not even known how many diseases or defects are covered under such broad popularized terms as those just mentioned.

The question now arises, "To what extent is an apprehended criminal emotionally or mentally ill?"

The man who sits at the window of a darkened room and shoots a person across the street may be a backward youngster shooting aimlessly; he may be a cunning individual attempting to rub out a competitor in typical racketeer fashion; or he may be a paranoiac shooting blindly and senselessly.

The act of shooting is identical in all three cases. But now we come to the problem of righting the wrong by judicial process so that it will (1) teach a lesson to the offender, (2) avoid repetition of the act, and (3) discourage others from committing similar misdeeds.

Taking these three possible offenders, we are first confronted with a backward or retarded youngster who on close examination, is obviously, unable to foresee the disastrous consequence of his shooting game. There is nothing negativistic in his background. There is no record, to use that farcical term, "criminal tendency" in his character, merely, on the other hand, a series of foolish trespasses against good sense. Turning a backward child —and some of these children are middle aged—over to a criminal or corrective institution could only arouse in him deep resentment and drive him finally to the commission of vicious and felonious acts against his own nature and society. He will not be improved by a corrective environment or any punitive administration, as he is thoroughly convinced of his innocence. Unavoidably, in any punitive institution he will become the butt of attacks by the all too nefarious, vicious and callous elements and come out at best a cowed but hate-filled person.

He will have been taught no lesson in the good life, but rather one in ugliness, and he is bound to repeat acts of foolishness—not the same, to be sure, for which he was punished, but others, for his is a foolish mind. There is a great need for a large social organization to carry on the re-education of retarded individuals, not only those of childhood age, but also those who are children in adulthood.

As for the determined and cunning assassin, whose back-

144

ground indicates a hardened and vicious attitude toward his fellow man, to put him in a common jail will be of little avail, for no one can teach this man a lesson that would make him look up and cry over what he is. As far as he is concerned, he is likely to continue to consider himself craftier than the authorities and capable of eluding apprehension. Confining him to the company of similar individuals will not lessen his self-esteem, but only make him more arrogant. He will think of ways to improve and perfect his antisocial talents, rather than drop them, and nothing goes on in those precious penal institu-'tions of ours which could make him a better man instead of a better criminal.

Finally, what of our third kind of offender, the paranoid? Jailing the felonious person who is either mentally or emotionally ill serves no practical purpose, except, perhaps, to deter those who do not suffer from similar ailments from the commission of crimes which are peculiar to the deranged. But then again, the normal person, even in his misdemeanor, will not demean himself to wrongdoing of the abnormal kind.

Certainly any lesson that incarceration may instill is lost on the demented or the addicted, and the emotionally unbalanced will not be discouraged by possible or even likely incarceration.

So while the vicious felon of set and incorrigible ways is best removed for life to a penal island, those who engage in grievous, dangerous and harmful acts to society because of their confused emotions and unbalanced minds, those whose crimes are rooted deeply in spiritual and physiological incompetence, should be dealt with as patients rather than as criminals, with patience in the full meaning of this word.

Mentally ill are not only those who stare and point in a catatonic state at blind walls, not only those who take flight in work and behavior into a nonexistent world of their schizophrenic imagination, not only those driven by their disturbed metabolism or infected bloodstream and deteriorated nervous system from anxiety to exhilaration and from exuberance to suicidal depression—not only those are insane against whose morbid minds humanity can thus far muster protection only by electric shock machines, chemical tranquilizers or hormonic shock therapy.

145

There are perhaps ten times as many insane out of the asylums as there are in them. Their souls are not sane who cannot endure life without having heroin, morphine, hashish or marijuana. Their souls are not sane who hunger more for alcoholic delirium than for daily food. Their souls are not sane who must exhibit their genitals to an unsuspecting public behind a park bench, in a dark doorway or on the steps of a public building, and there are many more female offenders in this respect than those of the other sex. Their souls are not sane who have grown year after year, schoolday after schoolday, and home day after home day in an ambience of malevolent hatred for minority races or religions. Such persons often commit overt acts of violence, a manifestation of their malformed minds, while the deliberate preachers of the hate gospel continue to ply their opportunistic trade under the protection of antiquated laws. Their souls are not sane who, finding love of the opposite sex repulsive, redirect their passions through the involuted channels of their own sex. Their souls are not sane who, because of a tender disposition and under the hammering of social pressure, are in despair over illness, injury or ineptitude, and stumble on the hard roads of daily life.

They are not sane—yet neither jury nor judge will rule them insane. Perhaps a new concept, a new term should evolve that would enable a more enlightened judiciary to make a clear distinction between recidivist, malevolent, hardened, antisocial criminals and those many who do what is prohibited, not because they are enemies of society, but rather because they are somehow victims of themselves. The human who does away with a newborn fetus because it came to life without arms and feet is not to be judged by the same panel and by the same paragraph as the mugger in the dark street killing a passer-by. Indeed, those persons whose failings and offenses originate deep in their mental, emotional or hereditary inadequacy should be judged not by officials of the court and not by their peers, but rather by their patrons. An organization of patrons is essential to deal with those who fail society not out of vice or viciousness, but out of weakness of body and soul. They need help, not punishment; they need guidance, not incarceration, not retention; they are poor, not pernicious.

146

Among the remarkable peculiarities of the last two or three hundred years is the existence of a segment of the population in every country and province which lives under specific rules of confinement, bound in time and bound in place. This imprisoned population lives in a state of bondage, as the individual may not leave his abode until his term of bondage has expired. In a way his position is similar to the Pharaonic or Assyrian slave living under a rigid work discipline without choice of vocation or avocation, doing his or her chores in exchange for a token reward, separated from kinfolk and friends and subject to a degrading discipline of his private life—if you can apply the words "private life" to prisoners, whose most intimate concern is subject to official public inspection.

At this writing by most reliable statistics, there are close to five million people housed in the prison compounds of the world. Of these five million, less than 20 percent are what we can refer to as vicious and violent repeated offenders against the safety of their fellow citizens. The great, overwhelming majority are merely persons who ran afoul of the law because of social, economic, or emotional pressure—to which must be added that many of the laws they ran afoul of are most unjustifiably on the books and most damagingly in effect.

While some hardened and aggressive criminals, that small core of the evidently incorrigible, are thus removed from coexistence amongst the rest of the citizenry, the many other occupants of our prison stables are reduced to slavedom for months, for years, for decades, or forever, and frequently for such paltry derelictions as inability to manage their cravings for narcotic smoke, or not knowing how to meet the economic requirements of daily life.

The last three centuries to which we euphemistically refer as the modern ones are the era of the world-wide enslavement of average citizens, young and old, male and female, either because of weakness in them or, more often, weakness in our system.

In the days of Pharaoh, men were enslaved for failing to pay the king's taxes. Our government still lives by the Pharaonic

147

principle,—only the enslavement is called workhouse imprison-ment. The rulers of the wild Assyrians thousands of years ago used to enslave a man for stealing from the nobles' gardens or storehouses. Our governments enslave people today for years at a time for theft or tort or larceny or fraud, regardless of the pressures crushing the unskilled or unprepared or unable. The Caesars of ancient Rome would send a man into the slave mines for sniffing at the secret leaves of Arabia; our states enslave the addicted or place them in chain gangs. Wherein do we differ from the barbarians, wherein is our despotism less virulent?

The lot of the slave on the Nile, on the Euphrates, on the Tiber was often better than that of the inmates in many of the jails of our day.

Our penologists and our sociologists have reiterated that our prisons are not reforming the inmates, but rather hardening them, and that the prison and our various forms of slave con-finement have not brought about reduction in crime or preven-tion of recidivism.

The original meaning of the word "punishment" is "cleans-ing," but long ago that concept of punishment evolved into its actual present-day meaning, namely, vengeance and terror.

If we expect with threat or terror to prevent crimes from being committed, our expectations have proven unwarranted. Excepting the incorrigibly vicious and violent, who don't belong in our society at all, as the insane do not belong, the rest of the inmates of our slave prisons are not there because they are un-duly aggressive; they are not there because they want to mur-der and kill and rob and plunder and mug. They are there be-cause they couldn't help themselves, and we have failed to help them. They are there because they are weak, not because they are evil. And they are there, finally, because some of our laws are worse than their alleged offenses.

If we want to rehabilitate and reform and better our in-mates, we must release them from the slave stables. We have to stop shaving their heads and dressing them in striped pajamas. We have to bring them back into our society and in the midst of our society have them make recompense.

Most of the failings for which we enslave people are common

148

to all, not only to those few, and some of the failings inherent to those few alone are in their minds, in their emotional lives, in their nerves, their tissues, and the chemistry of their bodies. What can cure them is not enslavement, not degradation and hourly humiliation, but a helping hand from people learned in respective professions.

Again we must ask:

Will the film actor lose his craving for the opiate by being thrown into a pen? Will the unbalanced girl drop her loose living by spending a year in a cell with old tarts? Will a storekeeper who borrowed money on an exaggerated statement become a better businessman by spending five years with hold-up men and muggers?

And all these thousand offenses against property—property of the state, property of the city, property of the big stores—are those who fail to respect the great god Mammon to be punished by enslavement for needing money and not always being able to manage within the letter of the law? And if they failed in respect to money, let them pay back money, as much as they can. Enslaving them will not bring back the money and will not make them money-wise.

The debtors' prison is back again, and more people are thrown into debtors' prison today for nothing but money offenses than ever before, when that dreaded confinement was called what it actually is: the poor man's punishment for being poor.

Many men have advocated improvement of our jails, from Cesare Beccaria to John Howard, from Pope Clement XI to Alexander Maconochie, from Benjamin Rush to Cesare Lombroso, but the improvement of slave quarters is not equivalent to the abolition of slavery.

And what happened to the slaves in ancient days when they were released? Many became destitute, many took the road of crime and many more sold themselves back into slavery.

Close is the fate of those slaves to that of the released prisoner today. Where shall he go? Where shall he turn? He may work for five years and walk out with fifty dollars, in many countries not even with that, although he could have earned

149

during those five years $25,000. Why should the inmate be robbed of his true earnings, and why should he not be given the opportunity to work at his skills? Why should a carpenter or a metalworker be paid $1 a week if he can earn $100?

If that interferes with the outside industries, so do all industries interfere with each other. A man who can earn $100 outside the prison should be able to earn the same $100 within the walls of his confinement.

And wouldn't it be wiser to make the man who failed stay on his job and pay for his failing with earned money instead of worthless time? Let the guilty do *work*, not time.

Even today the so-called work available in the prisons of the Western world is little more than pretence. They still knit blanket squares all over again.

Our penal slave system, abroad worse even than here, robs the inmate of his time, his earnings, and his rehabilitation and robs his victims, if any, of the restitution due to them.

A society that condemns an offender to enslavement cannot expect to have the freed slave find proper employment. To begin with, many of the offenders had problems in that same area of earning power. Through their confinement their problems have increased, not dwindled. It is easy to release a man with a thin envelope of bills and with the sage and stern advice to go straight.

If we enslave people because of their monetary difficulties, we owe it to them to assure their employment before we send them out into a hostile community.

We release prisoners on parole, which means on their word of honor to behave, and this after we have thoroughly dishonored them by enslavement. What parole actually constitutes today is a release of the prisoner into a world of hate, prejudice and suspicion, with the parole officer having no other obligation toward the parolee than to spy on him for possible infraction of further degrading regulations. The ex-prisoner, who to begin with had difficulty in keeping himself afloat, is thrown back into the raging ocean of life with the parole officer watching only to see if he will sink again.

150

The principle of probation, like that of parole, is highly ineffective if not substantiated by direct work and work guarantee on the part of the authorities. The indisputable slave existence led by prisoners makes them, in the eyes of the average employer or business contact, reprehensible or, at best, most unwelcome. The slave existence of the prisoner deprives him of dignity and self-respect, not only in his own eyes but more so in the eyes of possible employers, business associates, even friends and family, and until this system of enslavement ceases to exist, the released prisoner must be guaranteed proper employment by those who deprived him of dignity and respect. While some of the social work aspects of the probation and parole system are well-meant and commendable, they are highly inadequate to master the great problem of integrating the yearly army of ex-convicts into the social, business and work life of the community at large.

In summary, we must repeat:

If men are to be confined at all, they ought to work at full time, and if they work at full time, they should be paid the full wage, and that wage should be paid to them as they leave. The very society that took it upon itself to destroy the convict's business life, work life and family life, that very society owes the released prisoner full employment for at least as many years as it deprived him of it. The man in prison is entitled to a job like any other citizen, and the prisoner's work should be marketed like any other work, directly or indirectly under supervision of the authorities.

Almost five hundred years ago, the martyred Thomas More, one of the few truly great in history to give dispirited mankind trust in human courage and human kindness, wrote:

> For simple theft is not so great an offense that it ought to be punished with death. Neither is there any punishment so horrible that it can keep men from stealing who have no other craft whereby to get their living. . . . For great and horrible punishments are appointed for thieves, whereas, much rather, provision should have been made

151

for some means by which they might get their living; so that no man should be driven to this extreme necessity, first to steal, and then to die.

The majority of the adult inmates of our prisons are individuals who somehow stumbled on the road of economic life.

Whatever is needed to deter others from imitating their missteps or to lead the offenders back upon the right path, such measures can surely be carried out without the cruelty of execution, which the Communists practice, and without the cruelty of enslavement, such as we practice. As has been said by a great philosopher of law: "It isn't the severity of sentence that acts as a deterrent, but rather the swiftness and inevitability of its application."

Therefore, in this spirit, there is no need for the law to experiment in devious cruelties of humiliation and detention in order to accomplish its purpose. The law may safely become civil in civil matters and remain determined in brutal matters involving physical violence and demagogic malevolence.

Those who persist in living by the knife, the rod and the whip of racial incitement, let them be isolated with their lust for blood hate. But others, the civil offenders, let them not be relegated to the debtors' jail, but let them adjust their failings and falsifications in a civilized manner.

A million people commit these falsifications, a million people share these failings, but somehow these millions are wise to the pitfalls and invisible traps of legalism and manage to escape the misstep which can be detected.

There are a thousand ways to falsify truths in daily business life and in daily work life by cunning exaggeration and still escape the charge of fraud.

I do not propose indifference either to those who are fooling the people or to those many who are being fooled, but I do invoke the ancient maxim of the philosopher: "Nothing human is alien to me."

No human failing is alien to humanity at large. Let us not make an example of the frailty of one individual through his misdemeanor, since frailty is common to all men.

152

Certainly wergild has to be paid. Those who by scheme or coup have deprived their fellow citizens of their belongings have to make recompense. What I plead for is neither negligence nor indifference, but rather humane grace.

There is no grace in Leavenworth or Sing Sing.

There is no grace and no good purpose at all, because the inability to master economic success will forever elude some of our fellow citizens. That doesn't make them tigers or monsters to be caged; they merely lack the proper emotional, mental or social balance to overcome the obstacles of our rigid environment.

As the nobleman exclaimed, watching the criminal being led to the gallows, "There, but for the grace of God, go I."

Let everyone watching the jailbird being led away mark these words: "There, but for the grace of God, go I." Let us remove from those guilty of civil offenses the brand of criminality, the yoke of degradation, the stain of prison life, and let them work off the needed, the required adjustment in the continued privacy of their lives. Let them continue amid their families; let us not drive them to perversions by isolation with strangers of their own sex for insufferable years. Let us not destroy their families and themselves by deportation to slave mines or slave jails. Let us not undermine their business and work talents. Let us not make them subjects of despair and disdain. Let us be human.

Let us charge them and fine them to make restitution of property. Let them pay off their fines or work them off; if necessary, let us create adjustment workshops where they can spend the day working off their debts to society, but let them otherwise live freely with friends and family. Let us remove this stigma of prison enslavement. Why enslave a man because of property? And state property is no different from other property, because the state is no better than its people. No property is worth the price of human life, no property is worth the price of human enslavement.

THE SOCIAL PSYCHOLOGY OF PREJUDICE

NATHAN W. ACKERMAN, M.D.
Director of Professional Program
The Family Institute

Editorial Note

The deep roots of prejudice have withstood successive attacks through the centuries. The dynamics of prejudicial behavior baffle the mind capable of comprehending the structure of the atom. Yet prejudice is universal and is learned at the age of three or four by almost every child. There is a close affinity between prejudice, thought control, psychological torture, and character assassination. In the following article the author calls attention to the trends in the organization of our society which favor prejudicial behavior and issues a warning.

Dr. Nathan W. Ackerman is Clinical Professor of Psychiatry at the College of Physicians and Surgeons, Columbia University, and Director of Professional Program of The Family Institute in New York City.

Born in Russia, Dr. Ackerman was educated at Columbia University in New York City. He received his B.A. in 1929 and his M.D. in 1933. He has been on the faculty of the College of Physicians and Surgeons since 1945 and has been Visiting Professor at the Albert Einstein Medical School since 1962.

Dr. Ackerman has pioneered in the development of family diagnosis and therapy, and has written widely on the subject. His latest book, *Treating the Troubled Family*, has just been published by Basic Books. He is Chairman of the Editorial Board of Family Process and is a member of the editorial board of other professional journals. He has been regular and guest lecturer at many universities and was the recipient of the Adolph Meyer Award in 1959, and of the Award of the Eastern Group Psychotherapy Association in 1966.

•

THE SOCIAL PSYCHOLOGY OF PREJUDICE

"See that man over there?
Yes.
Well, I hate him.
But you don't know him.
But that's why I hate him." [1]

Here, in this small verse, lies the essence of prejudice; it is the fear of the unknown, the suspicion of the stranger in our midst. Prejudice is surely not caused by the accident of not knowing the other person; rather, it is the tenacious refusal to know and to trust the other that breeds prejudice.

As a form of social behavior, prejudice may be overt or covert; it may be crude or subtle; it may crop out like a weed in many guises and in many places. In the turbulence of the contemporary world, it gives rise to new problems and new dangers to the continuity of human relations.

Its manifestations are as old as human history. At no time has the social community been completely immune to or free of it. Its ubiquitous quality, its common and habitual features, however, in no way diminish its harmful consequences for society. At times, prejudice is a mild affliction; at other times, malignant. On occasion, it erupts with savage violence. It is highly contagious; as a communicable "disease," it occurs in both endemic and epidemic forms.

In this paper I propose to do the following: (1) Delineate the psychological mechanisms of prejudice; (2) Offer the hypotheses that there are common dynamic features between prejudice—psychological torture, thought control, and character assassination; (3) Draw an analogy between these behavioral tendencies and a master-slave pattern of human relations; (4)

1. Allport, Gordon, "The Roots of Prejudice," a quotation from *Life* on "The Ways of Hate," October, 1954.

Consider the implications of prejudicial behavior for group mental health.

The Psychological Mechanisms of Prejudice [2]

The functional purposes of prejudice are: (1) To restore a damaged sense of self; (2) To achieve secondary social, emotional and economic gain in order to fortify a threatened social position; (3) To flee from inner pain into a preoccupation with the external world.

Prejudice is not inborn; it is learned, as is any other social attitude. It does not appear in a child before the age of three or four years. It is the product of conflict and fear.

At the individual level, prejudice is a function of a basically weak, confused, fragmented sense of personal identity; it reflects disorder in the relations of self and others. It is exploited to fortify a precarious sense of self; it is associated with unconscious fear, self-hate and self-rejection. It involves a denial of negative personal qualities and a compensatory self-aggrandizement through attachments to symbols of power.

The prejudiced individual makes a special use of the group to implement defenses against anxiety. His identification with other persons often reveals a spurious quality; it is ungenuine, distorted and rigid. His effort to compensate a weak self through aggrandizing his position in the group is foredoomed because his perception of other persons is defective, because he has a low tolerance for conflict, is rigid in his social attitudes and has poor ability to learn from new experience. Thus, the urge to repair the damage to self-esteem miscarries.

There is no specific one-to-one correlation between prejudice and personality type. But prejudiced persons do disclose common kinds of emotional vulnerability: an injured sense of self, a feeling of weakness and exposure to further injury, a tendency to rigidity, a defective capacity for new social learning. Such persons vacillate between an image of self as big or

2. This section leans on an earlier study of prejudice, Ackerman, N. W. and Marie Jahoda, *Anti-Semitism and Emotional Disorder* (New York: Harper & Bros., 1950).

small, strong or weak, superior or inferior, important or unimportant.

They waver between a feeling of belongingness and a sense of isolation. Their attitude toward others is suspicious and ambivalent. Their relations with people tend to be temporary and lacking in genuine intimacy. They move between overdependent and overaggressive attitudes. They set up a false front of sociability and conformity. They are insecure, lonely, inwardly agitated. They experience constant fear of inner injury from an outer world perceived as harsh and menacing. They defend themselves against their fear through denial, projection, substitution of aggression for anxiety and the striving for magic power. They exploit these defenses for the purpose of intimidating others; the urge toward scapegoating is intense.

To such persons, difference is a constant threat. They interpret the different person, the stranger as a potential enemy. The difference of the other stirs in the self a painful reminder of deficiency. They demand, therefore, that everyone else conform. To comfort the self, they assault the wholeness of other persons. They externalize their conflicts and attack the surrounding world. There is, however, a strong tendency for these compensatory devices to backfire; they aggravate the very affliction they are intended to relieve.

In the case of anti-Semitic prejudice, a comprehensive examination of the relevant attitudes and intergroup relations demands consideration in four dimensions:

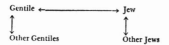

The definition of the interaction of Jew and Gentile remains incomplete unless it is viewed against the backdrop of the interaction of Jew with Jew and Gentile with Gentile. The development of an irrational hatred of the Jew rests on the matrix of a disturbance of the Gentile with his own kind. Where the Gentile requires to make a victim of the Jew, his relations with fellow Gentiles are always implicated. Where the Gentile has distorted relations with his own kind, he is apt to identify

157

with the Jew, envy him and be irrationally hostile toward him.

Similar considerations pertain to the emotional adaptation of the Jewish person toward Gentiles. Some Jews are the innocent victims of fanatical attacks. Others play a part in inciting the attack. When a Jew emotionally requires to be persecuted by a Gentile, he must in turn have a background of disturbed relations with his own kind. Where a Jew has distorted relations with his fellow Jews, he is apt to identify unconsciously with the Gentile and, at the same time, to offer himself as a victim. In irrational prejudice, members of both groups suffer.

In the case of anti-Semitism, the Jew suffers in a special way, but so does the Gentile. The victim and the assailant have a close, complementary relationship. The interaction and merging of selected elements of the identity of each member of this pair provides a matrix for the mechanisms of shared emotional illness, a kind of *folie à deux*. The attacker fulfills his sick self through the victim, the victim through his attacker.

For the relations of whites and Negroes, the culture provides an institutionalized pattern. The stereotype, in essence, is as follows: white and Negro are unequal in worth; the white is superior, the Negro is inferior; the white is the master, the Negro the slave; the white is the exploiter, the Negro the exploited. They are interrelated in an axis of domination-submission. They are bound in a pattern of interdependence and mutual need. The dependent, subordinate position of the Negro complements the superior status and prestige of the white. The Negro, in turn, claims the patronage, care and protection of the white.

Members of each group develop particular ways of dealing with anxiety about the different person, the stranger. As a white person matures and stabilizes his personal identity, he incorporates into it the fact of a socially inferior Negro group. He uses this fact in defining his image of self as being above the Negro; by excluding the Negro, he enhances his sense of security and his belongingness with his own group. However false may be this feeling of self-pride and superiority, it nevertheless contributes to the shaping of his identity as a white person. As a Negro matures and stabilizes his personal identity, he incorpo-

158

rates into it the fact of a socially superior white group. He too uses this fact in defining his image of self.

Unconsciously the white person may fear to be socially weak and inferior like the Negro. He may at the same time envy in the Negro the imagined qualities of superior physique, "carefree" existence, the zestful enjoyment of music and dancing, sexual abandonment, etc.

The Negro may unconsciously identify with those qualities of the white which symbolize status and power. He may desire to pass as white or dream of appearing as white.

Again, at a deeper level, to whatever extent the member of one group identifies with qualities attached to other groups, feelings of disloyalty and guilt are aroused in relation to his own group. Thus, patterns of cross-identification arouse anxiety-guilt and fear of loss of support from the own group.

In each case the individual strives to enhance his sense of adequacy by incorporating into his self-image the favored qualities of the contrasting group, while denying the disadvantageous qualities.

A shift in attitude of white toward Negro and Negro toward white is determined by the way in which an individual experiences the own self, the different self and the way in which parents, family and wider society structure the identity of each group.

Accordingly, the emotional and symbolic representations of difference may be perceived as a threat or as a complementation of the own self. Depending on whether the difference is experienced as a danger or an opportunity, the two groups may find a basis of greater affinity and identity, or discern a sharper conflict and threat of hostility.

When the traditional role relations of Negro and white are disturbed, there is an inevitable struggle to restore a state of balance and stability. Negroes and whites accommodate to a gradual change of relations with a minimum of anxiety and defensiveness. Sudden change exerts profound effects on the individual's emotional integration into his various roles in the community, with his own group and in relation to the different group. This may precipitate both a social and emotional crisis.

159

Members of both groups may cope realistically with crisis and adapt to the changed situation in a way that restores balance and promotes self-development. Or, they may react with excessive anxiety, failure of reality testing, destructive behavior and other signs of disorganization. In the latter event, self-esteem suffers a further injury.

What is feared is a reversal of traditional roles. In effect, Negroes and whites simply change places. The Negro becomes the master, the white the slave. The white dreads Negro revolt. The Negro is panicked by his fantasy image of ruthless retaliation. The white's fear of role reversal may lead to violence. He may conceal a damaged self with the facade of fanatic aggressiveness. He may mobilize the militancy of white against Negro. Or, if he feels betrayed by his own group, he may overidentify with the Negro and become belligerent on his behalf. He may adopt the Negro as a "mascot," a disguised way of expressing hostility to his own group.

The Negro may develop a false sense of power over white. He may react with depression, and withdraw from the scene of battle. He may simply "stay in his place."

A mutually healthy readaptation, using fully the opportunities for reality-testing, can ultimately lead to a more secure basis for self-esteem in both groups.

Always the issue is: will members of each group cling to the old pattern or choose the new? Inevitably comes the increasing awareness that each group needs the other, that both are part of the larger community, that co-operative relations, mutual acceptance and respect, in the end, add to the common good.

A full definition of the phenomenon of prejudice, therefore, requires a consideration of both intrapsychic and interpersonal forces. The proper unit of examination is the prejudicial person plus his social environment, anti-Semite plus Jew plus other Gentiles; or, in the case of anti-Negro prejudice, the white person plus Negro plus other whites.

The root of a prejudicial attitude is its antihuman quality. It is the urge to destroy the humanness of the other person. The prejudiced individual's fear of the stranger, like the child's fear of the intrusion of a sibling, is a product of the child's lack of security within his own family. The child's fear and hate of the sibling emerges in inverse proportion to his feeling of security with his own parents. The essential nature of the vulnerability pattern rests on the defective integrity of the self-structure, a defect in the sense of wholeness of self that is related to family group and surrounding community.

As indicated earlier, prejudice may emerge in a range of personality types, which, although different, may nonetheless have in common certain component elements of emotional weakness. Just as delinquency, alcoholism, narcotic addiction and psychosomatic disorders may be correlated to component reactions of personality rather than to specific personality types, so is prejudice similarly related to such component reactions. However, the defensive responses of such persons are both anachronistic and regressive. They are a distorted attempt to repair a damaged sense of self and to restore contact with other persons. The attempt fails its purpose, and, in the end, it magnifies the underlying feeling of exposure to attack and aggravates the difficulty of establishing genuinely close human relations.

The specific form of prejudice varies, of course, from one person to the next. The factor of psychological specificity may range from high to low. This depends on the idiosyncratic features of personal and social background and is shaped by the processes of interaction between the personal sources of anxiety and the qualities of the group situation.

Finally, it is to be remembered that prejudice occurs in both public and private forms. The public prejudices revolving about differences of skin color, religion and ethnic background are obvious. The private forms are rather more elusive. They emerge within the intimacies of family life [3] and appear superficially distinct from the conventional prejudices of the wider community.

For example, there are private prejudices for one sex against the other, for youth against elders, for money and power against spiritual and cultural values, for duty and discipline against freedom, spontaneity and pleasure, for brain against brawn, for

3. Ackerman, N. W., *Prejudice, Mental Health and Family Life* (New York: American Jewish Committee, 1961).

animals against people. Still other prejudices of this kind may atttach to qualities of tall and short, fat and skinny, to varieties of food, clothing, and habits of cleanliness.

Such personal forms of prejudice are patterned within the private life of the family group. Public prejudice in the larger community and private prejudice within the family are mutual and interpenetrating forces. The influence moves in a circular fashion, both from outside inward and from inside outward. Personal and familial types of prejudice often invade the public domain.

It is this private prejudice that provides the emotional energy, the driving force for the acceptance of the common prejudices expressed in the wider community against Jew, Catholic, Negro, Puerto Rican, etc. Families with intense, violent antagonisms may breed the fanatic fringe of bigot who incites organized violence against minority groups. In this way prejudice engendered in the intimacies of family living may feed fuel to the fire of the culturally given types of prejudice.

What remains mysterious in the nature of prejudice has to do with the relations between inner and outer experience, the relations of subject and object, individual and group. In essence, prejudice is an admixture of things that belong to the self and to others. It is the rejection and projection of some qualities of self, the introjection of others into self. It is thus a merging of parts of the individual and parts of the group.

The Common Features in Prejudice, Thought Control, Psychological Torture and Character Assassination

The dynamic significance of this problem may be viewed in broader scope if we ask ourselves several other questions: Is there not a close affinity between prejudicial behavior, mechanisms of thought control, psychological torture and character assassination? Can we not regard these forms of behavior as close cousins? It seems so to me. They all seem to relate basically to the dynamics of the pattern of master-slave relationship.

The close analysis of the unconscious motivations leading to prejudice reveals the sick germ of the impulse to impose thought control, to inflict pain and torture and to destroy the character of the victim. The extent to which these other motives enter the picture depends upon the intensity and irrational violence of the prejudice, and the receptivity and support for such actions provided by the social environment.

In other words, it is possible to see these several forms of behavior reflected on a single psychological spectrum, a motivational continuum which begins with the milder forms of prejudice, moves into its more severe expressions, to thought control, psychological torture, character assassination and culminating finally in annihilation of the victim.

It is an emotionally disordered society which sparks the explosive discharge of the terminal, irrational forms of destruction. The common dynamic feature which underlies this whole range of destructive motivation is a regressive pattern of master-slave relationship, a twisted expression of the striving to restore a symbiotic bond.

In this interpersonal pattern the master and slave interact parasitically. The power of one individual is aggrandized as the power of the other is crushed. The security and the strength of the one is enhanced at the expense of the other. The necessary condition is sacrifice. The sacrifice of one partner in this symbiotic bond is required to maintain the other. It is as if there is not enough strength, not enough food, not enough love; therefore, one must surrender to the other. For the implementation of this forced sacrifice, the tactic of intimidation is indispensable; the subordinate half of this unit, the slave, yields and appeases the master in order to survive.

We have here the paradox of one member of this pair progressively surrendering autonomy of self in order barely to stay alive. The slave sacrifices a part of himself, his personal integrity and his separateness in order to save what is left, simply the right of existence. So long as he lives, however, the aggrandizement and indulgence of the master remain parasitically dependent on the self-sacrificial attitude of the slave.

While the slave survives, he is a perpetual threat to the master. The master derives his whole existence from the willingness of the slave to play the reciprocal role. This is a shared omnipotence. The master commands, the slave obeys, but the slave also commands, and the master obeys. Should the slave become willing to risk his right of survival and turn defiantly on his master, the master's omnipotent power is forthwith destroyed.

The vulnerability of the position of the master can be likened to the emotional vulnerability of the person who is anti-Negro or anti-Jew. Both make defensive use of intimidation. Both are dependent for their precarious position on the willing weakness and submissiveness of the victim. The aggrandized position of the master is promptly placed in jeopardy if the victim proves unwilling to play the required complementary role.

The Implication of Prejudice for the Mental Health of the Group

In our time human relations are in a high state of turbulence. This is influenced by the changed relations of individual, family and community, which are a response to the advance of technology, the alienation of man from the satisfaction of work, the altered role of religion in the community. In this setting the security of the individual's position in the group is reduced. The task of establishing identification with the group is rendered more difficult and more precarious.

Under such conditions the emotional weaknesses which lead to prejudice are likely to be rather common and widespread. These weaknesses become exaggerated in a period of chaotic social change. The inner need of prejudice grows more intense and the unstable compensatory conformities with the group become caricatures of positive, healthy identification. Although basically false, this identification gives to the prejudiced person an illusory although temporary sense of superiority and omnipotent mastery. In this way the prejudiced person attempts to feel consciously more whole and more complete. Such considerations are relevant both to the conflict of Jew and Gentile and the conflict of Negro and white.

In our society we see these paired reciprocal roles: the controller and the controlled, the master and the slave, he who

164

makes the sacrifice and he who imposes it. In the society where there is social and political conflict and mass discontent, social forces emerge which reward and fortify the persons enacting these roles. As I see it, such trends contaminate the human relations pattern. They are an invasive threat to the emotional health of the community.

In seeking to understand the psychological roots of prejudice, it is not enough to ferret out its expressions in the individual on the one hand and its manifestations in the group on the other. In the production of prejudice, the dynamic interrelations of individual and group are of the essence. Prejudice is one of the functional consequences of a failure of mental health. People tending toward mental illness are prone to lean on prejudice. To stave off their own breakdown, they exploit prejudice as the weapon with which they try to break down other persons.

In the interaction of the individual and group, we see reflections of a striving toward the group in two ways: to obtain a protective cover for weakness, distortion and vulnerability of the individual personality; and, through parasitic attachment to the group, to achieve compensatory self-aggrandizement and power. With respect to inner sources of anxiety, the individual seeks to hide with a protective blanket his insecurity, guilt, damaged and confused sense of self, his loneliness, his fright and exaggerated sense of exposure to hurtful attack.

With respect to others, the striving is to exploit the group in order to substitute aggression for fear, to intimidate instead of cringing. The effort is clearly to build the self up by tearing another down. Surely these mechanisms are at the very core of the master-slave pattern of human relations.

This is the kind of maladaptive behavior that is mainly oriented to dependency and power. It reflects an arrest of personal development and regression to the omnipotent, coercive tactics of the rejected, helpless infant. This is "immaturity" in a truly malignant form. In some respects, such psychological mechanisms are reminiscent of those which are discerned in cases of perversion. The pervert is one who uses the instrument of sex not really to love the partner, but rather to enslave, degrade and injure the partner. What makes the perversion is not the nature of the sex act, but rather the perversion of the relationship from motives of love to those of destruction.

Are there conceivably certain trends in the organization of our society which foster this form of behavior? I believe so! There are elements in our group structure, influenced by a climate of unrestrained competition, which are oriented both to dependency and power drives. In such a group pattern, it is as if there is not enough of anything to go around, not enough security, food or prestige. It is rather as if one person has these things at the expense of another, since there is not enough for everybody. An emotional and social climate of this kind inevitably promotes an exploitive pattern of human relations, a master-slave pattern in which the gain of one signifies the loss of the other. In such a climate, in effect, one person lives off the other. There is no room in this setting for mutual understanding and respect, no room for genuine co-operation, and the provision of opportunity for all to grow to their full potentials in life.

Outbreaks of prejudice and social crises are close companions. The annihilation of the Jews in Europe may be as nothing compared to the possible devastation of a war between the white and dark-skinned peoples. In a time of social unrest we must be watchful for the rise of demagogic groups and fanatic leaders who stand ever ready to launch a new crusade of prejudicial destruction. The aim of such groups is to seize power, terrorize the public, subject the will of the people, and realign human relations in a regressive, master-slave design. It is imperative, therefore, that we understand the relations of prejudice and social change.

The age of space and nuclear energy is upon us. It offers limitless horizons for new adventure, new knowledge and new gains for the welfare of man. At the same time, it excites new fear and new temptation to aggrandizement and power. In this new age, shall we move ahead for the common good or passively allow a social climate of insecurity, fright and confusion, within which demagogues may launch a crusade for power, this time exploiting new instruments for the imposition of old forms of prejudice? One would need to be all things combined to find the answer—historian, psychologist, social scientist, philosopher and politician.

One thing is clear. The trend toward authoritarian values, the pressure to conformity, the aggrandizement of those in power and the subjugation of the others, move ever more tightly toward a twisted regressive master-slave version of human relations, a form of sick symbiosis.

At the same time, it aggravates prejudice, fosters thought control and character assassination and intensifies the disposition to breakdown, to mental illness, ultimately to malignant forms of group paranoia.

Is it later than we think? Do we have the antidote?

Acknowledgment

The article "The Social Psychology of Prejudice," was originally published in *Mental Hygiene*, Vol. 49, No. 1 (January, 1965), pp. 27-35. It is reprinted with the permission of the editor, Dr. Henry A. Davidson, and Dr. Ackerman.

EXISTENTIAL PSYCHOLOGY

BEN STRICKLAND, ED. D.

Director of Counselor Education, Texas Christian University

Editorial Note

Existentialism has pervaded most disciplines and has made a decisive impact on contemporary psychological thought. That it may provide a basis for the development of a true science of human behavior is one intriguing possibility suggested by Dr. Ben Strickland, an authority in the field of Existential Psychology.

Dr. Strickland is Associate Professor at Texas Christian University in Fort Worth, Texas, where his primary responsibility has been the direction of counselor education. He was born in McKinney, Texas and received his doctorate in education from North Texas University in Denton, Texas, in 1964. His current interests and activities include educational and psychological research, psychological counseling, consultation to school and community agencies, and a considerable involvement in local and national professional organizations. One of his most active interests is the application of philosophical concepts to the solution of behavioral problems, and he has devoted much of his time to philosophical research and writing.

•

EXISTENTIAL PSYCHOLOGY

Background

During the early part of the twentieth century there began to appear in this country some indications that the existing philosophical systems were to receive a challenge from Europe.

168

As early as the 1930's and possibly even earlier, existential overtones were appearing in literature and translations of the writings of such existential thinkers as Søren Kierkegaard were becoming readily available.

The initial acceptance of existential themes by Western philosophers was somewhat limited, possibly because of several factors. First of all, the relative nature of many existential themes was in direct contrast to the logical, analytical, and systematized format of existing philosophies. Secondly, the pessimism of some European existential writers was offensive to many Western scholars. Thirdly, much of the existential thought reflected the feelings of writers living in Europe at an age when that country was on the verge of collapse. Americans were not at that time concerned with the collapse of a government and were not, therefore, sensitive to the impact of such a dramatic experience as were the Europeans. Many American scholars were therefore prone to ask, "Who needs it?" Because of these factors, and possibly many others, it took more than a decade for the philosophy of existentialism to have any apparent effect on the fields of education, psychology, and religion.

Today there is ample evidence that existential thought has pervaded psychological, psychiatric, and psychoanalytic theory in this country. The field of existential psychology, for example, has experienced rapid growth during the last few years as a part of a "third-force psychology," to distinguish it from the psychological systems of behaviorism and psychoanalysis. The ever-increasing list of references and periodicals attests to the continually growing interest of American scholars in existential themes.

Contemporary existentialism is considered largely a creation of the genius of Søren Kierkegaard. It was Kierkegaard who first used the phrase "philosophy of existence" from which the term "existentialism" apparently evolved. His personal revolt against traditional philosophies and their supposedly degrading effect upon the individual, laid the foundation for contemporary existentialism.

The theme of the "individual," was not original with Kierkegaard, however, who considered Abraham of Biblical times to

169

be an example of a true individual. Some existential scholars feel that existential themes can be traced back as far as ancient Greece and the thoughts of Plato and others. It is precisely because of the divergent experiences and viewpoints of the various existential writers that existentialism is not a systematized or organized school of thought.

Existential themes have appeared throughout history during eras when there was concern for the status of the individual. Tillich (1914) has attributed the appearance of existential themes to threats made to individuality by either autocratic governments, technological advances, or rationalistic thinking. Kaufmann (1962) has also suggested that existential themes have appeared as revolts against traditional philosophy.

One of these early revolts which appeared to be of some significance was initiated by Kant who, according to Barrett (1962), is the "father of modern philosophy." Kant's revolt included the insistence that existence cannot be conceived by reason alone. Furthermore, because of the subjective nature of existence, it cannot even be explained by reason.

Even before Kant's protest, Pascal earned for himself the title of an existentialist because of his pessimistic and yet unrealistic view of man. Pascal viewed man as being in search of some direction in life, only to be continually confronted by his own miserable existence. The somewhat negative approach of Pascal might be compared to the pessimistic view held by Jean-Paul Sartre, the leading French existentialist.

As might be expected, disagreement is not uncommon among present existential writers and neither was it uncommon among 19th century writers. It was a disagreement, in fact, which apparently provided the stimulus for the development or evolution of modern existentialism. The disagreement existed between Kierkegaard and Hegel, the German philosopher, resulting in an attack by Kierkegaard upon the classical philosophy of Hegel.

Although Hegel was apparently interested in man's process of becoming, his primary concern was with understanding the world of rationality which he proceeded to accomplish by adhering to the universal reason external to man. He apparently felt that it was thought which produced existence; this being the opposite of Kierkegaard's belief.

Kirkegaard's attack upon Hegel aroused some interest in his own era, although the bulk of his forty-three literary works remained obscure until the early part of the twentieth century when they caught the attention of the German philosopher, Martin Heidegger and of the German School of Phenomenology represented by Karl Jaspers. Heidegger and Jaspers are considered by many existentialist scholars to be the architects of twentieth century existentialism.

In 1919 Jaspers published his *Psychologie der Weltanschauungen*, for which Kierkegaard's thought apparently formed the framework. It was Jaspers who apparently formulated the basis for contemporary existential analysis. The translations of Kierkegaard's works by Jaspers and Heidegger were a mile-stone in the history of existential thought.

The philosophy of Heidegger spread to France where it aroused the interest of Gabriel Marcel and Jean-Paul Sartre. Although the contributions of these Frenchmen were not duplications of Heidegger's philosophy, there was some similarity. Both Sartre and Heidegger, for example, were concerned with the misery of society in apathy and chaos. Sartre has probably enjoyed more success than any other existential writer despite some of his strong pessimistic overtones. One reason for his success might be attributed to the breadth of his writings which include philosophy, psychology, and various types of fiction. According to Barrett (1962), however, Sartre's writing does not represent the most significant contribution to existential philosophy.

The names of several other influential writers should be added to the list of contributors to existentialism. The following is a list of only a few such writers and the country of their origin:

Denmark	Søren Kierkegaard
Russia	Fyodor Dostoevsky
France	Jean-Paul Sartre Albert Camus, and Gabriel Marcel

Switzerland	Karl Barth
Germany	Karl Jaspers
	Martin Heidegger
	Paul Tillich
America	Reinhold Niebuhr
England	Gerald Hopkins

The writings of several American scholars are particularly appropriate to the field of existential psychology. These include Rollo May, Abraham Maslow, and Carl Rogers, to name only a few.

The preceding chronology will provide little more than a brief historical orientation to the philosophy of existentialism. More extensive historical information can be found in the contribution of Barrett (1962), Kaufmann (1962), Wild (1959) and others. Because existentialism is a combination of many philosophies or points of view, the works of several writers, past and present, should be reviewed in order to obtain an adequate understanding of major existential themes.

What is Existentialism?

As might be expected, there are several areas of agreement and disagreement to be found in the definitions of existentialism as presented by various writers. The following are examples of some of the more popular definitions:

1. Barrett and Aiken—"Existentialism is a philosophy that confronts the human situation *in its totality*, to ask what the basic conditions of human existence are and how man can establish his own meaning out of these conditions." (1962, p. 143)

2. Allan—"Existentialism (is) an attempt at philosophizing from the standpoint of the actor instead of, as has been customary, from that of the spectator." (1953, p. 3)

3. May—"Existentialism is the philosophical trend of thought which takes as its focus of interest the consideration of man's most immediate experience, his own existence." (1958, p. 170)

4. van Kaam—"Existentialism is the collective name of widely divergent existential currents of thought which . . . studies . . . the real concrete man, human life—not as an abstract quantity but here and at the moment in its lively quality." (1960, p. 6)

A cursory examination of these and other definitions would suggest that existentialism speaks either for a revolt against or a re-evaluation of tradition. Some writers describe existentialism as a reaction to a political system. Others consider it as a reaction to the negative aspects of technological development. Still others consider it a challenge to traditional philosophical systems. The extent to which one might feel that existentialism is either a revolt or a re-evaluation would probably depend largely upon the repertoire of the reader. Furthermore, an exposure to only a limited number of existential writers might cause one to feel that the primary emphasis of existentialism is political, economical, philosophical, religious, atheistic, or with emphases in several other possible directions. The one thing that would be difficult to conclude is that existentialism is a set of highly organized and systematized tenets. It is precisely the lack of organization which seems to be the source of much criticism and rejection of existential concepts. The existentialists contend, on the other hand, that it is precisely the absence of prescriptions which makes existentialism meaningful to each individual, for it is indeed the task of each individual to find the true meaning of existence for himself.

The impact of existential thought has been experienced in many areas, not the least of which have been those of religion, philosophy, education, psychology, and the arts. Because of the scope of these areas, it may well be said that existentialism has had and is now having an impact upon American life in general. The most obvious impact of existential thought can be seen in literature, art, and drama where existential themes are quite common. If one examines popular music, for example, existential implications are frequently present in song lyrics such as "On a clear day . . . and you'll see who you are."

Although it may seem that the psychologist is far removed from the areas of literature, art, and drama, it must be remembered that the truly effective psychologist has probably been exposed to several walks of life. Since the title of this chapter is Existential Psychology, however, the impact of existentialism on psychology and related areas will be given specific consideration.

Existential thought has been a two-edged sword in that it has both renounced and proclaimed. Any psychological theory or construct which is at all depersonalizing has been questioned and every area which encourages personalization has been supported to some extent. The result of such examination has been a somewhat different approach to psychological inquiry wherein possibilities are just as important as probabilities and ideographic research just as important as nomothetic research. Real and ultimate concerns in life have become the principal criteria for investigation.

It has been suggested that existentialism could possibly provide the philosophical bases now of limited development in psychology. Whether or not such is true remains to be proven although the increasing emphasis in philosophical aspects of psychology is quite apparent. In fact, one might well label an existential psychologist as a philosophical psychologist since practically all such scholars are concerned with some type of attitude or frame of reference. Such a categorization is not intended, of course, to offend the philosophical psychologists who are not existentially sympathetic.

In addition to the increased or renewed philosophical emphases, it seems quite obvious that at least two areas of impact have resulted either directly or indirectly from existential thought. The first of these areas is a new dimension in theory, specifically in relation to counseling, psychotherapy, and psychoanalysis. A number of theorists in these areas have emerged during the past decade. Probably the most prominent of these theorists is Rollo May whose publication *Existence* was one of the psychology classics of the 1950's. The Logotherapy of Victor Frankl might be considered the European counterpart to May's Existential Analysis. Although May's theoretical formulations concerning psychotherapy and psychoanalysis may not have been the first of their kind, certainly these have been the most widely quoted. Other exponents of existential therapy or analysis have been Medard Boss, Clark Moustakas, Avery Weisman, Werner Woolff, and Adrian van Kaam, to name only a few.

An examination of the techniques described by most existential therapists would reveal nothing revolutionary, although current literature reveals some departures in techniques from the traditional. The most important aspect is the attitude of the therapist rather than techniques which he might employ. This attitude is an expression of a concern for understanding the person as an individual living in a particular environment or world of experience. Existential analysis departs from traditional psychotherapy in that personal problems or syndromes which might tend to make man a series of fragmentations are of secondary importance in understanding the individual. The emphasis is on the importance of "knowing" rather than just "knowing about" an individual. The "I-Thou" relationship described by Buber seems to be an accurate representation of the relationship between the existential therapist and his client. Such a relationship involves an encounter between two or more people, rather than just an experience. Specific applications of existential therapy or analysis are explained in the works of May, van Kaam, Boss, Moustakas, Weisman, and Woolff.

A second major impact of existentialism on psychological thought has been evidenced in the development of a family of theories all of which are concerned with the development of man's potential. The family includes such titles as Ego Psychology, Humanistic Psychology, Phenomenology, and possibly several others. Because of the abundance of literature related to each of these theories it might be more appropriate to refer to these as schools.

The spokesmen for these schools have been such writers as Abraham Maslow, Erich Fromm, Gordon Allport, Carl Rogers, Paul Tillich, and several others. Among these writers the importance of personal growth or self-actualization has been paramount. Hall (1965) has suggested that the reason for the development of such schools has been man's disgust with himself, his environment, and philosophies or psychologies which tend to degrade his nature. This explanation seems appropriate when it is realized that this family of schools has allowed man to attain a uniqueness, worth, dignity, and importance heretofore possibly not achieved in the history of mankind.

The impact of the writings of the various humanists or phenomenologists has probably been more extensive than in any other area of existential development. The works of Maslow, Fromm, Allport, Rogers, and Tillich, for example, have become increasingly popular during the last few years even to business and professional people. This popularity is attested to by an increasing number of activities emphasizing such terms as self-actualization, development of potential, becoming, and the meaning of life. The optimism of the humanistic writers has apparently been somewhat contagious.

Major Tenets of Existentialism

An attempt to find a consensus of belief among the various existential writers would meet with some degree of frustration. No two major existential writers seem to share similar points of view as to which themes are most important or as to the degree of importance placed upon any particular theme. Thus it is easy to understand why the philosophy of existentialism is not highly organized and systematized.

As the original works of the various writers are examined, however, some areas of tentative agreement can be found. For the purposes of this discussion the major tenets will be considered those themes to which some consideration is given by several existential writers.

It should be remembered that the interpretations expressed herein are merely those of the writer and do not represent any ultimate existential truths. A person interested in understanding existentialism should read the works of several writers and synthesize from these works the concepts which are personally meaningful. To accept as unquestionable the works of any one existential writer would seem to refute at least one of the major tenets of existentialism; namely, truth, which must be understood by each individual through his own experience.

I. Individuality

Man is a unique animal. He possesses a superior potential to those of lower animals and by virtue of these can control and direct his life. Although many writers have voiced this point of view, the strongest advocate of individuality was probably Søren Kierkegaard, to whom individuality was a prime concern. He viewed individuality as a positive concept and described it as the extent to which one is realizing his potential. True individuality is, therefore, not beatnikish or bizarre. No matter how unusual a person may appear, external manifestation plays only a minor role in individuality. Physical features would not be a criterion for individuality because these are to some extent natural endowments; possessions which may not necessarily result from active pursuits. Individuality should be considered an accomplishment rather than an endowment or passive endeavor. It is a potential, a potential "to become oneself." This potential is not necessarily the potential to become a great orator or athlete for, according to Kierkegaard, "the greatest thing is not to be this or that but to be oneself, and this everyone can be." (1944, p. 150). Furthermore, it is "in every man's power to become what he is, an individual" (1962, p. 119).

Individuality may also be considered as an emergence. One does not just acquire individuality just as an oak tree does not acquire acorns. Individuality is an intrinsic potential which manifests itself as a result of a commitment to individuality. Paul Tillich has described this commitment as "self affirmation of the individual self as individual self." (1952, p. 113) For this commitment courage is needed. Thus individuality is "the courage to be as oneself."

Through positive growth experiences a person learns that he has certain potentials and limitations which become more specifically defined throughout life. It is his own potential or limitation with which an individual must be concerned. Otherwise he can never "become himself." This is not to discourage one from overcoming physical handicaps or setting high goals but rather to emphasize that coping behavior can quite obviously be obstructive to the development of one's own potential.

Individuality is both product and process. It is a product in that it reflects man's past experience. It is also a continual process in that man can never completely understand himself or completely realize his potential and thus is always confronted with the possibility of discovery and renewal. Man is always in process of "becoming."

Contemporary critics of existentialism see individuality as a somewhat negative concept wherein man is antisocial rather than social. Quite the contrary seems true from the existential point of view, however, for individuality does not develop in a vacuum. Man is a part of his environment; he cannot become human by himself, according to Jaspers (Kaufmann, 1962). Man must exist successfully in his environment for it is only through interaction with his environment that man is able to identify his potentials and limitations. The true individual according to Rogers (1963) seeks empathy rather than rebellion with the values of his culture.

II. Freedom

The development of individuality is both a responsibility and a freedom from an existentialist point of view. The freedom "to become," or the freedom to develop individuality, is the most important freedom of all. In addition to being a criterion for individuality, freedom is expressed by man's very existence, for life itself is a choice and to live is to exercise the freedom of choice, in choosing to live. What is left to the individual is the way in which he exercises freedom according to Price (1963).

Freedom may be viewed as an active concept which, without action, is merely another potentiality. The action context of freedom is also implied by Sartre in that, "man is nothing other than what he makes himself." (1947, page 18) Kierkegaard has further amplified the active aspect of freedom in his implication that a person has freedom only to the extent to which it is actively utilized, for man "can remain in his freedom only by constantly realizing it." (1944, p. 236) Freedom is therefore more than a mere recognition, it is a manifestation of the commitment to the task of becoming an individual.

Freedom is a psychic development, not a political decree. It must be more than a hypothetical construct; it must be an active belief. Freedom, according to Sartre, is the first condition of action. (1956) Freedom is actively initiated the moment a person recognizes that he has the freedom and responsibility for any change which might take place within him.

To some existential writers, freedom is more than a potentiality; it is an ultimatum. Man is not only free to choose, he must choose. To this extent, man is "condemned to freedom." (Wilde, 1963, page 163)

As might be anticipated, the emphasis and direction of freedom vary among the writings of existential scholars. Common to most writers, however, seems to be the feeling that although possibly influenced by the environmental conditions or restrictions, freedom does not originate within the environment; it originates within the individual. It is a matter of choice; to some extent a person can choose freedom or bondage.

Since freedom requires responsibility, to be unfree might be a more desirable choice to some people. Tillich (1952) and Fromm (1947) have provided descriptions of man as he attempts to "escape from freedom," in order to avoid risks and responsibilities. In this case, man evades his freedom being fearful of the consequences.

III. Responsibility

A necessary condition of freedom is responsibility. Sartre (1956) has described responsibility as "the logical requirement of the consequences of our freedom." Without responsibility, the concept of existential freedom seems somewhat meaningless.

Responsibility is considered by most existential writers to be an essential ingredient of man's existence. Because man is unique, he alone can be responsible for his existence and for the realization of his potential. Responsibility may also be viewed as an ingredient for growth since man is what he makes of himself.

The concept of responsibility is an increasingly important one in contemporary society. Man is reaching for more and more external freedom. Such a search seems paradoxical, however, because from an existential point of view true freedom is intrinsic rather than extrinsic. Furthermore, as man finds an external source of freedom he, in essence, has also found an external source of responsibility and thus may accept less responsibility for his own actions.

Existential freedom seems quite removed from irresponsibility. In fact, existential freedom is in reality an "unfree" concept. For in order to be free, man must also be responsible. He must be able and willing to accept the consequences of his freedom. Responsibility may be seen as the enabler of freedom.

IV. Choice

Individuality, freedom, and responsibility are acts of choice. Freedom, for example, is not determined genetically, politically, or socially but rather through active choices. The importance of choice cannot be overemphasized when it is realized that even life itself is a choice. An alternative to life always exists.

Ideally, choice implies action as well as freedom. Pragmatically speaking, however, a decision can be either active or passive. A person may either choose or choose not to choose. In either case, a choice has been made and man has no choice but to choose. According to Sartre (1947), man is condemned to choice.

Choice should be considered a continual process rather than terminal product. A person does not just choose to become an individual, for example, or to be free, and then let nature take its course. According to Kierkegaard (1941), genuine existence demands continual choice and renewal.

One result of choice is self-direction. Choice cannot, therefore, be considered either unidirectional or irreversible. The appropriate condition for a particular choice may change with the acquisition of additional understandings thereby making the original choice inappropriate.

The basis for choice is not necessarily a collection of objective data. Meaningful choices, according to Kierkegaard (1941), are "rooted in subjectivity." This is not to suggest that a person ignore all available information but rather to suggest that man use such information to establish such possibilities or alternatives which can then be evaluated and from which decisions can be made. The existential emphasis is not to refute objective data but to remind each individual that even the divisions of a yardstick are the result of subjective consensus.

Under normal conditions, man is always free to choose. Choice is always a possibility, even in very restricting environments. According to Frankl (1963) a person can be deprived of everything but the freedom to choose. Thus if the possibility of choice exists in a concentration camp, it would seemingly exist for all men.

The existential choice should not be confused with superficial choices. The choice to become an individual, for example, is the true existential choice rather than the mere choice of a particular suit or dress. Responsibility must accompany choice also. Unless man is able to accept the consequences of his choice, his choices can seldom be of an active nature. He must, instead, choose not to choose.

V. Identity

The stimulus for the existential movement was the increasing dehumanization of man in the contemporary society. One of the most tragic results of dehumanization from an existential point of view is the accompanying loss of identity which is an essential criterion for authentic existence.

Who, then, is man? Man is a being who possesses the potential of individuality, who can become an individual. The extent to which man does become an individual is determined by the extent to which he understands the meaning and importance of freedom, responsibility, choice, commitment, truth, anxiety, authenticity, and other similar concepts.

Identity inevitably focuses on the self which is the locus of man's existence. The self is a synthesis of possibility, limitation, awareness, acceptance, choice, freedom, objectivity, subjectivity, good, and bad. It is the synthesis of what man has been, what he is now, and what he can become.

The self is never a finished product for the process of self-development is never complete. The self must continue to be in process since man can never completely understand himself and can never discontinue his search for meaning.

VI. Subjectivity/Understanding

Man lives in a world of objective fact. Modern learning resources place a fantastic amount of knowledge within easy grasp of the average person. To the existentialist, however, there is a great degree of difference between objective knowledge and subjective wisdom or understanding. Kierkegaard has designed a law for self-development which suggests that unless less self-understanding is the result of increased objective knowledge, self-deterioration rather than self growth is the result (1941, page 47). From this point of view, understanding and knowledge can be two very different concepts, for when viewed as extremes the emphasis of knowledge can be external whereas the emphasis of understanding is internal. It is through inwardness, according to Kierkegaard, that man finds subjective understanding.

What is reasonable is not necessarily what is best for the individual. The task of each individual is not merely to assimilate knowledge about reality or about himself, but rather to search inwardly for the appropriate meaning of all available knowledge. Existence and knowledge may therefore be two very different things and, according to Kierkegaard, "to understand everything except for one's ownself is very comical." (1941, page 316)

Subjectivity does not discount objective data for man does not exist in a vacuum. Unless man exists successfully within an environment he does not really exist, from an existential point of view. Environmental data therefore provides much of the subject matter for existence. According to Jaspers (Kaufmann, 1962) man may attach symbols to objective data. These symbols constitute the subjective information essential to man's existence. It is through this subjective information rather than objective data that man develops understandings and is understood.

Existential reality is a product of subjective exploration rather than objective consensus. What is reality to one man is not necessarily reality to another. By the same token, what is rational to one man may not be rational to another. The importance of the irrational in every man's life receives emphasis from virtually all the existential writers. Nietzsche (Barrett, 1958), Kierkegaard (1941), Camus (1955), for example, have suggested that behavior be considered a protest against mere reason. It is through the emphasis on the irrational that man is able to develop subjective reasons for behavior. There comes a time in every man's life where he must act in the absence of logic or reason. At this time his behavior is directed more by feelings than by rational processes. Kierkegaard (1941) has described such behavior as "acts of faith" wherein a person charts his own path into the unknown. Such ventures are not uncommon to the existentialists, however, because man can never completely understand himself and frequently must act in the absence of appropriate evidence or information.

VII. Anxiety

An area of concern common to all existential writers is that of anxiety. As might be expected, however, there is some disagreement as to the source of anxiety, the emphasis placed upon anxiety, and the directional impact of anxiety. Anxiety may be seen as metaphysical or psychological depending upon the reference examined. Regardless of the emphases of the various existential writers, anxiety is apparently seen by most to be some state of disequilibrium within the individual or between the individual and his environment.

Most existential writers see anxiety as being inevitable. Heidegger (Barrett, 1962) described anxiety as a fundamental mood which is a natural result of man's existence in a world of uncertainty and his continual encounter with the unknown. Sartre (1956) saw anxiety as a fundamental uneasiness resulting from man's inability to realize his potentials and the necessity of making his existence more secure. Kierkegaard's (1941) source of anxiety was similar to that of Sartre in that the disequilibrium represented a difference between what man is and what man could become; between the real and ideal self. The similar emphasis of Kierkegaard and Sartre is somewhat interesting in view of their theistic and aetheistic views respectively.

In addition to the metaphysical explanations of anxiety presented by Heidegger, Kierkegaard, and Sartre, other writers have described anxiety from a psychological orientation. May, for example, has described anxiety as the "state of the human being in the struggle against that which would destroy his being." (1961, p. 83) He has described anxiety from an analytic point of view and has provided examples of persons experiencing anxiety in a psychotherapeutic relationship wherein a person considers his present existence and his potentialities.

From the foregoing it seems quite evident that the popular use of the term anxiety, which has somewhat negative emphases, is somewhat different from anxiety as expressed by the existentialists which has at least some positive aspects. Disequilibrium may in fact produce a healthy form of anxiety which could in reality be a source of motivation for change. Anxiety may, for example, cause a decrease in the separation of the real and ideal self, or it might provide the motivation for increased realization of potential.

Existential anxiety is paradoxical, for although anxiety may provide the motivation for change, change itself may produce disequilibrium. Change is usually accompanied by some degree of uncertainty and with uncertainty there is usually disequilibrium. Uncertainty is frequently accompanied by ambiguity which may also be a source of disequilibrium.

The positive anxiety about which the existentialists speak is seemingly growth oriented rather than being overwhelming or incapacitating. Furthermore, because man can never completely realize his potentials, existential anxiety would seem to be to some extent a perpetual ingredient of man's existence. Man must continually exercise his freedom through choice and certainly choice must be accompanied by uncertainty. From this point of view, anxiety would seem to be a prerequisite to individuality and authentic existence.

An interesting description of disequilibrium from a behavioral science viewpoint has been presented by Bernard, Ottenberg, and Redl (Schwebel, 1965). These writers have explained dehumanization as a result of man's reaction to the uncertainties of contemporary society, a position similar in many ways to that of existential writers.

VIII. *Experience/Confrontation/Encounter*

From an existential point of view, many commonly used terms are subject to re-evaluation and re-definition. "Experience" is an example of such a term. Since it may refer to a wide variety of meaningless and meaningful incidents, it does not necessarily meet the existential criterion of authenticity. For this reason the terms "confrontation" and "encounter" are frequently substituted for the term "experience."

A person's life can easily become a series of meaningless events in a society which places, by necessity, much emphasis upon automation and production. It is with this directionless existence that existentialism is concerned. Authentic existence contains significant, meaningful, enduring experiences which are called "confrontations" to connote impact and involvement. These confrontations may occur in the form of dialogue between people or in living thoughts and feelings. A person may experience a confrontation with nature, for example, in the form of extra vehicular activity in space. By the same token, a confrontation may occur in an accidental conversation between strangers. The time, place, and circumstance of confrontation is incidental; the impact of the event is the important aspect.

The difference between experience and encounter is described by May as being the difference between "knowing about" and "knowing" (1962). Knowing about a person, for example, is of much less importance than an authentic relationship with him. Marcel has made a similar distinction between encounter and experience in that encounter describes what is in a person and experience may describe only what is before a person (Barrett and Akin, 1962, p. 370). Both of these distinctions emphasize an inward search for meaning or reflection. It is through reflection according to Husserl (Barrett and Akin, 1962) that the intrinsic nature of an experience is understood or that an experience is transformed into an encounter.

Most existential writers describe encounter as the relationship of an experience between two individuals. Such an experience must of necessity be of an involved rather than a casual nature. The "I-Thou" relationship described by Buber would seem to be an excellent example of an encounter. This experience involves an interpersonal merger wherein two individuals become almost as one, resulting in a deep inner experience in which both come to know rather than just know about each other. The encounter would, therefore, seem to be a necessary ingredient of existential psychotherapy.

IX. Truth

The existential truths are not necessarily universal truths. The direction of man's existence is a function of the truths by which he lives and these truths are validated intrinsically rather than extrinsically. What is truth for one man may not be truth for another. It is through truth, therefore, that freedom evolves for until a person determines what is truth for himself he is bound by the truths of others.

Man finds truth as he determines what is personally meaningful and valuable. It is therefore the task of each individual to actively seek truth. Man cannot passively accept truth, according to Kierkegaard, for "truth exists for the particular individual only as he himself produces it in action." (1944a, page 123). Therefore, to preach truths and expect another to absorb these is sheer folly. When a person actively finds and accepts his truths he frees himself to become an individual; he is no longer an imitation.

The subjective nature of truth is emphasized by most existential writers. Existential truths cannot be equated with scientific truths, according to Jaspers (Kaufmann, 1962), for "truth consists precisely in that conception of life which is expressed by the individual," and since each individual is unique, no objective truth can be adequate for all individuals. (Kaufmann, 1962, p. 117) Furthermore, only the truths which edify are truths for each individual. (Kierkegaard, 1941)

The existentialist's emphasis on subjectivity is not intended to refute objective knowledge. Truth can be described as self-appropriated knowledge, emphasizing the importance of both subjectivity and objectivity in truth. The important thing to remember seems to be that truth cannot just be known; it must be experienced. It is not just a theory; it must be a belief.

The subjective and inward nature of truth makes it accessible to each person. Kierkegaard (1939) has suggested that the underlying principle of all truth is that each person is able to acquire it himself. This is not to suggest, however, that a person finds truth in isolation. Truth in fact must be attained through interaction with other people.

Truth must also be considered an approximation since each person is always acquiring new knowledge and new understandings. Truth cannot be classified as a definite sustaining body of knowledge as long as a person is engaged in a process of becoming an individual. The truths of man's existence will also be in process.

X. Commitment

One of the most popular existentialist concepts now in wide-spread use is that of "commitment." The number of possible definitions of commitment probably varies as much as the number of people using this term. It is important in this discussion to examine commitment as it is understood from an existential point of view.

Not only is commitment an important tenet, it is, according to Beck (1963, page 114) "the crux of existential philosophy." Since existentialism is concerned with man's existence, then commitment may be seen as the "crux" of existence. There is no real existence, according to Sartre (1947) without commitment. Furthermore, the lack of commitment is the real source of despair. The necessity of commitment to the individual and the futility which results from lack of commitment were vital concerns to Kierkegaard (1954) also.

Commitment is both the focal point and life force of existence. It is more than an attitude or feeling, for it demands action. It might, in fact, be viewed as the verb of philosophy, for if one really believes he must put his beliefs into action.

The direction or impact of commitment is a function of the truths by which an individual lives. External validation of commitment would therefore be somewhat difficult to accomplish. Each person must decide what is truth for himself and then decide how he will express this truth. Because of the uniqueness of each individual's experience, two people would not be expected to possess identical commitments. The relative nature of commitment among the various existential writers has been reviewed by Heinemann (1958) who lists atheism, theism, politics, philosophy and several others, as possible commitments of these writers.

It would seem impossible to place value upon the commitment of any one person. Likewise, it would be inappropriate to evaluate a commitment on the basis of any ultimate or universal truth. An interesting dialogue in relation to the nature and value of commitment has been conducted by Crawford (1966) and Winborn (1966) in which Winborn has suggested that the important aspect of commitment is centered around the individual and his search for meaningful existence, rather than to any one system of values to which any group might subscribe. From this point of view it seems that the "act" of commitment is much more important than the "direction" of commitment.

Since commitment is a choice it need not be considered terminal, unidirectional, or irreversible. Since any commitment is based on understandings, it seems logical that additional understandings or changes in understanding could affect a commitment. A commitment would therefore seem to be of a more tentative rather than terminal nature.

Operationally speaking, commitment may be either general, specific, or both. A person may be committed to individuality or authenticity, for example, and at the same time be committed to several more specific elements such as being a good parent, a good Christian, or a good athlete. It may be, in fact, that a general commitment requires several sub-commitments for reality-testing purposes.

Subcommitments may also be viewed as changes in direction within the general commitment. The commitment to authenticity, for example, would not be affected by a specific commitment from being a good parent to being a good husband or wife, as children grow up and leave home.

Changes in general commitments are also possible. As a person more clearly understands the essential elements of authenticity, he could become more realistically committed to authenticity.

An Existential Growth Model

One criterion for predicting the extent to which any concept will be accepted by any discipline is the extent to which this concept can be effectively communicated. Generally speaking, the more objective a concept is, the more easily it can be communicated. Subjective concepts, on the other hand, frequently do not lend themselves to effective communication because subjective meaning is dependent upon individual experience rather than group consensus. Two people, for example,

189

would probably have somewhat different understandings of concepts such as "becoming" and "being" because of different attitudes, feelings, values, experiences, etc. It is precisely this subjectivity which has limited the extent to which existential concepts have been communicable. Many of the existential concepts seem to be the epitome of subjectivity and thus a person who is annoyed by indefiniteness, ambiguity, and relativity of meanings could easily be offended as he attempts to wade through the subjective existential concepts. Thus, it is easy to understand the criticism to which existentialist scholars have been subjected when they have experienced difficulty in communicating an existential concept to the satisfaction of another person.

It seems probable that many existential concepts would defy widely accepted explanations and the person who must live with certainties would have some difficulty in understanding, much less accepting these concepts. This condition should challenge rather than exonerate existential writers, however. The future of existential thought would seem predicated, in fact, upon the extent to which existential writers develop a greater commitment to effective communication. Such a commitment would not require any person to prescribe meanings for all but rather to elucidate his understanding so that others might be able to more effectively synthesize their own understandings.

The following pages represent an attempt to synthesize certain existential tenets into a growth model. The purpose of such model development is twofold: (1) to show that some organization and objectivity is possible; and (2) to encourage existential writers to give less attention to theory development and more attention to the process of communication. Despite certain objective aspects, the model will be highly subjective because it is based on the understandings of the writer. The reader should therefore not accept the model as the only possible explanation of existential growth, but rather should use whatever understandings are developed from an examination of the model and with these develop a model of his own with which he feels comfortable. The model is presented therefore, as a possibility rather than a certainty and should be stimulative rather than palliative. All of the existential concepts previously described are implicit, although only four are explicit.

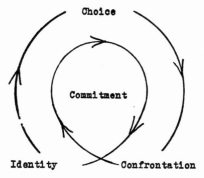

The helix shape is probably one of the more significant aspects of the model since the underlying principle of existentialism, if such exists, is that of continual process. Man is ever in process. He is continually changing, re-evaluating, growing, and becoming. The only product which could possibly be implied is that of additional understandings upon which additional changes might be predicated. Although man is a product of his experiences and his environment, he is always changing biologically and philosophically during his lifetime. The decrease in the direction of man's change is obviously heightened by an innumerable number of factors.

A second significant aspect of the model is the implication that the growth process is centered around or centers upon commitment. It is this commitment which is the directive force in man's life.

The arrows connote the sequence of the model. These do not imply, however, that identity, choice, confrontation, and commitment must occur in a fixed, lock-step manner. Such an assumption alone would make the model unacceptable. The implication is, rather, that all of these elements are necessary in a growth model, but that the sequence may vary. In some people the sequence would occur in a one, two, three, four pattern in which there is identity, then choice, then confrontation, then commitment. It seems more likely that all four of

191

these elements might occur more simultaneously as a person "becomes." Each element will be examined independently, however, for the purpose of clarity and understanding.

Although the model may be entered at most any point, it would seem more appropriate to begin with identity. By identity is meant an understanding of one's potentials and limitations; what one might possibly be able to do as well as what one might probably not be able to do. All areas of existence are included in identity—physiological, intellectual, social, emotional, and any other dimension which might be conceived. Identity is not fixed; it also is in process and changes as man more carefully and accurately understands his potentials and limitations. Furthermore, identity should not be seen as a limiting element. Just because man does not presently possess certain potentials, for example, should not imply that he is incapable of developing these potentials. Realistic self-appraisal is of primary importance in establishing identity.

As man establishes his identity, as he understands more thoroughly who he is and what he is capable of becoming, he is in the position of making realistic choices in relation to present and future goals. He can, for example, decide to improve present skills or develop new skills. On the other hand, he may choose to do nothing about certain areas of his existence. Even this, however, is a choice; for in essence, man has chosen not to choose. The important thing of course is that man has the freedom to choose and that realistic choices are predicated upon realistic understandings.

One important aspect of choice and freedom of choice is responsibility. Freedom must be accompanied by responsibility; otherwise the process of becoming is really nonexistent. As man chooses, he must accept the responsibility of the consequences of his choices. If man attempts to avoid the responsibility then his experience is of limited value.

The term "confrontation" must, therefore, be substituted for "experience" since it implies responsible involvement. Confrontation must be considered a form of reality testing wherein man evaluates the appropriateness of his choices through involvement

192

with others. Confrontation implies something deeper and more meaningful than experience; but, nonetheless, it is still a form of reality testing. Through this reality testing a person has an occasion to continually re-evaluate the appropriateness of his direction to his ultimate commitments.

On the basis of man's experiences or confrontations, he acquires evidence with which to develop real and meaningful commitments. A basis for commitment would seemingly be identity, choice, and confrontation. A commitment is much broader and deeper, seemingly, than the choice to become educated, marry, or select an occupation, although it seems possible that these might be considered parts of one's total commitment. An example of a total commitment might be to become a genuine or authentic person, in which case it should pervade all areas of a person's existence.

Quite obviously, a total commitment would not develop overnight and would not, itself, be a product. As a person gains greater understanding of himself and of the implications of authenticity, for example, his commitment to authenticity might take on different emphases. Since man is ever in process, so must his commitment be.

Growth is a gradual, directional process beginning at conception and supposedly ending in death. In order for a growth model to be of value, it must be adaptable to some extent to all ages.

The importance of effective parent-child relationships becomes increasingly clear when commitment is examined. It seems quite unlikely, for example, that an infant could develop a commitment to authenticity. On the other hand, the importance of a child's understanding something about himself, the decision making process and the consequences of certain decisions can not be overly emphasized. These factors provide the basis for future commitment.

The proposed model might be offensive to the more orthodox existentialists because of certain possibly naive assumptions underlying it. Hopefully, however, the model will be sufficiently abrasive to encourage others to develop more sophisticated models which might provide a more adequate understanding of human behavior and provide existential psychology with needed philosophical systems.

Research

One criterion for the longevity of any theoretical formulation is the extent to which it is researchable and in turn stimulates research. If quantity is a criterion, then a cursory review of existential literature would provide some basis for supporting the position that existential tenets are indeed researchable and stimulate research. During the last few years the quantity of existential literature both in reference and periodical form has greatly increased. The development which seems more interesting than quantity, however, is the revelation that existential questions can be empirically explored. This is evidenced by the fact that several research studies involving existential exploration have been conducted utilizing experimental research designs and statistical analysis.

The studies attempt to describe and understand the authentic person as he exists. No attempt is made to force man into a stereotyped existence or to desecrate or destroy the emphasis upon individual freedom. The contention of the researchers seems to be that if existence has essence, then it is worthy of more adequate understanding on the part of both participant and observer.

The greatest quantity of existential literature has been contributed by existential theorists and clinicians. In addition to describing man in his existential condition, techniques have been designed both to assist man in understanding himself and assisting theorists and clinicians in understanding man in specific environments. An existential approach to mental health, for example, was explored by Kotchen (1960). Using an existentially oriented inventory, he found that one distinction between mental patients and normal people was the degree to which they could find meaning in life. Similar results were obtained by Crumbaugh and Maholick (1964) who developed a "purpose of life" test which was designed from some of the

194

major emphases of Frankl's Logotherapy. These are only two of several research studies utilizing statistical analysis.

In addition to research involving comparisons, several clinicians have designed both individual and group techniques for existential explorations. Examples of individual and group techniques can be found in research of Garner and Jeans (1962) and Meigniez (1963) respectively. In both of these studies the emphasis is upon the individual in a particular environment, rather than as a particular technique. Possibility rather than necessity is the major emphasis.

Although current literature contains several examples of experimental research, such as those previously described, descriptive studies still exist in greater abundance. Probably the most extensive research is described in the works of existential theorists and/or clinicians such as May (1962), Boss (1963), Moustakas (1966), Weisman (1965), Woolff (1950), and van Kaam (1966). Existential periodicals such as the *Journal of Existentialism*, the *Review of Existential Psychology and Psychiatry* and the *Journal of Existential Psychiatry* provide ample evidence for the existence of prolific contributors utilizing descriptive methods.

The findings of current existential researchers have yielded expanded perceptions of man in his existential condition. Many of these findings have been the form of at least partially validated hypotheses, which seem to have some consensus among the contributors. One of the conclusions is somewhat paradoxical in nature; namely, that although every man is unique, his existential possessions are common to some extent to all men.

Retrospect and Prospect

During the past few years all disciplines have become increasingly aware of existing inadequacies in meeting the needs of contemporary society. Psychology and related disciplines have probably been most sensitive to inadequacies and needs since society has come to rely upon these disciplines in finding explanations and guidelines for personal growth and adjustment. If psychology is to continue its leadership role, two challenges

195

seem readily apparent. First of all, Psychology is no longer a self-sufficient discipline; it cannot exist alone. Secondly, greater strides must be made in the development of philosophy and methodology if psychology is to keep pace with other disciplines.

In the not too distant past it was assumed by the masses that the psychologist held the key to understanding human behavior. Few people would have considered calling on the services of a sociologist, anthropologist, or educator, for guidance concerning human behavior. Today the scene is changing. Multi- and inter-disciplinary emphases are the central focus of current thrusts in psychological thought. Psychologists are realizing that if indeed solutions are possible the resources of all available disciplines must be utilized and articulated. If psychology is to contribute to the development of a science of human behavior, such efforts must result in synthesis rather than fragmentations.

The diversity of emphasis and the lack of agreement now present in various fields of psychology do not seem characteristic of a true science of human behavior. Many leaders in psychology have emphatically insisted that much of the disparity can be accounted for in the absence of, among other things, an acceptable philosophical foundation. Existentialism seems to be one of the contenders for such a foundation. The success of Existentialism in becoming a corner stone for future psychological growth seems predicated upon one major factor; namely, the commitment of existential psychologists to the effective communication of the possibilities of existentialism in the development of appropriate rationale and methodology. Psychologists must do more than just criticize "what is" and just theorize as to what "might be." An understanding of possible approaches to implementation seems essential if people are to live existentially and not just discuss existentialism. This is not to suggest that rigid guidelines be established, however, which would revoke individual freedom. It implies instead that people be given assistance in understanding what possibilities exist through Existentialism and what is involved in authentic existence.

196

Obviously, this discussion of Existential Psychology can do little more than provide the reader with a limited understanding of Existentialism. It remains the challenge of Existential psychologists to develop ways and means for the effective communication of existential concepts.

It seems probable that the accomplishments of an interdisciplinary science of human behavior hold much more promise for meeting the challenges of contemporary society than do the accomplishments of several behavioral sciences. Since Existentialism seems to have pervaded most disciplines it is possible that it might provide a basis for the development of a true science of human behavior. This has yet to be proven, however. While it is apparent that Existentialism has made an impact upon contemporary psychological thought, it is difficult to predict the extent and direction of this impact upon future developments. Whether it is a passing fad or a stimulus for significant psychological thrusts yet remains to be determined. The true impact of Existentialism will probably not be known for at least another decade.

Bibliography

Allen, E. L. *Existentialism From Within.* London: Routledge and Kegan Paul, Ltd., 1953.

Allport, Gordon. *Becoming.* New Haven: Yale Univ. Press, 1963.

Barrett, William. *Irrational Man.* New York: Doubleday and Company, Inc., 1962.

Barrett, William, and Aiken, Henry D. *Philosophy in the Twentieth Century.* Vol. 3. New York: Random House, 1962.

———. *Philosophy in the Twentieth Century,* Vol. 4. New York: Random House, 1962.

Beck, Carleton E. *Philosophical Foundations of Guidance.* Englewood Cliffs, New Jersey: Prentice-Hall, Inc., 1963.

Boss, Medard. *Psychoanalysis and Daseinanalysis.* New York: Basic Books, Inc., 1963.

Buber, Martin. *I and Thou.* New York: Charles Scribner's Sons, 1958.

Camus, Albert. *The Myth of Sisyphus.* Translated by Justin O'Brian. New York: Alfred A. Knopf, Inc., 1955.

Crawford, Claude C. Commitment. *Personnel and Guidance Journal,* 1966, 54, 904-909.

Crumbaugh, James C., and Maholick, Leonard T. An Experimental Study in Existentialism: The Psychometric Approach to Frankl's Concept of Noogenic Neurosis. *Journal of Clinical Psychology,* 1964, 2, 200-207.

Frankl, Viktor, *Man's Search for Meaning.* New York: Washington Square Press, Inc., 1963.

Fromm, Erich, *Escape from Freedom.* New York: Holt, Rinehart, and Winston, 1947.

Garner, Harry H., and Jeans, Robert F. Confrontation Technique in Psychotherapy: Some Existential Implications. *Journal of Existential Psychiatry,* 1962, 8, 391-401.

Hall, Calvin. Personality Theory Revisited and Reevaluated. Paper presented to the American Personnel and Guidance Convention, April, 1965.

Heidegger, Martin. *Existence and Being.* Edited by Werner Brock. New York: Regnery, 1949.

Heinemann, F. H. *Existentialism and the Modern Predicament.* New York: Harper and Row, 1958.

Jaspers, Karl. *Man in the Modern Age.* Translated by Eden and Cedar Paul. London: Routledge, 1951.

Kaufmann, Walter. *Existentialism from Dostoevsky to Sartre.* New York: The World Publishing Company, 1962.

Kierkegaard, Søren. *Concluding unscientific postscript.* Translated by David F. Swenson and Walter Lowrie. Princeton, N.J.: Princeton Univ. Press, 1941.

———. *Philosophical fragments,* translated by David Swenson. London: Oxford Univ. Press, 1939.

———. *Either/or.* Vol. 2. Translated by Walter Lowrie: Princeton, N.J.: Princeton Univ. Press, 1944. (a)

———. *The concept of dread.* Translated by Walter Lowrie. Princeton, N.J.: Princeton Univ. Press, 1944. (b)

———. *The point of view for my work as an author.* Translated by Walter Lowrie. New York: Harper, 1962.

———. *The Sickness Unto Death.* Translated by Walter Lowrie. New York: Harper, 1962.

———. *Fear and Trembling.* Translated by Walter Lowrie. New York: Doubleday and Company, Inc., 1954.

Kneller, George F. *Introduction to the Philosophy of Education.* New York: John Wiley and Sons, Inc., 1964.

Kotchen, Theodore A. Existential Mental Health: An Empirical Approach. *Journal of Individual Psychology,* 1960, 16, 174-181.

Marcel, Gabriel. *Man Against Society.* Chicago: Regnery, 1952.

Maslow, Abraham H. *Eupsychian Management.* Homewood, Illinois: Richard D. Irwin, Inc., 1965.

———. *Toward a Psychology of Being.* New York: D. Van Nostrand, 1962.

May, Rollo, and van Kaam, Adrian. *Existential Theory and Therapy, Current Psychiatric Therapies.* Vol. III. New York: Greene and Stratton, Inc., 1963.

May, Rollo, Angel, Ernest, and Ellenberger, Henri F. *Existence.* New York: Basic Books, Inc., 1958.

May, Rollo, *Existential Psychology.* New York: Random House, 1961.

Meigniez, Robert. Group Therapy From the Existential Point of View. *Review of Existential Psychology and Psychiatry,* 1963, 1, 91-98.

Moustakas, Clark. *Existential Child Therapy.* New York: Basic Books, Inc., 1966.

Price, George. *The Narrow Pass.* New York: McGraw-Hill Book Company, Inc., 1963.

Rogers, Carl R. Toward a modern approach to values. Paper read at a symposium at The University of Houston, 1963. (b)

Royce, Joseph R. Psychology, Existentialism, and Religion. *The Journal of General Psychology,* 1962, 66, 3-16.

Sartre, Jean-Paul, *Being and Nothingness.* Translated by H. E. Barnes. New York: Philosophical Library, 1956.

199

————, *Existentialism*. New York: Philosophical Library, 1947.

Schwebel, Milton. *Behavioral Science and Human Survival*. Palo Alto, California: Science and Behavioral Books, Inc., 1965.

Tillich, Paul, Existential Philosophy, *Journal of Historical Ideas*, 1944, 5, 44-70.

————, *The Courage To Be*. New Haven, Connecticut: Yale University Press, 1952.

van Kaam, Adrian. *Existential Foundations of Psychology*. Pittsburgh: Duquesne University Press, 1966.

Weisman, Avery D. *The Existential Core of Psychoanalysis: Reality, Sense, and Responsibility*. London: J. and A. Churchill Ltd., 1965.

Wild, John. *The Challenge of Existentialism*. Bloomington, Indiana: Indiana University Press, 1959.

Wilde, Jean T., and Kimmel, William. *The Search for Being*. New York: The Noonday Press, 1962.

Winborn, Bob. Comment on Crawford. *Personnel and Guidance Journal*, 1966, 46, 909-910.

PSYCHOLOGY AND THE DEVELOPMENT OF HUMAN POTENTIALS

RALPH MASON DREGER, PH. D.

Professor of Psychology, Louisiana State University

Editorial Note

Only recently have psychologists given explicit attention to the general problem of personality change under the impact of varying circumstances. Deliberate attempts to alter basic personality structures are seen in the so-called "brain-washing" of prisoners of war. Now we are also coming to realize the deep-lying effects of forces as insidious as a system of segregation and conditions of cultural deprivation. Less obvious, perhaps, are the effects of economic, sociological, and technological changes now in progress.

Dr. Ralph Mason Dreger has been Professor of Psychology at Louisiana State University in Baton Rouge, Louisiana, since 1964. He has published many articles in scientific journals and is the author of the textbook *Fundamentals of Personality* (1962).

Dr. Dreger was born in Chicago, Illinois, on April 18, 1913. He received his A. B., *cum laude*, from Wheaton College in Wheaton, Illinois, in 1935; his B. D., with distinction, from Garrett Biblical Institute in Evanston, Illinois, in 1938; his M. A. from Northwestern University in 1939; and his Ph. D. from the University of Southern California in 1950. He is a member of Phi Beta Kappa.

Before accepting his appointment at Louisiana State University, Dr. Dreger served as a Methodist minister (1935-1947), a teacher of psychology and literature in the Adult Evening

High Schools of Los Angeles, California (1948), and Director of the Child Guidance and Speech Correction Clinic in Jacksonville, Florida (1960-1964). He was Instructor in Psychology at George Pepperdine College in Los Angeles (1948-1948), Assistant Professor of Psychology at Florida State University in Tallahassee, Florida (1949-1956), and Professor of Psychology, at Jacksonville University in Jacksonville, Florida (1960-1964).

Dr. Dreger has been active in many professional, civic, and religious societies. His publications and affiliations are detailed in *American Men of Science*. He served as President of the Southeastern Psychological Association in 1965-1966.

•

PSYCHOLOGY AND THE DEVELOPMENT OF HUMAN POTENTIALS

A. Introduction

Social psychology has been interested for many years in changes of attitudes under changing social conditions, and has developed a number of theories to account for the alteration or lack of alteration of attitudes under varying conditions (23). The more general problem—of change under the impact of changing social circumstances in personality, of which attitudes are only a part—has but recently been given explicit attention [e.g., Worchel and Byrne (89)]. It is to this more general problem that this paper addresses itself.

For the sake of those who are not familiar with the eclectic "working model" of the personality that the writer utilizes in both his theory and clinical practice, the following review capsulates the position set forth in the writer's text on personality (25). According to this view, personality consists of the organized functions of the individual. This definition is general enough that it can be adapted to any overall theory of personality. If one goes along with Gordon Allport (1, 2) and regards personality as contained within the skin, he may do so. If one is more sociologically oriented—for example, with Gardner Murphy (58) or Harry Stack Sullivan (84)—a concept of personality as partly interpersonal can utilize the definition. The author's own theory incorporates both "within the skin" concepts and roles; he cannot see how any understanding of individuality is possible if roles are considered as external to the personality, but he recognizes that not all authorities are in agreement on this point [see Allport (2)].

B. *The Model of the Personality*

The above concepts are encompassed in overlapping sets derived from various personality theories, all of which constructs serve as efforts to order the amazingly complex data of personality. First, use is made of an expanded Freudian scheme of dynamic structure—especially id, ego, and superego—as one classification of functions, and conscious-unconscious as another. Like others [e.g., Kluckhohn, Murray, and Schneider (47)] who have enlarged Freud's original notions, the writer has come to think of the *id* as the dynamic reservoir not only of evil intentions or amoral impulses, but also of intents acceptable to and encouraged by society, such as love, worship, air hunger, food hunger, and all metabolic processes or tissue needs. Presumably the inherited component is a large portion of the id. The drives or primary impulses are initially DNA (deoxyribonucleic acid) derived; we can say they are at the heart of the id as the id is at the heart of the personality.

Ego, which arises as a set of control functions to master and direct id energies and to gain control over stimuli arising outside of the organism, consists of at least five major subfunctions: perception, mastery of motility or of the motor apparatus, "binding" or controlling tension, judging or thinking, and synthesizing or attempting to harmonize the bewildering and often conflicting functions of the personality and aspects of the external world.

Last in Freud's schema, but not in the writer's, is the *superego*, a "precipitate within the ego" as Freud said. Superego is the set of functions developed as controls for the personality relating to the demands of society—both custom and conscience demands (27)—mediated first by the parents or parent-surrogates and later by siblings, peers, teachers, and others who can give or withhold love.

Finally, in this simplified classification of personality functions, there are the *roles* we enact in the world. These are interobject, mostly interpersonal, portions of the personality. If one thinks that roles are not organized functions of the individual and therefore parts of the personality, he may not have observed, as most clinicians have, parents and children in symbiotic relation to one another; he may not have perceived, although he may have seen, husband and wife combinations wherein the death of one causes the other to say, quite accurately, "Part of me died when he died." The roles of parent and child and the roles of truly married husband and wife are *inter*personal, not within the skin. Since the general topic of this paper relates to changes in personality accompanying social changes, the concept of role already commits the writer to the contention that changes in roles, mostly social changes, *are* personality changes, inasmuch as roles are integral portions of the dynamic structure of personality.

Going beyond id, ego, superego, and roles, again with Freud and a host of others, the theory of personality reviewed here cross-classifies personality functions into *conscious* and *unconscious*. As is mostly obvious, consciousness and unconsciousness overlap all other functions. Thinking and judging, affects, and ambitions may be either conscious or unconscious. By definition the hidden source of the personality's energies, the id, is unconscious. But all other functions may be either or both conscious and unconscious—even roles. Again, if one thinks roles are totally conscious, one has not observed a mother's reinforcing her child's dependency by subtle though entirely recognizable cues— mother role behaviors of which she is mostly unaware—or the role behaviors of Negro and white in interactions that they dimly perceive in themselves, if at all. One must also become familiar with the scientific literature on unconscious factors involved in enacting a role. This literature is too extensive to cite [*cf*. Sarbin (73, 74)], but it goes back at least to the theories of G. H. Mead (56) and the experimental studies of Solomon Asch (5) in the social modification of autokinetic behavior.

Some theorists, one must frankly admit, deny the reality of the conscious-unconscious classification of personality functions.

As far as can be ascertained, however, no one denies the reality of the distinction between central and peripheral functions, a cross-classification suggested mostly lucidly by Kurt Lewin (51). All that is needed is to call attention to phenomena with which we are all familiar to clarify what is meant here. The well-known congressional hearings on the Ku Klux Klan saw a procession of witnesses who, in effect, said, "I know, but I ain't sayin'." Central functions are those that we are unwilling or unable to reveal to others; peripheral functions are those that we are able or willing to disclose to others.

Again, another overlapping classification of personality functions divides them into *self-* and *not-self* or more precisely, in the writer's view, into *selves* and *not-selves*. There are those parts of our personalities, including our roles, that we accept as our own, and those that we reject. The former we subsume under a composite rubric, the self. Although it seems to go contrary to common sense and to the notions of many theorists to maintain that we have selves rather than a single self, the burden of proof rests on those who assert that all the disparate and contradictory functions we claim as "I," "me," or "mine" constitute a single, monolithic self. Roughly, though, we may say that personality can be divided into self and not-self.

One last category of functions completes the present image of the personality. Functions of the personality can be cross-classified into *traits,* sometimes called sets or dispositions or sentiments, or in the Allportian sense just plain traits of personality. These may be conscious or unconscious, or more likely both. They may be central or peripheral, or likewise more likely both. And they may share components of id, ego, super-ego, and roles. If one takes, for example, the trait of dominance-submissiveness, either factor-analytically derived or derived from a single scale test, it is not impossible by any means to show that it has drive (or id) qualities, that it has some measure of rational (ego) control processes, some superego aspects, and some role-taking properties, that it seems to possess conscious and unconscious characteristics, that it almost certainly is both central and peripheral, and that some features of this trait are acceptable as "mine," while others may be rejected as "not-mine." Traits like dominance-submissiveness may extend from the surface to the center of personality.

We should recognize two other dynamic considerations here that affect the general topic of social change and personality. Boundaries among all of the functions named above are both *permeable and flexible*. Some thoughts and affects, for example, may be conscious at one time and unconscious at others. Some aspects of our personalities we share with some other persons readily, and then slide them from the central to the peripheral region with other persons. At one time the author spoke with a teen-age girls' group on their psychosexual development. When the girls realized that this psychologist knew more about them in some ways than they knew about themselves, they began to listen and speak with freedom. The speaker became one of the girls among girls. Then one of the fathers came to get his daughter, entering the rear of the room very quietly and as unobtrusively as he could. But the spell was broken. The speaker was no longer one of the girls. The discussion continued, but the girls now concealed things that they had revealed when only "us girls" were present. What had been peripheral became central again. So, too, with other functions, the boundaries may be permeable.

From a sociological standpoint, the other consideration is important here: that is, that we may conceive of *external forces* impinging on the personality as so many vectors of force, moving the personality one way or another. If the forces approaching from different directions balance one another, the personality, as it were, goes nowhere. As is usually the situation, however, the forces do not balance one another, and the personality moves in a particular direction with a velocity that is the vector resultant of all the forces acting upon the personality.

Should anyone suppose that the personality is a helpless object moved willy-nilly by "external forces," he should pause to reconsider. The "*external* forces" are far and away only "external *forces*" insofar as *this particular personality* is concerned. Let the following incident illustrate: The author's oldest boy was with the Army in Viet Nam, then was removed to a

Japanese hospital with some type of ear trouble in one ear. But this ear is his one good ear. He assured his parents and his wife that he would be all right. However, when his letters arrived, the news came as a tremendous blow to his wife and parents. The writer's son has a son who was two years old, and the writer has a son who was also two years old at the time. It is almost certain the soldier's wife discussed her fears and worries in front of her 2-year-old, and so did the parents in front of theirs. Did the same news make the same impact on these youngsters as on the adults? To ask the question is to answer it. What for one person is a long and powerful social vector, to another is scarcely a glancing blow. On the other hand, all personalities may be moved by some external forces of which they may or may not be aware, forces that they cannot interpret as powerful or weak for they are not even unconsciously cognizant of them, or being cognizant of them interpret them correctly as objectively overwhelming. The point is that most "external forces" are not of this latter variety, but are only *forces* impinging upon the personality because that particular personality makes them so.

Here we have the complicated picture of personality with which we have to deal in thinking of social change and personality: Functions of the personality may be divided up into the three Freudian constructs, id, ego, and superego, to which are added role functions, then into conscious and unconscious, into central and peripheral, into self (or selves) and non-self, and into multitudinous traits. These overlapping groups of functions are not static, for a particular function may slip from one category to another. And acting upon the whole personality are external forces, or vectors of force.

The parallel between the position described above and European stratification theory [see David and von Bracken (22)] is, the writer is inclined to believe, not fortuitous. Although developed independently, the concepts outlined here are not any more truly independent than is stratification theory; both have been influenced by the raw data of personality. Since ancient times men have been forced to think of personality as having levels (what goes on in the "heart" is contrasted with more superficial, more readily observable behaviors). All the writer has done is to delineate more sharply among the levels that have been conceived at one time or another.

C. Social Changes in the Personality

What effect do social changes have upon the personality as conceived here? Just how far can social change change personality? A first answer may be given that reiterates a position stated before: Roles are interobject and interpersonal portions of the personality. *Therefore, any changes of roles are by definition social changes.* This principle cannot be emphasized strongly enough, for the man on the street and many scholars regard personality as a fixed entity inside the organism that somehow may be related to intelligence and attitudes and roles. This is not the view expressed here: personality *includes* intelligence, and *includes* attitudes, and *includes* roles. It is not just related to these functions; it *is* these functions among other things. Consequently, when the roles of an individual change, his personality changes. If he plays the role of a factory worker and he moves into the role of a supervisor, do not ask, "Has his personality *also* changed because his roles have changed?" for one cannot answer on these terms. Of course his personality changed when his roles changed, because *roles are part of the personality*. Insofar as roles may be changed, personality that consists in part of roles changes too. The degree of such change has to be determined by objective investigation. There has been some research along this line, but there has been mostly theorizing thus far [*cf.* Worchel and Byrne (89)].

Some of the reasoning employed in the preceding paragraph may seem circular: Personality is defined in a certain way, so that inevitably one must conclude that personality *does* change, because some social changes occur within the personality defined so as to include social functions. The only defense that can be given for such seeming circularity is that the concept of personality outlined above is a logical extension of interpersonal concepts of the personality that have arisen in the last

208

few decades; and all the writer is doing is pointing out the implications of these concepts.

D. *External Forces and Personality Change*

What about social changes that stem from what are identified above as external forces impinging upon the personality? Just how far can these alter the personality? Here let another general principle be stated: *roughly speaking, the closer to the center of the personality a function is, the more difficult is it for external forces to change it; and conversely, the farther from the center, the easier it is for external forces to change it.* By "closer to the center" and "farther from the center" the idea to be conveyed is that of progressing from id to roles, from unconsciousness to consciousness, from central to peripheral, and from self to not-self. Let us think, then, of how far social changes of an external nature can reach into and alter the personality.

Before doing so, a second possible *petitio principii* must be dealt with: If the functions of the personality were categorized into "closer to center" and "farther from center" on the basis of their vulnerability or invulnerability to social change, it would indeed be the case that the conclusion has been assumed in the premise. But such layers are not, at least substantially, defined by their responsiveness to social change. They are defined in some cases by their indispensability to the life processes, in others by their degree of concealment (conscious or unconscious), and in still others by the degree of investment or cathexis the individual has in them. While one cannot deny that in some instances the amount of resistance to social change is used as one criterion of centrality, in no case is the latter an essential criterion. Once again the circularity is only apparent. External social changes may be correlated with personality changes, but the latter are not necessarily defined by social changes.

1. Prenatal Social Influences

When one thinks of such social changes, one may be envisaging far-reaching sociological changes, poverty, unemployment, segregation and desegregation, mass migrations, war, and mass societal movements, such as the coming of Communism to Russia or Nazism to Germany. To be sure, these must be considered very seriously. But we begin much more modestly with the first social changes that occur in the life of an individual, those that take place in his intrauterine life. One may say the embryo or fetus has no personality—personality only comes after the child is born. Does it? Not according to the writer's definition: personality consists of the organized functions of the individual. Is an embryo an individual? Does he have organized functions? Then he is a personality.[2] By the end of the second month of gestation, when we usually say the embryo becomes a fetus, it is clear that there are individual differences among prenatal infants. But even before this time there are socially induced changes that affect the personality.

It cannot be considered trivial to say that social factors that could be different but that actually do occur make for personality changes even before the child is conceived. It is known now that malnutrition in the mother affects adversely the developing prenatal infant [see Mussen, Conger, and Kagan (59)]. Therefore, any social changes that generate conditions in which the mother's malnutrition reaches the point that her reserves are depleted also generate changes in the functioning of the child. We can think of a number of such social changes: wartime conditions, migration to barren places, general or spe-

2. Since someone may say that the unborn child has life but not personality, a distinction must be made between life and personality [cf. the author's discussion on this very point (25)]. The concept of personality *in utero* does not depend on a particular definition of personality. Almost any definition implies the concept. That definition which across the years has proved the most acceptable of all (1) certainly does: "Personality is the dynamic organization within the individual of those psychophysical systems which determine his unique adjustment to his environment" (1, p. 48); at the very least, by the time the fetus has developed a rudimentary nervous system, "psychophysical systems" exist.

cific famine conditions (especially if brought about by soil-depleting farming techniques), economic exploitation conditions, and so on. We have no way of knowing now just how much harm was done the unborn children of the Pilgrims in those hard months of their first implantation on the bleak New England scene. But we do know that socioreligious reasons moved the Pilgrims from the relative abundance of western Europe to this land. And if the results of controlled experiments on maternal malnutrition can be extrapolated to the Pilgrim mothers, we can only suppose some harm did occur to the infants conceived in those days.

Contraction of Rubella or German measles in the first trimester of pregnancy can result in physical or mental defects in the child. Rubella is an epidemic disease: in other words, it is socially promulgated. The Rh factor, as is well-known, is an important genetically determined blood chemical or chemicals found in about 85 percent of human beings. If an Rh-positive child is born to an Rh-negative mother, especially if the child is the second one, disastrous consequences to the child may result from the antibodies produced by the mother. But as with some *genetically determined* diseases, the mating of the mother and father comes about as a result of social factors, some purely accidental, some from societally determined assortative mating. If these two people or others so genetically constituted had not gotten together, the Rh incompatibility would not have occurred. So, too, if the Age of Tranquillizers had not been socially induced, several thousands of youngsters in western Europe would not now be known as thalidomide-deformed children. One could name a number of other purely physical agencies, with direct effect on the prenatal infant, that are easily seen to be as much the agents of a sociological change as they are of physics or chemistry.

Does the thesis, that the closer to the center the more difficult it is for external forces to change a personality function, hold in relation to prenatal socially induced personality changes? Generally, it appears to. The prenatal infant is initially primarily id, then very basic ego in his middle and later stages. The genes or the DNA molecules, genetic functions at the very

211

center of the embryonic personality, seem to be the least amenable to change, but in this embryonic state of the individual where they are still close to the surface of the personality they are subject to mutations from various outside agencies, radiation in particular [see Dobzhansky (24); McClearn (55); and Sinnott, Dunn, and Dobzhansky (80)]. As controls develop in relation to genetically determined energies, controls that may be called the embryonic ego, *they* are more subject to these outside influences and the id processes less so.

Even if one could not support the thesis of increased difficulty in changing central embryonic and fetal processes, if we can grant that the prenatal infant either has or is a personality, the major point to press home is that that personality is liable to be changed and the subsequent efforts noted when social forces are altered in such a way as to bring (usually indirect) influence to bear on the unborn child.

2. *Postnatal and Childhood Social Influences*

When we turn to the postnatal period, probably no one would deny that the young, even the newborn infant, has or is a personality. Here, on the one hand, someone may say the infinite plasticity of childhood is manifest. The tiny malleable creature can be molded, as John B. Watson asseverated many years ago, into anything the environment desires. Or on the other hand, another person may say that the infant is so close to being a gene-controlled creature, not much can be done to change him.

To the proponents of the first position it may be said that an ultra environmentalist optimism must be tempered by the results of controlled research. As far as deep-lying id and ego processes are concerned, the social experiences of infancy seem not to be very potent. In the reviews of the research literature by Bettye Caldwell on the effects of infant care (19) and of Yarrow and Yarrow (91) on early experiences, it appears that the primary personality characteristics, the temperament patterns, are fairly well built in.

For example, the fact that a child has been breast- or bottle-fed, or given considerable or little oral gratification, or has been toilet trained one way or another, of itself seems to be of little influence in altering so-called oral and anal temperament characteristics. Shades of Freud and Abraham! Further, the more general patterns of differences among infants, such as irritability and activity level, can be predicted with a fair degree of accuracy from infancy to at least the early preschool years, even though infants and toddlers may have been subjected to a host of differing experiences (85).

In addition, one cannot ignore the comprehensive studies of the relative influences of genetic and environmental factors on intelligence functions that are fairly central to the personality.[3] The best studies utilizing monozygotic twins compared to dizygotic twins keep offering the figure of between 70 to 80 per cent of the variance of intelligence test scores that may be attributed to heredity, and the remainder to environment [see Burt and Howard (17), and Nichols (61, 63)]. At least some of the specific factors of intellect, as well as general intelligence (Spearman's "g" factor), are subject to this same principle. In other words, social change as represented by altered social conditions, nutritional factors, differences in family and cultural patterns, and so forth have about 20 to 30 per cent of intelligence variance within which to work. These findings are in keeping with the thesis that the closer to the center of the personality a function is, the more difficult it is to change it.

In reference to the proponents of the second position—that the infant is so close to being gene-controlled that he can scarcely be changed at all—it may be stated that later developed functions, and especially those that do not become deeply buried by repressions, may yield to social changes to a marked degree, so that even relatively early vast personality alterations may take place [even in intellectual functions, if results of recent rat

3. The writer mentions this aspect because he knows the general interest in this area and not because he thinks it is of the *utmost* importance, important as it is. Kent Miller and the writer (29, 30) have tried to overcome the exceeding overemphasis on intelligence comparisons between Negroes and whites in the psychological literature by stressing temperament and social variables; but the writer does notice that the majority of citations to the 1960 *Psychological Bulletin* article refer to the section on intelligence.

213

experiments with environmental impoverishment or complexity may be extrapolated to man (70), though these results challenge some previous research]. These personality alterations may be, and in all likelihood usually are, the resultant of combined internal and external changes. But there is no requirement that social change has to be the sole determinant of a personality change, but may indeed be the precipitator or catalyst of such change, a necessary even if not a sufficient condition.

In this connection, as is often the case, reference to extremes of behavior, as in abnormal states of personality, clarifies a process that may not be seen so clearly in the less pronounced normal state. Anna Freud, Sigmund Freud's exceptionally brilliant daughter, has recently called attention to a phenomenon that proved distressing to psychoanalysts when they began longitudinal investigations of children. Some similarity between adult and childhood neuroses can be found in both symptoms and dynamics. But among the disappointments that analysts met

was the realization that in spite of all the links between infantile and adult neuroses, there is no certainty that a particular type of infantile neurosis will prove to be the forerunner of the same type of adult neurosis. On the contrary, there is much clinical evidence which points in the opposite direction. An example is the uncontrolled state of a four-year-old which equals in many ways that of a juvenile or adult delinquent insofar as both give free rein to their impulses, especially the aggressive ones, and both attack, destroy, and appropriate what they desire without regard for other people's feelings. For all this similarity, this early delinquent behavior need not turn later into a true delinquent state; the child in question may develop into an obsessional character or obsessional neurosis rather than into a delinquent or criminal. Many children who begin with a phobia or anxiety hysteria grow later into true obsessionals. Many with truly obsessional symptoms such as washing compulsions, ritualistic touching, arranging of details, etc., who resemble adult obsessionals in every way while they are young, are nevertheless predestined to develop in later life not obsessional neuroses but schizoid and schizophrenic states instead (37, pp. 151-152).

Anna Freud attributes these fairly fundamental changes to id and deep-lying ego operations. One would not wish to minimize these internal changes that result in such dramatic overtly observable, but deep, personality changes. Yet it is well to suggest also that the external world does not remain static while the child is maturing, so that a number of the personality changes to which Anna Freud refers may well stem in part from the child's changing world.

Yarrow and Yarrow (91) point out, for instance, that family structure and dynamics do not remain the same across the years. Every clinician with fairly extensive experience has probably had a similar experience to one of the author's. The clinic he headed dealt some years ago with a very bright boy of 9 with whom the author had the major therapeutic contacts. In fact, this boy was one for whom the clinic had to initiate activity group therapy, for play therapy was too infantile for him. Some years later the writer met the mother who told of the boy's quite substantial recent accomplishments. The writer said with some pride, "I think I can take credit for some of that." The mother paused for a moment, then candidly remarked, "I don't think that had a great deal to do with it. What I learned from the clinic about handling him I'm sure had a great deal more to do with it." Deflated, one therapist's ego balloon! While it is not necessary to admit that the carefully devised activity therapy had no effect, one can readily recognize that the change in child management practices in that home probably *did* have more to do with altering the boy's personality than did the therapy.

Not long ago a case was terminated with a 10½-year-old girl who had to be carried bodily for her second session from her car to the playroom, not because she could not walk but because she balked and locked herself in the car. Screaming and struggling all the way, she yielded only to superior force. Inside the playroom she made the welkin roar with her screams and high-pitched crying. She used language on the therapist that her mother did not know she knew. The least rabid of her epithets was "Prisoner!" and "Stupid!" For a number of sessions she continued her tantrums and tirades. Some sessions later, however, this same sweet young lady had arrived at the point where she could express liking for the therapist, adding in one period, as she looked up a bit shyly, "I even love you." She had repressed the knowledge that she loved the therapist by the next session; but after a somewhat stormy hour resulting from several factors, she made one pipe-cleaner figure for herself and one for the therapist. The changes that occurred in this girl—not limited by any means to the therapy hour—were not solely dependent upon her therapy contacts. Her parents drastically altered their management techniques as a result of clinical guidance, including the use of Ginott's *Between Parent and Child* (40). Family structure and dynamics may change, altering the personalities of children to a measurable degree.

Less dramatically, usually, but nonetheless effectively, for better or for worse nonclinical families change and personalities of youngsters change along with them. How much personality change results from so much change in the family *qua* family can only be conjectured at this time. Maturation effects are sometimes confounded with learning effects, as we may infer from experiments on "imprinting" [see Hess (42)], so that we may think something results from social factors when it is really the result of maturing functions. Yet even these could not mature without an appropriate environment.

The age and stage at which certain social experiences occur may make considerable difference as to their effectiveness in altering personality. Separation from parents has been taken as one very traumatic social experience that is supposed to alter a young child's personality profoundly. Yet Yarrow (90) has shown from going over the studies in this field that the effects of separation *per se* may not be traumatic for the very young infant, say in the first six months of postuterine existence, and even afterward may be more determined by events subsequent to the separation, such as being placed in an institution. However, some evidence exists for the conclusion that immediately observable behavior in the infant following a separation experience may not be a good indicator of the degree of disturbance that shows up later. Later separation at certain stages may be more disastrous than at others. A case known to the writer is that of a girl of 5½ whose mother died in the midst of the girl's partly expressed oedipal fantasies. The tremendous guilt aroused by the fulfillment of these fantasies of killing mother and marrying daddy was overpowering, so that profoundly disturbing patterns of affect and behavior showed up.

Whatever the directly traceable effects of early separation are, we have to keep in mind from the standpoint of our inquiry here *any* changes, including changes in roles of the child and his important others, prior to, accompanying, or subsequent to the parental separation itself are *social* changes; and whether their effects are equal to, or less than, or more than the actual separation, it is the social changes *of some kind* that are or bring about beneficial or deleterious personality changes, possibly reaching fairly deeply into the central portions of the personality.

3. *Social Influences in Early Adolescence*

Space does not permit further elaboration of the impact of social forces on childhood personality, or of their effects on the aging personality. But it is necessary to take time to discuss changes surrounding puberty and adolescence. Psychoanalysts (14, 37, 49), social psychologists (79), child psychologists (54), including Piaget and his followers (35), regard the beginning of the adolescent period as somewhat of a crisis, at least in our society. McCandless calls it "the fifth psychosocial crisis." Sherif and Cantril are close to psychoanalysis when they speak of the "re-formation of the ego in adolescence." Although there may be an overemphasis on adolescence as the period of *Sturm und Drang*, storm and stress, nevertheless it has been recognized for a long time that adolescence has been a crisis period in the West.

Some evidence has accumulated that in our era society has changed enough to make the period even more stressful yet.

Perhaps most potent is "the American sex revolution," as Sorokin (83) dubbed it. Probably, as a survey by the *National Observer* not long ago indicated, not much more premarital sexual freedom actually is present now than there was a generation ago [see Klemer (46)]. However, *attitudes* toward sex have changed in many ways [see Schur (75)]. And adolescents have to face a world that more than ever gives them equivocal guidance in sexual matters. Other forces of major magnitude impinge on the lives of young adolescents, such as a plethora of violence, mayhem, and murder on TV and movie screens, large scale financial crimes in high places, revolts against exploitation of oppressed peoples, and issues of peace and war brought to focus by Viet Nam.

Do these vast social changes alter the personalities of youth in the crises of puberty and early adolescence? One could cite opinion studies and questionnaire responses of youth relating to specific opinions and attitudes on one or another issue, studies that do indicate changes. And insofar as opinions and attitudes are personality functions, it is evident that youthful personalities have changed. However, deep changes in the adolescent personality probably do not occur primarily because of the vast social changes going on about the pubertal and early adolescent individual.

If we turn to recent intensive studies of adolescent personality undertaken by psychoanalysts (11, 14, 41, 49), which have been carried out in the present era, in the midst of all the social upheavals we find that they tend to support the long-held views of psychoanalysis (34) that the external world, while surely playing a part in the pubertal crisis, is not as important as the intra-psychic (the more central) functions in shaping the crises of this stage. Further, Quay and Quay (67), working with seventh and eighth graders, repeated the work of Peterson (64) that delineated the problem behaviors of middle childhood; they produced by factor analysis the same two factors in these pubertal youngsters that Peterson had found in latency age children and labelled "Conduct Problems" and "Personality Problems." From a practical, clinical standpoint this division into only two factors is nearly useless. But when Quay and Quay found the same factors in over 500 seventh- and eighth-grade children, and only one other weak factor apparently related to behavioral immaturity in the eighth graders, from a theoretical standpoint the results suggest that even today the pubertal child has not changed a great deal in his problem orientation from what he was in the prepubertal period. In other words, the storms of the present day have not inundated the pubertal youngster in his personality crisis period. Similar findings were obtained by the Behavioral Classification Project (26, 28, 32). The writer and associates discovered that among the many factors of child behavior, principally behavior problems, which they found among hundreds of clinical and normal children, only one, which was a specifically maturity-immaturity factor, was age-related among children 6 through 13 years of age.

The theory, then, that the tremendous social changes of today's rapidly moving world are not reaching the core of the young adolescent's personality with the devastating impact they might seem to have, is not groundless [see Klemer (46)]. That one of America's most respected authorities on family life agrees with this theory is support of an indirect nature. Blaine R. Porter writes of the present teen-ager, "Some four or five per cent (or even 10 per cent) get into trouble, and the trouble they get into is extremely serious. But considering the temptations, frustrations, and complexities to which they are subjected, and the confusion that surrounds them, the 90-95 per cent who do not get into trouble deserve congratulations" (65, p. 147).

4. *Social Influences in Later Adolescence*

In the latter years of adolescence more and more youth in our society attend college. From what one reads by alarmed adults in papers and magazines, atheistic and communistic professors are influencing young people toward evil ways. There must be some magical attribution of power to college professors at this point, for the research—to say nothing of a professor's chastening experience—does not bear out the vast influence ascribed to professors, either for good or ill. It is not that under college suasions changes do not occur, sometimes changes of a fairly dramatic nature, but it would seem that they do not ordinarily reach to the depths of the young person's personality.

Without any scientific study it can be seen that new roles are assumed when a young person takes up a college career; and older, established roles are altered, like those of being a son or daughter, a male or a female, and being an adolescent. As argued previously, changes in roles *are* changes in personality. Attitudes of some sorts are changed, partly by the impact of the teachers of a college or university, but mostly by the general atmosphere of the campus. A study colleagues and the writer carried out about a dozen years ago (31) showed that dating attitudes and practices may change radically in the first three months of college life. Other changes of this nature do take place, so that critics of higher education may confuse these changes with the more fundamental ones they think are taking place. The more fundamental functions, however, probably are not altered.

There has been, to be sure, a consistent showing that students in college become increasingly liberal in their religious thinking, decreasingly ethnocentric, and increasingly independent and unconventional [see Lehmann *et al.* (50), Prien (66), Sanford (71), and Webster (86)].

But even if these findings of change do mean that students are influenced toward more liberal *expressed attitudes*, it seems reasonable to believe that the inner core of the personality in which the beliefs are rooted may not change as a result of external social changes as much as might appear. One study of a generation ago (39), for example, runs counter to the general trend, finding that in several colleges students did *not* change in the direction of their professors' religious beliefs. And in the present decade Nichols (62) has carried out a four-year longitudinal study with three temperament scales on the National Merit Scholars in a large number of different colleges. As in previous studies, colleges are shown to be somewhat different from one another; and different curricula seem to have some differential effects. Some few temperament changes appear. But in general there has not been a great deal of change effected in the basic personality structure of students. Nichols concludes that the major portion of the differences found in his subjects could be attributed to events that happened before they entered college.

The student who has been a "hard shell conservative" seems to become what one minister friend calls a "hard shell liberal." Some students who adopt a liberal outlook in college may be only conservatives in disguise, for research (48) shows that the farther out of college many a man gets, the more conservative his views become.[4] The writer is reminded of a member of a faculty committee who was studying the drinking problem on his campus. This man said in one of the meetings, "My views are changing rapidly; I have a daughter ready to start in the university next year." Observation of the man's general behavior in the committee would lead one to believe that his liberal views on drinking have been overlaid on some much deeper convictions about the wrongs of drinking, views now beginning to reassert themselves. One cannot forget in assessing the impact of college on personality that the majority of Southern legislators, both national and state, who have been so consistently antiliberal in their legislative actions, are college-trained men who for four years at least were exposed to many influences that should have moved them toward liberal social attitudes.

4. Studies of persons 14 or 15 years out of college contradict the general findings of increased conservatism or interpret conservative trends or liberal trends as primarily a function of the changing times [see Bender (10), and Nelson (60)]. It is true that waves of conservatism and liberalism move across the land; one expects, then, that individuals will tend to go along with the times, whether they are in college or out. That one study (Nelson) shows a liberal trend from 1936 to 1950 and the other (Bender) a conservative trend from 1940 to 1956 should not be surprising (the McCarthy era was in the early 1950's). The main point of the text discussion is that college does not make the radical changes in personality that its friends and enemies hope or fear it does. There is no need to deny, or rather there is need to assert, that social changes do affect personality; but the superposition of college influence on the main societal trends seems to make not a great deal of difference. Relatively small shifts are reported in the study cited showing the liberal trend, and somewhat larger shifts in the other study showing conservative trends.

E. Central Personality Changes

Having said all these things about what cannot be changed by ordinary social changes in the development of the personality, to keep perspective we must hasten to reaffirm that such changes *can* occur under certain circumstances on a very deep level of the personality. Such changes are not impossible, they are only more difficult. Briefly, some of the circumstances and some of the changes that occur may be illustrated by the following.

1. Facilitated Behaviors

There are first what may be called "facilitated behaviors," as opposed to stress-induced behaviors. So much has been written about stress and its effects that we tend to overlook positive forces that may penetrate to the deeper levels of the personality and profoundly alter strata far from the surface. A book may reach the depths of one person, a sunset another, a mountain or canyon another, an opera or a person another. In all these the individual may be able to say "from the depths of his heart" that he has never been the same since "that experience." Granted that "that experience" (either one time or prolonged) is probably only catalytic, acting upon a concatenation of forces already in existence, the reality of the realignment of certain temperament patterns can only be doubted by challenging most of the evidence in many cases. Out of the many possible "facilitated behaviors" that could be discussed here, only a very limited sample can be taken.

For illustrative purposes, what happens under the influence of psychotherapy is important, not merely because some psychologists, psychiatrists, social workers, and others have invested a great deal of their lives in psychotherapy, and hosts of clients or patients have committed their destinies to it, but also because psychotherapy represents in miniature what facilitation if any can occur as a result of deliberately manipulating certain interpersonal variables in order to bring about more or less deeplying changes "for the better" in the personality.

222

It is difficult to assess the changes that may be brought about by psychotherapy (18, 52) in the underlying patterns of the personality. For many years it has seemed that psychotherapy cannot be much good in altering the personality, for the conclusions reached by Eysenck (33) in the early part of the fifties have stood unchallenged until recently. Eysenck surveyed the studies on psychotherapy up to that time and concluded that about two-thirds of those who had psychotherapy recovered, and that of similar persons who had not had psychotherapy about two-thirds recovered. More recently, however, a serious challenge (45) has been made to Eysenck's position that gives hope to those who engage in psychotherapy. They have felt all along that *something* of a more or less profound nature was happening to their clients in response to the social changes they were providing in the form of psychotherapy.

Of course, controlled research is the only way to ascertain whether the psychotherapist's feelings are justified or not. Every palmist and astrologer can point to some rather astounding "successes" achieved with his clients. Further, what sometimes seems like profound change may only be reduction in anxiety to a marked degree. On going over his records of cases he had seen in the last two years before leaving one university, the author discovered to his dismay that three young men, whose cases had been terminated on the basis of the usual signs employed in psychotherapy, had shown by their subsequent behavior on campus not to have been altered basically at all by therapy. Where before they had displayed psychopathic trends but had come for therapy because of anxieties they were experiencing, now they were displaying the same psychopathic trends without the anxiety.

Nevertheless, it does seem that some of the people who have undergone psychotherapy have had fairly central alterations in their personalities, if not of basic id processes, at least of deeper ego and other unconscious functions (36). Consider, for example, the woman who "had suffered many things of many physicians," having gone to a dozen physicians and renowned clinics with her psychosomatic problems; in three months' psychotherapy she found more help of a lasting nature than from all the physical therapies. Other cases from the files of other psychotherapists, complete with follow-ups, would demonstrate the same thing. As is true of any social process intended to facilitate behavior, it must be said of psychotherapy: that profound change does not occur in every instance does not mean it has not occurred in some instances.

Very closely related to psychotherapy, and indeed utilized by many psychotherapists, is hypnosis, which may be subsumed here under facilitating factors. Although the authorities who have written on hypnosis are legion, by far the most persistent researcher and critical authority in the field is Barber and his associates, with about half a hundred experimental and theoretical articles on the subject. The most salient publications (6, 7, 8, 9) dispel many myths about hypnosis. With some of Barber's contentions other authorities may differ,[5] but a number of his and others' experiments lead very strongly to several surprising conclusions: First, "hypnosis" itself is an unclear concept, sometimes meaning an independent variable, sometimes a dependent variable, and oftimes some unspecified combinations. Second, many subjects perform "hypnotic" behaviors without benefit of induction procedures. Third, the prior relation to the hypnotist seems to be very important in many cases. And fourth, the prior personality structure of the subject, and in particular his "suggestibility," appears to be a determining factor—whether they are "hypnotized" or not, some persons perform the feats of a presumably hypnotized individual at the behest of an experimenter. There are other conclusions to be drawn from Barber's work, but these are most pertinent to our quest.

If the foregoing conclusions are correct, "hypnosis" would seem to be a variety of interpersonal relation that would serve as a social change much the same as does psychotherapy. As far as the writer knows, despite many studies of "posthypnotic

5. Sarbin (72) some time ago had interpreted hypnotic behavior from a role theory standpoint. His conclusions appear to be similar to Barber's, especially as to the subject's relation to the hypnotist. Rotter, in discussing the role of the psychological situation from his Social Learning Theory standpoint (68), develops concepts that reinforce the interpretation of hypnosis as described by Barber.

suggestion," dealing primarily with retention of specified memory content, no studies have been made of long-term effects on personality organization, and especially any that might bear on temperament reorganization. Presumably, however, given a subject who is suggestible enough, a therapist with prestige yet with whom the individual relates well, and a continued "hypnotic" situation intermittently repeated long enough, we should expect far-reaching changes in the personality (to some extent in each of the dyad). Hypnoanalysis [see Arluck (4), and Wolberg (87, 88)] contains most if not all these ingredients; its proponents claim just such fundamental alterations in the personality as suggested above. As for drastic changes from one or a few sessions, the writer supposes ideal conditions of preparation in the subject's life would be needed—not an impossible condition, but unlikely in most cases.

As stated previously, other social experiences too numerous to mention may bring about substantial deep-level change in the personality. Whatever hapens, for example, in the understanding acceptance of a teacher's after-school conference with a pupil, may "make all the difference in the world" to the student. And what happens in a ministers' study may likewise produce such changes. The writer spent a number of years in the ministry. One of his most vivid memories of his pastoral work is of one morning during the Second World War when a professional man, not a member of his church but more often in attendance than a good many members, called. He said in an urgent tone, "Ralph, can I see you right away?" When he came into the study, he dropped into the chair across from the minister and said, "The only thing I can think of is that I want to kill myself." He went on, "I have everything to live for. I have a lovely wife and daughters. I have everything to live for." He repeated that same thought several times during the conversation. Since that time the writer has come to realize the significance of the repetition of this idea, but at the time of this story he did not understand it. The distressed man spoke of the band like an iron band he felt about his chest, and how he could not breathe because the band was tightening on him so. After the two had talked for a short while, the minister said, "Paul"—

that is not his name—"Paul, let us pray about this." So they knelt down at their chairs and the writer prayed briefly. Then the other began to pray. At first his words came out haltingly. Then he began to cry and he said, "I feel the band is loosening about my chest. I feel I can breathe again." In a short while he rose, they shook hands, and he left. It is not entirely clear just what happened that day. All that we do know is that this man was ready to take his own life, and that now nearly a quarter of a century later he has not done so. Possibly no *basic* alteration in this man's personality structure took place in response to introducing certain social change, but something fairly profound, at a deep, unconscious level, did take place.

2. *Stress-Induced Behaviors*

Just as "facilitated behavior" may be brought about by beneficial changes in society, so, too, central changes may be brought about by stress. Most biological and social scientists are familiar with Selye's (76, 77, 78) "general-adaptation syndrome." If a stress is prolonged sufficiently, the organism reaches the exhaustion stage and expires. This would seem to be a fairly extensive alteration in the personality. Such stresses may be physical, such as extreme cold or heat, or infection or pain. Even these may be the result of social processes, as in a war situation or a concentration camp. In fact, much that we know about reactions to stress came from studies made during wartime (82) and reports of former inmates of concentration camps (69). The results of deliberate attempts to alter the basic personality structures of prisoners of war, as in China's so-called "brain-washing" of American prisoners in Korea, are somewhat in doubt (44); but enough evidence has accumulated to recognize that some prisoners were deeply affected. Indeed, just being a prisoner of war may wreak profound havoc (20, 21). Likewise, although some returnees from concentration camps seemed not to have been deeply changed (3), the preponderance of evidence (12, 15, 53) suggests that the extreme stresses set up by a society bent on mass destruction,[6] stresses both physiological, psychological, and

6. This is a society organized for a heinous purpose. A disorganized society may likewise achieve evil ends [see Blumer (16)].

sociological, wrought alterations in central portions of personalities that can probably never be effaced in those who survived.

In recent years some investigators have been coming to realize the deep lying effects a system of segregation can produce in the personalities of those who are oppressed by it as well as in those who are the oppressors, or what changes may come when desegregation takes place. As one of the bishops of the Methodist Church in India said after he, an outcast, had become a Christian, "One of the most important things my becoming a Christian has meant to me is that I can meet a man and look him in the eye." We have to remember that slavery and segregation in this country were introduced as social changes and that the very depths of personalities were reached by these changes, so that, for example, both many whites and many Negroes came to feel that anything different would be immoral. Young Negroes who have been growing up in a different day may not understand [though some may, see Solomon and Fishman (81)] that some of the opposition—in fact, the most basic opposition—their elders manifested at the start of the Negro Revolution was not from fear of consequences, but from a conviction reaching deep into their unconscious minds that what their youth were doing is immoral. The same holds for a large number of white persons. Their antipathy or apparent indifference to the Negro's need for freedom may not stem from sadism or delight in having the fruits of exploitation, but from the feeling that associating with Negroes on an equal plane is just downright immoral. How far the social changes of the present will reach these underlying superego attitudes is a moot question, although some indications are that changes can be wrought (13).

F. Postscript

One last word about social change and personality: we are not at all sure how social change does bring about personality change, although some investigators have been theorizing for years about the matter, as Freud, Adler, and Jung all did.[7] A

7. The latest has just come to hand, N. Sanford's *Self and Society: Social Change and Individual Change* (New York: Atherton, 1966), whose aim is to provide a basis for planned action affecting individuals and groups.

more modern attempt (38) leaves the writer rather cold. When observable social changes are followed by observable personality changes (57), we may tend to think we have at least identified the causal relations. But as scientists have been warned again and again, correlation does not mean causation. What about the times when vast social change is not followed by the expected personality change (43)? And what about the vast personality change not preceded by any observable social change?

An instance of the latter may serve to bring humility to the ranks of those who are presumed to be authorities in the area of personality and social psychology. The man was a rancher friend with a fair-sized family. But he drank extremely heavily. In fact, he told the writer—and there was independent evidence as to the correctness of his figure—that he spent two hundred dollars a month on liquor for himself, not to entertain, but just for himself. And that was under price control. The figure would be at least double today. When this man's wife had a very unfortunate accident, the writer thought it might bring the friend to himself. But, no. Then his son had a serious accident, a truly horrible thing. Surely, the writer thought, the man would be reached. But, no, he kept on with his drinking. The exhortations of friends and even the help of others during his very trying times seemed to be of no avail. A year after the writer's family had moved from the community, the man quit drinking—just like that. No tapering off, no sanitarium "drying out," no religious conversion, no AA, nothing that could be seen—he just quit. What happened? The writer can only hazard some guesses about the cumulative effects of a string of misfortunes. But actually nothing is really known. In some ways we are not too far from that situation in our scientific position in respect to social change and personality in general. We are convinced that social change brings personality change. The writer is convinced, as are many, that the more central the personality function is, the more difficult it is to change.

Acknowledgment

The preceding article is adapted from a lecture delivered at Clark College, May 3, 1966, in the Clark College Winter and

Spring Lecture Series 1966, "The Social Sciences and the Development of Human Potentials." It was printed under the title "Just How Far Can Social Change Change Personality?" in *The Journal of Psychology*, Vol. 64, 1966, pp. 167-191. Permission to reprint the article was granted by the author and The Journal Press.

References

1. Allport, G. W. Personality: A Psychological Interpretation. New York: Holt, 1937.
2. ———. Traits revisited. *Amer. Psychol.*, 1966, 21, 1-10.
3. Allport, G. W., Brunner, J. S., & Jandorf, E. M. Personality under social catastrophe: Ninety life histories of the Nazi revolution. *Charac. Personal.*, 1941, 10, 1-22.
4. Arluck, E. W. Hypnoanalysis: A Case Study. New York: Random House, 1964.
5. Asch, S. E. Studies in the principles of judgments and attitudes: II. Determination of judgments by group and by ego standards. *J. Soc. Psychol.*, 1940, 12, 433-465.
6. Barber, T. X. Antisocial and criminal acts induced by "hypnosis." *Arch. Gen. Psychol.*, 1961, 5, 301-312.
7. ———. Hypnotizability, suggestibility, and personality: V. A critical review of research findings. *Psychol. Rep.*, 1964, 14 (Monograph Supplement 3-V14), 299-320.
8. ———. Experimental analyses of "hypnotic" behavior: A review of recent empirical findings. *J. Abn. & Soc. Psychol.*, 1965, 70, 132-154.
9. Barber, T. X., & Calverly, D. S. Empirical evidence for a theory of hypnotic behavior: Effects on suggestibility of five variables typically included in hypnotic induction procedures. *J. Consult. Psychol.*, 1965, 29, 98-107.
10. Bender, I. E. Changes in religious interest: A retest after 15 years. *J. Abn. & Soc. Psychol.*, 1958, 57, 41-46.
11. Bergen, M. A. Some observations of maturational factors in young children and adolescents. In R. S. Eissler (Ed.), *The Psychoanalytic Study of the Child (Vol. XIX)*. New York: Internat. Univ. Press, 1964.

229

12. Bettelheim, B. Individual and mass behavior in extreme situations. *J. Abn. & Soc. Psychol.*, 1943, 38, 417-452.

13. Bettelheim, B., & Janowitz, M. Social Change and Prejudice. New York: Free Press of Glencoe, 1964.

14. Blos, P. The initial stage of male adolescence. In R. S. Eissler (Ed.), *The Psychoanalytic Study of the Child* (*Vol. XX*). New York: Internat. Univ. Press, 1965.

15. Bluhm, H.O. How did they survive? Mechanisms of defense in Nazi concentration camps. *Amer. J. Psychother.*, 1948, 2, 3-32.

16. Blumer, H. Social disorganization and individual disorganization. *Amer. J. Sociol.*, 1937, 42, 871-877.

17. Burt, C., & Howard, M. The relative influence of heredity and environment. *Brit. J. Stat. Psychol.*, 1957, 10, 98-104.

18. Byrne, J. Assessing personality variables and their alterations. In P. Worchel & D. Byrne (Eds.), *Personality Change*. New York: Wiley, 1964.

19. Caldwell, B. M. The effects of infant care. In M. L. Hoffman & L. W. Hoffman (Eds.), *Review of Child Development Research* (Vol. 1). New York: Russell Sage Foundation, 1964.

20. Curle, A. Transitional communities and social reconnection: A follow-up study of the civil resettlement of British prisoners of war, Part I. *Hum. Rel.*, 1947, 1, 42-68.

21. Curle, A., & Trist, E. L. Transitional communities and social resettlement of British prisoners of war, Part II. *Hum. Rel.*, 1947, 1, 240-288.

22. David, H. P., & von Bracken, H. (Eds.). Perspectives in Personality Theory. New York: Basic Books, 1957.

23. Doby, J. T. Introduction to Social Psychology. New York: Appleton-Century-Crofts, 1966.

24. Dobzhansky, T. Mankind Evolving: The Evolution of the Human Species. New Haven, Conn.: Yale Univ. Press, 1962.

25. Dreger, R. M. Fundamentals of Personality: A Functional Psychology of Personality. Philadelphia: Lippincott, 1962.

26. ———. A progress report on a factor analytic approach to

classification in child psychiatry. *Psychiat. Res. Rep.*, 1964, No. 18, 22-58.

27. Dreger, R. M., & Barnert, M. Measurement of the custom and conscience functions of the superego. J. soc. Psychol. (in press)

28. Dreger, R. M., & Dreger, G. E. Proceedings of the Technical Assistance Project held at Jacksonville University, August 16-17, 1962. Behavioral Classification Project, Report No. 1. Jacksonville, Fla.: Behavioral Classification Project, 1962.

29. Dreger, R. M., & Miller, K. S. Comparative psychological studies of Negroes and whites in the United States. *Psychol. Bull.*, 1960, 57, 361-402.

30. ———. Recent research in psychological comparisons of Negroes and whites in the United States. Paper read at Southeastern Psychological Association, Atlanta, Georgia, April, 1965.

31. Dreger, R. M., Smith, W. D., & Wieland, R. G. Changes in dating attitudes and practices in the first three months of college life. Unpublished paper, Florida State University, Tallahassee, Florida, 1954.

32. Dreger, R. M., Reid, M. P., Lewis, P. M., Overlade, D. C., Rich, T. A., Taffel, C., Miller, K. S., & Flemming, E. L. Behavioral Classification Project. *J. Consult. Psychol.*, 1964, 28, 1-13.

33. Eysenck, H. J. The effects of psychotherapy: An evaluation. *J. Consult. Psychol.*, 1952, 16, 319-323.

34. Fenichel, O. The Psychoanalytic Theory of Neurosis. New York: Norton, 1945.

35. Flavell, J. H. The Developmental Psychology of Jean Piaget. Princeton, N. J.: Van Nostrand, 1963.

36. Frank, J. D. Persuasion and Healing. New York: Schocken, 1963.

37. Freud, A. Normality and Pathology in Childhood: Assessments of Development. New York: Internat. Univ. Press, 1965.

38. Gendlin, E. T. A theory of personality change. In P.

231

Worchel and D. Byrne (Eds.), *Personality Change*. New York: Wiley, 1964.

39. Gilliland, A. R. The attitude of college students toward God and the church. *J. Soc. Psychol.*, 1940, 11, 11-18.

40. Ginott, H. *Between Parent and Child*. New York: Macmillan, 1965.

41. Gyomroi, E. L. The analysis of a young concentration camp victim. In R. S. Eissler (Ed.), *The Psychoanalytic Study of the Child (Vol. XVIII)*. New York: Internat. Univ. Press, 1963.

42. Hess, E. H. Two conditions limiting critical age for imprinting. *J. Comp. & Physiol. Psychol.*, 1959, 52, 515-518.

43. Hilberg, A. The Destruction of the European Jews. Chicago, Ill.: Quadrangle, 1961.

44. Holt, R. R. Forcible indoctrination and personality change. In P. Worchel & D. Byrne (Eds.), *Personality Change*. New York: Wiley, 1964.

45. Kiesler, D. J. Some myths of psychotherapy research and the search for a paradigm. *Psychol. Bull.*, 1966, 65, 110-136.

46. Klemer, R. H. Student attitudes toward guidance in sexual morality. In E. M. Schur (Ed.), *The Family and the Sexual Revolution, Selected Readings*. Bloomington, Ind.: Indiana Univ. Press, 1964.

47. Kluckhohn, C., Murray, H. A., & Schneider, D. M. (Eds.). *Personality in Nature, Society, and Culture*. New York: Knopf, 1953.

48. Kuhlen, R. G. Personality change with age. In P. Worchel & D. Byrne (Eds.), *Personality Change*. New York: Wiley, 1964.

49. Laufer, M. Ego ideal and pseudo ego ideal in adolescence. In R. S. Eissler (Ed.), *The Psychoanalytic Study of the Child (Vol. XIX)*. New York: Internat. Univ. Press, 1964.

50. Lehmann, I. J., Sinba, B. K., & Harnett, R. T. Changes in attitudes and values associated with college attendance. *J. Educ. Psychol.*, 1966, 57, 89-98.

51. Lewin, K. Some socio-psychological differences between the United States and Germany. *Charac. & Personal.*, 1936, 4, 265-293.

52. Luborsky, L., & Schimek, J. Psychoanalytic theories of therapeutic and developmental change: Implications for assessment. In P. Worchel & D. Byrne (Eds.), *Personality Change*. New York: Wiley, 1964.

53. Luchterhand, E. Survival in the concentration camp: An individual or a group phenomenon? In B. Rosenberg, I. Gerver, & F. W. Howton (Eds.), *Mass Society in Crisis: Social Problems and Social Pathology*. New York: Macmillan, 1964.

54. McCandless, B. R. Children and Adolescents: Behavior and Development. New York: Holt, Rinehart & Winston, 1961.

55. McClearn, G. E. Genetics and behavior development. In M. L. Hoffman & I. W. Hoffman (Eds.), *Review of Child Development Research* (*Vol.* 1). New York: Russell Sage Foundation, 1964.

56. Mead, G. H. Mind, self, and society from the standpoint of a social Behaviorist (ed. by C. N. Morris). Chicago, Ill.: Univ. Chicago Press, 1934.

57. Merton, R. K. Social structure and anomie. *Amer. Sociolog. Rev.*, 1938, 3, 672-682.

58. Murphy, G. Personality: A Biosocial Approach to Origins and Structure. New York: Harper, 1947.

59. Mussen, P. H., Conger, J. J., & Kagan, J. Child Development and Personality (2nd ed.). New York: Harper & Row, 1963.

60. Nelson, E. N. P. Persistence of attitudes of college students fourteen years later. *Psychol. Monog.*, 1954, 68 (2), Whole No. 373.

61. Nichols, R. C. The inheritance of general and specific ability. National Merit Scholarship Corporation, Research Reports, Vol. 1, No. 1, Evanston, Illinois, 1965.

62. ———. Personality change and the college. National Merit Scholarship Corporation Research Reports, Vol. 1, No. 2, Evanston, Illinois, 1965.

63. ———. The National Merit twin study. In S. G. Vandenberg (Ed.), *Methods and Goals in Human Behavior Genetics*. New York: Academic Press, 1965.

64. Peterson, D. R. Behavior problems of middle childhood. *J. Consult. Psychol.*, 1961, 25, 205-209.

65. Porter, B. R. American teen-agers of the 1960's—Our despair or hope? *J. Marriage & Family*, 1965, 27, 139-147.

66. Prien, E. P. Personality correlates and changes in proworld-mindedness and antiworldmindedness following an intercultural experience. *J. Soc. Psychol.*, 1966, 68, 243-247.

67. Quay, H. C., & Quay, L. C. Behavior problems in early adolescence. *Child Devel.*, 1965, 36, 215-220.

68. Rotter, J. B. The role of the psychological situation in determining the direction of human behavior. In R. C. Teevan & R. C. Birney (Eds.), *Theories of Motivation in Personality and Social Psychology*. New York: Van Nostrand, 1964.

69. Rosenberg, B., Gerver, I., & Howton, F. W. (Eds.). *Mass Society in Crisis: Social Problems and Social Pathology*. New York: Macmillan, 1964.

70. Rosenzweig, M. R. Environmental complexity, cerebral change, and behavior. *Amer. Psychol.*, 1966, 21, 321-332.

71. Sanford, N. (Ed.). Personality development during the college years. *J. Soc. Issues*, 1956, 12, No. 4.

72. Sarbin, T. R. Contribution to role-taking theory: I. Hypnotic behavior. *Psychol. Rev.*, 1950, 57, 255-270.

73. ———. Role theory. In G. Lindzey (Ed.), *Handbook of Social Psychology, Vol. I. Theory and Method*. Cambridge, Mass.: Addison-Wesley, 1954.

74. ———. Role theoretical interpretation of psychological change. In P. Worchel & D. Byrne (Eds.), *Personality Change*. New York: Wiley, 1964.

75. Schur, E. M. (Ed.). *The Family and the Sexual Revolution*, Selected Readings. Bloomington, Ind.: Indiana Univ. Press, 1964.

76. Selye, H. A syndrome produced by diverse nocuous agents. *Nature*, 1936, 138, 32.

77. ———. The Physiology and Pathology of Exposure to Stress; a Treatise Based on the Concepts of the General-Adaptation-Syndrome and the Diseases of Adaptation. Montreal: Acta, 1950.

234

78. ———. Stress and disease. *Science*, 1955, 122, 625-631.
79. Sherif, M., & Cantril, H. The Psychology of Ego-Involvements. New York: Wiley, 1947.
80. Sinnott, E. W., Dunn, L. C., & Dobzhansky, T. Principles of Genetics (4th ed.). New York: McGraw-Hill, 1950.
81. Solomon, F., & Fishman, J. R. Youth and social action: II. Action and identity formation in the first student sit-in demonstration. *J. Soc. Issues*, 1964, 20, 36-45.
82. Sorokin, P. A. Man and Society in Calamity. New York: Dutton, 1942.
83. ———. The American Sex Revolution. Boston: Porter Sargent, 1956.
84. Sullivan, H. S. A theory of interpersonal relations—The illusion of personal individuality. Paper presented to the Society on the Theory of the Personality, New York City, May 3, 1944. Reprinted in H. M. Ruitenbeek (Ed.), *Varieties of Personality Theory*. New York: Dutton, 1964.
85. Walters, C. E. Prediction of postnatal development from fetal activity. *Child Devel.*, 1965, 36, 801-808.
86. Webster, H. Changes in attitudes during college. *J. Educ. Psychol.*, 1958, 49, 109-117.
87. Wolberg, L. R. Hypnoanalysis. New York: Grune & Stratton, 1945.
88. ———. Hypnotherapy. In J. L. McCary (Ed.), *Six Approaches to Psychotherapy*. New York: Dryden, 1955.
89. Worchel, P., & Byrne, D. (Eds.). Personality Change. New York: Wiley, 1964.
90. Yarrow, L. J. Separation from parents during early childhood. In M. L. Hoffman and L. W. Hoffman (Eds.), *Review of Child Development Research (Vol. 1)*. New York: Russell Sage Foundation, 1964.
91. Yarrow, L. J., & Yarrow, M. R. Personality continuity and change in the family context. In P. Worchel & D. Byrne (Eds.), *Personality Change*. New York: Wiley, 1964.

PSYCHODRAMA AND TRENDS IN
GROUP PSYCHOTHERAPY

J. L. MORENO, M. D.
Beacon, New York

Editorial Note

Psychodrama has been effectively used as a form of group psychotherapy but is not restricted to this application. Its advocates claim that it is successfully used wherever human relations are studied—by psychiatrists, psychologists, sociologists, and educators—by itself or in combination with other therapeutic methods. The word was coined by the author of the following article.

Dr. J. L. Moreno founded the social movement known as group psychotherapy in the United States in 1931. The first edition of his *Plan for the Transforming of Prisons into a Socialized Community* was published in August of that year and widely distributed by the National Committee on Prisons and Prison Labor (it was published in a second edition the following year, under the title *Application of the Group Method to Classification*). This was the first book ever written on group psychotherapy.

Dr. Moreno founded the International Committee of Group Psychotherapy in 1951 and serves as President of the International Council of Group Psychotherapy. His most recent book is *The International Handbook of Group Psychotherapy*. Some of his other publications are listed in the Reference section of this article.

PSYCHODRAMA AND TRENDS IN GROUP PSYCHOTHERAPY

1

A. Introduction

It is in the atmosphere of the great French Revolution that the First Psychiatric Revolution took place, the emancipation of the insane from chains, symbolized by Philippe Pinel (1793). Many modern recent innovations, like the open door, the day hospital, the night hospital, the halfway-house and the community clinic, can be considered as extensions and reverberations of that original rebellion.

The next important step, the era of the Second Psychiatric Revolution in the course of the nineteenth century, was the development of psychotherapy. It extended from Mesmer to Charcot and Janet, to the leaders of the psychoanalytic movement.

The era of the Third Psychiatric Revolution, with an "élan thérapeutique" of its own, is now in progress. While the changes brought about by the First Revolution were institutional, and those by the Second psychodynamic, the changes brought about by the Third Revolution are due to the influence of cosmic and social forces. They are further transforming and enlarging the scope of psychiatry. They made their greatest contribution with group and action methods, especially group psychotherapy and psychodrama. The changes are taking place in many fields, in technology, physiology, pharmacology, communication, mass psychiatry and sociatry. Their ultimate goal is a therapeutic society, a therapeutic world order which I envisioned in the opening sentence of my opus *Who Shall Survive?*, 1934, p. 3: "A truly therapeutic procedure cannot have less an objective than the whole of mankind."

B. The Third Psychiatric Revolution

Marx, Kierkegaard, Nietzsche, and Bergson may be considered among the forerunners of the Third Psychiatric Revolution, since their writings were a prelude to group and action methods. Karl Marx, for example, was a forerunner of industrial sociometry. Kierkegaard's religious fantasies, striving toward an heroic existentialism, were a prelude to action, to action techniques and psychodrama. Nietzsche, in *Zarathustra* and *Ecce Homo*, desperately tried to move into an heroic life. He was another forerunner of action. Although Kierkegaard and Nietzsche did not attain their hopes and dreams, they triggered a call to action. Another precursor was Henri Bergson, author of *L'évolution créatrice*, who paved the way for the modern concept of spontaneity.

Although these men lived prior to, parallel with, or after Freud, they belong in tempo and spirit to a later era, that of the twentieth century which was the century of many liberations—such as the Russian Revolution of 1917, of the masses of people from the economic fetters of their landlords and the bourgeoisie, the liberation of children from the fetters of their parents, the liberation of adolescents from the authority of their elders, the emancipation of women from their subordination to men, the revolution of sex and birth control, the emancipation of religion, revision of old mythologies, new interpretations of the bible to meet the demands of our age, modernization of the Catholic church and the Ecumenic Council, the wars of liberation in Africa and Asia, and the civil rights struggle of the Negroes in the U.S.A.

During the early years of this century, I formulated the concept of the encounter, which triggered me to a number of existential actions: liberation of the actor from the script—I broke into a theater during a performance and stopped it (1911), demanding that the actors throw away their scripts and begin playing their own selves; liberation of the minister from the bible conserve—I broke into a church during a sermon and stopped the minister, demanding that he practice love and charity in the here and now (1912); liberation of children from their parents—a forerunner of the sociometric test in a gathering of children and parents in which the children were given the privilege of choosing new parents or keeping their own (1909). In addition, I introduced role playing in the gardens of Vienna as a forerunner of psychodrama, group psychotherapy, mass psychiatry, and therapeutic theater. As conductor of psycho-dramas in the free setting of the Viennese gardens, I triggered a form of mass catharsis, anticipating the therapeutic television for the mass, mass group psychotherapy, and mass psychodrama, which are among the goals and strivings of the Third Psychiatric Revolution.

This revolution has many facets. The one is the psycho-physiological revolution, pioneered by Pavlov and Berger—the conditioned reflex and the electro-encephalogram. The second facet is the psycho-pharmacological revolution—pioneered by Sakel, Cerletti, Hoffman, and Delay, among others—with the development of insulin- and electro-shock treatment, the tran-quilizers and hallucinogens. The third facet is the psycho-tech-nological revolution, represented by space travel, automation, cybernetics, and the methods of birth control. The fourth facet is the mass media of communication—radio, motion pictures, television and their impact upon the behavior of individuals and masses. However, the final and most important facet is the development of group and action methods, because they facili-tated and integrated the benefits of all the revolutionary methods enumerated above—the physiological, pharmacological, techno-logical, and sociological—into a single package, so that they could reach and aid the masses of the people towards a mass psychiatry.

One of the greatest achievements of this era is the discovery of methods of measurement through calculated experimental methods—the measurement of small groups, the measurement of the brain, and the measurement of human relations. Social meas-urement, with sociometry as its exponent, established the first solid bridge beyond psychiatry into sociology. It proposed "sociatry," a concept of healing which transcends psychiatry. Sociatry aims at a science of the normality and pathology of large masses of individuals, of entire communities and nations, and perhaps, someday in the future, of the entire mankind. Psychiatric concepts such as neurosis and psychosis are not applicable to group and mass processes. A group of individuals may become "normotic" or "sociotic" and the syndromes pro-ducing this condition have been called "normosis" or "sociosis."

239

II
Early visions of group and action methods

A. Background of Psychodrama

As I was walking through the streets and beautiful gardens of Vienna, now more than half a century ago (1908-1914), a very anonymous and intensive young man, observing and playing with children, I had a vision which triggered my entire life-work and which gave me a precocious anticipation of the great changes which have since taken place in our world.

I meditated about the meaning of the universe and about my place in it. According to legend, Buddha, when he was reborn, did not return as Buddha but as Bodhisattva. Buddha, instead of fleeing from the world, moved into it to live in it and, if necessary, to change it. I remembered the efforts of Freud, whom I met in the Vienna Psychiatric Clinic (1912), to analyze himself and the world to its very depth and, like a modern Buddha, to find a way out of his misery. But if Freud would be reborn, would he continue to analyze himself, or would he take a new turn, as Buddha did, and become a psychoanalytic Bodhisattva? I asked myself: If an "analysis" is successfully terminated, what is the next step? One has to live! The technique of psychoanalysis may be good for an analysis on the couch, but what does it offer the cosmos into which we enter as modern Bodhisattvas? We need techniques of living. There must be methods of living which satisfy the deepest needs of personality, of our society and of the world. Psychodrama offers such methods. They are applied and are effective *hic et nunc*, "in the midst of life." We call these methods *psychodrama in situ*, that is, not applied within a therapeutic setting but in the "kairos of living," in the daily challenges and transactions within oneself between husband and wife, parents and children, around the dining table, in the bedroom, in the workshop, wherever life is lived productively (soliloquy techniques and monologues), assisted by role reversal, mirror, double, future techniques, etc. Illustrations for psychodrama in situ I have given repeatedly in my recent publications, *The Discovery of the Spontaneous Man*, 1956, *The First Psychodramatic Family*, 1964, and in my earliest writings (1911-

1925), such as my dialogues in a church setting, in a library setting, in a theater, in actu and in situ; the earlier period included a psychodrama in situ between a husband and wife, in a family setting in *Das Stegreiftheater*, 1923, pp. 74-78.

Two questions bewildered me and I could not rest until I found an answer: (1) How can I communicate with the entire world, with all people, and how can all people communicate with me? (2) How can this be done in the here and now? How can I emancipate myself from the past and create in the moment and for the future, with the people I encounter? Then and there the miracle happened, at least in my fertile imagination; the "encounter" took place: I met all the people and the people met me. I spoke to the people in India, in China and in America, in Africa, to the people in Russia and to the people in France. And they spoke back to me. I saw them and heard them and felt them.

As I see it now what happened to me was not exactly what we call delusion and hallucination; it was a healthy, goal-directed experience. It was rather an anticipation of the future which fifty years later has become feasible. I just saw the future and I was experiencing it, without telegraph and radio, without tape recordings and without computers, without mass two-way television, without any of the miracles of the machine being at my disposal. Because I had that vision, I began to work so as to make that vision come true. I began to work on electro-magnetic fields and developed the radio-film (radio-telephone tape recording). I worked with small groups and developed interactional and co-actional group psychotherapy. I began to work on the invisible underground of mankind and developed sociometry. Then came psychodrama, as a climax.

B. Background of Group Psychotherapy

After freeing the children from their parents' rigid views of life I knew intuitively every next step I should make in order to bring the new world to realization. I looked after the weakest links in the chain of our social existence and found the most vulnerable and helpless victims—in the streets of Vienna—the prostitutes. I followed them into their sexual ghetto, Am Spittelberg (1913), in which they lived in small groups in individual houses. The question was: what can be done to free them from their chains and to give their life true meaning? They wanted to appeal to the sexual appetites of men and sell their bodies to them. The answer was simple: as the body is their property, give them the privilege to do whatever they wish to do with their body, give them freedom of sex. But I found out rapidly that to establish sex as a commodity met with enormous resistance and the barriers were practically unsurmountable. The logical step seemed to be to follow the spirit of our time and put the problem on an economic basis. We established a "union of prostitutes," just as there are other labor unions. But the revolution of complete sexual freedom appeared to be a greater revolution still than the revolution of the proletariat. The labor unions of the communist and socialist parties did not recognize them as equals; the religions and their charity organizations did not accept them unless they were willing to give up their identity and look for respectable occupations. We had meetings from time to time in their houses during which economic and legal problems were first discussed. Gradually their personal sufferings became the most important aspect of the meetings. Their emotional needs pushed the idea of a labor union into the background and group psychotherapy "in situ" took over. It is interesting that what was an absurdity and a paradox in the Vienna of 1913 has taken a novel appearance in our time. What is the meaning otherwise of the "sexual explosion" of today except a further move towards the freedom of the body?

Modern group psychotherapy started in the sexual ghetto of Vienna, in a natural setting, in situ (1913), and not in clinical settings, as it developed in the U.S.A. in the nineteen thirties, where professional experts—psychiatrists, psychologists, social workers, etc.—took over therapeutic leadership.

The forerunners of the modern group psychotherapy movement of professional groups took different forms in various cultures. In early Christianity it grew out of the monasteries in which comparatively small groups of monks or nuns lived in intimate ensembles. Although the value systems and aims were

242

religious, the results were often unconsciously therapeutic. It was to save the soul and not to heal the sick. The idea of mental illness is a modern concept. One monk helped another within the religious ritual of the monastic hierarchy (see J. L. Moreno, *Application of the Group Method to Classification*, 1932, and *Who Shall Survive?*, 1934).

It is interesting to compare the autonomous group movements of lay people in our time, the movement among the prostitutes in Austria, 1913, with the Alcoholics Anonymous Movement (A. A.) in the U.S.A., 1934, and the Synanon Movement among drug addicts, 1960. The movement among the prostitutes started with the principle of "affirmation" and "acceptance" of the body as an indisputable property of every woman, so to speak as the first natural law. They did not want to give up sex as a commodity, but to be recognized as having the professional and legal right to practice prostitution. The tendencies in the autonomous movements in the U.S.A. are quite different. Similar to the early Christian movements to heal the soul from impurities, also the modern movements in the U.S.A. express themselves in *denial* rather than *affirmation*. This trend expresses itself in diet; do not eat what you like and as much as you like, but follow dietetic rules. Do not drink alcoholic beverages because they make you sick. Do not take drugs because they make you pathological. Do not indulge in sex, because it's immoral unless it is sanctioned by marriage. We see here the old value conflict between upholding the natural law and the natural rights of the body and mind, the sanctity of food, of sleep, of love, of creativity, versus the tendency to control them and restrain them by principles which are unnatural or at least unproven as to their validity.

C. Background of Sociometry

When the first World War broke out in 1914, I was employed by the Department of the Interior of the Austro-Hungarian monarchy as an Officer of Health in a camp, a community of refugees near Vienna. My determination to find new solutions to difficult social problems found here a fascinating and unexplored target. I recognized that just as the prostitutes lived in two worlds, the community of Mitterndorf had an official and an invisible part. In order to resolve the tensions between these two aspects of this sick community I began to make graphs of the structure of every house, "sociometric diagrams," and gradually developed the system of sociometry which has become a basic science of sociology.

D. The Triadic System, Sociometry—Group Psychotherapy—Psychodrama

I merged group psychotherapy, sociometry and psychodrama into a single system: the Triadic System.

The triadic system is the integration of three theories: the science of the group, the science of sociometry and the science of action. These are interrelated and indispensable to one another.

1. The first discovery was that interaction of individuals in groups has a therapeutic potential. Such interaction can lead to indifference, to violence and destruction, but also to integration and catharsis. The result was the concept of "therapeutic interaction" (one man a therapeutic agent of the other) and interactional, coactional group psychotherapy, which has become the foundation of all forms of group psychotherapy.

2. Therapeutic interaction found a solid scientific basis in the science of sociometry.

3. The greatest benefits accrue to group psychotherapy and sociometry through the action methods, therapeutic psychodrama, psychodrama in situ, and behavior training.

The experimental methods of group and action therapy did not prosper in university laboratories; they require the open communities as fields of testing and research. One can distinguish between two directions of experimental methods: (a) in the atmosphere of a university laboratory for instance, Pavlov's experiment, and (b) in the atmosphere of the open community, as sociodrama, group psychotherapy, sociometry, family therapy, etc.

244

Conditions of the open experiment are: the visible body in space, in the here and now, real life, on the spot, in situ, the group, action and interaction, acting out, action and social catharsis.

III—*The Scientific Method and Group Psychotherapy*

A. *Philosophy of Group Psychotherapy*

The first question which can be raised is: why group psychotherapy? Adjustment may make human relations sterile. Maladjustment may make them more spontaneous. A sane world may be stereotype, an insane world may be creative. The question: Why good psychotherapy? falls into the same category as the question: Is eating, sleeping and reproduction necessary? They are a matter of survival. Living in groups is also a matter of survival. There is no alternative, to live in groups or not to live in groups, we are existentially stuck. Group therapy is a process which goes on regardless of whether it is done by means of scientific methods or not. The answer is that ongoing, unorganized group psychotherapy can be improved by scientific methods.

The second question is: if the individual is only a fragment or a part of reality, what is real and more comprehensive? Our answer was that however real the individual is, the group is a greater reality and includes it. Mankind is a greater reality still than the groups and the universe at large includes all individuals, all groups, and all possible mankind. In my philosophy the essence of the universe was its creativity-spontaneity. The development of physical and cultural conserves, with the latter getting the upper hand more and more, led to the pathology of man, who became deficient as a spontaneous and creative agent. The objective of group psychotherapy became, therefore, to stimulate and train man's spontaneity and creativity, in the vehicles in which he naturally exists, that is, in groups.

With different connotations, Burrow asked the same question. His answer was: the individual is an illusion, the race—phylum —is the real reality. We have to analyze the group through phyloanalysis and return the I into the phylum. Burrow's query was how to integrate individual man into the bio-racial groups from which he has separated himself.

The neurosis of man has been visualized by the theoretical forerunners of group psychotherapy in various ways. It can be best expressed in terms of the fundamental process of alienation from reality. For Marx, who can be considered as a forerunner of theoretical group psychotherapy, the cause of the neurosis is the *economic* alienation of man, the fragmentation of man's productivity in the work process. For Burrow the cause of the neurosis is *biological* and *phyloanalytic* alienation of man, the separation of his I from the total phylum. According to my system the cause of neurosis is the *cosmic* alienation of man, his alienation from the essential meaning of the universe, its primary creative processes. It stands to reason that the philosophy envisioned by these early leaders would determine to a large extent the type of method which they sponsored and the kind of operations they considered significant. Marx found it indispensable to solve the economic alienation of man by a social revolution in which the working man becomes the top figure in the hierarchy of values. Burrow turned from verbal group therapy to the study of the distortions of the physiological condition of the individual produced by his separateness. He engaged, therefore, in physiological experiments and abandoned the group vehicle. I saw a remedy in developing methods which would train and re-train the behavior of individuals and groups in terms of their spontaneity and creativity. I claimed that the economic and the biological neurosis of behavior are interlocked and related to the more primary neurosis of spontaneity and creativity.

B. The Scientific Method and the Therapeutic Group

The trends which dominated the group psychotherapy movement from its inception are: a) the interactional trend; b) the analytic trend; and c) the activist trend, psychodrama, sociodrama, role playing and allied forms.

All group psychotherapists have come to agree that a *science of the therapeutic group* is basic to "scientific" foundations of group psychotherapy.

But how is a science of the "therapeutic" group possible? It is often considered in conflict with the demands of pure basic science. The advent of sociometry and group psychotherapy has had a revolutionary impact upon the orthodox, customary meaning of the scientific method which John Stuart Mill developed after the model of the physical sciences. Mill had come to the exasperating conclusion that the experimental method can not be applied to the social sciences, their subject matter being too complex; eo ipso, it could not be applied to a science of the group, thus making group psychotherapy an anecdotal, second-class science. My argument was (see my *Sociometry, Experimental Method and the Science of Society*, 1951) contrary to the model postulated by physical science that group research, whether under laboratory or in situ conditions, *must* appear of *consequence* to the subject. The subjects must be motivated, they must expect to be helped, or potentially helped, by the process. If the subjects are cold themselves, uninvolved in the outcome of the research, it has no tangible validity. The very fact that the methods of group psychotherapy are so constructed that the patients are subjectively participating, involved in the process and expecting beneficial results from it, has given the patients the "status of research actors" and the experimental method in social science a new slant. Every group psychotherapy session (analytic, discussional or psychodrama) is an experiment. Cold laboratory experiments carried out by academic social psychologists with subjects who are unmotivated and uninvolved from within their own depth, are of questionable value. In this context, indeed, we are in full accord with Mill, only that we replaced the skeptical conclusion of Mill by positive conclusions and by carrying out experiments in natural and laboratory settings.

The earliest task of sociometry and of sociometric group therapy was to construct a group psychotherapy experiment and a comparable control group which permitted rational evaluation and measurement. All schools of group psychotherapy have explicitly or implicitly followed this thought, trying whenever possible, to go beyond the anecdotal evaluation of the group process and to set up experimental situations.

C. *The Small Group vs. the Large Group*

The majority of studies to date have been made with small groups of from three to ten persons. The earliest conscious, analytic determination of the size of a small group was made in my Sing Sing Prison study in 1931. The number of participants was *seven*. "Forty-seven prisoners, inmates of Sing Sing Prison have been charted. From them, seven men have been selected and assigned to a possible group, 'Group I.' A double analysis is that of two analyzed together; a triple analysis, that of three analyzed together but of no more than such number of persons as can know one another intimately." But seven is by no means final; any number between three and ten or more has been recommended. The number changes with the criterion of the group.

In the context of family therapy, for instance, when an entire family is treated, we must accept the number of members in the family, whether it is three, ten or whatever. Here the number of participants is determined by the specific family and changes from case to case.

Another barrier to the rigid number of participants has arisen in groupings which represent "intimate ensembles." It is often therapeutically indicated to permit participation of a larger number because they share, for instance, the same hospital ward. The same is true in collective forms of psychodrama where social problems are treated. In St. Elizabeth's Hospital, for example, as many as fifty to sixty patients are treated simultaneously. In the course of such sessions every patient of the group can be reached.

But the greatest need for innovation and extension has come from the more recent efforts of the author to combine group psychotherapy and psychodrama with the mass media of communication like motion pictures and television and to give the benefit of therapy to the largest possible number of individuals.

It is obvious that we have to pursue the goal of mass psycho-therapy with the greatest possible caution; the therapeutic and ethical responsibilities are far greater than in small group psy-chotherapy. We are aware of the first revolutionary step beyond individual-centered therapy, made now more than fifty years ago and which has proven so fruitful. We have been able to overcome, to some extent, the resistance of the individual-centered schools. The approach to the large group is, of course, a new challenge to our inventiveness and courage. It is a second revolutionary step to extend the size of the group so that any number of individuals can be included without being limited by size. In order to accomplish this, an objective "reanalysis" of the therapeutic situation has to be made and new methods have to be invented. The question is how to move within a national therapeutic framework from small group psychotherapy to mass psychotherapy and mass psychiatry. There is no reason why we should fear that forms of individual psychotherapy will be neglected and become unnecessary. On the contrary, there is good reason to assume that the three dimensions of psycho-therapy, individual psychotherapy, group psychotherapy and mass psychiatry, will parallel and stimulate each other.

IV—The Need for Mass Psychiatry

When the need for mass psychiatry emerged in our time, there were two questions: (1) Why is the need for mass treat-ment greater and more urgent *now* than perhaps at any other time in history? (2) By what methods can we reach the masses effectively?

Let us first answer question one: The development of mass media of transportation and communication has projected and filtered into every home innumerable ideas, perceptions and per-suasions which have reduced the influence of the immediate family and the primary group (Cooley). It is not an accident that the sociometrists have introduced the term "tele" which means "influence at a distance" as the basic concept of com-munication. Of course, mass media such as television and mo-tion pictures are influences at a distance, but they are notoriously one-way relationships. Therefore, it is implied in the tele concept that two-way relationships be established between two individuals, however far distant from one another, so as to restore the intimacy which exists in the dyads of the family group.

But what instructions should we give the technologist as to the minimum requirements the television instrument must fulfill in order to be useful for some form of group psychodramatic therapy? The television production would have to be so arranged that every viewer could communicate with the therapist and the protagonist in the broadcasting station. In other words, the present one-way has to be transformed into a "two-way" television system. Just as in a typical psychodramatic session in which every member communicates with every other, or with the therapist, a psychotherapeutic television system must permit every viewer to see every other viewer in action as if they were in the same social space. Even if other requirements are not met, this is a minimum.

Question two has been answered in two ways: (1) By the known methods which have proven effective with small groups; (b) By methods which can reach large masses of people, in the literal sense, the entire living community.

Among the methods which are being developed in our time to reach large masses of people is the therapeutic theater, which is increasingly following the psychodramatic group model.

In Paris, in collaboration with the Italian producer, Roberto Rossellini, I made a few years ago (1956) a psychodramatic motion picture sponsored by the French Government Radio and Television. In the French Cinema, the producer, Rouch, has approached psychodramatic rules many times in his productions. In the U.S.A. an increasing number of television productions apply psychodramatic techniques. These are all signs of the time, indicating how mass media of communication are used for therapeutic aims.

The television-psychodrama is at present the future method *par excellence*. But other, better methods may emerge in the future. The commandment is that all beings be included in the therapy, all mankind.

In the psychodrama of small action groups, in the synthetic group formations in clinics, in natural groupings like families and community settlements in forms of psychodrama in situ, on the spot, in the here and now, the small group approach has spread all over the world and is practiced in many varieties. The treatment of large masses, consciously or unconsciously, is already in full swing in many places or waiting to be organized in an overall system of operations. The treatment of the entire living humanity, which was at the time of *Who Shall Survive?* an utopian dream, is moving now towards becoming a practical reality.

Every group psychotherapy session can be viewed as a modified Stegreiftheater, a modified theater of spontaneity. The original dictum of the psychodramatic process was that there are "no" spectators permitted in the theater of psychodrama. All participants are to play their own roles and to switch roles with every member in the group, each acting out his perception of the other fellow. The idea of psychodrama, reaching back to the dimmest memories of earliest civilizations, presents the first modern model of mass psychiatry. Although the "public" sessions of psychodrama are limited in the numbers of people who could participate in person, they contain the seed which could be taken up by the mass media of communication, especially by television, to be developed further into the televised psychodrama.

V—Synthesis and Future Objectives

We must face realistically all the fronts in the group psychotherapy movement; scientific, clinical, cultural, political, its growth as well as its spread. The movement has become easily the most popular and influential among the psychotherapies of our time. But in the rapid spread there is danger that the movement may go out of hand. The many trends and sub-forms, although a sign of productivity and progress, threaten to break it up from within into fragments.

Group psychotherapy is striving to attain the status of a vigorous science in its own right. But in the work of many practitioners it is still immature and parasitic, leaning upon other disciplines for its concepts and terminology—psychoanalysis, group dynamics, and existentialism, to name a few.

The three mysteries to be combatted are: 1) psychoanalytic mysticism—the mysticism of the individual psyche as the sole source of group analysis; 2) group mysticism—when the group becomes a self-propelling entity independent of the individuals who comprise it; and 3) existential mysticism—when existential concepts are used instead of those gained through empirical investigation.

Acknowledgment

Dr. Moreno's article incorporates materials published in a recent work which he edited, *The International Handbook of Group Psychotherapy* (New York: Philosophical Library), 1966. References, based on materials found in the same volume, have been compiled by the editors of this volume.

References

Abrams, O. Effects of group therapy upon certain personality characteristics of a selected group of institutionalized male sex offenders. *Dissert. Ab.* 1953, 13, 114.

Bassin, A. Effect of group therapy upon certain attitudes and perceptions of adult offenders on probation. *Dissert. Ab.* 1958, 18, 2241-2.

Beletsis, J. Jr. Group psychotherapy with chronic male schizophrenics: an evaluation of the frequency of group psychotherapy sessions as a factor affecting the results of the therapy. *Dissert. Ab.* 1956, 16, 1170-1.

Brown, P. M. A comparative study of three therapy techniques used to effect behavioral and social status changes in a group of institutionalized delinquent boys. *Dissert. Ab.* 1957, 17, 674-5.

Burrow, T. *Science and Man's Behavior.* New York: Philosophical Library, 1953.

Cadman, W. H., Misbach, L. & Brown, D. V. An assessment of roundtable psychotherapy. *Psychol. Monog.* 1954, 68, 384, 48 pp.

Clampitt, R. R. An experimentally controlled investigation of the effects of group therapy. *Dissert. Ab.* 1955, 15, 2292-2293.

Corsini, R. J. *Methods of Group Psychotherapy.* New York: McGraw-Hill, 1957.

Cowden, R. C., Zax, M. & Sproules, J. A. Group psychotherapy in conjunction with a physical treatment. *J. Clin. Psych.* 1956, 12, 53-56.

Daniels, M. The influence of the sex of the therapist and of the cotherapist in group psychotherapy with eighth grade behavior-problem boys, comparing results achieved by a male therapist, by a female therapist, and by two therapists in combination. *Dissert. Ab.* 1958, 18, 1489.

DiGiovanni, P. A comparison between orthodox group psychotherapy and activity group therapy in the treatment of chronic hospitalized schizophrenics. *Dissert. Ab.* 1959, 19, 3361.

Ends, E. J. & Page, C. W. Group psychotherapy and concomitant psychological change. *Psychol. Monog.* 1959, 73, #10, whole no. 480, 31 pp.

Feifel, H. & Schwartz, A. D. Group psychotherapy with acutely disturbed psychotic patients. *J. Consult. Psychol.* 1953, 17, 113-121.

Fisher, B. An investigation of the effectiveness of group therapy for the remediation of reading disabilities. *Dissert. Ab.* 1953, 13, 590-1.

Fleming, L. & Snyder, W. U. Social & personal changes following non-directive group play therapy, *Am. J. Ortho.* 1947, 17, 101-116.

Francus, J. B. A comparative study of two therapeutic methods of treating the significant relatives of hospitalized schizophrenics. *Dissert. Ab.* 1955, 15, 1898.

Foulkes, S. H. and E. J. Anthony. *Group Psychotherapy.* New York: Penguin Books, 1957.

Franklin, G. H. The effect of group therapy on the attitudes toward self and others of institutionalized delinquent boys. *Dissert. Ab.* 1958, 18, 1104-5.

Friedmann, A. *Progress in Psychotherapy.* Vol. I. New York: Grune and Stratton, 1956.

Funk, I. G., Shatin, L., Freed, E. X. & Rockmore, L. Somapsychotherapeutic approach to long-term schizophrenic patients. *J. Nerv. Ment. Disease.* 1955, 121, 423-437.

Gerstenlauer, C. Group therapy with institutionalized male juvenile delinquents. A comparative evaluation of the effects of group therapy on some aspects of institutionalized male juvenile delinquents. *Dissert. Ab.* 1959, 10, 101-3.

Harriman, B. L. Influence of group-centered therapy and mental health films on attitudes of prisoners. *Dissert. Ab.* 1956, 16, 1494-1495.

Harrow, G. S. The effects of psychodrama group therapy on role behavior of schizophrenic patients. *Group Psychotherapy.* 1951, 3, 316-320.

Haskell, M. R. Psychodramatic role training in preparation for release on parole. *Group Psychotherapy.* 1957, 10, 57-59.

Jones, F. D. & Peters, H. N. An experimental evaluation of group psychotherapy. *J. Abnorm. Soc. Psychol.* 1952, 47, 345-353.

Kahn, S. *Psychodrama Explained.* New York: Philosophical Library, 1964.

Klonoff, H. An explanatory study of the effect of short-term group psychotherapy on attitudes of tuberculosis patients. *Dissert. Ab.* 1955, 15, 290-291.

Knox, W. J. Acceptance of self, other people, and social conformity as a function of group therapeutic experiences. *Unpub. doct. dissert.* Pennsylvania State University, 1958.

Lassar, B. T. A study of the effects of group discussion on the attitudes of mothers toward their cerebral palsied children: an investigation of the attitudes of mothers of celebral palsied children and the effects of group discussion on these attitudes. *Dissert. Ab.* 1957, 17, 676-7.

Lindemann, J. E. The process and efficacy of short-term nondirective group psychotherapy with hospitalized schizophrenic patients. *Ab. Doc. Dissert.* Penn State Coll., 1953, 17, 690-694.

Klapman, J. W. *Group Psychotherapy, Theory and Practice*, 2d edition. New York: Grune and Stratton, 1959.

Luchins, A. S. *Group Therapy, A Guide.* New York: Random House, 1964.

McCann, J. R. A technique to facilitate acceptance and its relationship to interaction during group psychotherapy. *Dissert. Ab.* 1956, 16, 576.

Meiers, Joseph I. *Origins and Development of Group Psychotherapy.* Beacon, N. Y.: Beacon House, 1945.

Moreno, J. L., *Psychodrama Volume I,* third edition 1964, Beacon House, Beacon, N.Y.

Moreno, J. L. *Psychodrama Volume II,* Beacon House, Beacon, N.Y., 1959.

J. L. Moreno, M.D., Chapter on Psychodrama, *American Handbook of Psychiatry,* Basic Books, 1959.

Moreno, J. L. *The Theater of Spontaneity.* Beacon, N. Y.: Beacon House, 1947. The German original appeared in 1923.

Moreno, J. L. *Application of the Group Method to Classification.* Washington, D.C.: National Committee on Prisons and Prison Labor, 1932.

Moreno, J. L. *Who Shall Survive?* Washington, D.C.: Nervous and Mental Disease Publishing Company, 1934.

Moreno, J. L. *The First Book on Group Psychotherapy.* 3d edition. Beacon, N. Y.: Beacon House, 1956.

Moreno, J. L. (ed.). *The International Handbook of Group Psychotherapy.* New York: Philosophical Library, 1966.

Mullan, H., and M. Rosenbaum. *Group Psychotherapy, Theory and Practice.* New York: Penguin Books, 1957.

Newburger, H. M. The effect of group therapy upon certain aspects of the behavior and attitudes of institutionalized delinquents; the evaluation of certain aspects of behavior and attitudes toward self, others, and some social institutions following group therapy. *Dissert. Ab.* 12, 597-8.

Newburger, H. M. & Schauer, G. Sociometric evaluation of group psychotherapy. *Group Psychotherapy* 1953, 6, 7-20.

Peters, H. N. & Jones, F. D. Evaluation of group psychotherapy by means of performance tests. *J. Consult. Psychol.* 1951, 51, 363-367.

Peyman, D. A. R. An investigation of the effects of group psychotherapy on chronic schizophrenic patients. *Group Psychotherapy.* 1956, 9, 35-39.

Renouvier, P. *The Group Psychotherapy Movement.* Psychodrama and Group Psychology Monograph No. 33, 1958.

Roman, M. Tutorial group therapy: a study of integration of remedial reading and group therapy in the treatment of delinquents. *Dissert. Ab.* 1955, 15, 1761.

Sacks, J. M. & Berger, S. Group therapy techniques with hospitalized chronic schizophrenic patients. *J. Consult. Psychol.* 1954, 18, 297-302.

Scire, H. G. Changes in behavior and personality following use of chlorpromazine and reserpine: adjunct, group therapy: comparison of the immediate administration of a chemotherapeutic program with group therapy administered after delay, i.e., after a period of exposure to group therapy. *Dissert. Ab.* 1959, 19, 3222.

Semon, R. G. & Goldstein, N. The effectiveness of group psychotherapy with chronic patients and an evaluation of different therapeutic methods. *J. Consult. Psychol.* 1957, 21, 317-322.

Shatter, F. An investigation of the effectiveness of a group therapy program, including the child and his mother, for the remediation of reading disability. *Dissert. Ab.* 1957, 17, 1032.

Sheldon, D. & Landsman, T. An investigation of nondirective group therapy with students in academic difficulty. *J. Consult. Psychol.* 1950, 14, 210-215.

Singer, J. L. & Goldman, G. D. Experimentally contrasted social atmospheres in group psychotherapy with chronic schizophrenics. *J. Soc. Psychol.* 1954, 40, 23-37.

Temmer, H. W. An investigation into the effects of psychotherapy upon habitual avoidance and escape patterns displayed by delinquent adolescent girls. *Dissert. Ab.* 1958, 18, 304.

Wilcox, G. T. Changes in adjustment of institutionalized female defectives following group psychotherapy. *Dissert. Ab.* 1957, 17, 402.

Wright, F. H. An evaluation of the candidate employee programs in the rehabilitation of psychiatric patients. *Dissert. Ab.* 1957, 17, 1604.

Yormak, B. B. An investigation of behavior changes following general semantic training of neuropsychiatric patients. *Dissert. Ab.* 1957, 17, 402-3.
256

LSD-TYPE DRUGS AND PSYCHEDELIC THERAPY

SANFORD UNGER, PH.D.
(with the assistance of the Spring Grove
Psychedelic Therapy Research Group:
Albert Kurland, John Shaffer, Charles Savage,
Sidney Wolf, Robert Leihy, O. Lee McCabe, and
Harry Shock)
Spring Grove State Hospital

Editorial Note

In recent months LSD has become a household word. Widespread misuse of LSD-type drugs has at times had tragic consequences which have obscured their potential use as therapeutic aids in the treatment of neuroses and psychosomatic illness. Clinical investigators continue, however, to show a growing interest in the theory and practice of therapy based on controlled use of these drugs. The following account of the so-called "psychedelic" procedure suggests that patients who fail to respond to other forms of treatment may be helped by psychotherapy incorporating the administration of these drugs.

Dr. Sanford Unger is Chief of Psychosocial Research of Friends of Psychiatric Research, Inc., Spring Grove State Hospital, Baltimore, Maryland, and Chief Therapist of the Psychedelic Therapy Research Program. He began LSD work at Spring Grove in 1963 on official loan from the National Institute of Mental Health, where he served, from 1960-1964, as Research Psychologist in the Laboratory of Psychology.

Dr. Unger received his B.A. degree from Antioch College and his M.A. and Ph.D. degrees from Cornell University. In 1958-1959, he was a Senior Fellow of the Cornell Graduate

School. In 1959-1960, he was Chairman of Psychology at Shimer College.

Dr. Unger has published papers in developmental and neuropsychology as well as the area of psychedelic therapy. Recently, he authored "LSD: The Spring Grove Experiment," a guide to the CBS television documentary being distributed by McGraw-Hill Text-Film Division.

•

LSD-TYPE DRUGS AND PSYCHEDELIC THERAPY

"Considering the state of our knowledge, we still do not seem sufficiently daring and experimental about therapeutic tactics . . . we know so little about the process of helping that the only proper attitude is one of maximum experimentalism" (Meehl, 1955, p. 374).

In the search for new techniques which might enhance the efficacy of psychotherapy, LSD-type drugs have been claimed or conceived for some time to hold unusual promise (see Unger, 1963; 1964). The development and systematic assessment of psychedelic therapy, incorporating a procedure of high-dose LSD administration first reported by Osmond (1957), has been underway at Spring Grove State Hospital for over three years. Although complete data are not yet in, all present results from this work point to the following conclusions:

(1) that trained personnel can implement the psychedelic procedure with relatively high safety; and

(2) that its judicious use can importantly and perhaps uniquely facilitate the achievement of a variety of psychotherapeutic objectives.

Psychedelic Therapy

a. Nomenclature and Overview. *Psychedelic therapy* refers to an overall theory and practice of treatment. The *psychedelic procedure*, alternatively called "the session" or the LSD session, refers to a specialized set of techniques for programming and guiding the reaction to LSD (or an LSD-type drug) within the context of ongoing psychedelic therapy. (Thus, a patient may receive psychedelic therapy for six months but have only one LSD session.) The psychedelic procedure is expressly designed to produce the *psychedelic reaction*. The psychedelic reaction may occupy only intermittent minutes of the full 10-12 hours of an LSD session; however, such episodes, characterized, subjectively, by profound meaningfulness and an extraordinary depth and intensity of positive emotion, are the hallmark of psychedelic therapy. In other (non-drug) contexts, such reactions have been referred to as "peak," "identity," or "conversion" experiences, or "encounters." The emergence of psychedelic therapy as a distinctive treatment form is based on the reliable reproducibility of the psychedelic reaction.

At present, psychedelic therapy is composed largely of strategies and tactics of treatment; theory development has been sketchy. In general, pathological functioning in the patient is presumed to have been determined by the reinforcement history which would have predisposed toward root "defects" in the self-system (self-image, self-esteem, self-trust, sense of basic worth), and associated value-attitude distortions and "inadequacies." The major effort of psychedelic therapy is reconstructive, premised on the possibility—via the psychedelic reaction—of rapidly establishing and then consolidating the patient's functioning on a core of positive self-acceptance and regard.

b. LSD and the psychedelic reaction. In dosages of 200 mcgms. or more, LSD produces a 10-12 hour period of unusually striking, varied, and anomalous mental functioning; the range of possible effects and/or episodes of reaction is panoramic. Certain dimensions of possible reactivity are therapeutically irrelevant (e.g., sensory changes); others are of distinctly antitherapeutic consequence (e.g., panic or terror, or psychotic reactions). The major dimension of therapeutic relevance of drug-altered reactivity is the affective or emotional sphere; intense, labile, personally-meaningful as well as ego-transcending emotionality is uniformly produced, with periodic episodes or "shock waves" of overwhelming feeling.

It is perhaps needless to note that the use of LSD is not

predicated on any conventional drug or chemotherapeutic model. In the context of psychedelic therapy, the LSD session is undertaken only after the therapist 1) has gained intimate knowledge of the patient's developmental history, dynamics, defenses, and difficulties; 2) close rapport has been established; and 3) the patient has been specifically and comprehensively prepared for the procedure. The therapist, in a demanding and arduous role, attends the patient throughout the entire period of drug action. The purpose of the high-dose LSD session is not conceived as diagnostic or uncovering but rather as corrective and remedial. Overall, beyond forestalling or attenuating anti-therapeutic developments. the psychedelic procedure is designed to program and guide the evolving episodes of experience so as to regularly achieve meaningful catharsis, reciprocal inhibition of anxiety, conflict resolution, emotionally-validated insight, attitude redirection, elevated self-esteem, and deepened philosophical perspective.

The *rapidity* with which major changes in certain aspects of a patient's psychological picture may be accomplished is one of the unique advantages of psychedelic therapy. As indicated, the pivotal event in accomplishing this turnabout is conceived to be the psychedelic reaction. While paroxysmal electrical activity triggered by LSD in limbic systems (Monroe, 1957) is guessed to constitute the key neurophysiological substrate of psychedelic reactivity, such reactions are not simple drug effects. Rather, they seem to be a complexly-determined outcome of adequate (high) dosage, structured preparation, therapeutic session management, and selected auditory input.

The effects of the first several hours of a psychedelic session are non-specific and pervasive: perseverative preoccupations and emotional distress patterns are "broken" or fragmented; subsequent recall for this period is nearly always poor. During the fourth to fifth hours, psychedelic reactivity usually appears at peak intensity (though this is somewhat unpredictable). With skillful handling, the remainder of the session may be stabilized in an elevated mood state—psychotic and other turbulent phenomena are no longer spectres. Resistance (defensiveness) is much reduced; psychodynamic resolution may proceed efficiently, and depths of positive interpersonal emotion may be mobilized and reeducatively explored.

The short-term consequences of a stabilized psychedelic reaction are often quite remarkable. Mood is elevated and energetic; there is a relative freedom from concerns of the past, from guilt and anxiety; and the disposition and capacity to enter into close interpersonal relationships is enhanced. This psychedelic "after-glow" generally persists for from two weeks to a month and then gradually fades. The therapeutic challenge has revolved, first, on reliably producing the psychedelic reaction, and then more importantly, on learning to utilize this extraordinary, "paranormal" phenomenon as a fulcrum of enduring personality reconstruction.

c. Advantages. As already indicated, the rapidity of meaningful impact is one principal virtue of psychedelic therapy. Within a matter of a month into therapy, for example, persisting depression may be relieved, generalized anxiety and preoccupying distress reduced in salience, and constructive motivation established. The patient may already be able to resume his position in society, while therapy proceeds in increasingly productive fashion.

The significance of a rapid and radical benign alteration in the patient's pattern of functioning, while it would seem of general value, is crucial in the treatment of alcoholism. Conventional therapy has been singularly unsuccessful with this patient category as the very nature of the condition, the inability to maintain sobriety, has seemed utterly to compromise the possibility of therapeutic progress. Hence, the especial affinity and relevance of psychedelic therapy for the alcoholic patient is apparent.

Another advantage, as it has emerged during the course of our work, has been the apparent effectiveness of psychedelic therapy with culturally-deprived patients of low intelligence. Needless to note, these patients are very poor candidates for conventional therapy. The route to emotional re-education represented by the psychedelic procedure, however, seems not at all prejudicial against individuals of poor verbal skills or sophistication.

Additionally, other patients who ordinarily would be considered exceedingly difficult or inappropriate candidates for conventional treatment, by virtue of their inability to enter into a therapeutic relationship (e.g., sociopathic and other personality disorders), may apparently be engaged by the psychedelic procedure and continue much more meaningfully and effectively in therapy.

d. Safety. In view of the oft-expressed concern about the dangers of LSD, although it has been repeatedly shown that trained personnel can use the drug without danger (see Cohen, 1960), the safety record at Spring Grove had best be mentioned. Despite severe pathology in many of the approximately 175 cases treated, there has been only one adverse reaction, and that occurring in a schizophrenic patient in remission, was readily reversible by standard chemo- and psychotherapy. In addition, it may be worthy of note, in view of persistent concern about LSD abuse, that not a single patient treated at Spring Grove, to our knowledge, has engaged in subsequent illegitimate use of the drug.

In-Progress Research

After a somewhat extended period of exploration and development, during which time 69 alcoholic and seven neurotic patients were treated (see Kurland *et al.*, 1967), two controlled studies of the efficacy of psychedelic psychotherapy were initiated. Both studies, still in progress at the present time, are about 2/3 through the clinical phase; both utilize double-blind methodology, both cover an active treatment period of six months.

In the study of psychedelic therapy with alcoholics supported under PHS Grant 7 M.H. 08074, volunteer patients hospitalized in the Spring Grove alcoholic rehabilitation unit are randomly assigned to experimental and control groups. All testing and treatment is exactly the same for both groups with the single exception being the dosage of LSD in the implementation of the psychedelic procedure. Under strictly double-blind conditions, control patients receive 50 mcgms. of LSD, considered to be an active placebo dose in that it is inadequate to produce the psychedelic reaction. The experimental group receives 450 mcgms. This dosage differential is maintained through any repeat sessions deemed indicated by clinical judgment throughout the active treatment period. Follow-up contact, assessment, and evaluation, performed entirely independently of the clinical staff, is accomplished for all patients at six months, twelve months, and 18 months after entry into the program. The objectives of this study are to systematically assess whether and in what dimensions or degree the psychedelic (high-dose) procedure materially affects the outcome of therapy with chronic alcoholic patients. Over 60 patients of an anticipated 99 have completed or have been started in active treatment in this program. Recently, for purposes of this presentation, the blind was broken on the cases who had passed the first six-month evaluation point. (Note: The blind was broken in such a way as not at all to contaminate the continuing evaluation). Out of a total of 29 patients who had been located and interviewed, ratings of global improved adjustment were over twice as high in the experimental as compared to the control group, with the rate of complete abstinence in the experimental (high-dose) group running well over 50 per cent.

The study of psychedelic therapy with neurotics, supported under PHS Grant MH-11001, in fact includes a diversity of patient types: severe depressives, sociopaths, and borderline cases. The objectives and methodology of this study are similar to those outlined above, with the addition of another comparison group. Patients referred by ward psychiatrists, acceptable to the study, are randomly assigned to 1) an intensive group psychotherapy condition, and to 2) experimental or 3) control psychedelic therapy groups, with the controls receiving the active placebo (50 mcgm. dose) and the experimentals receiving 350 mcgms. under double-blind conditions and with all other treatment and evaluation considerations being identical. Nearly 60 patients of an anticipated 99 have either completed or are in process of completing the six-month treatment period. While clinical impressions are favorable, data are not yet available from this study; hence, it may prove of value to examine the MMPI's of the first seven patients who comprised an open psychedelic therapy pilot study prior to the controlled phase. These patients covered a range of diagnoses, and in two cases had had many years of prolonged hospitalization. Composite MMPI Profiles (see Fig. 1) show their pretreatment status, their

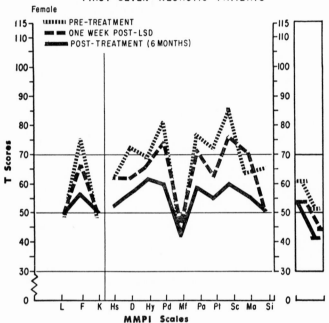

Figure I

improvement after the first high-dose LSD session (about one month after beginning psychedelic therapy) and their status at the end of the six-month treatment period. Patients were released from the hospital as soon as seemed clinically advisable and carried through the treatment period as out-patients, with brief rehospitalization if and when needed—four of the seven patients did have at least one additional LSD session. All of the patients, to present knowledge, have done well since the close of active treatment; none has been rehospitalized.

Case Illustration

In order to illustrate the details of the therapeutic process, it is the intention to present the case of one of the pilot study "neurotic" patients, N-5. Though no case is "typical," this one recommends itself because of unusual difficulty; it demonstrates both the strengths and limitations of the treatment. As well, the patient wrote an especially articulate account of her first session, conveying more effectively than can discursive discussion the nature and impact of the psychedelic procedure.

Pre-treatment Assessment

Prior to the initiation of therapy, upon referral to the program by the ward psychiatrist, a social history is taken and psychometric testing performed; relevant data are summarized below.

Patient N-5: Social History

"This is patient N-5's fourth admission to Spring Grove. She is a 23 year old Baltimorean, unmarried, but has one child—a one and a half year old son. This young woman had an unpleasant and unhappy childhood. Her father deserted the family when she was an infant. She describes her mother as being cold and indifferent.

"By age 14 she had been found delinquent by the Juvenile Court of Baltimore County, spent six weeks at the girls' training school, and was put on probation. At age 16, by the order of that court, she was committed to Spring Grove and remained over one and a half years. The diagnosis was Adjustment Reaction, Childhood. When discharged she began a pattern of loose and promiscuous living.

"At age 20, while working at a private psychiatric institution, she met an alcoholic patient with whom she eloped from

265

the institution. She lived with him off and on for over two years. Twice within one year, in 1963, she was admitted to Spring Grove. The diagnosis was Depressive Reaction. In 1964 she had four months of private psychiatric treatment.

"For several months before this admission to Spring Grove she says that she 'ran wild.' She held a clerical job in a downtown office but was out every night frequenting all the night spots and was neglectful of the baby. She blandly admits being promiscuous and ultimately became very depressed. She was arguing with everyone constantly, was crying, and upset. Finally, she voluntarily came to the hospital.

"This young woman recounts events in her background coldly and casually—in a detached manner. The impression is that her demeanor is very unpredictable."

Patient N-5's pre-session Raven I.Q. score was 94. Her MMPI profile is shown in Figure 2. Clinical evaluation of the MMPI follows:

"The profile of this patient suggests the presence of severe psychopathology. Primary elevations are on scales measuring psychopathy and unusualness of thought content. Secondary elevations are on scales measuring depression and anxiety— 'psychic pain,' in short. Diagnostically, this is the profile of a personality disorder, currently experiencing severe anxiety and depression. Reality contact appears tenuous, and psychotic episodes are a distinct possibility. Poor judgment and impulsive acting-out are likely characteristics. The relatively low *Mf* score in the presence of the other scale elevations suggests masochistic feminine attitudes."

Pre-Session Therapy

"We have much to learn about peak experiences: their differentiation from some brands of psychotic experiences which subjectively appear very similar, their different contexts and the preconditions of their occurrence and of their dynamic effectiveness. Should we at any time incorporate similar exceptional states into the

266

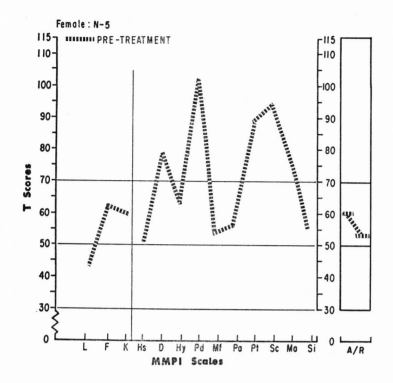

Figure 2

therapeutic process—e.g., through the use of consciousness expanding drugs—I believe that patients would have to be prepared for them just as they must be prepared to make effective use of insights . . . to be prepared means having a real need for new answers; it means expecting them and knowing concretely how to put them to use, the *right* use, and realizing clearly that one might be tempted to put the experience to neurotic uses. Unless exceptional experiences are integrated with the pattern of health, the very fascination they arouse can actually divert the person from the task of reorganizing his life . . ." (Angyal, 1965, p. 297).

The treatment program begins with the patient intensively engaged in near-daily psychotherapy. Although a brochure of information and expectation-structuring articles on the use of LSD in treatment is given to the patient for outside reading, the forthcoming session itself is largely ignored during this period. With the therapist assuming the role of compassionate taskmaster, concentrated and repeated attention is focused on tracing and delineating the influences and determining factors in the emergence of the patient's self-system and related attitudes and assumptions—pinpointing their dynamic involvement in unproductive, self-defeating behavior patterns. The therapist, via his commitment and concern, also transmits his belief in the capacity of the patient to establish his functioning on a foundation of positive self-acceptance—in a world perceived, not as alien, but as a source of potential satisfaction.

Pre-session therapy with patient N-5 filled out the developmental picture as follows: The predominant influence in the patient's first five years was the maternal grandmother; the patient's mother worked and was largely out of the home. The grandmother pampered the child in a manipulative way, demanding loyalty to herself rather than the mother. The patient's most vivid recollections from this stage of childhood were of squabblings at the dinner table, and her own consistent refusal to eat unless she was literally spoon-fed by the grandmother.

When the patient was five years old, her mother began a new courtship. The grandmother, disapproving, issued dire warnings to the patient about its consequences—effectively training the child to dislike and fear her prospective stepfather.

The patient's mother did marry, and amidst great turmoil, a move was made to an apartment shared with the stepfather's mother, that is, N-5's step-maternal grandmother. The patient's new grandmother, from the very beginning, openly disliked and resented her. She was irked by the overcrowding—the patient, at this time, shared a bedroom with the grandmother—and she engaged in vicious verbal abuse of the child.

Two sons were born to the new couple in rapid succession. When N-5 was about eight years old, she attempted to drown one of her infant half-brothers in the bath tub—which was only narrowly averted by the stepfather. At this point also, a full-blown pattern of stealing, indiscriminate lying, and like rebellious behaviors emerged in the child. She recalls only feelings of hate for the stepfather and stepgrandmother; she did periodically try, though unsuccessfully, to win the mother's affection and approval by occasional conformity. By age 10, after setting a fire in the kitchen of her home, the patient ran away for the first time.

The feelings of self-disgust and self-hatred in patient N-5 were profound; as she described herself, "I am filled with filth." Increasingly, during three weeks of pre-session therapy, she seemed definitely to be engaged and reached, with the development of a modicum of insight. The therapeutic relationship approached to as good rapport as seemed possible at the time.

Pre-Session Preparation

"Vergil guided Dante into the Inferno and returned him safely, chastened and enlightened. Those who would use LSD should do as well for their patients" (Savage, 192, p. 434).

Largely, "expectations" regarding the LSD session are structured by outside readings, although the therapist, also, implicitly, reinforces the hope that there are resources of strength and goodness within the patient whose existence has been buried by the pathogenic influences and pathological functioning of the past. It is the aim, primarily, to see that such potentials are revealed. At the same time, the pathways to such desired objectives, it is conveyed, may be difficult to negotiate and require courage and faith.

Specifically, in the pre-LSD preparation several key issues are worked through and emphasized.

The patient is enjoined that "LSD does not put anything into him"; that it alters the experience of oneself by unlocking "silent" and closed-off areas, but that "everything that he experiences comes from him, reflects what is *in him*, makes manifest some aspect of his functioning or potential." Further, the

269

patient is assured that there is nothing within that he cannot face; nothing that can emerge that cannot be "handled," that does not have meaning, that cannot be understood with beneficial result.

The patient is enjoined against excessive discussion, intellectualization, or analysis—rather, he is told to "just be," to let the music carry him. (In LSD dosages of 200 mcgms. or more, the capacity for normal ego functioning and "volitional" control is much attenuated; especially in the first three to four hours of a session, efforts at prolonged verbalization or logical formulation are likely to lead to distressed confusion.)

The patient is prepared for the possibility of unusual somatic effects, for fear reactions (either general or specific), for depression, and for the dynamic significance of "distrust," as well as other potentially alarming, frightening or antitherapeutic reactions or developments.

Insofar as it is possible, the patient is literally rehearsed for the course and conduct of the session day, including a brief exposure, while wearing a sleep shade (designed to cut down on the distracting instability of the external visual world), to stereophonic headphones. The importance of music in programming an LSD session should not be underestimated; next to his knowledge of the patient and the established relationship, music is probably the therapist's most important tool in guiding the course of the session. Music not only "speaks" a direct emotional language but, in addition, choral and vocal selections contain specific verbal-symbolic (attitudinal) input.

As a final item of the pre-session preparation, the course of therapy is reviewed. The dynamics of the patient's difficulties and "disorders" are summarized, along with reinforcement of hopefully identified, if heretofore submerged, potentials.

The Session

"Emotions grasp vitally that of which thoughts are merely a pale reflector; they are concrete value experiences and thus are the springs of our actions. Insight can pave the way to change only if, seeing the state of affairs differently, we also come to *feel* differently about it. . . . Insights accompanied or followed by a strong and appropriate emotional response—one might call them *vital insights*—have the best chance of becoming effective, at once or in time" (Angyal, 1965, p. 271).

For the therapist, the session is arduous, often exhausting—but very rewarding. Along with a female nurse, the therapist spends the 12 hours of the session day in constant attendance on the patient. The nurse keeps a time-indexed record of the patient's statements and significant events, including the musical selections; this is given to the patient at the end of the day and usually helps in the session write-up requested of all patients.

Patient N-5 received a total LSD dosage of 300 micrograms —200 in a first administration, followed by an additional 100 an hour later. Her report, slightly edited, follows.

Patient N-5: LSD Session Report

"I must admit that in the beginning, I was quite apprehensive and more than a little afraid. The nurse had come and got me at about eight-thirty. I felt a little more comfortable when I got in the treatment room where I had spent so many hours in therapy. When the doctor came in I was even more comforted as I knew he understood and would be there to help and guide me.

"I drank my LSD at 8:45. From that point on time had no perspective. The doctor, the nurse, and I looked at some pictures of myself and my family. I began to feel dizzy and wanted to lie down. Then the thought occurred to me that I'd better go to the bathroom first. When I got up the floor seemed to tilt and roll. It wasn't an unpleasant sensation, however. I came back from the bathroom and the eye shades and earphones were put into place. The doctor squeezed my hand and suddenly I wasn't afraid anymore. I drifted with the music and was at one with the music.

"My sense of touch became very intensified. The

blanket that was covering me became alive. I remember touching my face and feeling every particle of my skin.

"I was drifting with the music and I had the sense that I was dying. I was at my funeral. I could smell all of the flowers. I cried, but I didn't want to escape from the feeling. I somehow knew that I had to die in order to be born again.

"The music was stopped and the eyeshades and earphones removed. The colors in the room were vibrating and alive. I talked with the doctor and asked him if I had died. I was still crying.

"I lay back down and the shades and earphones were put in place. Again, I drifted with the music.

"Suddenly my body seemed to grow very warm. I felt with every sense of my being that I was in Hell. My body grew warmer and warmer, then suddenly burst into fire. I was afraid, then the doctor took my hand. I lay there and let my body burn up. The fire seemed to cleanse me. Then all sensation seemed to fade and I asked to sit up.

"The doctor showed me some pictures. One was called the Guardian Angel. To me, at the time, it represented a mother and child. I said with amazement, 'It's me. I'm crying. My baby!'

"All at once, after all the doubts and fears, I knew I was a mother and that I loved my child!

"The earphones and shades were put back in place and the music playing was 'The Lord's Prayer.' There must have been a short pause in the music but to me it seemed an eternity. I said, 'Don't stop it. God is whole in me.' At this point, I felt as if God were holding me in His arms and revealing Himself to me. I smiled and said, 'I've found Him, I've found Him!' I had such a tremendous sense of peace and well being. After so many years of running alone and afraid, God was now with me.

"The music stopped and I lay relaxed and said, 'But I found a reason for it all.' God's place in the universe, in the world, and in myself seemed so clear. He is love and He is life. He is in everything. And finally, at long last, He was also in me.

"I looked at a picture of my son and I felt an overwhelming sense of love and for the first time gratitude for my motherhood. I was crying but crying with joy and thankfulness. I wiped away the cleansing, wonderful tears.

"I then looked at a picture of myself when I was fifteen. I knew that the girl in that picture never was; the person was never real. I tore up the picture and pointed to myself. 'This is what she is.' I was on the road to discovering myself.

"It was now 11:20. I had been under the LSD for only three hours, however, it seemed as if it had been eternities. I had no sense of time. I can remember at one point asking the doctor what time it was and he answered, 'Twenty minutes to eternity.'

"I lay relaxed and smoked a cigarette. I was shown a picture of the Christ Child and His mother. I said with wonder, 'She's not afraid of Him—I'm not afraid!' It had been fear of love that had kept me from loving my son.

"The earphones and shades were put in place and again I drifted with the music. I had a tremendous sense of life and living. I exclaimed, 'I'm alive! All the twenty-three years I had been here I had never really been alive. I had only existed!' The music again paused and again I said, 'Don't let it go away. I don't want it to go away!'

"Then, the music changed. The record was Mahalia Jackson. The sound pounded around me. It seemed as if the music was trying to consume me. I knew fear, stark, naked fear. Fear was all around me, covering me. The music shouted at me and vibrated through me. I tore off the earphones and shades and shouted, 'Turn it off!' It was as if it didn't stop, it would destroy me.

"The doctor turned off the music and blessed silence filled the room. I said, 'I don't think I've ever been so afraid!' I knew then that I was running away. My words

273

were, 'I was running away, wasn't I? I was all the way back in Hell and I wasn't afraid. What frightened me? I was never so afraid!'

"The doctor talked to me of fear and fear of fear. I realized that I had been consumed with fear all my life. He said, 'This is the time. Let's go toward it.' I said, 'I'm afraid—I don't want to go.'

"Then, suddenly, I knew that I had to face whatever there was to come. It was now or never. I held to the doctor's hand and said, 'Don't let me run anymore.' I was too tired to run anymore.

"The music again took over and I felt comforted. I relaxed and was just one with the music.

"When the music stopped, I looked about the room and the colors were alive. They glowed. I wanted a purple glass that was on the table. I wanted to feel the color. I seemed to be one with the soft glowing purple.

"I went to the bathroom and looked out the window. The earth seemed to vibrate with life. I exclaimed, 'It's alive! It's a wonderful world. I don't have to run anymore.'

"Back in the treatment room the rose seemed to radiate life. I felt it, smelled it, savored it.

"Again the shades and earphones were put into place and I drifted with the music. The record was 'Oh Come Immanuel.' Again, I had the sense of being with God. He was holding me in His arms and He was revealing life to me. Then suddenly, light was all around me, and love, wonderful, overwhelming love, was all around me.

"I could love and be loved. After so many years of wandering I had come home. My words were, 'I walked with God, completely with God. I know what love is. I have *so much* to give. I've been so empty—that's not important now.' I was crying for joy and thankfulness. I had received the most priceless gifts there are—the gifts of life and love. The music continued and I cried, 'I'm crying for joy!'

"The music stopped, and I removed the shades and earphones and sat up. The doctor gave me a mirror. I

274

looked and saw myself. I radiated love. I said, 'I see love, so much love. It was there all along. Oh, I love me!

"I know now where I was. I was at the beginning of my life. I had just been born. I was alive! After twenty-three dead, wasted years I had been born. Thank God I was finally alive! I said in awe, 'I don't have to run anymore. I can be with myself—it's so wonderful, so wonderful. I'm so thankful. I can just feel it all over me.'

"Again, I went back with the music and knew only joy. The music flowed over me and I was elated. The sound flowed through every fiber of my body. The music stopped and I laughed and laughed with pure joy. I asked for a drink of water and it was nectar. I cried, 'I want to embrace the whole world. I found God—it was so important. I'm not alone any more. I'll never be alone again.' I looked at a picture of my son, and felt as if I would burst with love.

"Again I listened to the music. When it stopped, I looked at a picture of my mother. The hate I had once felt dissolved and I knew only compassion. I said, 'I feel so sorry for her.'

"I went again to the bathroom and this time the sun came in through the window and I travelled up the rays and went into the sun. It was warm and dancing and vibrating with golden color.

"Once again I returned to the couch and listened to the music. When the music stopped, the doctor and I had sandwiches. I ate a salami sandwich and relished every bite. I can truthfully say it was the best thing I've ever eaten.

"Later, the doctor and I went for a walk and I literally discovered the world. I saw, smelled, and touched the trees, flowers, and grass. I touched the bark of a tree and felt the life running through it feeding the deep green leaves. I touched the grass and it felt like velvet. The soft warm air embraced me. This was life; this was my world and I was at home.

"We returned to the treatment room and continued to

listen to music. The music seemed to reach and awaken a depth in me that I never knew existed. When Beethoven's ninth was playing, I was completely at one with the music. With each note I seemed to soar to higher heights.

"At about 9:00 p.m. I returned to the ward and drifted off into a dreamless sleep. When I awoke, the next morning, I saw my rose on the nightstand and for the first time in my life, I thanked God that I was alive."

Post-Session Assessment

"A neurotic individual carries in himself a secret concept which may be stated as: If people knew all there was to know about me (that is, my 'bad unconscious'), they would think that I was a pretty unpleasant, worthless individual. . . . Under LSD some actually experience walking into the shadow and finding a great inner light. . . . The result . . . is that the individual has a new, total view of himself. He sees that he has good in him, that he has value. He finds that he can like himself more, that he can love himself. Such positive changes towards one's self also alter one's view of other people, for one's concept of others is always colored by the way one sees himself. If the individual accepts himself more, trusts himself more, loves himself more, he can also trust others and love others to a greater degree" (Downing and Wiegant, 1964 p. 191).

On the day following the session, and for a while thereafter, N-5 was described as "radiant" (the psychedelic "after-glow"). She reflected, as William James would have it:

"A feeling of being in a wider life than that of this world's selfish little interests . . . An immense elation and freedom. A shifting of the emotional center towards loving and harmonious affections. . . ." (James, 1902, p. 289).

N-5's post-session Raven I.Q. tested at 112—a significant increase over the pre-treatment score of 94. Her MMPI, administered one week post-session, is shown in Figure 3 below; the evaluation follows:

276

"Post LSD-session, marked improvement has taken place in a number of symptom areas. Depression and anxiety have both been reduced to within normal limits. Perhaps even more striking, however, has been the reduction in psychotic elements. Reality contact appears firm and there is no longer any suggestion of an imminent psychotic break. However, although the patient is undoubtedly more psychologically comfortable, in view of the continuing indications of an 'acting-out' personality disorder, any long-range prognosis must be guarded."

Post-session Therapy

"For the majority of patients, the task of recovering falls into two parts: getting well and staying well" (Angyal, 1965, p. 256).

The fundamental aim of the psychedelic procedure is to frontally assault the negative assumptive systems which have mediated an essentially unproductive contact with life. The profound, directly-confronted, corrective emotional experiences of a session pave the way for the establishment of psychological functioning on a positive foundation. However, for the majority of patients, this is just the beginning.

The therapeutic task remains of effectively reinforcing the patient's commitment to his discovered potentials, of consolidating a set of stable "self-equilibrating" reactions, which will call the patient back to his "new identity" whenever relapses into old thought and feeling patterns occur. At the same time, habits of constructive growth must be widened and entrenched, ensuring an increasing range and frequency of such positive emotional states as satisfaction, joy, and love.

Through a continuing reinforcement period, sometimes gently, sometimes forcefully, unequivocal commitment is engendered to *the basic assumption:* that life can make sense and provide satisfactions. Periods of depression and anxiety are seen for what they are: part and parcel of the human condition, to be expected, but not to be unnecessarily prolonged or perpetuated. In times of stress, patients must learn, "take one day

277

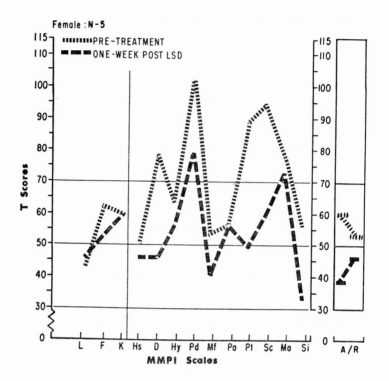

Figure 3

at a time," making that day as good a day as possible by remaining open and attentive to the opportunities for positive emotional experiences that are offered; additionally, to be clinically perceptive to other people as well as themselves—to be compassionate and constructive in human relationships, seeing beneath objectionable "defensive" behaviors, and understanding them in others as one has learned to understand and forgive in oneself. And over and again: the basic, affirmative commitment to life, to growth toward stability in inner comfort, zest, and self-respect.

In the days following the session, any tendencies toward euphoria must be firmly moderated. Integration of gains, it is reiterated, requires time, self-discipline, and increased self-knowledge. As soon as possible after the session, the patient begins writing a detailed account of its significant events in order both to "imprint" major accomplishments and to provide an enduring record which may often or occasionally be re-read.

Presuming that a sufficient degree of improvement has been achieved, patients are returned rather quickly to the community, and therapy continues on an out-patient basis. Patient N-5, after obtaining a job and inexpensive living quarters, left the hospital several weeks after her session. During her hospitalization, her son had been placed in a foster home through the auspices of a welfare agency, and with the patient's consent, this arrangement was continued. She ended an ill-starred affair that had been begun before therapy, visited her child regularly, and eagerly awaited and desired therapeutic appointments. She tried, with moderate success, to live according to the credo: Do not do anything for which you will dislike yourself. At the same time, she read avidly and entered into several wholesome social activities.

Nevertheless, she grew increasingly restive with the tedium of her job, despaired of really making something of her life, and at such times, would relapse into manipulative and destructive behaviors.

Her mother, who had heretofore disowned her, "allowed" her to return home for the Christmas holiday. She reacted to "Christmas with mother" with renewed feelings of deep unworthiness. Leaving the family home in a depressed state of mind, she entered into a casual sexual liaison which "filled her with self-revulsion." Shortly thereafter, arrangements were made for rehospitalization, specifically for further intensive therapy and another LSD session.

As has been frequent in our experience, the second session was very different from the first; repeat sessions tend to be more psychodynamic and less psychedelic in content. Although, before the session, there had been considerable "working through" of her decision to have her son adopted, feelings of guilt and remorse over her plan of action and past treatment of the child emerged explosively. She was finally able to accept, though late in the session, that such feelings came from and reflected a basic "goodness" in her. Persistently, she was haunted by a sense of frightening isolation and feelings that she could never escape from her past—which mocked her present aspirations and marked her as evil and dirty. Working through these feelings, resolution emerged with deep emotional insight into her own developmental dynamics: she grasped at core levels the relation and transition between the loneliness, fright, hurt, and rejection that she experienced as a child, and the hard, bitter, unfeeling, self-destructive adolescent she became. Again, she could finally accept that while she *feared* that she was "all bad," that these were just fears, that she (the essential self) was not her fears.

There was no psychedelic reaction, and no after-glow. At the end of the session, the patient was exhausted but relieved. She had been stripped bare, she felt; she had faced her deepest fears, without distortions or fantasies, and she had clearly seen into her own developmental dynamics and the vicious circles of destructive thought and behavior in which she had been caught.

The confrontation of the second session seemed to complement the discoveries of the first. During the postsession period, stable self-acceptance and self-compassion appeared to consolidate.

Within a week after the session, N-5 left the hospital; her six-month therapy period was at an end, and subsequent therapeutic contacts were less than sporadic. In closing accounts, it may be noted that ward nursing personnel, long familiar with the patient, considered the changes which had taken place in her to be very impressive.

Follow-up

Patient N-5 occasionally wrote to her therapist in the months that followed. One letter began: "Happy anniversary to me." It was one year after the *first* session, and since it sheds light on the significance of the psychedelic reaction, the first paragraph of the letter is reproduced:

"Do you realize that exactly one year has gone by since

the most memorable day of my life? At this time last year, I was enraptured in divinity. I guess I still am only it's not as magnified. There's just a warm place deep inside me. A place that knows that I'm a part of everything and everyone. A place that knows beauty and love. A place that reaches blindly and without question toward the infinite. A place that is at peace even while the rest of me is at war. And no matter what happens, that place will be there forever and ever."

The last follow-up interview with the patient, conducted 15 months after her initial entry into therapy and nine months after the conclusion of therapy, reported on her course and status as follows:

Patient N-5: Follow-up Interview

"After her second LSD session, the patient went to work as an aide at a private mental hospital, where she lived in. While there, she met and befriended a young male patient of very good family background. A satisfying relationship developed and was continued after the patient's discharge.

"During this time, N-5 consented to the adoption of her son. She states that she worked out her guilt over this matter and feels sure that it was in the best interests of the child.

"Shortly thereafter, in a church wedding, and with the consent and approval of the groom's parents as well as her own, she was married to the aforesaid ex-patient. From that time to date, she has had a more satisfying and meaningful adjustment than ever in her life.

"At times, there have been rough spots in her relationship with her husband, who is finding his own way since his hospitalization. However, there have been no insurmountable problems and this period has been stable. She seems to feel more sure of herself and more comfortable than this interviewer has ever seen her before. She does have a health problem, though. In the past month, she has lost 15 lbs. and is seeing a physician regularly. He has diagnosed that she has an ulcer of the colon.

"All in all, she is adjusting well."

"We have no faith in human nature, if you mean that men are naturally good or naturally prepared to get along with each other. We have no truck with philosophies of innate goodness—or evil, either, for that matter. But we do have faith in our power to change human behavior" (Skinner, 1948, p. 196).

While the psychedelic therapy program has now seen a goodly number of treatment-resistant patients display sustained change, in a beneficial direction, over a wide spectrum of behavioral functioning, a major limitation or disadvantage of the psychedelic procedure had best be noted. It revolves on the lengthy period of action of LSD. The session places a very heavy burden on the therapist, and as well, unorthodox schedules are necessary for all clinical personnel. This drawback would seem to render the procedure, as presently implemented, difficult of accommodation or assimilation to existing treatment facilities on a wide scale without great cost.

A number of shorter-acting LSD-type compounds have been identified and tested in recent years: shorter-acting derivatives of psilocybin and psilocin, CEY-19 and CZ-74, as well as the chemically-related drugs diethyltryptamine (DET), dipropyltryptamine (DPT), and dimethyltryptamine (DMT). The agents are mentioned above in decreasing length of average period of action, ranging from 3½ hours (CEY-19 and CZ-74) to 40 minutes (DMT).

Szara, the discoverer and most persistent worker with the tryptamine series, has expressed the hope "that the shorter acting dialkyltryptamines (DET and DPT), which produce qualitatively the same effects as LSD-25," could effectively and conveniently replace the much longer acting LSD-25 (1965). Clinical trials with DPT and DET, with alcoholics, along modified psychedelic therapy lines, have already been performed by Szara and his co-workers at St. Elizabeth's Hospital in Washington, D. C., with promising outcome (see Vourlekis, 1966). Both test data and clinical impressions strongly indicate that the psychedelic reaction may be regularly and reliably produced with these compounds in doses of around 1.0 mg./kg.

Leuner, probably the most experienced clinical LSD investigator in Europe, reporting his experimental trials with CEY-19 and CZ-74, concluded: "These new drugs would seem to be suitable to replace the known hallucinogens in experimental psychiatry and psycholytic therapy." He added: "There is little risk involved in their use in out-patient treatment" (1965).

One major objective of anticipated future research is to explore and develop a psychedelic procedure which, utilizing a short-acting LSD-type drug, might be more readily and widely implemented.

Though it is clear that maximally safe work in this area requires specialized experience and training, LSD-type drugs apparently hold major psychotherapeutic import. Certainly, all present indications call for expanded systematic exploration of techniques of harnessing and utilizing their possibilities in planned (therapeutic) "reprogramming" of nervous system circuitry.

Acknowledgement

Research reported in this paper was supported under PHS Grants Nos. MH-0874 and MH-11001, administered by Friends of Psychiatric Research, Inc.

References

Angyal, A. *Neurosis and treatment.* New York: Wiley, 1965.

Cohen, S. LSD: side effects and complications. *J. Nerv. Ment. Dis.* 1960, 130, 30-40.

Downing, J. and Wiegant, W. Psychedelic experience and religious belief. In Blum, R. and associates, *Utopiates.* New York: Atherton Press, 1964.

James, W. *The varieties of religious experience.* New York: Modern Library, 1902.

Kurland, A., Unger, S., Shaffer, J., Savage, C., Wolf, S. Leihy, R., and McCabe, O. Psychedelic therapy (utilizing LSD) in the treatment of the alcoholic patient. *A. J. Psychiat.* 1967, in press.

Leuner, H., and Baer, G. Two new short-acting hallucinogens of the psilocybin group. In Bente, D. and Bradley, P. (eds.) *Neuropsychopharmacology*, Vol. 4. Amsterdam: Elsevier, 1965.

Meehl, P. Psychotherapy. *Ann. Rev. Psychology*, 1955, 6, 357-378.

Monroe, R., Heath, R., Mickle, W., Llewellyn, R. Correlation of rhinencephalic electrograms with behavior: a study on humans under the influence of LSD and mescaline. *EEG Clin. Neurophysiol.*, 1957, 9, 623-642.

Osmond, H. A review of the clinical effects of psychotomimetic agents. *Ann. N. Y. Acad. Sci.*, 1957, 66, 418-434.

Savage, C. LSD, alcoholism and transcendence. *J. Nerv. Ment. Dis.*, 1962, 135, 429-435.

Skinner, B., *Walden two*. New York: Doubleday, 1948.

Szara, S. Background information on the pharmacological and clinical data of N.N.-dialkyltryptamine derivatives. 1965, unpublished.

Unger, S. Mescaline, LSD, psilocybin and personality change: a review. *Psychiatry*, 1963, 26, 111-125.

Unger, S. LSD and psychotherapy: a bibliography of the English-language literature. *Psychedelic Rev.*, 1964, 1, 442-449.

Vourlekis, A., Faillace, L. and Szara, S. Psychotherapy combined with psychodysleptic tryptamine derivatives. 1966. Presented at the Fifth Collegium Internationale Neuropsychopharmacologicum, Wash., D.C.

PSYCHODIAGNOSTIC TESTING

MOLLY HARROWER, PH.D.
Professor, Graduate Faculty
New School for Social Research

Editorial Note

Psychodiagnostics covers a large area and has great worth in some of its applied aspects, particularly in counseling and personnel work. The author of the following article asserts that psychodiagnosticians should expand the psychodiagnostic unit, understand more completely the interaction of its components, and accept responsibility as leaders in multi-disciplinary research.

Dr. Molly Harrower is Visiting Professor of Psychology in the Graduate Faculty of the New School for Social Research in New York City. Her main activities, however, lie in psychodiagnostic testing, therapy, and research in the clinical field. In this connection she has recently completed a large scale follow-up study of some 2000 patients seen psychodiagnostically and has correlated the success of the therapeutic effort with the degree of mental health potential as shown in the tests.

Dr. Harrower came to this country to study with Professor Kurt Koffka, the well known Gestalt psychologist. She has been on the faculty of Wells College, New Jersey College for Women, and Temple University Medical Center. She has been a Consultant to the Department of State, and a member of the Technical Advisory Committee, the Air Surgeon's Office.

Dr. Harrower has published ten books and 80 articles in the experimental and clinical field. She devised the Harrower Inkblots and developed the Group Rorschach and Multiple Choice Test.

PSYCHODIAGNOSTIC TESTING

By implication, the title of this volume, New Outlook in Psychology, suggests that each of its chapters will be concerned with the newer aspects of the subject or topic covered. My assignment then, is really to acquaint the reader with the "new vistas" in psychodiagnostic testing or, more specifically, to discuss the new roles and responsibilities that are opening up for the psychodiagnostic tester, or psychodiagnostician, as he is more frequently called.

But this immediately raises the question, how new? Or, new with respect to *what?* And this in turn prompts the query: How well acquainted is the general reader with the old or traditional aspect of diagnostic testing? For it is clear that without a baseline to give the needed perspective, the newness may not appear as important growth and development in the field at all.

Let me therefore set the stage, for those of us who work continuously in an area of service or research, sometimes forget that our basic tenets, our plan of working, the household words of our speciality are often quite strange and meaningless to others. I will begin therefore by answering three questions which that useful hypothetical entity, the intelligent reader, might well ask. First, *how does psychodiagnostic testing differ from other forms?* The use of the word "diagnostic" indicates a medical, rather than a vocational or educational frame of reference. It springs from the fact that Herman Rorschach, a physician and psychiatrist, in developing his now famous ink-blot test, called it a method of psychological diagnosis. One of his major aims was to show that from the inkblots alone one could "diagnose" the presence of various forms of mental illness. Rorschach, as a matter of fact, was caught up in the thinking of his day. It did not occur to him to go beyond the accepted classifications schizophrenia, manic-depressive, obsessional neurosis, hysteria and the like.

What tests are used in psychodiagnostic testing?

The psychodiagnostician rarely uses a single instrument or

technique, and is apt to speak of his battery of tests. He may also refer to the methods he uses as the Projective Techniques, a term introduced in 1939 by Lawrence Frank. (1) Amongst these one is almost sure to find the Rorschach inkblot test, the Thematic Apperception test developed by Murray, graphic techniques such as the drawing of the human figure, drawing of a family, drawing of an animal, drawing of the most unpleasant thing that can be thought of. (2) (3) One will also find some version of the sentence completion test and almost invariably one of the intelligence tests such as the Bellevue-Wechsler which can be used not only to establish the intellectual level, but also to pick up meaningful deviations from the standard answers which may give clues to the areas in which the individual is not thinking objectively. Less often used, but in my opinion a very valuable test, is the Szondi.

A third question which may well be asked is *what does the psychodiagnostician actually do?* It is here that we can make a bridge between the past and the emerging future. For in defining the old role it will become clearer what possibilities exist for the years to come.

The traditional role in the past decades of the psychodiagnostician was something like this. His patients were referred to him by therapists, psychiatrists and analysts. He rarely saw them again or knew anything of their therapeutic fate. Thus a certain type of all important learning and feed-back experience was not available to him. He was an independent assessor, not involved in clinical details, needed to make impartial judgments. He had an important task in picking up early and subtle distortions in thinking, which might not have broken through into everyday speech. However, he was rarely asked or encouraged to demonstrate mental health potential co-existing with the more attention-getting psychopathology. In following this line of duty he was constantly forced to do violence to the rightness of the raw material in the tests, because his final answer had to be in psychiatric terms. That is, while asked to assess the individual by special psychodiagnostic tools he still had to use the restricting and hampering psychiatric classifications for the final summations.

In speaking of new vistas in psychodiagnostic testing, therefore, we are concerned with how this traditional role, this way of functioning, may be changed and supplemented. I will discuss this from six different vantage points and I have formulated them in terms of responsibilities, rather than in terms of the more passive approach, which I somehow feel is implied in looking at a "new vista." Any advance it seems to me is a combination of waiting for the time to be ripe, and accepting the challenge of taking the appropriate action.

First, then, comes the responsibility of developing our own diagnostic classification system, one which will include mental health potential and will be free of those outworn and symptom-based psychiatric concepts.

Secondly, we should accept and expand our roles as psycho-diagnostic-therapists, as persons equipped with a peculiar area of insight into the dynamics and problems of the patient.

Thirdly, we must assume the responsibility of expanding the psychodiagnostic unit, which has traditionally been the testing of one person, expanding it to include that individual's marital partner, perhaps his entire family, or the group members with whom he works.

Fourthly, we must put ourselves, as therapists, under the psychodiagnostic microscope in order to understand better our successful and unsuccessful therapeutic interactions.

Fifthly, we must be more mindful and aware of the pertinent community problems of our day, we must break sacred tradition in the methods of testing if by so doing we can contribute to live problems.

Finally we must accept the role of spark plug and initiator in experimentation and multidiscipline research in the whole area of psychotherapy and diagnosis.

And so back to point one. The responsibility which I have felt most keenly in recent years has been the need to establish a projective classification system, a scale, or as it turned out, two scales, of mental health potential, both derived exclusively from the scores on the projective tests. It was to this end that I stopped my practice for three years and embarked on a follow-up of 1600 patients in order to be able to correlate the results of therapy, as assessed by their therapists, with the degree of mental health potential, or lack of it, as reflected in the tests. (4)

It has always seemed to me highly unsatisfactory to have to give the ultimate summation of test findings within a different frame of reference from that in which the examination took place. The projective tests deal in symbolic patterns and below the surface phenomena, yet we have been forced to come up with psychiatric classifications which are based on observable symptoms and pathological behavior. The lack of our own system of classifying test look-alikes (persons with similar projective gestalten) has hindered research and has relegated us to a subordinate position.

The classification scheme which I have recently developed can be described in this way: It was found that the scores which an individual has made on a battery of seven tests can be summated in such a way as to be placed somewhere along the line on one of two scales of personality endowment or mental health potential.

These scales have been called the Homogeneous and Heterogeneous scales of mental health potential. The former is based on scores from the seven projective tests, each of which has been handled at approximately *the same "level" of achievement.* The second scale, on the other hand, reflects a total test performance containing a *marked discrepancy* between high endowment in some tests or areas, and poor performance, lack of endowment, or disturbance as reflected in others.

The various steps in the two scales have been named as follows:

Homogeneous endowment	Heterogeneous endowment
Very Superior	Gifted, with Problems
Superior	High Potential, with Problems
Within Normal Limits (+)	Gifted, but Disturbed
Within Normal Limits	Potential, but Disturbed
Within Normal Limits (−)	Disturbed, but with Potential
Mediocre	Disturbed
Impoverished	Very Disturbed

The Homogeneous Scale

Very Superior, Superior, Within Normal Limits Plus. The first three positions on the Homogeneous Scale can be spoken of together in that each, in varying degrees, indicates above average personality endowment in all measurable test areas. Persons whose total test performance can be categorized under any of these three headings will have shown themselves to be above average in endowment or will have displayed above average ability in all the tests contained in the personality battery.

Essentially, the persons in these three groups have shown a balanced and uniform performance, leading one to postulate a balance of acceptable personality assets. For example, they are to a more than average degree warm and outgoing toward others. They combine adequate intellectual control with freedom and spontaneity. They possess inner resources, depth, and intuitive sympathy for others. Such persons will show both creativity and a capacity for routine work. They are the psychologically fit, showing no constitutional weaknesses in the psychological framework.

On this analogy with physical fitness, one can say that though individuals in these test groups may at times become somewhat disturbed psychologically—even the basically physically healthy person can catch the grippe—they will not become chronically ill because of inherent psychological weaknesses.

Within Normal Limits. The persons so categorized are the psychologically average citizens, those with no outstanding defects or difficulties, but with no great psychological potential. They performed all the tests well enough to get by satisfactorily. The Within Normal Limits test scores are, so to speak, a baseline above which we may look for various degrees of additional richness in the personality and below which we may expect some problems to arise simply because the individual lacks substance or richness.

Within Normal Limits Minus, Mediocre, Impoverished. We can speak of these three positions on the scale together in that, again in varying degrees, the persons who fall into them have reflected below average endowment in all the seven tests given in the battery. The uniformity we have spoken of before is found in these below average sub-groups. As the name implies, the Impoverished group reflects a bare minimum of those measurable qualities listed previously. Persons in this group show little emotional warmth, a complete lack of imagination or creativity, an inhibition of all spontaneity and flexibility. Interestingly enough, such persons are frequently of the highest intelligence, an important fact showing that intellectual endowment does not necessarily go hand in hand with the facets of the well rounded personality that our scale attempts to measure.

The Heterogeneous Scale

So much, then, for the three key positions on a scale of performance throughout the variety of tests.

The need to construct a second scale of personality endowment—which we have called a Heterogeneous Scale—comes from the fact that many persons cannot be classified as possessing Above Average, Average, or Below Average personality endowment because the various component parts making up that endowment are not all of a kind. Some persons, for example, show giftedness, richness, or great potential in some areas and at the same time clearly exhibit disturbed functioning or acute problems in others.

On the second scale it is possible to distinguish two, rather than three major divisions. There are those persons whose giftedness (or high potential) runs parallel to what we have called *problems*, as opposed to those who—as measured by some tests —have equal giftedness or high potential but show profound *disturbance* or serious pathology as measured by other tests.

Gifted-Problems, High Potential-Problems. Concerning the first two positions in this scale—the Gifted with Problems and the High Potential with Problems—the emphasis is on the positive component. These two positions are comparable to the above average categories on the Homogeneous Scale. Many of the qualities we mentioned when describing persons in the Very Superior, Superior, and Within Normal Limits Plus groups may also be found here. However, a person in the Gifted with Problems or High Potential with Problems categories will show in one or two areas that a consistently high level has not been achieved. It may be, for example, that an over abundance of creative imagination leads to withdrawal into fantasy rather than into constructive, outgoing activity. In such individuals, the important balance factor—namely, the need for warm relationships with others—may be absent.

Regardless of what the "flaw" is, the poor showing on one or two aspects of the tests will stand out in sharp contrast to the giftedness or the potential shown in the rest.

Our prediction for the persons whose test scores place them in either of these categories is a favorable one, provided that circumstances do not trigger the particular problem to an excessive degree.

Gifted-Disturbed, Potential-Disturbed, Disturbed-Potential, Disturbed, Very Disturbed. As soon as our classification has to include the word "disturbance"—be it combined with giftedness or with potential—our predictions for success in any area must be hedged with "ifs" and "provided such and such does not occur."

In varying degrees, those persons whose test findings must be classified as including a disruptive or disturbing element, are subject to internal sabotage. Their brilliance, their giftedness, their energy, their creativeness may be undermined from within.

Finally, when the disturbing elements obscure all but a fragment of the personality as at the lower end of the Heterogeneous Scale, our prognosis must be a somewhat pessimistic one, unless some form of therapeutic intervention can be guaranteed.

I should add that I have no fervent belief in the details of the two scales which I have formulated. By that I mean the definitions of the specific scoring which demarcate each of the categories may well have to be changed. I do advocate strongly, however, that psychodiagnosticians accept the responsibility of developing and adopting some scale which can include within it the most talented and balanced individual and the most inadequate and impoverished one, a scale which can reflect varying degrees of disorganizing and disruptive forces combined with varying degrees of healthy potential.*

* Details of the scoring necessary to fit each of these positions on the scale will be found in *Psychodiagnostic Testing: An Empirical Approach.*

A second role which requires changing, sharpening and developing is that of the psychodiagnostician as a therapist with peculiar qualifications. By this I do not mean clinical psychologists pursuing the recognized forms of therapeutic procedure, analysis, psychoanalytically oriented therapy or group therapy, this is no longer a "new vista" for this is an established fact. Rather I am speaking of making more explicit the peculiar insights which, by virtue of an exhaustive projective battery, the psychodiagnostician-therapist has in regard to the patient's problems and to the patient's pattern of thinking and responding.

In formulating this method in 1956 (5) and again in 1960 (6) I may have masked its full therapeutic potential by settling for the noncontroversial term, at that time, of projective counseling. I did this because I did not wish to be dragged into the boiling cauldron of emotions pertaining to whether or not psychologists could do psychotherapy! The name however is actually unimportant. Those of us who do both psychodiagnostics and therapy know that the psychodiagnostician when he becomes a therapist, possesses a thousand cues from the raw material of the test findings which no report which he can write, however detailed, can ever pass on to another person.

Because we are now established therapists with secure practices, it seems to me we are called on to contribute more actively and creatively to the therapeutic armamentarium. One such way is by a more systematic combination of psychodiagnostics and therapeutic insights.

The details of this technique will, as I mentioned earlier, be found elsewhere, but a few words may make my point clearer. Projective counseling or projective therapy has several facets. The patient's test "productions" (that is, his response to the Rorschach cards, his answers to the incomplete sentences, his TAT stories and the like) can be used in the therapeutic hour much as one would use dreams. They can be used, for example, by getting the patient to free associate to them or to interpret them in the light of the particular problems he is facing. To give a very simple example: Patient X sees on the Rorschach card III "two hostile women." At a point in therapy where she is complaining of the "hostile" persons in the office in which she works, the therapist brings up her answer to card III and asks her to think about it. The discussion then turns about the fact that she has projected hostility onto the meaningless inkblot, created hostility out of its nothingness. When such an interpretation is properly timed it may be enormously revealing. The patient may be willing to accept this information about herself, coming as it does, from her own lips.

Projective therapy may also mean that the therapist, knowing from the inside, as it were, the basic mental health potential of an overtly disturbed person, may be able to ride out what might otherwise be a therapeutic crisis with a greater equanimity. An enormously gifted woman whom I have recently treated showed a fiercely explosive color score on the Rorschach. However, to counterbalance it she showed extraordinarily good control (CF 16, but F% over 50). The fact that I knew this allowed me to take in stride occasional outbursts of violent weeping, various psychosomatic symptoms which were quite transient, and to keep going with a rather direct interpretive brief therapeutic approach which has proved very successful.

Projective therapy can also be used effectively in the confrontation of their respective Summary of Test Findings to couples with marital problems. (See page for a copy of the Summary of Test Findings.) This type of confrontation is very successful when there are comparable degrees of health and disturbance in each partner. It should not be undertaken when there is a real discrepancy in terms of the severity of the disorganizing processes in the couples' records.

My third point concerns the change and expansion of the psychodiagnostic unit, the fascinating field which opens up when the testing is not only of one individual, the patient, but of the person or persons most closely connected with him.

In 1954 I reported a study of 40 marital couples seeking help, the essence of whose various domestic conflicts I was fascinated to discover, were reflected in the interrelation of their test scores. (7) (8) Quite apart, however, from marital conflict, when only one person is seeking help, it would seem to me that it is imperative in the planning of treatment to have the partner's record. Take for example Miss Four and Mrs. Three who consulted me because of various inhibiting anxieties

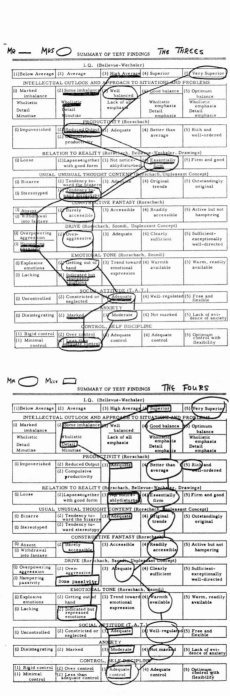

Mr ___ Mrs ○ **SUMMARY OF TEST FINDINGS** THE THREES

I.Q. (Bellevue-Wechsler)

(1) Below Average	(2) Average	(3) High Average	(4) Superior	(5) Very Superior

INTELLECTUAL OUTLOOK AND APPROACH TO SITUATIONS AND PROBLEMS

(1) Marked imbalance	(2) Some imbalance	(3) Well balanced	(4) Good balance	(5) Optimum balance
Wholistic	Wholistic	Lack of all emphasis	Wholistic emphasis	Wholistic emphasis
Detail	Detail		Detail emphasis	Detail emphasis
Minutiae	Minutiae			

PRODUCTIVITY (Rorschach)

(1) Impoverished	(2) Reduced Output / (2) Compulsive productivity	(3) Adequate	(4) Better than average	(5) Rich and well-ordered

RELATION TO REALITY (Rorschach, Bellevue-Wechsler, Drawings)

(1) Loose	(2) Lapses together with good form	(3) Not noticeably disturbed	(4) Essentially firm	(5) Firm and good

USUAL UNUSUAL THOUGHT CONTENT (Rorschach, Unpleasant Concept)

(1) Bizarre	(2) Tendency toward the bizarre	(3) Adequate	(4) Original trends	(5) Outstandingly original
(1) Stereotyped	(2) Tendency toward stereotypy			

CONSTRUCTIVE FANTASY (Rorschach)

(1) Absent	(2) Barely accessible	(3) Accessible	(4) Readily accessible	(5) Active but not hampering
(1) Withdrawal into fantasy				

DRIVE (Rorschach, Szondi, Unpleasant Concept)

(1) Overpowering aggression	(2) Over-aggressive	(3) Adequate	(4) Clearly sufficient	(5) Sufficient-exceptionally well-directed
(1) Hampering passivity				

EMOTIONAL TONE (Rorschach, Szondi)

(1) Explosive emotions	(2) Getting out of hand	(3) Trend toward emotional expression	(4) Warmth available	(5) Warm, readily available
(1) Lacking	(2) Indicated but repressed emotions			

SOCIAL ATTITUDE (T.A.T.)

(1) Uncontrolled	(2) Constricted or neglected	(3) Adequate	(4) Well-regulated	(5) Free and flexible

ANXIETY

(1) Disintegrating	(2) Marked	(3) Moderate	(4) Not marked	(5) Lack of evidence of anxiety

CONTROL, SELF DISCIPLINE

(1) Rigid control	(2) Over control	(3) Adequate control	(4) Adequate control	(5) Optimum control with flexibility
(1) Minimal control	(2) Less than adequate control			

Mr ○ Miss □ **SUMMARY OF TEST FINDINGS** THE FOURS

I.Q. (Bellevue-Wechsler)

(1) Below Average	(2) Average	(3) High Average	(4) Superior	(5) Very Superior

INTELLECTUAL OUTLOOK AND APPROACH TO SITUATIONS AND PROBLEMS

(1) Marked imbalance	(2) Some imbalance	(3) Well balanced	(4) Good balance	(5) Optimum balance
Wholistic	Wholistic	Lack of all emphasis	Wholistic emphasis	Wholistic emphasis
Detail	Detail		Detail emphasis	Detail emphasis
Minutiae	Minutiae			

PRODUCTIVITY (Rorschach)

(1) Impoverished	(2) Reduced Output / (2) Compulsive productivity	(3) Adequate	(4) Better than average	(5) Rich and well-ordered

RELATION TO REALITY (Rorschach, Bellevue-Wechsler, Drawings)

(1) Loose	(2) Lapses together with good form	(3) Not noticeably disturbed	(4) Essentially firm	(5) Firm and good

USUAL UNUSUAL THOUGHT CONTENT (Rorschach, Unpleasant Concept)

(1) Bizarre	(2) Tendency toward the bizarre	(3) Adequate	(4) Original trends	(5) Outstandingly original
(1) Stereotyped	(2) Tendency toward stereotypy			

CONSTRUCTIVE FANTASY (Rorschach)

(1) Absent	(2) Barely accessible	(3) Accessible	(4) Readily accessible	(5) Active but not hampering
(1) Withdrawal into fantasy				

DRIVE (Rorschach, Szondi, Unpleasant Concept)

(1) Overpowering aggression	(2) Over-aggressive	(3) Adequate	(4) Clearly sufficient	(5) Sufficient-exceptionally well-directed
(1) Hampering passivity	Some passivity			

EMOTIONAL TONE (Rorschach, Szondi)

(1) Explosive emotions	(2) Getting out of hand	(3) Trend toward emotional expression	(4) Warmth available	(5) Warm, readily available
(1) Lacking	(2) Indicated but repressed emotions			

SOCIAL ATTITUDE (T.A.T.)

(1) Uncontrolled	(2) Constricted or neglected	(3) Adequate	(4) Well-regulated	(5) Free and flexible

ANXIETY

(1) Disintegrating	(2) Marked	(3) Moderate	(4) Not marked	(5) Lack of evidence of anxiety

CONTROL, SELF DISCIPLINE

(1) Rigid control	(2) Over control	(3) Adequate control	(4) Adequate control	(5) Optimum control with flexibility
(1) Minimal control	(2) Less than adequate control			

which they were experiencing. It transpired in addition that Miss Four was in constant indecision as to whether or not to marry her fiancee or call the engagement off. Mrs. Three, it also became evident, was in a state of constant indecision as to whether or not to continue in her marriage although this overtly was an acceptable one to both partners. Test findings on Miss Four's fiancee (taken by another psychodiagnostician so that I did not meet him for well over a year) revealed him to be an extraordinarily gifted and stable individual. In the findings it seemed to me he could be counted on to remain content with his decision to marry Miss Four and to be a person who could almost function as a co-therapist in allowing the patient to live out some of her problems in their premarital life together without affecting his major decision.

The husband of Mrs. Three, however, appeared as an equally disturbed individual, that is, someone whose problems were almost the exact mirror image of those of his wife. Where she was fiercely aggressive he was completely hampered by passivity. Where she was dominant and masculine in her approach he was retiring, gentle and feminine.

It was quite clear that no amount of work with Mrs. Three could accomplish a positive result unless Mr. Three were also able to tackle his difficulties. Thus the decision was made to get him into treatment with a therapist of his own.

The two charts which are included here show the relationship of each pair one to the other. The scores of Miss Four's fiancee, it will be seen as it were, envelop and support her. His scores reveal him to have achieved a richer and more mature status in all the measurable areas. The Threes on the other hand reflect their interrelated problems indicating the need for the independent treatment in order to achieve their goals. This couple will be discussed in greater detail in a subsequent publication. They have been followed for two years and re-testing shows some startling improvements at the deepest levels.

Testing both partners or testing the family opens up exciting new vistas. Along these lines one should also mention the important new technique of interaction testing developed by Roman and Bauman. (9) This I believe, has very far-reaching implications for the study of families and small groups and even community problems. In the interaction technique the couple not only gives their independent responses on the Wechsler or the Rorschach but then attempt to achieve a compromise, in selecting a common answer which both will agree to. A brief summary of some of their latest findings may be given here.

Under the impetus of new community mental health legislation, there will be a great deal of pressure to accelerate the development of knowledge in the area of family and small group diagnosis. With the technique of Interaction Testing, Roman and Bauman have begun to explore the usefulness of applying traditional, clinical diagnostic procedures like the Wechsler-Bellevue, Rorschach, TAT, etc. with their proven usefulness in individual diagnosis to married couples, families, and small groups. They have found that these techniques with minor modifications can be enormously useful in generating clinical insight into group and family dynamics and appeared to have pioneered in the development of standardized procedures and the evaluation of reliability of test results. This latter activity is focused on the marital I.Q. and its dynamics. As they have used it, the marital I.Q. represents the pro-rated verbal I.Q. score derived from comprehension and similarities subtests of the Wechsler-Bellevue as these scores are obtained from married couples. They have collected data on samples that include: a) 65 normal couples; b) 50 so-called pathological couples, that is, couples having one member who has been hospitalized for acute psychiatric disturbance and c) 16 couples from the 50 "abnormals" who were re-tested two years after hospital discharge. Some of the highlights of their findings are:

1) The I.Q. obtained by the couple has the same order of reliability as that of individuals, approximately .85.

2) Intellectual efficiency, a score reflecting the effectiveness with which the couple pools the individual resources that they bring to the task, is likewise a reliable measure of the couple as a unit.

3) In contrasting the groups of couples who are normal with those having a nonpsychotic patient member and those having a psychotic patient member, it is found that interaction I.Q. does not distinguish among the three groups, but intellectual efficiency does significantly distinguish among the three groups in that normals are the most efficient intellectually; couples with a neurotic member second, and poorest in efficiency are couples having a psychotic member.

4) Dominance patterns in decision-making of couples is likewise a reliable characteristic of the couples. In general, husbands dominate more than wives; nonpatients dominate more often than patients; and the brighter spouse dominates more often than the less bright spouse.

5) In the follow-up study of 16 couples two years after discharge of one spouse, it was found in analysis of dominance behavior that the original findings for husband dominance and brighter spouse dominance still obtain, but the former status of patient is no longer a significant variable in determining dominance behavior. Thus, the technique seems to respond to changes in a social status or social role, that is, patient or non-patient.

6) In the 16 cases comparing couples before and after family treatment, it was found that the interaction I.Q. was significantly increased on post-testing, while the individual I.Q.'s did not change significantly. While the meaning of this finding requires further controlled study, it seems to suggest the exciting pos-

sibility that we can produce and detect changes in group functioning which are not reflected in similar ways in the functioning of the individual members.

Interaction Testing seems to point to a very promising line of development; namely, the differentiation diagnostically of couples, families and small groups in ways that may be quite relevant for different kinds of intervention and therapeutic effort. While Roman and Bauman have not collected systematic treatment data, they and their associates have had some dramatically positive experiences following confrontation of couples by their test behavior in which couples can see instances of irrational and pathological interaction and domination, utilizing essentially conscious and pre-conscious material which is relatively unthreatening to the couples as they examine their own decision-making behavior. (10)

Despite these pioneering efforts, however, by and large, we have not moved into the habit of thinking in which we demand that the test material of the marital partner be included, even if there is no domestic problem, or require that the whole family's test findings be studied when considering a disturbed child or adolescent. The isolation of the test findings is all the more interesting in an era where so much emphasis has been placed on family therapy, group process and group therapy.

Let us take a quick look at the fourth new vista of emerging responsibility. I would call this the need to study our own psychodiagnostic selves. How do our test profiles as therapists compare with those of our patients? The lack of testing which we have done on psychodiagnosticians and therapists suggests a blind spot that has worried me for a long time. Several pilot studies which I have undertaken with groups of private practitioners, with a group at the Department of Psychiatry at Temple University in Philadelphia and now at the Post Graduate Center in Manhattan have convinced me that there are some fascinating similarities in the test findings of therapists and those patients with whom they feel themselves to have worked most successfully.

The findings here are still too tentative to be discussed but I feel that this area is wide open for courageous research. It need not be limited to what can be done in institutions for it seems to me any psychodiagnostician who is also a therapist could make his own study on himself and his patients.

This idea has received an added impetus for me during the last few months due to the number of patients who have come self-referred with the explicit request to be tested and placed therapeutically on the basis of their test findings. Granted that this is a small and sophisticated group of the total population, nonetheless it is an important one. I have long matched patient and therapist by hunch, but it seems to me there is no longer need to stay always at the hunch level.

The fifth point I will make relates to the need to break away from the accepted, the same, the "establishment" in the psychodiagnostic field, if by so doing we can contribute to more vital problems.

I am thinking, for example, of some studies of mine which have been in progress now for over 10 years. One of our religious denominations, the Unitarian-Universalists, are interested in getting psychological tests on their candidates for positions in the church. They attempted to raise funds to send these candidates, perhaps some 30 to 40 a year, to my office for testing, but this proved too expensive since the candidates came from all over the country. We then passed through a two-year period where I journeyed to various parts of the United States and administered a group battery of tests with the candidates who could be collected in that area. Even this, however, involved too much hardship and difficulty for the students who had to travel. Finally, under pressure, I developed a self-administering battery which has now been in use for the last seven years. Because of the follow-up study which we were able to make, this procedure has really passed out of the experimental or trial stage. While this may evoke an image of "testing by mail" which appears dangerous to say the least, it is really nothing of the sort.

The material or package consists of a 52-page test booklet and a loaned set of the Rorschach cards. This booklet allows the individual to take, and record his responses to, the Szondi, the Rorschach, the sentence completion, four tests from the verbal Bellevue-Wechsler, four pictures concerning which stories can be written along the lines of the TAT and pages for three graphic tests. The instructions are as follows:

Here is an overall statement about the tests you will take.

The first test is called the Szondi. The instructions for it are given on Pages 2-3. You will repeat this assignment until you reach Pages 12-13.

The next test is the Rorschach Inkblot Test. You will have received a set of the ten inkblots along with this booklet. Turn over inkblot No. 1 and, on Page 15, record everything which you feel it reminds you of. What does it look like? What do you see there? On Page 14 you will find a small duplicate drawing of the inkblot to which you have responded. This is to be used as a map on which you should chart those areas of the blot which you used in your answers. Continue in the same way for all ten inkblots until you have reached Page 33.

On Pages 34-35 you will find some incomplete sentences. Finish them any way you wish. (Holsopple-Miale)

On Pages 36, 38, 40 and 42 you will find various questions which have to be answered on Pages 37, 39, 41 and 42. (Bellevue-Wechsler)

On Page 43 you are instructed to draw a person any way you wish, and on the following page a person of the opposite sex.

On Page 45 you should draw the most unpleasant thing which you can think of. State underneath the drawing what your idea was.

On Pages 46, 48, 50 and 52 you will find some pictures. Your task is to write a short story of what is happening in

PICTURE I

each of these scenes (what has happened, what is happening and what will happen). Write the story on the blank page opposite each picture. (T.A.T.)

By using this material, I have over the last 10 years, been able to test every candidate seeking to enter the Universalist-Unitarian Church and to make a thorough follow-up study on the success or failure of the minister with reference to the original test prediction. (11) (12)

The charts on page 58 in which the scores of the couples designated as the Threes and the Fours have been recorded are another way in which it is possible to embark on large scale projects which involve the assessment of many records in a short space of time. Obviously to write a detailed report on a hundred persons in a short space of time would stump even the most vital psychodiagnostician. Yet these summaries can be made relatively easily for the tests can be scored by assistants at a lower echelon leaving the "principal investigator" to place the scores on a summary sheet within a few minutes. The summary sheets are meaningful after a brief interpretation, to persons from other fields and in scanning large populations they allow the test look-alikes to stand out promptly.

What I am conveying by mentioning these two rather divergent illustrations is that we should be free to alter both our method of conducting tests and our ways of passing on our information, depending on the contribution we can make to the larger issue.

And so to my final point. Our new vistas should include the psychodiagnostician assuming the role of initiator of multidisciplinary research programs in the therapeutic field.

When I talked over plans of my follow-up study, in which I would attempt to get information on 1600 patients previously tested over a 12-year period, I was repeatedly warned by concerned professional friends about the hazards and the unlikelihood that busy therapists would fill out my questionnaire. Yet of the 200 therapists approached, 196 responded. And of the 1600 questionnaires sent out, 1463 were returned filled out! Many therapists made the spontaneous comment that the fact

303

that this investigation was organized by someone from a slightly different vantage point, made cooperation easier. I was equally struck by the willingness of so many therapists to take part in the therapist-patient projective program. The psychodiagnostician is in some sense less bound to his patient than is the full-time therapist, and should use this perspective and lack of deep personal involvement to instigate joint research projects.

In summary then, our "new vistas" for diagnostic testing should include an era of an autonomous frame of reference for our test results, a scale of health potential on which the richest and the poorest projectively endowed citizen can be recorded. We should contribute more actively to the development of varying forms of therapy, particularly in the use of our own tools as insight-giving material. We need to expand the psychodiagnostic unit, to understand more completely the interaction of patient-patient, patient and well-partner, patient and therapist. We need to discard out-worn methods and traditions if by so doing we can find a place in the vital problems of the community, and we need to accept responsibility as leaders in multi-disciplinary research. It looks like an exciting decade ahead.

References

1. Lawrence Frank: *Projective Methods*, Charles C. Thomas, Springfield, Illinois, 1948.
2. Harrower, Molly: The Most Unpleasant Concept Test. *Journal of Clinical Psychology*, Vol. VI, No. 3, 1950, pp. 213-233.
3. Harrower, Molly: The Most Unpleasant Concept Test: A Graphic Projective Technique for Diagnostic and Therapeutic Use. Chapter in *The Clinical Application of Projective Drawings*, Ed. H. Hammer. Charles C. Thomas, Springfield, Illinois, 1958.
4. Harrower, Molly: *Psychodiagnostic Testing: An Empirical Approach*, Charles C. Thomas, Springfield, Illinois, 1965.
5. Harrower, Molly: Project Counseling–Psychotherapeutic Technique, *American Journal of Psychotherapy*, Vol. X, No. 1, pp. 74-86, January, 1956.

6. Harrower, Molly: *Creative Variations in the Projective Techniques*, Charles C. Thomas, Springfield, Illinois, 1960, Chapter 16.
7. Harrower, Molly: The Measurement of Psychological Factors in Marital Maladjustment. *Texas Reports on Biology and Medicine*, Vol. 12, Number 1, pp. 72-85, Spring, 1954.
8. Harrower, Molly: The Measurement of Psychological Factors in Marriage in *Neurotic Interaction in Marriage*, Ed. Victor Eisenstein, Basic Books, 1956.
9. Roman, M. & Bauman, G.: Chapter in *Creative Variations in the Projective Techniques*, Charles C. Thomas, Springfield, Illinois, 1960.
10. Personal Communication.
11. Harrower, Molly: Psychological Tests in the Unitarian Universalist Ministry. *Journal of Religion and Health*, Vol. 2, No. 2, January, 1963.
12. Harrower, Molly: Mental health potential and success in the ministry. *Journal of Religion and Health*, 4: No. 1, 1964.

PSYCHOLOGY AND THE GIFTED CHILD

JOSEPH L. FRENCH, ED. D.

Professor of Special Education and Educational Psychology
The Pennsylvania State University

Editorial Note

At a time when the pursuit of excellence assumes new importance in light of national goals, the gifted child again becomes a focal point of research in educational psychology. Dr. French's survey of recent findings points up the two-sided nature of the problem of developing the talents of superior individuals: identification of potential talent and effective cultivation of this talent. The chronic underachiever, generally a product of a home environment which stunts intellectual growth, poses a challenge to the investigator concerned with unleashing a vast reservoir of human talent.

Dr. Joseph L. French is Professor of Special Education and Educational Psychology at The Pennsylvania State University in University Park, Pennsylvania, where he directs the graduate programs in School Psychology. He is the editor of *Educating the Gifted: A Book of Readings* which was published in 1959 and extensively revised in 1964, the author of numerous journal articles and the *Pictorial Test of Intelligence*—a scale for assessing severely physically handicapped as well as physically typical children.

He has studied attitudes of secondary school and college youth toward television instruction and has been the principal investigator in projects designed to study physiological and psychological correlates of stress in young children responding to items in an intelligence test and to study attitude, personality and interests of high school dropouts of high mental ability.

Professor French holds degrees from and was on the faculty of Illinois State University at Normal and the University of Nebraska. He moved to The Pennsylvania State University from the University of Missouri. He is a Fellow in APA, a member of SRCD, APGA, CEC, and AERA, and an associate editor of two professional journals.

•

PSYCHOLOGY AND THE GIFTED CHILD

Providing ideal learning conditions for all school children has been the principal concern of educators for a long time. Every few years someone or some event causes attention to be focused on students with superior potential for learning. During the late fifties and early sixties there was renewed interest in the gifted.

The terms "gifted" and "talented" usually refer to those with intellectual or academic capabilities that exceed a majority of their age mates. But in a way all children have gifts, for there are gifts and talents other than those that are academic in nature. We have all seen persons who are quite unusual in their ability to arbitrate or express affection. Others possess unique physical characteristics, exceptional musical qualities, or mechanical ingenuity. Sometimes several or all of these characteristics are found in one individual. Perhaps these talents are not really gifts but a product of an individual's inherited capability and his interaction with his surroundings. In this chapter our concern is for the intellectually or academically talented individual, however he has attained this classification.

In a critique of research trends in the education of gifted children Gallagher (1964) introduces the reader to the problems of the gifted as follows:

> The achievements of intellectually superior individuals do not equal the sum of the achievements of any number of less talented people. The definition of a genius as "a person who does easily what no one else can do at all" is appropriate here. One can not evaluate Michelangelo by saying that he is equal to 20 painters of inferior rank,

or Einstein by saying that his work approximates the combined products of 30 run-of-the-mill physicists. These rare individuals are invaluable; they produce something that no other collection of persons can produce. The same generalization holds true at lower intellectual levels. No collection of persons of below-average intellectual abilities can match the contribution of the best individual physician, college professor, or executive. Attempts to use to the utmost the intellectual resources of the society can result in incalculable benefits, not only to the individual but to the society as a whole. . . .

Environment can have either an inhibiting or an encouraging effect on the development of intellectual talent. Such an assumption places a heavy responsibility on the culture and the education system, but it is also an exciting one for the educator and the social scientist. The concept of "intelligence" as a genetically determined trait has been replaced by the concept of a pliable and plastic intellect which is responsive to the environment in which it is placed. The place of genetics in intelligence has not been denied; rather, the place of environment and its interaction with genetics has been reaffirmed.

Other implications of this newer concept are that (a) the prediction of future intellectual ability must take into account past environmental and probable future environmental experiences; (b) any classification of giftedness should be tentative and should be used for present educational planning rather than for prediction; (c) the younger the child the more plastic his abilities; (d) prediction of future performance should not be ruled out, but the complex nature and problems of such prediction should be fully realized.

In the vast array of articles pertaining to intellectually and academically talented students, it can be seen that some authors describe the top one per cent of our population as gifted while others are concerned with any student who can profitably complete a college education. Many leaders in the National

Education Association consider those individuals whose measured ability places them in the upper 15 to 20 per cent of our population, or those who have IQ's in the vicinity of 115 and above, to be academically talented.

The use of an intelligence test as an operational definition of intelligence seems justified only to the extent that the abilities measured by the test are themselves important and valuable in this culture. Giftedness is inseparable from its social and cultural environment. Socially deprived children are not handicapped by a test; rather their handicap is described, in part, by the test score just as a scale reflects the weight of an undernourished waif.

In the current literature one finds reference to several means of identifying talented students, but only individually administered intelligence tests can identify very intellectually capable students. When group intelligence and achievement tests are used without the individual tests, only academically talented students are located. Many underachievers are missed. The use of tests which can be used with groups of students often merely certify able students rather than identify students with high potential. The students with hidden talent are not located by tests (Wrightstone, 1960) and are not found until an enriched environment helps them bloom. Intelligence tests seldom identify students who have high potential in the performing arts. Torrance (1960) and Getzels and Jackson (1958) have located other significantly high achievers (but less pleasing students in the classroom) with various tests of creativity. They have found two-thirds of the students with high standardized achievement test scores and high creativity test scores to have lower IQ's than others of similar achievement. These lower IQ's, however, range above 115.

In the foregoing paragraph I have tried to make a case for four groups of gifted students, namely:

1. The intellectually capable but not necessarily academically able,
2. The academically able who must be intellectually capable,

309

3. The student with hidden talent brought out, not by tests but by opportunity and strong (and often new) desire to produce, and
4. The highly creative student who has the minimal intellectual capability (IQ of 115), plus an added factor.

Any classification of talents should be flexible and subject to revision. But, more than that, those identified must be thought of as "possessing high potentiality" rather than "assured of achievement" through membership in a designated group. It is unrealistic for anyone to expect each member of a "talented group" of children ultimately to attain extreme success as judged by traditional criteria such as eminence, professional accomplishment, or the production of creative ideas. This reality should not keep us from searching for programing that will more effectively meet the unique needs of all children.

The topic of identification of the academically able and intellectually capable is discussed in several other sources (National Education Association, 1961; Pegnato and Birch, 1959; Gallagher, 1960; French, 1964; and De Haan, 1957). The definition provided by Paul Witty in 1940 still stands as the most popular. He defined the gifted as "one whose performance in a potentially valuable line of human activity is consistently remarkable." Such a definition allows for great variation from researcher to researcher and makes a summary of research difficult because so few studies are directly comparable. For the remainder of this chapter our concern will be with the intellectually capable and/or academically talented (able) individuals. The performing artists in athletics, music, and art; the craftsmen or those with skill in cooking, carpentry, etc.; and skilled technicians with great potential for careers in business and industry will not be discussed in this chapter even though they may be very appropriately labeled as talented.

Some of the problems inherent in identifying the gifted in our society have been identified by Freehill (1961), who reminds us that brightness is much less obvious than dullness because 1) gifted people are capable of average performance; 2) many gifted people do not live in situations that bring forth ingenious verbal or academic behavior; and 3) gifted responses are marked by *appropriateness* and/or by the fact that they are stimulated by *small* clues which may or may not produce unusual behavior or performance. After a brief look at educational provisions, other topics will be reviewed.

The gifted need some time for daydreaming, for listening to records, for talking on the telephone, or for watching television productions. No one can rush along producing at a higher than his normal level every waking moment. Ambitious parents and teachers should not drive a student faster than his efficient operating level. Additional or supplementary activities for the gifted are necessary because their "gifts" allow them to operate efficiently at a higher than typical level. To push them beyond that level is unhealthy but it is also unhealthy to keep them from operating at that level.

As provisions for the gifted are discussed, the word "equality" frequently enters the conversation. And although many people accept with little question the desirability of provisions other than those for all students in the areas of athletics, music, speech and the handicapped, there is often concern about making unique provisions for individuals in the area of academics. A large number of people feel that when it comes to general learning in school, everyone should go through the same steps, and everyone should take just as many steps even though researchers have indicated for quite some-time that individuals vary in their education needs, that some people need more practice than others, and that some people are ready to move on to new learning experiences much earlier than others. We have long tried to establish that identical education experiences for each person attending a school are not desirable and that the same experiences for each person are not an indication of equality. Only as we provide for each child according to his needs are we providing for each child equally and democratically.

In few areas has weighty and consistent research been so neglected for a score of years as in the area of acceleration. Such authors as Terman (1954), Pressey (1954), Worcester (1956), McCandless (1957), Justman (1953, 1954) Barnette (1957), Meister (1956), Gowan (1958), Shannon (1957), and

Tyler (1957) approve various forms of "natural progress." The evidence that the effects of acceleration are favorable rather than unfavorable is becoming increasingly abundant.

"Grouping" is simply a term used to denote the way in which students are combined for instruction. Students have been combined for instruction by ability for years upon years. Even in the one-room rural schools all of the students in the room did not receive the same instruction. They were provided with instruction as the teacher had time to work with them at their level of instruction. As the schools grew in size the students were grouped according to their chronological age which in effect is grouping by ability.

Now, years after the first consolidation began, many people wonder if something can be added to chronological age and geographic location of the home to make the instructional groups such that a teacher can spend more time working with each pupil regardless of his intellectual ability.

Grouping according to English ability has been the practice in many secondary schools for a long time. In recent years grouping by ability in other subjects has increased. Over half of the secondary students are in schools with some form of ability grouping. Such administrative organization allows the teacher to start teaching at the competency level of the students and to carry them as far as possible in the year. Appropriate texts and other materials can be used with each group.

By maintaining several sections of each course at the same time of day scheduling difficulties are minimized. An ability grouping procedure in several subjects allows a student who has high ability in English to enroll in one of the advanced courses for that year as well as courses for middle ability students in other subjects. Although it would be unusual, this student might be in a lower level English course and a high level course in another subject the next year if such placement was appropriate for his growth pattern. A given student can enroll in the same level of instruction for each course on his program.

In elementary systems with one teacher providing all the instruction for the children in each classroom, grouping has been more difficult; but some school administrators with two or more sections for each grade have been able to reduce the difference in all areas when they place all of the very able students on the basis of their reading ability and intelligence test scores in one class and all of the children with very low scores in the other class. Such grouping in the elementary school does not do away with the need for grouping within the classroom in which two and possibly three reading and arithmetic groups are formed which may or may not contain the same students.

Although certain advantages have been discovered in grouping elementary and secondary children, a system has not been developed that will allow the teacher to provide instruction without giving attention to some individual differences. As Cornell pointed out so well in the mid-thirties "The results of grouping seem to depend less upon the fact of grouping itself than upon the philosophy behind the grouping, the accuracy with which grouping is made for intended purposes, and the differentiations in content, method, speed and techniques of the teacher as well as more general environmental influences." (Cornell, 1936, p. 304.)

Narrowing the ability range does not result in consistently greater achievement without specifically designing varied academic programs for the various ability levels (Goldberg and Passow, 1962). Following a long series of observational tours a group of educators from the Southern Regional Education Board concluded as follows:

Observers of special programs come quickly to the conviction that grouping of students according to ability for at least pertinent portions of their school experience is eminently desirable at every grade level. The mere grouping of pupils does not make a program, nor does absence of grouping necessarily mean that a program is absolutely ineffective. Nevertheless, ability grouping greatly increases the school's power to effect a marked improvement in the process of education. . . .

Ability grouping makes possible many teaching and

313

learning experiences which can not be accomplished in the typical classroom. This can be seen again and again in specially composed classes in all parts of the country. (Ward, 1962, p. 73).

Virtually the same observations were made after studying bright elementary age children in "regular" classes (Gallagher et al. 1960).

A demonstration of grouping and acceleration is provided in the organization of the St. Louis schools. As the students in St. Louis advance from the kindergarten, they are placed in a primary group. Rigid classification lines for the grades have been abolished, and the students progress through the basic educational experiences at a rate determined by their own characteristics. This plan is called the "Primary Pool," and the student stays in the primary pool until he is ready to profit from instruction at the fourth grade level. Some students progress through the primary pool much more rapidly than others, and of course, some progress much more slowly than others. Upon entering the fourth grade, students in the top one per cent of the fourth grade population in intelligence can be placed in one section. As the students in this section progress through the grades, the work normally introduced in higher grade levels is offered as the students are ready for it. By the time the students enter high school they have completed much of the freshman year program as well as many enrichment projects. By the time the students finish the secondary school they have completed much of the academic work usually accomplished in the first year of college, yet most of the students have remained in the public schools through kindergarten and 12 years. Other communities, even with much smaller school systems, have been able to obtain similar results.

When grouping is attempted on the basis of ability as well as on chronological age, good tests of achievement and ability are necessary. Testing for such purposes has improved considerably in the last few years. But even so, an individual who possesses a good understanding of test construction and test interpretation is necessary to make the optimal use of the results.

In any learning situation the concept that one holds of himself and of others in regard to ability to learn is to a large extent determined by the teacher. Sometimes unrealistic concepts develop when the students are grouped either by chronological age or by academic ability.

When students are grouped by their chronological age, it is very easy for some of the brighter students to consistently produce work that is superior to the others of the class. It is then easy for them to develop the belief that they can succeed with little effort in most of their ventures. This attitude is sometimes disastrous as they move through the academic process and competition increases. A major cause of underachievement in collegiate work is brought about by the attitude that only a little effort will be necessary to satisfactorily complete the assignments. When students easily excel in the elementary and secondary schools, it is very easy for them to develop attitudes of snobbishness. Because they are successful with such little effort, it is hard for them to realize why others can not be equally successful. On the other hand, when the students are grouped by ability, the fact that they know that they are in a high ability section sometimes causes them to develop the same snobbish ways. The attitudes and actions of the teachers and parents are very important in determining the attitudes and actions of the students under either condition.

Ability grouping provides a compromise between the old "pass or fail concept" with the "social promotions policy" to produce a healthier learning climate because grouping provides more time for learning experiences directed by the teacher at a level at which the student can learn efficiently. The students are grouped so that enrichment for groups is easier (than for individuals) and natural academic progress can be maintained with good results for all children and the gifted can be accelerated without omissions in their program.

Since today there is more to learn than there was yesterday, and tomorrow there will be more to learn than there is today, we need to find the most efficient ways of transmitting our knowledge to students. Provisions for the gifted child demand an accurate assessment of intellectual and academic characteristics of each child so that an educational program can be tailored to fit the needs of the student. Such a procedure is desirable for every child no matter the gifts he possesses.

In a study of ninth grade English classes, Drews (1959) found that the slower students read more, recited more, were more confident, liked school better, and were more accepted socially and intellectually in homogeneous groups. Superior students wrote more compositions, did more research, discussed at a more mature level, used more difficult words, expressed more complex and abstract thoughts, and were more interested in learning in homogeneous than in heterogeneous groups. Evaluations of this type indicate the superiority of grouping. Mere comparison of achievement test scores is not enough. When students of all ability levels are working with students of like ability, desirable changes in self concept may occur. There is no evidence to support the idea that grouping will have ill effects on the social or personal attitudes or behavior of children and youth. Neither does broad range grouping foster greater mutual acceptance among children of various ability levels.

Any practices that are introduced must be perceived only as means of moving toward the goals of the total program. New practices or modifications which are undertaken without this total program concept will waste money, personnel and the enthusiasm of learners. Whatever is planned "must be effected in terms of a sound social philosophy, on the basis of the psychological facts of the case, in terms of the unique realities of the local situation, and on the basis of any research findings that may be relevant." (Newland, 1961, p. 522).

From a thoughtful review of all that was studied by the Southern Regional Education Board's Project for Education of the Gifted Committee, the following principles have been formulated as those which characterize excellent programs (Ward, 1962):

1. Particularization of objectives
2. Staff training
3. Community interpretation

4. Systematic pupil identification
5. Distinguishable curricular experiences
6. Flexible pupil deployment
7. Comprehensiveness and continuity
8. Progressive program development
9. Financial allocation
10. Radiation of excellence

If the gifted individual is to be productive and innovative, the culture must encourage personal independence and autonomy. But our emerging values tend to reward conformity and cheerful compliance with the *status quo*. If the gifted person is to realize his endowment and potentialities, he must work hard and sacrifice present ease for future achievement. Such attitudes are difficult to foster in a society that blares out "Fly now-pay later" through the popular communication media.

Under the leadership of Charles Bish, the National Education Association has published more than a dozen monographs dealing with Mathematics, Science, English, Foreign Language, Social Studies, Music, Art, Business and Economics, Education, Elementary Education, Guidance and Administration for academically talented students. It is impossible to deal with curricular topics such as these in this chapter and unnecessary since these monographs and other published by professional associations are available.

Perhaps the greatest piece of research concerning the gifted was started in 1921 by Lewis Terman (1954). It was his purpose to find the traits that characterize children of high IQ and to see what kinds of adults these children become. He was moderately successful. (The study will continue until 2010 due to the farsightedness of Professor Terman.) Although his method of screening prior to individual testing was poor, he has provided a magnificent supply of good quality data relating to the top one per cent of our academically able children and youth. In his study of 1500 subjects located in California he provides data to dispell much of the unfortunate folklore surrounding talented youth. Terman found academically able children of high IQ to be generally superior to unselected students in physique, health, social adjustment, attitudes, and achievement. As his study progresses, we are finding that the intellect of his subjects in adulthood remains high and keeps expanding. We also see that general intelligence measures at six to ten years of age tell a great deal about achievement thirty years later. It is unfortunate that Terman or one of his followers could not have foreseen the need for a similar study of creativity, underachievement, and individuals who attain an IQ in the top one per cent of the population in later years but who were below that point in early childhood.

The high general achievement of children with high intelligence is emphasized in current research. In all reports the average general achievement of children with above average IQ's exceeds the average general achievement of randomly selected groups.

Most gifted children report favorable attitudes toward school (Abraham, 1957), but a greater percentage of the less gifted like school, school facilities, and teachers just as well or better (Dye, 1956).

Several researchers reported reading characteristics of the gifted. Hildreth (1958) found the gifted read more books and make more careful selection of those they read. Abraham (1957) agreed that the gifted like to read and read well, but felt that they frequently make trite choices.

Bliesmer (1954) compared the reading abilities of bright and dull children of comparable mental ages. Junior high school students with IQ's of approximately 84 were compared with children in grades three and four who had similar mental ages and IQ's of 116. The younger, bright children demonstrated significant superiority in listening and reading comprehension, locating and organizing factual details, recognizing main ideas, and drawing inferences and conclusions. However, the two groups were similar in word recognition, word meaning, and reading rate.

Kolstoe (1954) conducted a similar study, but his conclusion about oral vocabulary differed from the preceding one. He found a significant difference favoring the older dull children on the Wechsler Intelligence Scale for Children subtest of comprehension and he concluded that bright children are not superior to their older, mental age mates in vocabulary.

The understandings gifted children have about time and size relationships have been explored. According to Dixon (1958) gifted children react to perceptions regarding size instead of being unduly influenced by expectations built up in previous experiences. As mental age increases, a significant increase in score involving concepts of present time was noted by Farrell (1953) but this did not affect scores involving past, future, or complex time. Studies concerning the relationship of visual and auditory perception with intellectual capability have not been found. The generally superior position of the gifted would suggest a positive relationship.

The adjustment of gifted individuals has been of considerable concern to parents and teachers recently. Fortunately, we are outgrowing the idea that the bright and gifted are eccentric and destined to lead poorly adjusted lives. But as we outgrow some of the misconceptions which have hindered public acceptance of giftedness, we are learning more of the complexities involved in the personalities of the gifted. The very characteristics of giftedness cause some adjustment problems.

Early development, wide interests, and ease of understanding help gifted children to solve their problems more quickly, but also create many problems. In the studies that have been reported so far it has been found that gifted children are on the whole superior to the average in personal adjustment. Terman and Oden found their large sample to be well adjusted socially both in childhood and adulthood. Moreover, in comparing the people in their study who possessed the highest IQ's (1 out of 1000) with those of relatively lower IQ's (1 out of 100), they did not find more maladjustment among those with the highest IQ's. Leta S. Hollingworth, however, found that children with the highest IQ's (1 in 1000) are likely to have special adjustment problems. Most studies have indicated that the truly gifted person is usually endowed with a superior physique and mind. His physical vitality and his mental ability enable him to deal with stresses and to correct undesirable emotional conditions or personality trends. Another characteristic of the gifted is a superior capacity for self diagnosis which, whether it is evidence of adjustment or a step toward adjustment, probably requires a fairly high degree of intelligence. Despite their superior insight and adaptability, some gifted individuals are so emotionally disturbed that they fail to make a satisfying social or personal adjustment. Almost all of the problems of the gifted result from the blocking or denial of normal satisfactions.

Like other children, the gifted must be considered and treated as individuals. There are two reasons why investigations do not always reveal the role of intelligence in personal adjustment: (1) The sampling may not have included emotionally unstable bright children, who would have been unable to show their true capacity on the tests, and (2) the major measures of personality that have been used may also be, to some extent, measures of intelligence.

Gifted children sometimes experience feelings of inferiority even though they are superior in many ways. A gifted child is especially likely to feel inferior in developing physical skills or in other activities which require much practice before he becomes proficient. When he loses interest in thinking, playing, and working at the relatively immature level of his chronological peers, he sometimes withdraws from social contacts and engages in solitary pursuits. The ability to deal with problems by reasoning is so highly valued that it is sometimes used to excess. Such is the case when the gifted child uses his intelligence to gain the approval of parents and teachers but in so doing overemphasizes the intellect and fails to receive the greater gratifications based on emotional acceptance and belonging. Other causes of poor adjustment are parental or teacher pressure and exploitation, and the opposite reaction by adults: indifference and neglect. Poor school achievement is also associated with adjustment problems, but that aspect of the problem is considered later in a discussion of underachievement. Each case has its own peculiar combination of factors which are likely to be complexly interrelated.

Compared to average children, gifted children and youth receive higher grades and have more positive attitudes toward school. They participate in more extracurricular activities and have more hobbies and out-of-school interests. As a group they have more positive character traits, are better satisfied with peer relations, and are more confident of their general and social ability than are other children (Lessinger and Martinson 1961; Barbe 1955; Gallagher 1958a, 1958b; Strang 1956; Gowan 1956, 1960b; Elicker 1956; and Lightfoot 1951). Feldhusen and Klausmeier (1962) found a significant negative correlation between anxiety and intelligence of fifth grade children. They believe that gifted, more than average and retarded children, can assess realistically the actual dangers of a situation and find ways of overcoming them.

In the past decade several researchers re-examined the conclusion that the gifted are chosen more often than others when a large group of children are asked to name the students whom they like best. In a study by Liddle (1949) of 4500 children in grades four through six, intellectual talent was found to be positively related to social talent and negatively related to maladjustment. The sociometric ratings of high achieving students were compared with those of low achieving students in a study involving all 294 children in an elementary school (Grace and Booth, 1958). The high achieving students were among the best liked by their classmates and the low achieving students were among the least liked in all grades.

Miller (1956) compared 120 fourth and sixth graders who were classified as superior, typical, and retarded in intelligence. The children chose the superior students as friends to a significantly higher degree. The typical and retarded were next most wanted in that order. Although the superior students tended to underestimate their own status in the group, they were significantly more accurate in their self estimates than either of the other two groups. In another study, Martyn (1957) has shown that acceptance of the gifted is no different from that of others, although this may depend upon community and other local factors. However, those students in the top one tenth of one per cent have more difficulty in attaining peer acceptance (Barrett, 1957, Gallagher, 1958a, Sheldon, 1959).

The diversion of energies from intellectual to athletic and social pursuits by good students in response to peer pressure not only constitutes a loss in preparation time to the most talented individuals but tends to attract persons of mediocre ability into intellectual pursuits (Coleman, 1960). It is a well accepted belief that social approval of the gifted will improve their classroom behavior (Williams, 1958). In a report begging for replication in various settings Mann (1957) found that arranging gifted and other students together in school did not provide relationships significant enough to be called friendships. Hamilton (1960) and Justman and Wrightstone (1956) found among parents, teachers, and children, more favorable attitudes toward programs for the gifted in proportion to their understanding, relationship, and involvement in it.

A number of important insights into the attitude of adolescents toward academic brilliance were formulated by Tannenbaum (1962). He found academic brilliance and average ability were rated equally as personal attributes except when being brilliant required a greater than average amount of time devoted to school work and a lack of interest in sports. In such cases average ability was more highly prized. Studiousness *per se* was rated a less acceptable attribute than non-studiousness in all but one of the communities surveyed. Although academic excellence has, perhaps, increased in value in this culture, it is a long way from the top of a value scale. Tannenbaum concludes that "insofar as verbal stereotypes reflect face-to-face relations, these results suggest that academic brilliance, in-and-of-itself is not a stigma in the adolescent world. However, when it is combined with relatively unacceptable attributes, it can penalize its possessor severely" (p. 68). In many communities there is a danger of gifted students yielding to peer pressures and masking their talents in order to relieve these pressures.

The gifted child is first of all a child with a child's problems of development. Although the academic needs of the gifted vary from those of the generality, the social needs of all people are much the same. All need recognition, acceptance, and affection. All need to be appreciated by associates and superiors. Gifted children need to be appreciated by their classmates, teachers, and parents. Too often gifted children are left to "go it alone." Many gifted children hide their talents because their associates (including parents and teachers) begin to "pick their brains" instead of appreciating them as persons or working cooperatively with them. Research methodology will probably be improved in this area and other studies will be conducted.

Although academically able students as a group do not show excessive personal or social difficulties, there are suggestions in the literature that the kinds of problems exhibited by the able may be different from the generality. Some of these differences are generated by the more rapid rate of physical and psychological development. To illustrate some of the problems mentioned above, let us look at the measurement of interest.

Educators and psychologists know less about the interests of the gifted than such other major characteristics as achievement and intellectual development. In determining what role the assessment of interests should play in the total talent-identification program Passow (1955, p. 27) suggested that school personnel should consider "in what way if any . . . students with outstanding ability in a given field differ in their interest patterns from less talented students active in the same field."

Vocational interests have received sporadic treatment in the growing maze of literature pertaining to gifted students. Super (1957, p. 224) believes that vocational interests "are best defined in terms of the methods used to assess them" and that of these methods, interest inventories "have so far proved best." He also states that "vocational interest is important largely in determining direction and persistence of effort, but not, apparently the amount of effort."

In summarizing a number of studies concerned with the relationship between intelligence and interests, Roe (1956, p. 94) reports "correlations ranging from about —0.40 to +0.40. The relation is affected by sex, amount of education, occupation, the type of intelligence test, and the type of interest." Strong (1943) reports higher positive correlations occurring between scientific and linguistic interests and intelligence; and negative correlations between intelligence and social welfare, business contact, and business detail interests.

Later Strong (1955) questioned the appropriateness of correlational technique for showing true relationships between interests and intelligence. Despite the low correlations, he felt that ability must be important in the development of vocational interests. Although not specifically concerned with interests, Naomi Stewart (1947) indicated in her study of World War II Army personnel records that there is a clear occupational hierarchy with respect to Army General Classification Test Scores. Her report was consistent with World War I data and other studies including standardization data for most intelligence tests.

In reporting an analysis of scores from the Strong Vocational Interest Test used with National Merit Scholarship Corporation winners and runners-up, Lawrence Stewart (1959) found the scholars to possess interests which were less intense and consequently spanning a wider range than those recorded by a more representative sample of college students. Stewart postulated a less intense interest because the subjects recorded fewer primary and reject patterns than are normally found. This observation supports Strong's (1943) report on Terman's gifted group. The Terman group had fewer very high scores (A's) than a more representative student group.

Stewart (1959) felt that a reasonable explanation is that the interests of the high-ability students are less clearly differentiated from those of men in general than are the interests of more typical student groups, or . . . that high-ability students have a large number of interests which are spread over different areas. Another possible explanation for Stewart's scholars is that to qualify for inclusion in the NMSC group the students had to be more "well-rounded" than those in the more representative groups. He concluded that "the findings indicate that special pattern norms are necessary to describe the interests of high-ability students."

A study by French and Steffen (1960) involved the Kuder and undergraduate education majors. The wider interests of intellectually superior youth were observed here also.

The diversity of interests expressed by these students warrants further consideration and investigation of interest patterns recorded by groups with various collegiate majors as well as groups in other colleges of education.

324

The data reported above substantiate the belief that the gifted possess a greater range of interests and that gifted students differ in their interest patterns from their less gifted occupational peers. Adequate interpretations of these patterns have not been developed. These findings also support the belief that the educational and occupational opportunities for the gifted are usually greater than for others.

Such an analysis is possible for each area of personality but the studies are great in number and consequently outside the scope of this paper. Excellent and current reviews of pertinent literature can be found frequently in the *Review of Educational Research*.

Information on gifted girls and women is in general sketchy. There are far more studies about males than females. Many studies do not report results by sex and many important areas have not yet been investigated. Unfortunately it is very difficult for women to plan realistically to use their intellectual talents in a wide variety of fields. Although few women are able to utilize their talents as physicians, architects, engineers, lawyers, or bankers, bright females are making some inroads into professions requiring brainpower. Employment of women is related to education. In a recent report (USOE, 1965) it can be seen that 72 per cent of women having five or more years of higher education were in the labor force as were 53 per cent of those with four years of college. In contrast, 45 per cent of women who had completed only high school held jobs or were actively seeking them. As college enrollment booms the proportion of female enrollees declines, however.

The study of underachievement is of continuing concern. Under the editorship of Leonard M. Miller, the U. S. Office of Education published a monograph (Miller, 1961) on underachievement with the following definition:

> The underachiever with superior ability is one whose performance, as judged either by grades or achievement test scores, is significantly below his high measured or demonstrated aptitudes or potential for academic achievement.

Such a broad definition is necessary because of the maze of literature. Much of the difficulty in defining underachievement stems from attempts to compare one study with another when the groups of subjects have been working on different academic levels, with different levels of ability, and with different levels of achievement. To confuse the issue even further, different criteria of achievement and ability have been used.

Shaw (Miller, 1961, Ch. 2) has produced an excellent summary of the research concerning underachievement and a considerable number of pertinent studies. The types of underachievement described below come from the work of Shaw.

Underachievers should be categorized as chronic or situational. The chronic underachiever may be defined as one who consistently, from one year to the next, performs below the level of which he is capable. This consistency may not show up equally in all classes, but his underachieving performance will be both general and consistent. The situational underachiever is one whose underachieving behavior is short lived and the cause can generally be discovered quite readily. The lowered academic performance which sometimes follows a serious illness, the upset caused by the death of a parent, the physical and psychological problems accompanying growth spurts in adolescence, the personal problems which evolve when a child attempts to break away from overprotective parents and many other similar kinds of situations all may be productive of academic underachievement which may be relatively short in its duration.

Most educators consider nearly all underachievers as being transitory. Recent research, however, has revealed that this is not true. Most underachievers at the high school level have been underachieving from an early age (Barrett, 1957; Shaw and McGuen, 1960). Failure to recognize the difference between the two kinds of underachievement in research studies where relatively short term indices of achievement have been used has undoubtedly led to further confusion in research findings. Failure to recognize these differences in a treatment or a remedial program would likewise have confusing effects.

Still a third general type of underachievement is hidden

underachievement. Hidden underachievement can be divided into two general categories. The first category is created by the fact that some underachievers do poorly on most group intelligence as well as achievement tests. This is a particularly difficult kind of underachievement to detect and the teacher's judgment is often important. Students of the highest capability sometimes illustrate the second type of hidden underachievement which is equally difficult to diagnose. Their grades and achievement test scores lead one to believe that these individuals would perform far above the level of most students, and indeed they do. These students are test wise and when they enter collegiate institutions which are highly restrictive in their admittance policies, they still earn grades on tests equal to those of their peers but actually perform below the level of other students in spite of having high enough test scores to do the work.

The results of the current research studies on academic underachievement can be considered most applicable to chronic underachievers who are getting low grades but relatively high achievement test scores. This situation has arisen because most investigators made no attempt to differentiate among types of underachievers but lumped them together, and in most undifferentiated groups of underachievers, the chronic underachiever who received low grades but high achievement test scores will predominate.

In studies of the home backgrounds, parental attitudes, and child-rearing practices of fathers and mothers of underachievers the existence of some significant differences between families of achievers and underachievers has been observed. Underachievers tend to come from homes where the parents have less education and less favorable attitudes toward education than do the parents of achievers.

Personality characteristics of underachievers have been studied but no conclusive agreement is found among the results of various studies on the question of whether or not underachievers are more poorly adjusted generally than are achievers (New York City Talent Preservation Project, 1959; Shaw & Brown, 1957; Liebman, 1954). However, there are a number of specific characteristics upon which different investigators appear to agree. One of the most promising aspects of the personality of underachievers studied has been that of self-concept. There is rather general agreement that underachievers generally are more negative in their attitudes toward themselves than are achievers. There is also evidence to indicate that they tend to be more hostile and negative in their evaluations of others (Nason, 1958; Portland Public Schools, 1957 and 1959; Shaw & Brown, 1957; Kurtz & Swenson, 1951). These findings are in contrast with the superficial picture often presented by the underachiever of an aggressive, self-assured individual.

While research has revealed the answer to some of the questions posed by underachieving behavior, many of the most basic questions remain still to be answered. The search for specific traits which characterize underachievers as compared to achievers has not been particularly rewarding.

Another type of "underachievement" is the often observed high school dropout of high mental ability. Although the dropout rate is continually diminishing, eight to 10 per cent of all dropouts have IQs of 110 or above. In percentages this appears to be small but in actual numbers more than 1800 such students withdrew from Pennsylvania high schools in 1964-65 (French and Cardon, 1966). Nearly 500 had IQs of 120 and 80 had IQs of 130 or more. These figures are impressive when it is recognized that Pennsylvania has one of the lowest dropout rates in the country.

Some frequently mentioned correlates of school withdrawal were not substantiated in the findings of this study. Noticeably absent from the dropout data are indications of frequent school transfers, early part time employment, unemployment upon leaving school, generally low parental education, and lower parental employment status. What is noticed is that dropouts differ from persisters in such areas as personality, interests, educational skills, and family orientation toward school processes.

The male dropouts, when compared with the persisters, were found to be more uninhibited and happy-go-lucky. Although they tended to be easy going, their actions were marked with deliberateness and frankness of speech. The dropout boys were more assertive, independent, unconventional, and rebellious than the persisters. Their overall response pattern would suggest that they fell well within normal limits with regard to their mental health.

The girls dropping out of school for reasons other than marriage were very similar to the boys. However, two-thirds of the girl dropouts in this study were pregnant, married and/or planning to marry when they withdrew.

The girls who withdrew because of pregnancy and/or marriage were far less socially oriented than the persisters; they were less prone to seek social recognition. Also, they were more inclined to work alone, preferring things or words to people. These girls could be described as tending to be shy and retiring. Their personality pattern would indicate reason to suspect proneness to poor social adjustment in junior and senior high school.

Seldom did dropouts express attitudes which were opposite to those of persisters. The differences found were generally a matter of degree. Both the male dropouts and persisters, for example, believed that their parents considered school to be important; the dropouts were not as implicit however. Male dropouts did not demonstrate a truly negative attitude toward the schools. They did point to a number of areas which they found to be difficult to accept. They often expressed concern that schools are not preparing students for the "real" world. Lack of student involvement in the selection of courses to be taken was considered to be handicapping, for they felt that students best know their own needs and expectations. There also appeared to be an emotional gap between the male drop-outs and their teachers. The dropouts were not inclined to describe their teachers as being well prepared, knowledgeable with regard to subject matter, or concerned about the feelings and needs of the students. "Favoritism" was a problem listed by a number of dropouts. Dropouts tended to complain about having to conform to the school setting. More than did the persisters, they stressed the importance of being able to be an individual.

The attitudes of the unmarried female dropouts were similar

to those of the boys. They also expressed the notion that school training did not meet their needs as related to their vocational or professional goals. Although these girls also appeared to be estranged from their teachers, they seldom referred to unfair treatment or favoritism.

The married female dropouts were more similar to persisters than to unmarried female dropouts in their attitudes. They did not appear to feel that teachers were partial in their treatment of students or to be unhappy with their courses. They did, more so than the persisters or unmarried female dropouts, feel that their parents were dissatisfied with the school setting.

References

Abraham, W. A Hundred Gifted Children. *Understanding the Child,* 1957, 26:116-120.

Barbe, W. B. Evaluation of special classes for gifted children. *Exceptional Children,* 1955, 22:60-62.

Barnette, W. L. Advanced credit for the superior high school student. *Journal of Higher Education,* 1957, 28:15-20.

Barrett, H. O. Intensive study of thirty-two gifted children. *Personnel and Guidance Journal,* 1957, 36:192-194.

Bayley, Nancy, & Oden, Melita. The maintenance of intellectual ability in gifted adults. *Journal of Gerontology,* 1955, 10:91-107.

Birch, J. W. Early school admission for mentally advanced children. *Exceptional Children,* 1954, 21:84-87.

Bliesmer, E. P. Reading abilities of bright and dull children of comparable mental ages. *Journal of Educational Psychology,* 1954, 45:321-311.

Bonsall, Marcella, and Stefflre, B. The temperament of gifted children. *California Journal of Educational Research,* 1955, 6:162-65.

Coleman, J. S. The adolescent sub-culture and academic achievement. *American Journal of Sociology,* 1960: 65:337-47.

Cornell, Ethel L. *The grouping of pupils.* The thirty-fifth yearbook of the National Society for the Study of Education. Chicago: University of Chicago Press, 1936.

De Haan, R. F. Identifying gifted children, *School Review*, 1957, 65:41-48.

Dixon, J. C. Reactions of superior and feebleminded children to an illusion. *Journal of Genetic Psychology*, 1958, 93:79-85.

Drews, Elizabeth. *The effectiveness of homogeneous and heterogeneous ability grouping on ninth grade English classes with slow, average, and superior students.* U.S.O.E. Cooperative Research Report, 1959.

Drews, Elizabeth. What about the gifted child? *Michigan State University College of Education Quarterly*, 1957, 3:3-6.

Dye, Myrtle G. Attitudes of gifted children toward school. *Educational Administration and Supervision*, 1956, 42:301-308.

Elicker, P. E. Our brightest high school seniors. *NEA Journal*, 1956, 45:225.

Enochs, P. D. *An experimental study of a method for developing creative thinking in fifth grade children.* Unpublished doctoral dissertation, University of Missouri, 1964.

Farrell, M. Understanding of time relationships of five-, six-, and seven-year-old children of high IQ. *J. Educ. Res.*, 1953, 46, 587-594.

Feldhusen, J. F. & Klausmeier, H. J. Anxiety, intelligence and achievement in children of low, average, and high intelligence. *Child Development*, 1962, 33:403-409.

Freehill, M. F. *Gifted Children.* New York: Macmillan, 1961.

French, J. L. (Ed.) *Educating the gifted: a book of readings.* Revised edition. New York: Holt Rinehart and Winston, 1964.

French, J. L. and Steffen, H. H. J. Interests of gifted adolescents. *Personnel and Guidance Journal*, 1960, 38:633-636.

French, J. L. & Cardon, B. W. *Employment status and characteristics of high school dropouts of high ability.* University Park, Pa.: The Pennsylvania State University, 1966.

French, J. W. Evidence from school records on the effectiveness of ability grouping. *Journal of Educational Research*, 1960, 54:84-91.

Gallagher, J. J. Peer acceptance of highly gifted children in elementary school. *Elementary School Journal,* 1958, 58:365-470.

Gallagher, J. J. Social status of children related to intelligence, propinquity, and social perception. *Elementary School Journal,* 1958, 58:225-31 (b).

Gallagher, J. J. *Analysis of research on the education of gifted children.* Springfield, Illinois: Office of the Superintendent of Public Instruction, 1960.

Gallagher, J. J. *Research trends and needs in educating the gifted.* Washington, D.C.: U. S. Government Printing Office, 1964.

Gallagher, J. J., Greenman, Margaret, Karnes, Merle & King, A. Individual classroom adjustments for gifted children in elementary schools. *Exceptional Children,* 1960, 26:409-422 and 432.

Getzels, J. W. & Jackson, P. W. The meaning of giftedness. *Phi Delta Kappan,* 1958, 40:75-77.

Goldberg, Miriam L. & Passow, A. H. The effects of ability grouping. *Education,* 1962, 1-6.

Gowan, J. C. The underachieving gifted child: a problem for everyone. *Exceptional Children,* 1955, 21:247-49, 270.

Gowan, J. C. Achievement and personality test scores of gifted college students. *California Journal of Educational Research,* 1956, 7:105-109.

Gowan, J. C. Recent research on the education of gifted children. *Psychological Newsletter,* 1958, 9:140-144.

Gowan, J. C. Factors of achievement in high school and college. *Journal of Counseling Psychology,* 1960, 7:91-95.

Gowan, J. C. The present state of research on the able. *Exceptional Children,* 1960, 27:3-5.

Grace, H. A. & Booth, Nancy Lou. Is the gifted child a social isolate? *Peabody Journal of Education,* 1958, 35:195-196.

Guilford, J. P. Factors that aid and hinder creativity. *Teachers College Record,* 1962, 63:380-392.

Hamilton, N. K. Attitudes towards special education programs for gifted children. *Exceptional Children,* 1960, 27:147-150.

Hildreth, Gertrude. *Teaching Reading,* New York: Holt, Rinehart, and Winston, 1958 (ch. 24).

Hobson, J. R. Mental age as a workable criterion for school admission. Presidential Address, Division 16 Psychological Association Convention; September 1956 and also found in *Educational and Psychological Measurement*, 1963, 23:159-170.

Justman, J. Personal and social adjustment of intellectually gifted accelerants and non-accelerants in junior high schools. *School Review*, 1953, 61:468-478.

Justman, J. Academic achievement of intellectual gifted accelerants and non-accelerants in junior high school. *School Review*, 1954, 62:143-150.

Justman, J. & Wrightstone, J. W. The expressed attitudes of teachers toward special classes for intellectually gifted children. *Educ. Admin. Superv.*, 1956, 42, 141-148.

Kolstoe, O. P. A comparison of mental abilities of bright and dull children of comparable mental ages. *Journal of Educational Psychology*, 1954, 45:161-168.

Kurtz, J. J. & Swenson, Ester. Factors related to over-achievement and under-achievement in school. *School Review*, 1951, 59:472-480.

Lessinger, L. M. & Martinson, Ruth A. The use of the California Psychological Inventory with gifted pupils. *Personnel and Guidance Journal*, 1961, 39:572-575.

Liddle, Gordon. Overlap among desirable and undesirable characteristics in gifted children. *Journal of Educational Psychology*, 1949, 49:219-223.

Liebman, M. Our best minds were running errands. *NEA Journal*, 1954, 43:35-36.

Lightfoot, Georgia F. Personality characteristics of bright and dull children. *Contributions to Education* 969: New York Bureau of Publication, Teachers College, Columbia University, 1951.

Mann, H. How real are the friendships of gifted and typical children in a program of partial segregation? *Exceptional Children*, 1957, 23:199-201.

Martyn, K. A. *Social acceptance of gifted children.* Unpublished doctoral dissertation, Stanford University, 1957.

McCandless, B. Should a bright child start to school before he's five? *Education*, 1957, 77, 370-75.

Meister, M. Cooperation of secondary schools and colleges in acceleration of gifted students. *Journal of Educational Sociology*, 1956, 29:220-227.

Miller, L. (Ed.) *Guidance for the Underachiever with superior ability:* Washington, D.C.: U. S. Office of Health, Education, and Welfare, 1961.

Miller, R. V. Social status and socio-emphatic difference among mentally superior, mentally typical, and mentally retarded children. *Exceptional Children*, 1956, 23:114-119.

Nason, L. *Academic underachievement of gifted high school students*. Los Angeles: University of Southern California Press, 1958.

National Education Association and American Personnel and Guidance Association. *Guidance for the academically talented student*. Washington, D.C.: National Educational Association, 1961.

New York City Board of Education. *The NYC talent preservation project; an interim report:* August 1959.

Newland, T. E. Programs for the superior: happenstansical or conceptual? *Teachers College Record*, 1961, 62, 513-523.

Passow, A. H. The maze of the research on ability grouping. *The Educational Forum*, 1962, 281-288.

Passow, A. H., Goldberg, Miriam, Tannenbaum, A. J. & French, W. *Planning for talented youth*. New York: Bureau of Publications, Teachers College, Columbia University, 1955.

Pegnato, C. V. & Birth, J. W. Locating gifted children in junior high school. *Exceptional Children*, 1959, 25:300-304.

Portland Public Schools. *A report summarizing four years of progress by the cooperative program for students of exceptional talent*. Portland: the authors, 1957.

Portland Public Schools. *The gifted child in Portland*. Portland, Oregon: The Schools: 1959.

Pressey, S. L. That most misunderstood concept, acceleration. *School and Society*, 1954, 79: 59-60.

Roe, Anne. *The Psychology of Occupations*. New York: J. Wiley and Sons, 1956.

Shannon, D. C. What research says about acceleration. *Phi Delta Kappan*, 1957, 39:70-72.

Shaw, M. C. & Brown, D. J. Scholastic underachievement of bright college students. *Personnel and Guidance Journal*, 1957, 36:195-99.

Shaw, M. C. & Grubb, J. W. Hostility and able high school underachievers. *Journal of Counseling Psychology*, 1958, 26:46-66.

Shaw, M. C. & McCuen, J. T. The onset of academic achievement in bright children. *Journal of Educational Psychology*, 1960, 51:103-108.

Sheldon, P. W. Isolation as a characteristic of highly gifted children. *Journal of Educational Sociology*. 1959, 32:215-221.

Stewart, L. H. Interest patterns of a group of high-ability, high achieving students. *Journal of Counseling Psychology*, 1959, 6:132-139.

Stewart, Naomi, AGCT scores of Army personnel grouped by occupation. *Occupations*, 1947, 26:5-41.

Strang, Ruth. Gifted adolescents' views of growing up. *Exceptional Children*, 1956, 23:10-15.

Strong, E. K., Jr., *Vocational interests of men and women.* Palo Alto, California: Stanford University Press, 1943.

Strong, E. K. *Vocational interests 18 years after college.* Minneapolis: University of Minnesota Press, 1955.

Super, D. E. *The psychology of careers.* New York: Harper and Brothers, 1957.

Tannenbaum, A. A. *Adolescent attitudes toward academic brilliance.* New York: Teachers College, Columbia University, 1962.

Terman, L. M., & Oden, Melita. *The gifted child grows up: twenty-five years' follow-up of a superior group. Genetic studies of genius IV:* Stanford, California: Stanford University Press, 1947.

Terman, L. M. The discovery and encouragement of exceptional talent. *American Psychologist*, 1954, 9:221-30.

Terman, L. M. & Oden, Melita, *The gifted group at mid-life; thirty-five years' follow-up of the superior child. Genetic*

335

studies of genius, V, Stanford, California: Stanford University Press, 1959.

Torrance, E. P. Current research on the nature of creative talent. *Journal of Counseling Psychology*, 1959, 6:309-16.

Torrance, E. P. et al., *Assessing the creative thinking abilities of children*: Minneapolis: University of Minnesota, Bureau of Educational Research, 1960.

Torrance, E. P. Creative thinking of children. *Journal of Teacher Education*, 1962, 13, 488-460.

Tyler, Leona. Studies on motivation and identification of gifted pupils. *Rev. Educ. Res.*, 1957, 27, 291-299.

U.S.O.E. *Counseling girls toward new perspectives*, Washington, D.C. U. S. Government Printing Office, 1965.

Ward, V. S. (Ed.) *The gifted student: a manual for program improvement*. Charlottesville; Southern Regional Education Board, 1962.

Williams, Meta. Acceptance and performance among gifted elementary school children. *Education Research Bulletin*, 1958, 37:216-20.

Witty, P. Some characteristics of the education of gifted children, *Educational Administration and Supervision*, 1940, 26:516.

Witty, P. (Ed.) *The gifted child*. Boston: Heath, 1951.

Worcester, D. A. *The education of children of above average mentality*. Lincoln: University of Nebraska Press, 1956.

Wrightstone, J. W. Demonstration guidance project in New York City. *Howard Educational Review*, 1960, 30-237-251.

EXPERIMENTAL PSYCHOLOGY AND THE PROBLEMS OF AGING

SHEILA M. CHOWN, PH.D.

Lecturer in Social and Industrial Psychology, Bedford College

Editorial Note

The specter of old age haunts an ever growing number of men and women from all walks of life. Their fate in many instances will be determined by advances in gerontology or the scientific study of the phenomena of aging. Dr. Chown calls for an interdisciplinary approach to the solution of the problems of the Older Person, who "has more to offer to the science of Psychology than that favorite subject, the College Student."

Dr. Sheila M. Chown has been Lecturer in Social and Industrial Psychology at Bedford College in London since 1961. She obtained her Bachelor of Science degree from London University in 1953 and her Ph.D. from the University of Liverpool in 1957. Her doctoral dissertation was on the development of occupational choice.

Dr. Chown's research has been on intellectual changes with age and the interaction of these with personality and attitudes, particularly as displayed in rigidities of performance and outlook. She has also engaged in industrial research on attitudes and working conditions. She worked full time from 1956 to 1960, and has worked since on a part-time basis, in the Medical Research Council's Unit for Research on Occupational Aspects of Aging, in Liverpool, England. Some of her publications are listed in the References at the end of this article.

EXPERIMENTAL PSYCHOLOGY AND THE PROBLEMS OF AGING

Introduction: Social and Cultural Factors in Aging

Many practical problems of aging such as adapting to re-tirement and making new living arrangements in widowhood, are worsened by cultural expectations and social attitudes. Research on retirement, for example, shows that many men do not enjoy it and feel discarded by society, without any vital role to occupy their time. Housing arrangements for the elderly seem to be viewed differently by the old and middle-aged. One study showed that middle-aged people thought the elderly should remain independent and hence should live alone (Britton, Mather and Lansing, 1961). The other, in a different area of the United States but dealing with the same broad income bracket, discovered that the elderly themselves regarded having to live alone as a sign of rejection (Brown, 1960). The old may manage to stand up to feelings of social rejection—for in-stance, retirement does not have a deadly impact (Emerson, 1959; Thompson, Streib and Kosa, 1960)—but few people think of old age as the happiest time in their lives (Dean, 1960).

The topic of social interaction has particularly concerned the Chicago sociologists and psychologists: they have produced the theory of disengagement (Cumming and Henry, 1961). They think that successful agers gradually withdraw from active social life, and become less emotionally involved with other people. At first sight this does not seem to be the pattern of aging fol-lowed by many outgoing people, who seem to continue to be actively involved with others to a great age. In a recent study (Neugarten, Birren and Krines, 1966) successful middle-aged managers were interviewed about their work habits, and some backing for the disengagement theory was found. These men were constantly dealing with people in their work, but said that they had come to rely more on their subordinates for ideas and to give less attention to the personal problems of their subordinates. Thus the nature of their social interaction differed from that of younger men, though the amount of it did not. Results such as these could be used to suggest many useful alterations to conditions of life reached by elderly people.

But the theoretical and experimental psychologist wishes to look beyond the emotional and social concomitants of aging and to identify underlying age differences in ability. He is interested in three approaches and, particularly in the area of cognitive differences with age, he is beginning to see some results from all three. The psychologist first needs to have accurate descriptions of capacities at each age, together with data as to the variance in behavior found in each age group. He will wish to check his data from cross-sectional studies with longitudinal results. Second, he will want to undertake probing work to find out what aspects of performance cause most difficulty to older people, and how those aspects can be eased for practical purposes like retraining (Belbin and Belbin, 1966). Third, the psychologist will be interested in the elusive search for a theory of aging in terms of physiological or biochemical changes which might lead either to attempts to turn the clock back for individuals by suitable chemical treatment, or more likely to accurate diagnosis and prognosis of a person's life expectancy.

Normative Approach

Comparatively few researchers have collected test scores from adults representative of different age groups. Test norms are usually based on young adults' scores. Intellectual ability as measured by the Wechsler Adult Intelligence Scale has of course been quite thoroughly investigated with respect to age (Wechsler, 1955). 'Hold' and 'don't hold' subtests which rely respectively more on previously learned material and more on present problem solving ability have been consistently identified by other workers too (summarised by Riegel and Riegel, 1962). Moreover, in a number of studies, a single principal component seems to play an increasingly dominant part in performance, relating subtests in the old which were independent in young adults (Cohen, 1957; Nordvik, 1966). It is tempting to assume that this factor is physiologically based; but it has failed to yield its identity yet; short term memory and speed have been names given to the factor in different researches. American work has shown that norms for the WAIS may vary slightly from one section of the population to another (Levinson, 1960, 1962) so even here care is necessary in interpretation.

A normative study using a wider range of tests has recently been carried out in Liverpool, England (Heron and Chown, 1966-7) and will serve as an illustration of the survey-type which is demanded in this field. In all, 300 men and 240 women from the general population in the age range 20 to 80 were tested, with 50 men and 40 women included in each age decade. They were selected randomly from volunteers except that they were matched for socio-occupational class between age decades and they reflected the occupational class of the total population in the Liverpool area. Subjects were given a number of cognitive tests (Raven's Progressive Matrices, 1938; Elithorn's Perceptual Mazes, 1955; Clément's Digit Code, 1961; Reitan's Trail Making test, 1958; Heron's Digit Span test, 1967; and the Mill Hill Synonyms Vocabulary test, Raven, 1938). They completed two personality inventories (the Heron Personality Inventory, 1956, scored for Introversion and Emotional Stability; and the Wesley Rigidity Inventory, scored according to Chown, 1960, for Flexibility). Certain physiological measures were taken (systolic and diastolic blood pressure, and forced expiratory volume), and a number of physical attributes were recorded (height, weight, and grip strength). In all, each subject underwent four hours of testing, broken into two sessions.

Norms were reported for each test, in terms of the 75th, 50th and 25th percentile scores for each age decade. Across the different age groups, Introversion scores increased slightly but non-significantly, and so did Emotional Stability scores. Vocabulary increased slightly with age group. On all tests except those three, markedly lower median scores were found in the older groups. On the Wesley, older people ticked fewer Flexible items, and were more alike than the young. On all other tests, the variance in scores was greater in the older group.

All the cognitive tests intercorrelated quite highly; Matrices, Mazes, Digit Code and Trail Making more highly than Digit Span and Vocabulary.

Two questions remain about normative data which have been collected from different individuals representing different

340

age groups. One is, quite simply, whether it is valid to assume that age differences reflect true age changes. Cultural changes over the years in teaching methods, length of schooling, attitudes to tests, familiarity with experimental approaches, etc. might account for apparent age declines found in cross-sectional work. (However, in that case, why not age differences in all tests?) It is customary to point out that longitudinal work is needed to confirm cross-sectional findings, and indeed such work is already under way in a number of centres, in North Carolina (Busse, 1966), California (Jones, 1966), and Germany (Riegel, 1966). Interpretations from longitudinal work are also having to be made with some reservations, however, because there is growing evidence that those who live to be old tend to have made higher scores originally on cognitive tests than those who die in their fifties and sixties. (Jarvik, Kallman and Falek, 1962; Riegel 1966). This selective death rate suggests that we can only have fully representative information about the top scorers in the population. This in turn suggests that previous cross-sectional studies of age decrement curves may have underestimated decrements in the oldest groups, since the younger groups' averages will have been lowered by inclusion of the potential nonsurvivors. More work needs to be done on the selective death rate. We do not know whether it also operates before the fifties and sixties are reached, nor even whether it is any more than an artifact due to testing some people as they experience the fall in score likely a short time before death (Kleemeier, 1961).

The second question is, what use can be made of normative data. There are many occasions when we need to know how a man can perform on a novel task compared with another man. It may be valid to disregard age and compare raw scores—but due to his older age one man is likely to have more stored information at his command than the other and in many real life situations this might outweigh the lack of ability to deal with the truly novel. There are however other occasions when it is definitely desired to know how a man stands with respect to his own age group, and for this, detailed age norms are necessary. On a test like Trail Making for example, an elderly man may take two or three minutes to do the alternation number-letter series, and yet be within normal limits for his age; judged by young norms alone, he might have been classified as brain damaged. However, it might be a more diagnostic use of age norms if one were to look at change in a man's standing over the years with respect to his own age groups. In such work as that by Kleemeier (1961) the sudden fall in intelligence test results shown by some of the elderly subjects turned out to be an accurate predictor of death some six months to two years later. Deterioration curves more steep than normal might be revealing at earlier ages too: does deterioration occur gradually or in fits and starts, and can it be linked to any personal or physiological or physical trauma? These questions, as yet unanswered, indicate the part which normative data can play in future research.

Normative data are no more than a first step along the path of science. They provide some idea of what to expect from people, but little or no idea of why changes occur.

Analytic Approach

The second step in work on aging consists in attempts to look at age differences in performance in an analytical way, to try to find by experiment just what capacities alter with age, and to see how much each contributes to a given test performance. Experimental studies of learning and problem solving will be taken as examples of this approach.

A. Learning

In the learning process there are probably a number of stages, failure at any of which may cause deterioration in learning performance. Material to be learned has to be perceived; then put into a short term storage system; then reinforced and possibly related to previously learned material until a more permanent memory trace has formed. This trace also has to be stored (and may be distorted in the course of time); later, the memory has to be retrieved from storage in a situation where recognition or recall is required; lastly an appropriate response has to be made. Welford (1959) outlined this sequence and pointed to the need for controlled study of different parts of it.

1. *Short term memory*—The measurement of short term memory in the old has presented problems. The Digit Span test of the Wechsler shows very little alteration with age, and is often classified as a 'hold' test. Even in memory disordered patients, digit span does not seem much affected. It must be assumed that the kind of immediate, parrot-like memory tapped in the Digit Span test is not the same as the short term memory for news, names and appointments which begins to fail in middle age. Some delay is needed between giving the stimulus and asking for the recall, in order to tap that kind of short term memory. However, in experimental terms it is not easy to keep the delay constant or to control rehearsal of the material during the delay.

Both can be done by the method of dichotic stimulation, first used by Broadbent (1957) to study short term memory in young people. He fed stories of digits simultaneously to each ear, at a speed of two per second. The subject was asked to repeat first the digits heard by one ear and then the digits heard by the other. It was found that few errors were made in the first list recalled, but more errors were made in the delayed list heard by the second ear. Numbers were not often transposed between the lists, a fact which led Broadbent to suggest two memory systems, one which deals with immediate material and the other which stores material for a short time. (Later workers have found transposition).

Inglis (1965, 1966) has used dichotic stimulation in a series of experiments with elderly people and with memory-disordered patients. His findings have been that on the whole, the first-ear list is well recalled at all ages, though a slight fall-off occurs in the upper age groups. The second-ear list is progressively worse recalled by the older age groups. Memory-disordered patients produce poorer second-ear lists, but show little impairment on first-ear lists. These results fit in with what is known of ordinary memory for digits and short-term memory which is known by real life observation to deteriorate with age. The neat design of these experiments means that subjects serve as their own controls. What is managed successfully in recall of material heard by one ear might be expected in recall of material heard by the other ear, and differences in motivation between age groups (often put forward to explain learning decrements with age) cannot be used to account for dichotic listening results.

But objections have been put forward to the dichotic listening experiments on two main counts. The first was that in Broadbent's original experiments and Inglis's subsequent experiments, subjects were allowed to select which ear's-worth they reported first. Thus subjects might (if for instance lacking in confidence) have deliberately attended to one ear's worth and ignored the other. The fall-off in 'memory' for the second ear's-worth would then reflect 'lack of attention' rather than 'lack of memory' (Craik, 1965). The second objection also concerned the subjects' selection of which ear's-worth he reported first. Experiments on cerebral dominance and dichotic listening by Kimura (1963) showed that subjects had an ear preference, physiologically based on brain development. Right-handed people are usually right-eared. Subjects might thus be reporting their preferred ear first, and the age fall-off might be the result of an interaction between memory and inevitable ear-preference.

Inglis (1966) and Craik (1966) have both carried out experiments which provide evidence on these points. Inglis, using subjects over the age range 20 to 70, gave dichotic stimulation under two conditions. First, subjects were told beforehand which ear's-worth to recall first (left and right ear first were tested). Second, the same subjects were only told after they had heard the digits which ear's-worth they were to reproduce first. Under both conditions there was no consistent ear bias, and the difference between the right and left ears was smaller than the difference between the first and second lists.

Craik used the same two test conditions, but used two sets of subjects for the two experiments, and presented the numbers at a slower rate (90 per minute). When he warned subjects over the age range 20 to 70 which list to reproduce first, he found that the first ear's-worth, regardless of whether it was left or right, was reproduced better than the second. When subjects aged 20 to 30 and 60 to 70 were given instructions only after hearing the series, he found an interaction between order and ear. The right-ear-second lists were reproduced better than left-ear-second lists, and also better than left-ear-first lists. (Age differences occurred in first-ear lists as well as second-ear lists in these experiments: rate of presentation effects and subject sophistication both need further research.)

On the basis of these results it looks as though people can learn the dichotic listening technique; that naive subjects are likely to show a stronger ear preference than practised subjects; that left to themselves, people prefer to attend to their right ear, but given other instructions they can attend to their left ear instead. However, practised subjects seem able to attend to both ears and to reproduce either list first on demand, and in this situation, the right-ear-second list shows a marked fall-off with age in accuracy.

The task could be a useful instrument for future research, at least provided subjects are given practice on it before their scores are used. Inglis now hopes to link performance on it to performance on learning tasks. Apart from attempts to correlate these two, it should be possible to match groups of young and old subjects for dichotic listening, and then study their learning ability for long-term material. This technique might enable us to sort out the differential age effects of short-term memory upon long-term registration.

However, it must be remembered that digits provide a limited range of items, with only nine possibilities on each occasion. Their 'surprise value' in information theory terms is small. What would happen to span of apprehension and age if material other than digits were used? The alphabet has a limited but larger range of items. Nonsense syllables have a practically unlimited range. Would the dichotic listening results still obtain if these materials were used instead of digits?

Where sequential probabilities in the material are uneven, still more complications might ensue. Craik (1966) has suggested that with age there may be less ability to chunk or code information, so that short-term memory for meaningful material might show greater age differences than memory for non-sense material.

Meanwhile, it can be taken as highly probable that some of the apparent difficulty in learning found with age is due to impairment of the short-term memory storage system: less material gets through this intact in older people, and therefore less is available to consolidate in long-term memory.

2. *Long term retrieval and response*—The work on short-term memory leads naturally into a consideration of long-term memory; the registration in the long-term system, storage, and retrieval and response stages of learning.

In the best classical tradition, work has been mainly carried out using paired associate learning of material with low association values. For example, Arenberg (1965) looked at errors in performance by older subjects. His learning tasks consisted of paired associates, two consonants acting as the stimulus and a familiar word as the response. A dependent variable was the time for which the stimulus was presented alone. One group of subjects saw each stimulus for 1.9 seconds, and a matched group for 3.7 seconds. Both groups then saw a blank screen for 1.8 seconds, and then stimulus and response were exposed together for 1.8 seconds. Arenberg used highly intelligent subjects in his first experiment, 32 in their twenties and 32 in their sixties. Half of each age group had the long stimulus presentation, and half the short. Young subjects did better than old ones, and moreover, young subjects were not much affected by stimulus presentation times, but older subjects made fewer errors under the longer times. Errors could be due to failures in registration, interference with traces due to quick follow-on by the next stimulus, or errors in retrieval or response.

Arenberg's second experiment endeavoured to cut out the retrieval and response explanations of errors. His subjects were 16 men in each of four age-pace groups, (32 men aged 18 to 21, and 32 aged 60 to 77). All were unemployed men of comparatively low education, but all had raw scores on the WAIS of 20 or above and all were literate. Two rates of stimulus presentation were used, as in the first experiment. However, interspersed among the conventional trials were self-paced response trials, in which the subject was given an unlimited time to respond. Results were compared on the self-paced and ordinary presentations in each group. If retrieval and response time limitations account for apparent fall-off in learning with age, then the older subjects should have better results given 1.8 or 3.7 seconds plus unlimited time than with only 1.8 or 3.7 plus a further 1.8 seconds to respond. In fact, with the slower stimulus presentation time, little difference in the number of errors was found between timed and self-paced responses. With the faster time, more difference was found, but not a significant one. Larger differences in number of errors were found between fast and slow presentation rates and between young and old than between self-paced and limited time responses.

While it can be shown that response times of a simple type (reaction times) do alter slightly with age, and that association times also increase with age, in these experiments by Arenberg retrieval and response times do not seem to be the crucial factor causing the age differences in learning. If stimulus presentation times were reduced to less than those used by Arenberg, it is likely that significant age differences in performance would occur; but at least it has been shown that even when retrieval and response decrements are ruled out as explanations, decrement in learning paired associates still occurs. Is registration or interference with registered traces the crucial factor? Arenberg's experiments do not allow us to decide. As he points out, the longer presentation time could let subjects rehearse more, or respond more actively to stimuli, or allow more consolidation of the memory traces before interference from the next stimulus.

3. *Long-term retention*—Work on long term retention has not been very common as yet, and this is easy to understand since it involves testing old and young subjects on memory for the material at the end of the learning period, and then retesting them after some considerable interval of time.

In an experiment with trainee post office sorters, Chown, Belbin and Downs (1967) were able to test retention after three days with some of their middle-aged and young subjects. The middle-aged group consisted of men aged 35 to 49, and their young group of men aged 20 to 34. Subjects were given 12 minutes to learn the associations between 20 villages and their appropriate counties (five villages from each of four counties). The material was presented in the form of programmed instruction booklets; one version demanded active thought from the subjects and the other matched version needed only rote learning. At the end of 12 minutes, the subjects were given a random list of villages and asked to fill in the counties from memory. There was no time limit. The young did equally well after both programmes. The middle-aged equalled the young after the active, discovery programme, but were worse after the rote programme. Three days later, without warning, the same random test list was presented to all available subjects, 39 middle-aged and 36 young ones. (Twenty-four men had completed the course early and left, and one had been rejected: thus on the whole those who took the retention test were poor learners originally, concentrated below the median score for the total sample.) During the three days the subjects had been open to heavy potential interference. On the immediate learning test these young subjects did equally well after both programmes (active, median 11; rote, median 12). The active programme was better than the rote one for the middle-aged (active, median 9; rote, median 7-8). On the retention test, young subjects showed some fall-off (active, median 8; rote, median 10), but the middle-aged appeared to retain what they had learned very well indeed (active, median 9; rote, median 7).

More work needs to be done in the area of retention, preferably using subjects covering the whole range of age and learning ability, from whom subjects matched for immediate learning scores can be drawn. The experiment quoted above, however, suggests that it is at the stage of registration rather than retention that most of the age deficit in learning occurs in the middle-aged.

4. *Interference from previously established traces*—A further suggestion has been made that the old find more difficulty in long-term registration of new material because it has to displace previously established material. Alteration in motor skills is usually regarded as more difficult for the old than learning a completely new skill; for example, Kay's work (1954) showed

that the correction of errors in a psychomotor task was more difficult for the old than the young.

However, a recent piece of research by Canestrari (1966) suggests that this may not be the cause of difficulty in long term registration of paired associates. Using word association test norms, he sorted out two extreme groups of subjects, those who gave common responses to words on the list (and kept to common responses) and those who gave original responses (and kept to original responses). Subjects in their early sixties and subjects in their late 'teens were included in each group. It was expected that 'common' responders would have more difficulty than 'original' responders in forming new associations, particularly when these were of low associative strength, and that the difficulty would be worse for the old than the young. Subjects were asked to learn at their own pace one or other of two paired associate lists; the same ten stimuli were used in each list, but in one case the responses were extremely common ones and in the other, very rare. The three variables considered in the analysis were age, common/original response groups, and common/original lists. The old had lower WAIS vocabulary scores than the young, and both groups of old subjects did less well than the young on learning both lists, particularly on the 'original' list. However, the common and original responder groups did not differ significantly from each other in learning ability overall, nor when considered for the two age groups separately, nor was there a significant interaction between respondent groups, age and list. Original responders did do better on original lists, but age did not impose any extra handicap on the common responders— they were not subject to extra interference from previously well established responses.

These experiments all help to suggest that the basic alterations with age in learning come in the loss of ability to register new associations first in the short term and then in the long term memory store (perhaps as a result of short term decrement). Interference by existing or subsequent traces is not the fundamental cause of the difficulty. It is often supposed that short term reverberation dies away within it due to the build up of inhibition. Whether or not this supposition is correct, it seems likely that one given instance of stimulation has less effect on the short term memory system of the old, so that either an ordinary stimulus has to be repeated many times or the stimulus level has to be raised to get an effect in the old equivalent to an ordinary stimulus input in the young. An illuminating analogy has been provided by D. J. Stewart (personal communication), who likens short term memory to a taut piece of elastic—one twang keeps a new piece reverberating well, but the same twang given to an old piece hardly affects it. Practical help for older learners might be given by intensifying the stimulus, and this has been tried so far in two ways. Belbin, Belbin and Downs (1966) have shown in their work with trainee sorters that 'discovery' techniques bring the learning performance of the old up very close to that of the young. Hulicka (1965) was able to improve learning of paired associates by providing meaningful mediating material or extra associations. She had previously found that older subjects do not seem to use such mediators spontaneously, but there is evidence that, given training, old subjects can make excellent use of visual or auditory mediators (Hulicka, 1966; Canestrari, 1966). The physiological mechanism of long term memory is also far from certain yet, but it seems likely that some physical or chemical change occurs (such as growth of dendrites, or change in RNA) and that sufficient stimulation has to be given over a long enough time to allow such semi-permanent changes to take place. The problem now seems to be one for physiologists to unravel.

B. Problem Solving

Problem solving behaviour is beginning to be subjected to analytic experiments, but an extra difficulty in this area is that the experimenter eventually needs to discover the methods by which his subject operates. He is unlikely to be content for long with knowing whether the subject has the right or wrong answer, but will wish to discover how the decision was reached.

With certain reservations already mentioned it has been established that there is a fall off with age in ability to solve problems which involve new material. From Chown's (1961) study of the rigidities and age it seems that there are large type-specific and non-age related components in all so-called rigidity tasks, but that there also appears to be a common component running through many 'rigidity' measures and through Raven's Progressive Matrices Intelligence test. Several types of rigidity were involved, and the tasks used to measure them ranged through motor, perceptual, numerical and verbal. A likely common element might be 'set'. (Another might have been 'speed of work', but this seemed to become an important common element only in the group of subjects aged sixty and over.)

1. *Set*—The hypothesis that the poorer cognitive performance of older people is due to inability to alter 'set' from one line of reasoning to another is backed by some direct evidence from an open-ended problem situation. Stevens (1960 and personal communication) asked her subjects to think aloud as they tackled a problem, and the older ones did try fewer avenues in all, while more older subjects were unable to leave their initial false hypotheses.

Inability to shift 'set' has also been demonstrated in older people in perceptual experiments (Talland, 1959) and in the water jar test (Heglin, 1956). Bromley (1956) found that his older subjects were not able to regroup the Shaw test three dimensional figures in as many acceptable ways as younger subjects.

Brinley (1965) thinks that where the old have full control of a 'set' (i.e., reaction time experiments with fixed preparatory interval) their performance will improve with practice and may come to equal that of young subjects. (Murrell, 1966, has recent data which shows that this is so for choice reaction time.) But where the 'set' can only be for a category of response, where meaningful material is involved or an open-ended answer has to be given, 'set' does not always seem to help the old.

Brinley himself (1965) compared performance on shift and non-shift tasks of a simple verbal and numerical type. The old were not disproportionately hampered on the shift tasks if measures of speed were considered. The older subjects did make more errors in the shift tasks, and in this sense could not cope with the shift material as successfully as with the non-shift material.

It seems worth pointing out that success on Brinley's shift tasks could be achieved with the aid of a complex 'set', (for a series of three types of response in repeated order) which would require memory of the order and of position reached in the series. The errors of the old can be explained by quick decay of their short term memory, so that they could not hold the complex three-part 'set' in mind and return to the correct point in it after each subtask, though they could easily hold and use the simple single loop 'set' where no short term memory is really involved.

The inability to get out of a rut and think of fresh hypotheses in problem-solving tasks cannot be explained so readily by short term memory deficit. We can join Cattell (1946) and hypothesise an 'inability to alter nerve parthways' as he did when he originally discussed perseveration and disposition rigidity, but a more productive approach for psychological research might be to think in terms of inability to scan information in long term memory. It would be interesting to find the comparative effect of courses in creative thinking on young and old subjects. Would these aid the old in problem solving tasks as did Hulicka's introduction of mediators in paired associate learning?

2. *Logical thinking and negative instances*—Inability to shift 'set' is not the only apparent cognitive difficulty with age; logical thinking is difficult too. Jerome (1962) reported that older subjects were less inclined to follow logical procedures to discover which buttons to press in which order to put on a light. Lack of logic was present even when subjects had been given careful training and were encouraged to record their attempts so that they did not have to rely on memory. Jerome noted that buttons with complex functions and especially those which acted as inhibitors of part of the action of another button caused the most difficulty to the old. His older subjects were all retired from professional work, and in their youth must have been at least as intelligent and used to logical thinking as his

young student group. However, formidable levels of task were reached quickly, and a simpler task would be needed for work with less intelligent subjects.

Wetherick (1965, 1966) recently made up a simple test of logical thinking which presented groups of letters from which a common concept had to be deduced. He found that older subjects had more difficulty than younger ones in using 'negative instances.' These should have been used to disprove a given hypothesis, but were often used instead as though they confirmed it. Very interestingly, this age effect occurred even when subjects of different ages were matched for their current performance on Raven's Progressive Matrices.

Inclusion of inhibitory actions and negative instances both add complexity to comparatively simple situations. If a computer were programmed to carry out either Jerome's or Wetherick's tasks, the programs would have more stages in them on those tasks which older people find more difficult.

3. Complexity and channel capacity—If we wish to think in terms of inability to hold in mind several aspects of complex material at once, it seems natural to turn to the mathematics of information theory and the notion of channel capacity. Unfortunately, most existing intelligence tests do not lend themselves to an information theory analysis. While it would be possible to tease out how many logical aspects must be considered in each test item, it would not be possible to weight them for overdetermination or for ease of perception. If, however, the difficulty level of each item is considered instead of its information content, useful information about aging may be obtained. Furneaux (1952) used this approach in his work with letter series, when he developed 'speed' and 'level' tests of intelligence with young subjects. The difficulty of solving any item he took to be proportional to the log of time taken to solve it; he found that the slope of the difficulty/log speed graph was similar for all his subjects, though the intercept varied according to whether a subject was dull or bright. Whether the slope would also be similar for subjects of different ages has still to be tested, and work is now under way on it.

A number of researchers (Birren et al. 1963; Chown, 1961)

have found that performance on intelligence tests seems to be more related to performance on tests of psychomotor speed in old subjects than in young subjects, as though lack of speed either acts as a limiting factor only in the old or reflects lack of intelligence only in the old. However, the handicap imposed on older subjects by speed limits on Raven's Progressive Matrices is not so great as might be expected (Chown, 1966). It looks as though older people, when they know they are being timed, use their time in a way almost proportional to that of younger people; and reach their final score in only a little longer than a young person would take to reach the same final score. We cannot be sure without further investigation that the time spent on errors (which contributes to the time taken though the errors do not affect the score) is equivalent for the different age groups, but at the moment it does look as though, though the total is lower for the old, the rate of working is not differentially lower for the old.

It is interesting that in the area of choice reaction time with one type of stimulus only, slopes of speed of reaction plotted against $\log_2$ number of equiprobable choices seem to be parallel for different age groups (provided subjects are only allowed to see the stimulus for a short time). The slopes have not been proved parallel in conditions where extra stimulus time has been allowed, or where complex 'meaningful' material has been used as the stimulus (Welford 1962).

Problem solving techniques and strategies in different age groups still require much research. At the moment we can only summarize the main decrements in problem solving performance. Older people are less able to produce hypotheses for testing out; they can hold fewer aspects of a situation in mind at once; they take longer to deal with material they can hold in mind. In many problem solving situations, short term memory deficit may also hamper the old. Additional complexity makes a problem harder; if the complexity involves deduction from negative instances, the old may be disproportionately handicapped. Most changes with age are, however, proportional; no extra impediment appears to be introduced by age, and the performance of an older person and a suitably chosen young person will be very comparable in nearly all respects. But the individual older person is probably aware of the decrements in his own performance, and this indeed seems a likely reason for his desire to take his time over decision making if he can.

Physiological Approach

The problem for the physiological gerontologist is a two-fold one. He is faced with the job of explaining the mechanisms of memory, learning ability and problem solving ability in young people, and accounting for differences in performance within an age group. Then he has to explain how these mechanisms alter with age and account for fall-off in performance in the old.

A. Brain abnormalities

At the moment it is chiefly among the very old and mentally sick that physiologists have tried to correlate the state of the brain with ability to carry out psychological tasks. On the whole this has been done at a fairly general level. Attempts have been made to link memory disorders with loss of brain cells and presence of senile plaques or other abnormalities; but these attempts have been unsuccessful because cell loss and presence of abnormalities have been found as frequently in normal aged as in memory disordered ones (Hassler 1965).

Lack of oxygen supply to the brain has been suggested as the prime cause of age changes in intellect. There are difficulties in measuring the normal supply of oxygen in the older person, and it has not proved possible to show that lack of oxygen is the definite culprit (Birren et al., 1963). However, it has been shown that about a third of young people deprived of oxygen show 'old' patterns of EEG wave (Rossen et al., 1961); and on the other hand, that people with arteriosclerosis but with hypertension do not show the EEG abnormalities found in arteriosclerotics (Obrist and Henry, 1958). The behavioural abnormalities which occur under oxygen deprivation do seem to mimic those which occur in old age and the euphoria in the oxygen-starved does not quite agree with the increased caution, over-harsh judgment and liability to depression of the elderly (Van Liere and Stickney, 1963).

Diffuse brain damage has been suggested as a possible cause of intellectual deterioration. On most tests, such damage seems to 'age' performance by about 25 or 30 years (Reed and Reitan, 1963; A. D. M. Davies, 1966), but some differences in test results occur between young brain damaged and old normal subjects for which it is difficult to account. In particular, the young brain damaged do better than the old normals on Raven's Progressive Matrices; although the test is sensitive to both brain damage and age it is differentially sensitive. The Mill Hill Synonyms Vocabulary test, on the other hand, proved to be sensitive to brain damage but not to aging (A. D. M. Davies, 1966). It is difficult to see why these differences should occur if the mechanisms underlying both conditions are similar.

B. *Autotonic nervous system changes*

It has been demonstrated that certain physiological homeostatic mechanisms are balanced differently in the old and in the young. Resting adrenalin level is higher in the old, for example, while psychogalvanic response level is lower (Shmavonian et al., 1965). On the whole, stressful stimuli cause less alteration in the homeostatic systems in the old, and absolute levels of response do not reach those of the young. The different resting levels could be due to age changes in the immediate tissue concerned with the function, or to age changes in the general cardiovascular system, or to underlying changes in part of the nervous/endocrine system, say the hypothalamus, which controls the functions. Possibly changes in many physical systems contribute to the establishment of a new balance; this could account for the fact that changes appear to be specific to each system, and not intercorrelated between individuals.

Since perturbations in each system under a given level of stimulation are less in the old than the young, the old are commonly thought to be less 'aroused' by stimuli—but it has to be remembered that the perturbation occurs against a different basic level, so that it may not be a straightforward matter

356

of comparing young and old, but rather of comparing those with different resting balance systems. At the moment, experiments on 'arousal' in the old are most easily interpreted on the assumption that the old are less 'aroused' (D. R. Davies, 1966). That stimuli should make less impact on the old seems to tie in well with the evidence from short term memory experiments.

C. Central nervous system changes

'Arousal' has also been used in a different sense, linked to the notion of activity within the central nervous system rather than the autonomic system. It is supposed that within the CNS a certain amount of activity is necessary as a background if perceptual stimuli are to be dealt with adequately, but that too much activity has a hampering effect. It has been suggested that more random firing occurs within the CNSs of the old than the young, and that in certain boring situations with few external stimuli, this could lead to the old remaining more alert than the young. However, too much random firing within the CNS would be likely to make it more difficult for the subject to distinguish the effects of a stimulus; and hence in most situations the old would be more likely to produce a higher number of false positive judgments. This is an attractive theory, outlined by Welford (1965). However, Tune (1966) has found that in a vigilance task, older people made more commission errors than young ones especially so on the task with rarer signals (the less arousing task). This result goes directly counter to the theory that nervous system noise in the old (if it exists) can be equated to greater CNS arousal, and we must consequently await further tests of the theory with great interest.

At first sight it seems possible to apply Decision Theory techniques to data on vigilance performance to test whether the older person is reacting as though there were more 'noise' in his CNS. Briefly, Decision Theory postulates that in the 'no-signal' state the basic firing of the nervous system results for the subject in a probability curve of 'NO' decisions, from certain to uncertain. When a signal is present, the probability curve moves upwards, representing 'YES' decisions from uncertain to certain. The whole curve always moves up by an amount equal to the signal (Swets et al., 1961). There is an overlap between the 'YES' and 'NO' curves, and judgements made within the limits of the overlap will consist of correct decisions, false positives and false negatives. The point fixed for the decision verdict by the subject can be shown to depend upon the 'pay-off': if false positives are penalised, the subject will move his decision point so that he includes less of them. He will inevitably make more false negatives as well.

The horizontal axis of the decision theory graph represents 'firing rate' in this case. With older people, the 'NO' and 'YES' signal probability curves will both occur at a higher firing rate, further to the right along the axis. But two high firing rates are not likely to be so easily differentiated as two low rates, so the probability curves for the older people are likely to have a greater variance than those for younger people —and greater overlap. If this is so, then judgement rates of old and young will differ in all circumstances: (1) if the old keep their false positive rate down to that of the young, then their errors of omission will be greater than for the young; (2) if the old keep their omission errors low, they will include more false positives than the young; (3) if they choose a balanced position, both types of error will be equal but more numerous than for the young.

The difficulty is that contra-indications will be few: (1) the old should never make fewer total errors than the young; (2) total errors should never be less on rarer or quieter signals than on obvious ones.

Many psychological theories of aging are as yet pseudo-physiological; they suggest mechanisms which may be at work in the aging nervous system, but it will need interdisciplinary work between psychologists and physiologists to see whether such mechanisms can actually be found. Each discipline can suggest hypotheses to the other—each must rely on the findings of the other if gerontologists are to keep their theories within the bounds of possibility.

Adaptation

One generalization about age decrement seems to be possible. It is that channel capacity is lower in the older person so that any simple stimulus uses up proportionally more of his available capacity and a complex psychological stimulus may be too great for him to grasp without plenty of time.

The individual has to cope with this reduced channel capacity in his daily life, and in fact shows remarkable powers of adaptation. If complex material is less easily grasped it is sensible to take more note of information which turns out to be irrelevant (Rabbitt, 1966). If change of set is difficult, then it is adaptive to prefer old ways of doing things and to like routine (Chown, 1960). If correct decisions about stimuli are now harder to make, then it is wise to display cautious behaviour (Craik 1962) and to use extra stimulation time if possible before reacting (Botwinick et al., 1958). Gerontologists are prone to talk as though the elderly display nothing but decrements in cognitive tasks, whereas their behaviour is really adaptive to decrement—and sometimes in such things as caution and personality rigidity they behave over-adaptively. In time, it may be possible to prevent occurrence of the underlying decrements, but meanwhile the older person can be assured that he has more to offer to the science of Psychology than that favorite subject, the College Student, and that Psychology will soon have quite a lot to offer him.

References

Arenberg, D. "Anticipation Interval and Age Differences in Verbal Learning." *Journal Abnorm. Soc. Psychol.*, 70, 419-425, 1965.

Belbin, E., and Belbin, R. M. "New Skills in Middle Age." (*Proceedings, 7th Internat. Congress Gerontology*, Wiener Medizinischen Akademie, 1966.)

Belbin, E., Belbin, R. M. and Downs, S. "Age and Translation Processes." *Bulletin, Internat. Assoc. Applied Psychol.*, 1966.

Birren, J. E., Butler, R. N., Greenhouse, R. N., Sokoloff, L. and Yarrow, M. R. (Eds.) *Human Aging*. Bethesda, Maryland: U.S. Dept. of Health, Education and Welfare, 1963.

Birren, J. E., Riegel, K. F. and Morrison, D. F. "Intellectual Capacities, Aging and Man's Environment." In C. Tibbitts and W. Donahue, (Eds.), *Processes of Aging*. New York: Atherton Press, 1963.

Botwinick, J., Brinley, J. F., and Robbin, J. S. "The Interaction Effects of Perceptual Difficulty and Stimulus Exposure Time on Age Differences in Speed and Accuracy of Response." *Gerontologia*, 2, 1-10, 1958.

Brinley, J. F. "Cognitive Sets, Speed and Accuracy of Performance in the Elderly." In A. T. Welford and J. E. Birren, (Eds.), *Behavior, Aging and the Nervous System*. Springfield, Illinois: Charles C. Thomas, 1965.

Britton, J. H., Mather, W. G. and Lansing, A. R. "Expectations for Older Persons in a Rural Community: Living Arrangements and Family Relationships." *J. Gerontol.*, 16, 156-162, 1961.

Broadbent, D. E. "Immediate Memory and Simultaneous Stimuli." *Quart. J. Exp. Psychol.*, 9, 1-11, 1957.

Bromley, D. B. "Some Experimental Tests of the Effects of Age on Creative Intellectual Output." *J. Gerontol.*, 11, 74-82, 1956.

Brown, R. G. "Family Structure and Social Isolation of Older Persons." *J. Gerontol.*, 15, 170-172, 1960.

Busse, E. W. "The Effect of Aging upon the Central Nervous System." (*Proceedings, 7th Internat. Congress Gerontology*, Wiener Medizinischen Akademie, 1966.)

Canestrari, R. E. "Age Differences in Verbal Learning and Verbal Behavior." (Unpublished paper, Colloquium, Semmering, 1966.)

Canestrari, R. E. "The Effects of Commonality on Paired-Associate Learning in Two Age Groups." *J. Genet. Psychol.*, 108, 3-7, 1966.

Cattell, R. B. "The Riddle of Perseveration. I, Creative Effort and Disposition Rigidity. II, Solution in Terms of Personality Structure." *J. Personality*, 14, 229-267, 1946.

360

Chown, S. M. "A Factor Analysis of the Wesley Rigidity Inventory: its Relationship to Age and Nonverbal Intelligence." *J. Abnorm. Soc. Psychol.*, 61, 491-494, 1960.

Chown, S. M. "Age and the Rigidities." *J. Gerontol.* 16, 313-362, 1961.

Chown, S. M. "The Effects of Time Limits on the Assessment of Intelligence: a Comparison of Age Groups." (*Proceedings, 7th Internat. Congress Gerontology*, Wiener Medizinischen Akademie, 1966.)

Chown, S. M., Belbin, E., and Downs, S. "Programmed Instruction as a Method of teaching Paired Associates to Older Learners." J. Gerontology 1967.

Clément, F. "Recherches sur le vieillissement d'un Groupe Professional Homogène." *Revue Française de Gérontologie*, Février, 1-27, 1961.

Cohen, J. "The Factorial Study of the WAIS between Early Adulthood and Old Age." *J. Consult Psychol.*, 21, 283-293, 1957.

Craik, F. I. M. "The Effects of Age and the Experimental Situation on Confidence Behaviour." *Bull. Brit. Psychol. Soc.*, 47, 21, (Abstr.), 1962.

Craik, F. I, M. "The Nature of the Age Decrement in Performance on Dichotic Listening Tasks." *Quart. J. Exp. Psychol.*, 17, 227-240, 1961.

Craik, F. I. M. "Comment on Dr. Inglis' Paper at 7th Congress of Gerontology."

Cumming, E. and Henry, W. E. *Growing Old*. New York: Basic Books, 1961.

Davies, A. D. M. "Decline in Test Scores as a Function of Aging and Brain Damage." (*Proceedings, 7th Internat. Congress Gerontology*, Wiener Medizinischen Akademie, 1966.)

Davies, D. R. and Treacher, A. C. C. "An Experimental Study of Impulsivity and Autonomic Lability in Older and Younger Subjects." (*Proceedings, 7th Internat. Congress Gerontology*, Wiener Medizinischen Akademie, 1966.)

Dean, L. R. "Aging and the Decline of Instrumentality," *J. Gerontol.*, 15, 403-407, 1960.

Elithorn, A. "A Preliminary Report on a Perceptual Maze Test sensitive to Brain Damage." *J. Neurol. Neurosurg. Psychiat.*, 18, 287-292, 1955.

Emerson, A. R. "The First Year of Retirement." *Occup. Psychol.*, 33, 197-208, 1959.

Furneaux, W. D. "Some Speed, Error and Difficulty Relationships within a Problem Solving Situation." *Nature*, 170, 37, 1952.

Hassler, R. "Extrapyramidal Control of the Speed of Behaviour and its Change by Primary Age Processes." In A. T. Welford and J. E. Birren (Eds.), *Behavior, Aging and the Nervous System.* Springfield, Ill.: Charles C. Thomas, 1965.

Heglin, H. J. "Problem Solving Set in Different Age Groups." *J. Gerontol.*, 11, 310-317, 1956.

Heron, A. "A Two-Part Personality Measure for Use as a Research Criterion." *Brit. J. Psychol.*, 47, 243-251, 1956.

Heron, A. and Chown, S. M. *Age and Function.* London: J. and A. Churchill, 1966-7.

Hulicka, I., and Grossman, J. "Age Group Comparisons for the Use of Mediators in Paired Associate Learning." Paper presented at Eastern Psychological Association, Atlantic City, 1965.

Hulicka, I., Sterns, H. and Grossman, J. "Age Group Comparisons of Paired Associate Learning as a Function of Paced and Self-Paced Association and Response Times." (Unpublished paper, 1966.)

Inglis, J. "Immediate Memory, Age, and Brain Function." In A. T. Welford and J. E. Birren (Eds.), *Behavior, Aging and the Nervous System.* Springfield, Ill.: Charles C. Thomas, 1965.

Inglis, J., Ankus, M. N. and Sykes, D. H. "The Long Term Development of Short Term Memory." (*Proceedings, 7th Internat. Congress Gerontology*, Wiener Medizinischen Akademie, 1966.)

Jarvik, L. F., Kallman, F. J. and Falek, A. "Intellectual Changes in Aging Twins." *J. Gerontol.*, 17, 289-294, 1962.

Jerome, E. A. "Decay of Heuristic Processes in the Aged." In C. Tibbitts and W. Donahue (Eds.), *Social and Psychologi-*

cal Aspects of Aging. New York: Columbia University Press, 1962.

Jones, M. C., "The California Longitudinal Studies." (*Proceedings, 7th Internat. Congress Gerontology,* Wiener Medizinischen Akademie, 1966.)

Kay, H. "The effects of Position in a Display upon Problem Solving." *Quart. J. Exper. Psychol.,* 6, 155-69, 1954.

Kimura, D. "A Note on Cerebral Dominance in Hearing." *Acta Otolaryngol.,* 56, 617-618, 1963.

Kleemeier, R. W. "Intellectual Changes in the Senium, or Death and the IQ." (Presidential address, Division on Maturity and Old Age, Amer. Psychol. Assoc., New York, 1961.)

Levinson, B. M. "A Research Note on Subcultural Differences in WAIS between Aged Italians and Jews." *J. Gerontol.,* 15, 197-198, 1960.

Levinson, B. M. "Jewish Subculture and WAIS Performance among Jewish Aged." *J. Genet. Psychol.,* 100, 55-68, 1962.

Murrell, K. F. H. "The Effect of Practice on Reported Age Differences." (*Proceedings, 7th Internat. Congress Gerontology,* Wiener Medizinischen Akademie, 1966.)

Neugarten, B. L., Birren, J. E. and Kraines, R. J. "Psychological Issues of Middle Age." (*Proceedings, 7th Internat. Congress Gerontology,* Wiener Medizinischen Akademie, 1966.)

Nordvik, H. "A Tentative Reinterpretation of Results from WAIS Studies in Gerontology." (*Proceedings, 7th Internat. Congress Gerontology,* Wiener Medizinischen Akademie, 1966.)

Obrist, W. D., and Henry, C. E. "Electroencephalographic Findings in Aged Psychiatric Patients." *J. Nervous Mental Disorders,* 126, 254-267, 1958.

Rabbitt, P. M. A. "An Age Decrement in the Ability to ignore Redundancy." (*Proceedings, 7th Internat. Congress Gerontology,* Wiener Medizinischen Akademie, 1966.)

Raven, J. C. *The Mill Hill Vocabulary Scale.* London: Lewis, 1938.

Raven, J. C. *The Progressive Matrices Test.* London: Lewis, 1938.

Reed, H. B. C. and Reitan, R. M. "A Comparison of the Effects of the Normal Aging Process with the Effects of Organic Brain Damage on Adaptive Abilities." *J. Gerontol.*, 18, 177-179, 1963.

Reitan, R. M. "The Validity of the Trail Making Test as an Indicator of Organic Brain Damage." *Percept. Motor Skills*, 8, 271-276, 1958.

Riegel, K. F. "A Longitudinal Analysis of Socio-Psychological Functions." (*Proceedings, 7th Internat. Congress Gerontology*, Wiener Medizinischen Akademie, 1966.)

Riegel, R. M. and Riegel, K. F. "A Comparison and Reinterpretation of Factor Structure of the W-B, the WAIS and the HAWIE on Aged Persons." (*J. Consult. Psychol.*, 26, 31-37, 1962.)

Rossen, R., Simonson, E. and Baker, J. "Electroencephalograms during Hypoxia in Healthy Men; Response Characteristics for Normal Aging." *Arch. Neurol.*, 5, 648-654, 1961.

Shmavonian, B. M., Yarmat, A. J. and Cohen, S. I. "Relationships between the Autonomic Nervous System and Central Nervous System in Age Differences in Behaviour." In A. T. Welford and J. E. Birren (Eds.), *Behavior, Aging and the Nervous System*, Springfield, Ill.: Charles C. Thomas, 1965.

Stevens, R. V. J. "Some Aspects of the Relations between Verbal Fluency and Age." *Brit. Psychol. Soc. Bull.*, 13, 41, (Abstr.), 1960.

Swets, J. A., Tanner, W. P. and Birdsall, T. G. "Decision Processes in Perception." *Psychol. Rev.*, 68, 301-340, 1961.

Talland, G. A. "Age and the Effect of Anticipatory Set on Accuracy of Perceptions." *J. Gerontol.*, 14, 202-207, 1959.

Thompson, W. E., Streib, G. F. and Kosa, J. "The Effect of Retirement on Personal Adjustment: a Panel Analysis." *J. Gerontol.*, 15, 165-169, 1960.

Tune, G. S., "Age Differences in Errors of Commission in a Type of Vigilance Task." (*Proceedings, 7th Internat. Congress Gerontology*, Wiener Medizinischen Akademie, 1966.)

Van Liere, E. J. and Stickney, J. C. *Hypoxia*. Chicago: University of Chicago Press, 1963.

Wechsler, D. "Manual for the WAIS." New York: Psychological Corporation, 1955.

Welford, A. T. "Psychomotor Performance." In J. E. Birren (Ed.), *Handbook of Aging and the Individual*, 562-613. Chicago: University of Chicago Press, 1959.

Welford, A. T. "Age Changes in Times taken by Choice, Discrimination and the Control of Movements." In C. Tibbitts and W. Donahue (Eds.), *Social and Psychological Aspects of Aging*. New York: Columbia University Press, 1962.

Welford, A. T. "Performance, Biological Mechanisms and Age: a Theoretical Sketch." In A. T. Welford and J. E. Birren (Eds.), *Behavior, Aging and the Nervous System*, Springfield, Illinois: Charles C. Thomas, 1965.

Wetherick, N. E. "Changing and Established Concept: a Comparison of the Ability of Young, Middle Aged and Old Subjects." *Gerontologia*, 11, 82-95, 1965.

Wetherick, N. E. "Intellectual Deterioration with Age in the Normal Adult Individual." (*Proceedings, 7th Internat. Congress Gerontology*, Wiener Medizinischen Akademie, 1966.)

THE PSYCHOLOGY OF LEISURE

ALEXANDER REID MARTIN, M. D.

Psychiatrist, New York City. Former president, Association
for the Advancement of Psychoanalysis

and

RICHARD LEE HALL, ED. D.

Director of Upward Bound Project, Southeastern State College

Editorial Note

Ten years ago Clifton Fadiman noted that the existing state
of confusion regarding leisure was so great that, far from knowing any of the answers, people did not even know the questions
to ask. Still today increasing numbers of individuals are not
prepared emotionally and psychologically for free time, and
problems of maladaptation are intensified rather than solved by
developments which shorten the work week. The authors of
the following paper believe that our society will ultimately be
judged by "the extent to which free time is used to activate
and realize our inner creative resources."

Dr. Alexander Reid Martin was born in Chicago and educated in Belfast, Glasgow, and London. He holds the Diploma
in Psychological Medicine from the Royal College of Physicians
and Surgeons. In 1966 he completed his forty-third year in the
practice of psychiatry. He has been Chief of Service, Sheppard
and Pratt Hospital, Baltimore, and Resident Psychiatrist at the
Payne-Whitney Clinic, New York Hospital. For twenty-eight
years, he has been Psychiatric Consultant to the Children's Aid
Society of New York City and has developed an in-service
training program for Youth Club personnel. Active in many
youth organizations, he has served as Consultant to the Presidential Commission on Outdoor Recreation Resources (1961)
and as Chairman of the National Committee on Leisure Time

and Its Uses of the American Psychiatric Association (1949-61). Beginning in 1926 with the *British Lancet,* he has contributed many articles on psychiatry and psychoanalysis to major scientific journals here and abroad. Over the past twelve years he has concentrated his interest on leisure and recreation and on the problems of man's creative adaptation to the free time that lies ahead. Dr. Martin, in addition to other activities, maintains a private practice in psychiatry and psychoanalysis in New York City.

Dr. Richard Lee Hall was born in Chickasha, Oklahoma, and educated at Oklahoma State University, the University of Tulsa, and the University of Oklahoma, where he received his doctorate in psychology in 1966. He is now Assistant Professor of Psychology and Director of the Upward Bound Project at Southeastern State College in Durant, Oklahoma. He has distinguished himself as a teacher, counselor, and research director in the Tulsa Public Schools (1956-1965) and as President of the Oklahoma Personnel and Guidance Association. Recently his work with the Upward Bound Project has brought him national recognition.

•

THE PSYCHOLOGY OF LEISURE

Technological advances which are rapidly changing the face of the physical universe also confront man with new challenges and new opportunities in the social and behavioral sciences. The psychology of leisure is a fertile field for investigators concerned with new problems created or intensified by the virtual elimination of other problems which had persisted through the centuries—disease, poverty, hunger, drudgery, and fatigue. In recent years increases in productivity and wages have been matched by decreases in the total number of hours which the American worker devotes to his job and by a significant increase in his hours of leisure. Within the next decade, according to Boris Pregel (1959), the work week will be reduced to twenty hours. Various groups have already suggested that the traditional week-end be extended to three days and the annual vacation for workers to six weeks. Freed from enslavement to the machine which first threatened to rob him of his human qualities, the modern worker now faces the challenge of adjusting to problems issuing from his newly won freedom.

These problems are rooted in changes brought about by the transition from an agrarian society to an industrial urban society. Children were an economic asset when they worked on farms and helped their parents to attain family goals, but their gainful employment was drastically reduced by the spread of industrialization and the enactment of appropriate legislation. The family ceased to function as a unit in which the interests and values of individual members were subordinated to the welfare of the group as a whole, the father became a bread-winner and spent much of his time away from the other members of the family, the mother became a housewife or accepted gainful employment, and organizations outside the home assumed many of the economic, protective, educational, and recreational functions of the family.

The transfer of both production and consumption of goods to outside agencies, the introduction of appliances and products designed to minimize time devoted to the performance of household tasks, and the growth of service industries have contributed to the emancipation of the housewife and her children. As industrial and technological advances provide each member of the family with the opportunity to enjoy additional hours of leisure, the ranks of the retired continue to expand. The vast increase in this segment of the population during the past three decades has resulted from greater longevity as well as earlier retirement, and in the future medical advances may provide physicians with new means of prolonging human life. The use which American youth make of their free, unstructured time is of utmost importance to society as a whole, and helping men and women of all ages to spend their free time wisely and well becomes a problem of national concern.

To gain a clear notion of leisure, we must begin by understanding and setting aside our prejudices that come from overvaluing the world of work. A new philosophy which transcends the workaday world will dispel that "gospel of work" which regards all leisure as something to be paid for, to be earned, to be deserved, or, as a reward for labor and sweat. The proponents of this philosophy are still with us. They falsely equate leisure with sloth, idleness, and laziness. Margaret Mead (1957) says, "The belief that leisure has to be earned will die hard." Sebastian de Grazia (Maddox, 1966, p. 125) is also pessimistic about the possibility of free time becoming discretionary time. He gives three reasons for his pessimism: "(1) the absence of a strong cultural tradition of leisure; (2) a preoccupation with the accumulation of 'things' and with wanting 'things' which cost money, work, and time and hence lead to moonlighting, overtime, and a working wife rather than to the development of a tradition of leisure; and (3) the suspicion that leisure may be beyond the capacity of most people." The positive result—acceptance of free time as discretionary time—would be self-fulfillment.

Concepts of Leisure

Technological sciences and medical sciences have given us free time, but they have not given us leisure. We have too much time and too little leisure. A multibillion dollar market has been created for the so-called "Leisure-time Activities" with most participants not spending this time truly at leisure. The popular term "leisure time" is a misnomer. Playtime, playgrounds, and playthings are in abundance but we have no assurance that they are being used for play.

Ambiguity and inconsistency characterize attempts to define or describe leisure. The time element is stressed in the dictionary definitions and the etymology of the word. No mention is made of the inner quality of the experience. The confusion between leisure time and leisure itself is still evident. Needed is an identifiable entity that would lend itself to valid scientific investigation.

Martin (1962, p. 216) presents three examples of the confusion between leisure and free time:

(a) The University of Chicago, some years ago, had a television panel entitled "The Tyranny of Leisure." What they discussed was the tyranny of free time.

(b) Russell Lynes wrote an article, 'The Pressures of

Leisure.' What he dealt with were the pressures of free time.

(c) Franz Alexander, world-famous psychoanalyst, in a recent book informs us that 'increased leisure has changed the nature of modern man . . .' Alexander (1960) is really referring to the changes modern man has undergone in his struggle to adapt to more and more free time.

Misconceptions and inconsistencies about leisure are evident. Clifton Fadiman (1957) said that our present state of confusion regarding leisure is so great that, far from knowing any of the answers, we do not even know the questions to ask. Lexicographers have not made a clear differentiation between time for leisure and leisure itself. Webster defines leisure as "time free from employment, time free from engagement, freedom." Etymological authorities disagree by tracing the word to a Greek root, "scola" and the Latin and Old French roots meaning license, permission, and excessive liberty (Partridge, 1958).

The Committee on Leisure Time and Its Uses of the American Psychiatric Association has accumulated various quotations and descriptions of leisure. Among the more famous quotations are (Martin, 1964):

Socrates: "Leisure is the best of all possessions."

Aristotle: "The goal of education is the wise use of leisure."

Cicero: "Leisure with dignity is the supremely desirable object of all sane and good men."

Hobbes: "Leisure is the mother of philosophy."

Bertrand Russell: "To be able to fill leisure intelligently is the last product of civilization."

Martin (1962, p. 218-19) offered the following descriptions of leisure in an attempt to clarify and give the concept some degree of identity:

Leisure is not the inevitable result of spare time, a holiday, a weekend, or a vacation. Leisure is a particular state or condition of mind and being—more specifically, an actively receptive condition of the whole personality to open up to all stimuli from within and without. The personality is not passive or detached, but wholly engaged in this process. During leisure, the mood is one of affirmation in contrast to idleness, during which the mood is a negating one.

We have a natural tendency to enter into this actively receptive process periodically throughout our lifetime. In this respect and others, leisure is similar to the psychobiologic phenomena of psychomotor relaxation and sleep. In all three, their beginning and their duration are not subject to direct conscious control, but are determined unconsciously when outer and inner conditions are favorable.

It has been said that leisure is only possible to the extent that a man is at one with himself and also at one with the world, that is, insofar as he is not possessed by his inner and outer conflicts . . . Again, leisure demonstrates . . . the innate power of the human personality to step beyond the workday world, to transcend, as it were, the workday frame of reference . . . (Pieper, 1952).

E. D. Hutchinson's (1941) research on Creative Insight gives a conception of leisure as having positive function. The creative process follows a rhythmic pattern through the phases of (1) preparation, (2) incubation, (3) illumination, and (4) verification. Incubation and illumination are part of the leisure process. Preparation and verification are part of the work process. Work and leisure complement each other. In addition, leisure is not the opposite of work in the sense of being opposed to work.

Suppression of the Capacity for Leisure

Another misconception about leisure is that everybody works for and welcomes this free time and is ready for it. A great majority of our people are not emotionally and psychologically ready for free time. Many become uneasy when they have free time; others continue to work to avoid it. Unhealthy adaptations result from the unpreparedness of our people for free time.

Historically Western man has suppressed the capacity for leisure. The wise men of the past looked upon the following as resulting from giving man too much time with nothing to do: idleness, boredom, subversiveness, civil unrest and rebellion. The philosophies from the Victorian era and doctrines such as Calvinism found their strongest expression in the suppression of our capacity for leisure. These obsolete philosophies are a part of our workaday world.

Increased free time has not created any essentially new behavior; problems and reactions have become intensified and increased. Symptoms of individual maladaptation are: excessive guilt, compulsive behavior, psychosomatic symptoms, depression, increase of anxiety, suicide, and self-alienation. Ferenczi's (1926) "Sunday Neuroses" is a prototype of a prevalent and characteristic maladaptation of our present society. Research in Europe indicates an increase in depression and suicides during holidays and vacations. The increase in juvenile delinquency reflects the unpreparedness of youth for large measures of free time.

Martin (1962, p. 217) attributes our unpreparedness for free time to suppression of the capacity for leisure rather than to something we failed to learn or to something we failed to obtain during our upbringing. Our inherent capacity for leisure meets powerful cultural taboos and philosophies which lead to its suppression. The author emphasized that this capacity for leisure is not something that can be superimposed, or that we acquire from the outside through experience. It is a buried and disused attribute that we have to rediscover in ourselves. It is something we lost during our development.

Several authorities from various disciplines support the assumptions of childhood possession and exhibition of the capacity for leisure, suppression of the capacity, and loss during our development. Hans Selye (1956) attributes much of our over stressful life to the loss of the capacity of leisure we had as children. Lord Rushholme (1959, p. 6), High Master of Manchester Grammar School, said, "The chief goal of our schools and universities should be the rediscovery of leisure." Logan Smith (1945, p. 71) said, "If you are losing your leisure, look out—you may be losing your soul."

Within our disciplines is found cultural suppression. All psychological and psychiatric research on the creative process has been confined to the work phase. The leisure phase has been ignored. Reflected is our over-concern for work as a social function and our disregard for work as a psychobiological function.

Martin (1964, p. 30) issues this challenge, "how much of the forthcoming free time we can, or should, spend at leisure, how much at psychobiological work, and how much under social compulsion. Certainly, in the fruitful use of free time, our innate capacity for autonomous effort will manifest itself . . ."

Manifestations of the Capacity for Leisure

According to Martin (1962, 1964) a person who has retained his capacity for leisure *invariably* possesses and, at different times and in different degrees, will exhibit the following:

(a) A capacity for play of the body, mind, and feelings.

(b) A capacity for play with others.

(c) A capacity for wondering, marveling, contemplation, reflection, and meditation.

(d) A capacity for affirmative attentiveness, looking and listening, and for being actively receptive to music, poetry, and the arts.

(e) A capacity for general relaxation of the whole person, which we could call psychosomatic relaxation.

(f) A capacity for sleep.

These manifestations can be regarded as different variations of and intensities of the leisure process. There seems to be a close relationship between a person at sleep, a person in a state of psychosomatic relaxation, and a person at leisure. With limited valid scientific investigation about the three, our knowledge of them is basically empirical. Their dynamic similarity needs to attract research attention.

Patterns Which Suppress Our Capacity for Leisure

Five cultural patterns will be noted which have a suppressive effect on our capacity for leisure. These are exaggerated and intensified patterns of everyday living. The patterns never occur in isolation but are functionally interrelated.

1. Frictionless Pattern. This pattern can be traced to its roots in childhood and youth. Leisure manifests itself in all forms of physical interplay. A healthy friction can be seen in physical contact, contact sports, competitive games and recreation. With the passing of years the friction changes from physical life to include intellectual life. It helps to serve the leisure function of refinement, self-fulfillment, and self-improvement.

Parental misunderstanding of youthful interplay and consequent early interference with an essential leisure process results in the frictionless pattern. The healthy, happy "roughhousing" of youngsters too often becomes invested with malevolence by compulsive, anxious parents and consequently is forbidden. This frictionless pattern tends to make leisure less and less possible. The pattern is glorified in our society as "togetherness."

2. Fear of the Unconscious. Free association, the process of relaxing control and giving thoughts and feelings spontaneous expression, is in every respect and in essence a leisure process. Compulsive control which prevents this natural leisure process from asserting itself stems from fear of the unconscious. In many ways our rearing and our culture determine and perpetuate this fear of the unconscious. There are psychological determinants of this fear. It protects our illusions and Olympian aspirations, but it prevents us from feeling deeply. It perpetuates our avoidance of leisure and stifles all creative activity and growth.

3. Compulsive Pattern. Compulsions are considered to be reactions which always have a must or imperative quality about them. Contrast the man who *must* win at all costs with the man

who *wants* to win. Also, included are those reactions that come under the influence of obligation, expectation, and demand. When those driven by compulsion have free time, they not only have to avoid leisure, but they have to set up another authority, and thus exchange an objectively imposed compulsion for some subjectively imposed compulsion. In avoiding leisure, the individual avoids his real self.

4. Conditional Pattern. Work and leisure naturally complement each other in the healthy growth process. But with self-alienated individuals, their natural work-cycle becomes completely subordinated to a socially-motivated work-leisure cycle. Work becomes the payment penalty or punishment for leisure, while on the other hand, leisure becomes the reward for work. They have great feelings of guilt if they are not always doing something practical, sensible, and useful.

5. Superintellectual Pattern. Compulsive use of the intellect to repress the sensual and emotional is familiar to all. We have failed to note how much of this pattern is characterized by great glorification of the mind at work, and complete contempt and rejection of the mind at play. These individuals convince themselves that solely through intellectual work, intensive thinking-through, and logical reasoning, they can reach any solution and find all the answers. Intellectual work is not enough. Free play of our whole being, which can only take place when we are at leisure, is an essential and natural phase of every creative process.

Preparedness for Leisure

The above patterns of everyday living perpetuate maladaptation to free time and thereby increase emotional unpreparedness for it. Martin (1964, pp. 36-40) suggests ways to increase psychological and emotional preparedness for leisure. The results should be a lessening of need to resort to perpetual self-alienation as a means of adapting to free time.

1. We must recognize and define leisure's essential function in personality development and vividly stress the indispensability of leisure in every creative process.

375

2. We must become aware of those patterns in our culture which have a helpful or harmful effect upon our leisure, in order to promote those that are helpful and avoid perpetuating those that are harmful.

3. We must reaffirm our faith in man's unconscious being as the organ through which he lives his spiritual life, as the fount of poetry, music and visual arts, and as innately healthy, constructive, and indispensable to all creativity. We must accept the new scientific principles of physical indeterminacy and break away from sole adherence to the mechanistic determinism of Newtonian science and from the belief that man is wholly subject to exact and predictable mechanical laws. Those compelled to adhere strictly to the laws of physical determinism find it difficult to experience true leisure.

4. We must cultivate a humble-minded attunedness to nature and to our own nature. This means loving and listening to children; and, particularly loving and listening to the child in one's self—to what, so often, seems impractical, irrelevant, and nonsensical. Acceptance of the unconscious which accompanies leisure goes along with a capacity for humor, for humility—and a love for the beginning of things.

5. We must encourage a more poetic approach to life, as one means of off-setting and avoiding the compulsive materialism and literal-mindedness so characteristic of many who cannot truly enjoy their free time. This compulsive literal-mindedness, so often glamorized as being logical, practical, and objective, serves as a resistance to relaxing, wondering, marveling, contemplating, and to other expressions of leisure necessary for creative growth. We must, of course, always be prepared to take things literally, but this is not enough. There is always something that transcends the literal, which we admit when we say that man cannot live by bread alone.

6. We must encourage that healthy interpersonal friction which is a vital and natural manifestation of leisure, and recognize the formative influence of all physical and intellectual interplay, competition and conflict with others. We need to appreciate the influence of this interplay in generating the creative spark, and realize its essential role in differentiating the

"self" from the "not-self," thus increasing our sense of uniqueness and identity, and so strengthening the real self. Acceptance of noncompulsive physical conflict, sport, games and competition as natural manifestations of leisure in childhood and youth insures our capacity to accept, in adult life, intellectual friction, and also the friction of our inner conflicts.

7. We must develop clearer conceptions of progressive education so that we recognize that real work and real play do not overlap. Some proponents of progressive education are inclined to balk at the idea of hard work, agony, sweat, and tears. They strive to convert work into play. They fail to see that intense work complements play and leisure in every creative process. They also substitute cooperation for competition, and regard all conflict and friction as destructive. They do not distinguish between compulsive friction to *prove* oneself and healthy friction to *improve* oneself; between competition for the sheer pleasure of it, competition to become more fit for work, and compulsive competition. Such misconceptions and confusion mainly arise from a failure to see true play as a manifestation of leisure and failure to differentiate compulsive work and play from our inherent capacities for work and leisure.

8. We should avoid rigid adherence to what we can call a Conditional Philosophy. This philosophy places *all* life on a conditional basis and completely negates all unconditional love and unconditional giving. If you take the right road, you get a piece of cheese; if you take the wrong road, you get a shock. Thereby we all become highly conditional beings. Life becomes just one maze after another, with no exits. The gift outright, free and unmerited, becomes inconceivable and thus there is no conception of leisure, sleep, play, and interplay as blessings to be enjoyed, but only as rewards to be earned. Without Grace, considered either in its narrow or exalted sense, there can be no creativity, but only improvisations.

9. Education should consider a holistic rather than a dualistic approach to man's nature, behavior, and growth. This basically assumes that the whole, or healthy man although assailed by inner conflicts, is "lord of all counter positions." He possesses inner conflicts but is not possessed by them.

Such a holistic conception would transcend the present-day narrow and limited conception of a workaday world, and would provide an entirely new frame of reference in which work and leisure would in no sense oppose each other. Neither would have preference, primacy, or supremacy, but their perfect complementation would be recognized as essential to growth. One main direction of that growth would be towards greater and greater consciousness of our wholeness and uniqueness.

10. Finally, and of transcending importance, we must become aware of our total immersion in a philosophy which permeates and dominates all the thinking and behavior patterns of our western culture and is largely responsible for the aforementioned five patterns, which so seriously affect our leisure. This philosophy has as its sole and entire frame of reference the world of work. But this workaday world is rapidly becoming smaller and will shrink to a twenty-hour work week within the next decade.

We are crossing the threshold into a totally new world, equipped with an obsolete philosophy. Oliver Lodge reminded us that the last thing a deep-sea fish discovers is salt water. We, too, remain unaware of our habitual ways of thinking. We are unconscious victims of outmoded sequences and patterns of living, which keep us wholly unprepared for our forthcoming adventure in free time.

The accelerative rate of evolutionary change and growth causes rapid obsolescence of our tools and instruments of thought. Never at any time in the history of western culture has this been more true than today, when we consider the radical change that has taken place almost overnight between the old workaday world and the new world, where we have more free time than we know what to do with. Where, yesterday, our concern for mental health led us to those who were underprivileged, exploited, overworked and "poverty-stricken," today, we are forced to turn our attention to those who are "leisure stricken."

Implications

New insights into the role of leisure in assuring wholesome personality adjustment to free time suggest a positive approach to mental hygiene. This new, positive approach might circumvent barriers erected by those opposed to current psychiatric concepts and by false notions associated with terms currently used in educating the public in mental health. In any event, a multi-disciplinary approach to preparedness for leisure seems necessary since a single individual frequently requires the services of several agencies and institutions. The findings of researchers in the medical and social disciplines should be combined and used to evolve new procedures for helping individuals of all ages to adapt to creative use of free time, for only preparedness can bring about the full realization of their creative potential. Carrying the concept of a multi-disciplinary approach to preparedness for leisure a step further, one might say that the five disciplines identified by Martin (1962) as those having major roles to fulfill in formulating a philosophy of leisure in an aging population—religion, industry, psychiatry, education, and recreation—have much to contribute jointly to the solution of problems involving the creative use of free time at any age. For example, the housewife who becomes an alcoholic as a result of her inability to adapt to the free time now available to her is a familiar figure in contemporary society. Juvenile delinquency is rooted in another maladaptation to free time.

The success, the strength, the enduring quality of our democratic society will be determined and judged, not by the amount of free time we give ourselves, but by the extent to which we use that free time to activate and realize our inner creative resources and to develop and promote the dignity and uniqueness of the individual.

References

Fadiman, C. Boredom, brainstorms and bombs. *The Saturday Review*, 1957, 40 (35), 7-27.

Ferenczi, S. *Further Contributions to the Theory and Technique of Psycho-Analysis.* London: Hogarth Press, 1926.

Hutchinson, E. D. Nature of insight. *Psychiatry*, 1941, 4, 31-43.

Maddox, G. L. Retirement as a social event in the United States. In J. C. McKinney and F. T. de Vyver (Ed.) *Aging and Social Policy.* New York: Appleton-Century-Crofts, 1966.

Martin, A. R. The fear of relaxation and leisure. *Amer. J. Psychoanal.*, 1951, 11 (1), 42-50.

Martin, A. R. Self-alienation and the loss of Leisure. *Amer. J. Psychoanal.*, 1961, 21 (2), 156-65.

Martin, A. R. Urgent need for a philosophy of leisure in an aging population. *J. Amer. Geriat. Soc.*, 1962, 10, (3), 215-224.

Martin, A. R. Man's leisure and his health. *Bull. N.Y. Acad. Med.*, 1964, 40 (1), 21-42.

Mead, M. Pattern of leisure in contemporary culture. *Ann. Amer. Acad. Pol. Soc. Sci.*, Sept. 1957.

Partridge, E. *Origins.* New York: Macmillan Co., 1958.

Pieper, J. *Leisure, the Basis of Culture.* New York: Pantheon Press, 1952.

Pregel, B. Energy, economy, and society in transition. *Trans. N.Y. Acad. Sci.* 21 (*Series* 2), 1959, 206-19.

Rushholme, Lord James. Address before Westminster Medical School. *London Times*, October 6, 1959.

Selye, H. *The Stress of Life.* New York: McGraw-Hill, 1956.

Smith, L. *All Trivia.* New York: Harcourt Brace and World, Inc., 1945.

THE PSYCHOLOGY OF MODERN ART

RUSSELL EISENMAN, PH. D.

Assistant Professor of Psychology, Temple University

Editorial Note

Although art can be studied in a scientific manner, previous attempts in this direction have been meager and the psychology of art has not yet received its rightful place in psychology. Dr. Eisenman stresses two areas of importance for understanding art: the relationship of creativity and art, and complexity as a variable in creativity, art, and personality research. He concludes that our art preferences and aesthetic tastes can yield fundamental insights of unlimited use in studying personality.

Dr. Russell Eisenman is Assistant Professor of Psychology at Temple University in Philadelphia, Pennsylvania. He has published extensively in the areas of creativity, aesthetics, birth order, and personality.

Dr. Eisenman obtained his B.A. degree from Oglethorpe University in Georgia in 1962, his M. S. in psychology from the University of Georgia in Athens, Georgia, in 1963, and his Ph. D. in clinical psychology from the University of Georgia in 1966.

Interest in creativity and aesthetics has led Dr. Eisenman into research in several areas, including studies of perceptual preferences of schizophrenics and a recently completed study of flexibility, independence of judgment, and other variables in relation to perceptual preferences for complexity-simplicity. He has also done research on birth order as related to personality and other variables. Some of his works are listed in the References at the end of this article.

•

THE PSYCHOLOGY OF MODERN ART

Definitions

The reader of this chapter should be aware of the author's interpretation of the words in the title.[1] First, since this paper is concerned with the "psychology" of modern art, and not the "philosophy" or "history" of the subject, particular emphasis will be placed on empirical investigations of the problem. This is not to imply that experimental research is the only true path to understanding art. Instead, the emphasis on the empirical investigations of modern art is based upon the author's personal experience with this approach, as well as the belief that empirical studies can help us understand art. Philosophical and historical views of art are also helpful, but not within the scope of this paper. Second, the word "modern" implies the lack of concern with past events. But, someone has said that there is nothing new under the sun, so perhaps nothing is ever truly modern. As used here, "modern" means that the focus is on recent research. Finally, "art" has something to do with products which result in admiration and pleasure because of their beauty or skillful execution (English & English, 1958). Such a definition of art is admittedly vague, but it gives us some idea of what we are considering.

"Modern art" often implies work by Salvador Dali, Jackson Pollock, and other abstract or radically different artists. This paper does not endeavor to provide an understanding of the work of specific modern artists. Emphasis is placed on psychological investigations of art, which should have some relevance, though perhaps indirect, for understanding contemporary art. This paper will focus first on creativity, including theory and methodology, and then turn to complexity, which has become a major variable to be considered in research on creativity, art, and personality.

1. I wish to express my grateful appreciation to my friend Jerome J. Platt, and to my wife and friend Fran, who read and criticized earlier drafts of this paper.

382

Suppose someone is an artist. Does that make him creative? To many, art is a creative endeavor, and the mere fact that one is an artist means that one is creative. Such a simple-minded view of creativity seems undesirable, and is not held by the vast majority of creativity researchers. However, if researchers do not commit this "sin of commission," they often fail to differentiate between creativity in general and creativity in a particular field. Such a "sin of omission" would be a true virtue if it were the case that creativity is a general trait. In other words, if the creative artist is also a creative scientist, and a creative thinker, and a creative cook, and a creative athlete, then creativity is, apparently, a rather general kind of ability. Either you have it or you do not. Or, it may be that the creative artist, while not particularly creative in other fields, has in him the potential for creative accomplishment in many other fields to a much greater extent than the non-creative artist. This view of the creative artist as having "potentially high creativity in other fields" is often implied even if it is seldom stated explicitly. The alternative to the above viewpoints would be to conclude that creativity is basically *field specific*; someone's creativity in a particular field may tell us little about his creativity in some other field. Whether or not creativity is relatively field specific is a matter for empirical investigation, but those who think of creativity as a general trait should be aware of their assumptions. By failing to take cognizance of this problem, theorists have often omitted any consideration of what should be clearly stated, namely, the fundamental assumptions or hypotheses held by the investigator.

Consider a study of the kind often done to investigate creativity. Fischelli and Welch (1947) had art students and non-art students recombine ideas into something different. For example, words were combined into sentences and pieces of furniture were combined into new arrangements. The artists were superior to the non-art students. Does this mean that artists are superior in the recombination of ideas into new structures? If we answer "yes" then it sounds as if we are concluding that artists, for whatever the reason, tend to be more creative than the rest of the population. To answer the question intelligently, we must consider the specific procedure employed by Fischelli and Welch. When we look at their study closely it becomes apparent that artists were superior to non-artists because many of the tasks were artistic in nature. Artists did better than non-artists on tasks involving artistic principles, which is quite different than saying that artists were more creative, or were superior in recombining ideas. As Bereiter and Freedman comment on this study:

> . . . this finding points up a difficulty with which studies of this sort must contend: as one gets into more narrowly defined mental abilities, it becomes harder to measure them in a way that is not prejudiced in favor of special kinds of training (1962, p. 567).

What, then, is an adequate criterion for creativity, artistic or otherwise? Everyone seems to talk about creativity, but no one has an adequate definition of it. It is very easy to give some arbitrary definition of creativity, but it is very difficult to find some definition which seems to be obviously appropriate. Could it be that layman and researcher alike often talk about something which they call "creativity" without having an adequate definition in mind? The answer seems to be "Yes!" Creativity is considered good and desirable, and everyone has some sensitivity to what the word means; but, very frequently, no one bothers to define the term before using it. Consequently, creativity means different things to different people, and the only way to analyze various approaches is to be certain that the word is explained in terms of the particular theorist or researcher. Mackler and Shontz (1965) have mentioned trait, psychoanalytic, associationistic, Gestalt, existential, and interpersonal theories of creativity. Each will be briefly reviewed with emphasis, where possible, on what the theory has to say about creativity in art.

Divergent Thinking and Trait Theory: The Guilford Approach

Guilford has said, "It is in divergent thinking that we find the most obvious indications of creativity" (1957, p. 112). If divergent thinking is the hallmark of creativity, it should be fairly easy to devise tests of divergent thinking and thereby have a way of measuring creativity. This is precisely the approach taken by Guilford and his associates, who conceive of creativity as a group of aptitude traits which, taken together, define what we mean by creativity (Guilford, 1959). Divergent thinking is one kind of intellectual operation, and involves the production of different responses in order to solve a particular problem which has no one correct answer. Guilford (1959) gives the example of supplying a number of words for "low." One could say "depressed," "cheap," "degraded," and so forth, and all would be correct. This is divergent thinking because, unlike having to multiply four times two, there is no one particular answer which satisfies the question. If there were, the task would involve convergent thinking, as in the four times two problem.

Guilford studies traits, which are defined as relatively enduring ways in which one individual differs from another. Guilford and his colleagues have tests given to subjects; the tests are then analyzed for factors which intercorrelate with each other (factor analysis) and the resulting factors or traits provide the basis of description. For example, Guilford (1959) reports such traits as ability to see problems, word fluency, and spontaneous flexibility associated with creative thinking. Fluency, flexibility, and originality are all seen as belonging to the general category of divergent thinking, whereas the trait of sensitivity to problems is seen as belonging to the "evaluation" rather than the "divergent thinking" domain. Guilford's creative traits have been validated by relating them to samples rated as creative; the tests of creativity seem to have validity, as shown by low but significant correlations with ratings of creativity.

Psychoanalytic Theory

Kris (1952) has spoken of regression in the service of the ego. This psychoanalytic view is important because regression has frequently been considered part of autistic, uncontrolled thinking, and thus sure to result in lack of productive accomplishment. But, the individual's figural or symbolic abilities may be increased if he can regress in the service of the ego, which means that he is open to experiences of all kinds, including fantasy. If fantasy is properly used, it can enhance the person's utilization of autistic or primary process material. Thus, fantasy is not necessarily a disruptive, harmful influence. This view is in marked contrast to the traditional emphasis upon logical thinking as the only proper means of productive thinking or problem solving.

Various authors (e.g., Barron, 1963; Kris, 1952; Pine & Holt, 1960; Stark, 1966) have written of the value of fantasy, adaptive regression, autistic thinking, and the like. A study by Schmiedler (1965) is related to this issue, especially as it pertains to the acceptance of visual imagery. Schmiedler administered questionnaires of visual imagery and creativity to students in introductory psychology courses. The creativity measure was a subset of items on the Barron Independence of Judgment scale. She found that subjects who accepted their own judgments were also willing to accept visual imagery which supposedly conveys unconscious and preconscious impressions. Thus, creativity and adaptive regression are related, according to Schmiedler's (1965) inferences from her findings.

Now, let us bring the art student back into the picture. A comparison of art students, science students, and engineering students (Schechter, Schmiedler, & Staal, 1965) found that art students reported more dreams, had more imaginativeness associated with their dreams, and scored higher on the Barron Independence of Judgment scale (shortened version) which was considered a measure of creativity. Thus, the personality of the artist may be oriented toward regression in the service of the ego, whereby one is able to return to earlier, more primitive modes of thinking, and to utilize such thoughts in a constructive manner, e.g., creative artistic production. This research is somewhat indirect, but at least it was done. Since psychoanalysts are more often theorists than empirical researchers, many psychoanalytic assumptions are never empirically studied in a controlled, scientific manner.

Association Theory

We turn now to the associative theory of creativity. Mednick (1962) is perhaps the best representative of this theory. Briefly, he believes that creativity is the ability to form remote associations. Given the words "rat," "blue," and "cottage," the creative individual should be able to respond "cheese." The word "cheese" is a remote association which is also useful in the sense that it links the other words together in some meaningful fashion. Many have emphasized originality as being the primary component of creativity. Mednick's approach is consistent with such an emphasis on original, unique, novel, or remote thinking.

Obviously, the person who is able to fantasize is going to have some lead over non-fantasizers in the ability to form remote associations. Also, since the associations must be meaningful, some control is demanded; just any kind of association will not do. This is similar to the approach taken by Hitt (1965; Hitt & Stock, 1965) who found that both original and logical thinking were useful in the production of creative ideas. Hitt has studied scientists and engineers, so his work might seem out of place in a consideration of creativity and art. But, since no one has been able to demonstrate whether creativity is field specific or general over all fields, creativity research on non-artists remains relevant.

Wallach and Kogan (1965) studied the relationships of intelligence and creativity in children, stressing the value of high intelligence and high creativity coexisting within the same person. Four cognitive groupings were suggested:

1. High creativity-high intelligence children are said to exercise both control and freedom, and thus have the optimal qualities necessary for either adult-like or child like behavior.

2. High creativity-low intelligence children are in angry conflict with themselves and their school environment, and only blossom forth in stress-free environments. Perhaps, the conformity and convergent thinking demanded by schools results in few rewards for children who are creative but not especially high in intelligence.

3. Low creativity-high intelligence children are addicted to school achievement, and do quite well in terms of grades and other measures of academic excellence which leave out creativity.

4. Low creativity-low intelligence children are basically bewildered, and must engage in all kinds of defensive behaviors in order to meet the strains inherent in what they perceive as a very demanding environment.

When creativity is formulated in general terms, artistic or nonartistic accomplishment can be subsumed under the four categories. It is only when we attempt to specify what makes a particular individual creative in a particular task that it is necessary to become very specific and state that we are considering artistic or some other kind of achievement.

Existential Theory

Existential theories of creativity are not related to art in particular, although existentialists may analyze artists in terms of creativity and existentialism. May (1965) states that creativity is bringing something new into birth, and distinguishes between "art as artificiality" and "true art." He objects to some psychoanalytic approaches to creativity because of the reductionist approach often taken by psychoanalysts. That is, analysts tend to reduce creativity to some other process, and in so doing often overemphasize the neurotic patterns of creative individuals. As usual, May has some provocative ideas which, however, have not been translated into any significant amount of experimental research. Whether this is due to the vagueness of existential language or the limitations of scientific research in the face of global statements about the nature of man is debatable.

Gestalt Theory

Gestalt theorists have emphasized that piecemeal accounts of anything are artificial, and that the human organism responds to the totality of things. Thus, Gestalt theory is heavily grounded in perception. Wertheimer (1945) has shown how Gestalt theory may be applied in productive thinking, and Kohler (1947) has summarized theory and experimentation in the Gestalt framework. Certainly a theory which claims to explain perceptual phenomena is of interest to anyone studying art, since so much of the artist's work involves his perceptions and his transformation of these perceptions into an artistic product. Gestalt theorists have claimed that much of perception is essentially a natavistic phenomenon in which the person responds in an unlearned fashion to stimuli which he encounters. The reader interested in the natavism-empiricism controversy should consult Hochberg (1963).

Interpersonal Theories

Of great importance for artistic creativity as well as creativity in general is what Mackler and Shontz (1965) have termed interpersonal theories of creativity. There seems to be a great deal in common for such interpersonal theorists as Fromm (1959), Maslow (1959), Rogers (1959), and Torrance (1962, 1965). All of them emphasize the importance of social forces, and state that there is a need for self-actualization of some sort for the full development of creative capacity. In other words, all the so-called interpersonal theorists emphasize the need for a flexible, non-punitive environment which will allow the individual to maximize his growth. Torrance has been the major "interpersonal" experimenter, and his research has time and again shown that the creative child faces many obstacles from an environment which does not take kindly to those who fail to conform. These theorists have paid much attention to the personality of the creative person, although Torrance (1965) defines creativity in terms of sensitivity to problems, deficiencies, and gaps in knowledge; identification of the difficulty; searching for solutions, making guesses, or formulating hypotheses about the deficiencies; testing and retesting the hypotheses and modifying them; and, communicating the results. Although, on the face of it, Torrance's approach sounds terribly biased in favor of scientific as opposed to artistic creativity, he states

389

that not only is his paradigm more related to artistic and literary creativity than to scientific production, but also that his research has focused more on activities related to art, music, writing, and creative dance than to scientific creativity. If Torrance is correct, the differences between artistic and scientific kinds of creativity may be slight, and the findings in one area may hold much for the findings in the other. Torrance's tests of creativity have been used in many research endeavors, which indicates his firm attempts to combine theoretical and empirical approaches.

The Getzels and Jackson Study

No discussion of recent creativity research would be complete without consideration of Getzels and Jackson's (1962) study. These two researchers have perhaps done more than anyone else to emphasize that intelligence and creativity are not the same thing, and that intelligence is not the great god many have assumed it to be. Getzels and Jackson studied children who were in the top 20 per cent of intelligence but not creativity, and students who were in the top 20 per cent of creativity but not intelligence. Criteria can be found in their book *Creativity and Intelligence*. One test involved having children draw a picture of playing tag in the school yard. If the boys or girls drew a picture of children playing tag this was considered an orthodox response, indicative of low creativity. A highly creative response occurred when the subject approached his tasks from an unorthodox or original standpoint. For example, one highly creative response was that of a boy who drew prison guards shooting prisoners. Another was a drawing of a school yard, without any people present. The emphasis was on the buildings, and what children had written on them. This subject wrote on his picture that it was ghosts who were playing tag.

Getzels and Jackson found important differences between their "intelligent" and "creative" subjects. The highly creative subjects were more original in various ways compared to the high I. Q. group. Also, school achievement was just as good for the highly creative children, suggesting that intelligence has been overemphasized in considering factors necessary for school success. In other words, for some children tests of creativity could predict academic success better than tests of intelligence. Most shocking is the fact that the teachers of this school preferred the high I. Q. subjects over the more original, creative students. The non-conformity of the creative children may have been a threat to their teachers. Historically, the most important result of the Getzels and Jackson (1962) study was their review of studies showing only moderate or negative relationships between measured creativity and I. Q. and their emphasis on their findings which showed that creativity should be considered in domains once thought to be reserved to I. Q.: school achievement, originality, and various personality characteristics.

Unfortunately, besides having unusual groups those very high in one attribute but not in the other—the Getzels and Jackson study had other weaknesses (Barron, 1965; Wallach & Kogan, 1965) including the absence of truly low I. Q. students, and the fact that their creativity tests correlated just as highly with I. Q. measures as with each other. These methodological weaknesses suggest that Getzels and Jackson may not have successfully differentiated between intelligence and creativity. Thus, their results should be taken with a grain of salt. However, their study is extremely important since it gave I. Q. a well-deserved kick in the pants, and pointed out the need to consider creativity as an important independent variable in academic performance.

Complexity: An Important Variable for Creativity, Aesthetics, and Personality

The Harvard mathematician Birkhoff (1933) devised a formula of aesthetic measure. According to his formula, simple stimuli are the most pleasing, in contrast to complex forms which Birkhoff considered unpleasing. If Birkhoff had been successful in finding a formula which expressed aesthetic preferences in general, a great advance in the psychology of art would have been achieved. Unfortunately, his formula does not appear to be accurate. For one thing, Birkhoff was misled by the belief that the eye follows the angles of a figure; the more complex the figure, the more eye movements necessary to view it. If this theory of eye movements is true, perhaps simple forms which can be immediately appreciated would be more aesthetically pleasing. The trouble with such reasoning is that the eye does not follow all the angles of a viewed form. It is simply not necessary for the eye to take in each and every angle by making eye movements which correspond to that angle. In fact, a single brief glance will often be as effective as a period of visual inspection for recognizing visual configurations (Mooney, 1958, 1959). A second fallacy in the assertion that immediately appreciated forms will be more pleasing is the fact that the human organism does not always most appreciate that which can be easily attained. Man may seek out difficult situations which expose him to novelty and to stimuli which are only comprehended over a long period of time (White, 1959). Related quests for novelty and exploration also occur in animals (Fowler, 1965).

There is another reason why Birkhoff (1933) may have thought he had an accurate formula which expressed the aesthetic preferences of everyone. This is his implicit philosophical position of objectivism, or the belief that things, far from being relative, have absolute value and meaning. In other words, a certain stimulus is, in and of itself, beautiful, and such a judgment is not dependent upon the values or beliefs of people who view it. As I have pointed out elsewhere (Eisenman & Coffee, 1964), objectivism is implied by Birkhoff's attempt to devise an aesthetic formula which would have universal application.

An alternative approach to objectivism would be to claim that different kinds of groups will prefer different sorts of things, dependent upon such things as their personality, values, upbringing, etc. Eisenman and Coffee (1964) had art students and mathematics students express preferences for polygons which all had six points. Since all 10 polygons had the same number of points, one kind of complexity was kept constant.

However, five of the forms were symmetrical, while the other five were asymmetrical. The results showed that there were striking differences between the kinds of polygons preferred by the art students and by the mathematics students. Every single one of the art students chose an asymmetrical polygon as the most preferred figure, while every single one of the mathematics students chose a symmetrical figure as most preferred. Further, the other choices of the students revealed the same thing: art students preferred asymmetrical polygons while mathematics students preferred symmetrical polygons.

The results of the Eisenman and Coffee (1964) study suggest that the aesthetic preferences of a given individual may depend upon certain characteristics of that person, a point which was apparently alien to Birkhoff's thinking. Further, the fact that the mathematics students preferred the symmetrical figures suggests a possible reason why Birkhoff felt that simpler forms were more preferred than complex figures. Since he was a mathematician, Birkhoff may have been predisposed to prefer simpler stimuli. This makes sense if we conceive of the symmetrical polygons as being simpler than the asymmetrical ones. According to this formulation, Birkhoff generalized his own preferences to the world at large via his formula of aesthetic measure.

Is the objectivist approach totally lacking in any defense? It appears that many notable students of aesthetics subscribe to such a philosophical view. Their main line of defense would seem to be that evidence showing consistency of aesthetic choices across cultures (e.g., Pratt, 1961) suggests that something universal is occurring. Aside from this kind of evidence, research seems to support a subjectivist or relativistic approach, which would appeal to the abundance of evidence showing different aesthetic choices based on different characteristics of the person doing the choosing.

Some of the best evidence that aesthetic preference varies with personality factors has emerged from the finding that perceptual preferences can be described by a bipolar factor ". . . which opposes a preference for perceiving and dealing with complexity to a preference for perceiving and dealing with simplicity, when both of these alternatives are phenomen-enally present and when a choice must be made between them" (Barron, 1953, p. 163). This complexity-simplicity dimension was independently discovered by Eysenck (1941a, b) and by Welsh (1949).

Will a person in the field of art respond more favorably to complexity or simplicity? The Eisenman and Coffee (1964) study suggests that the answer is complexity. However, since personal characteristics of the person are alleged to make a difference, it was deemed desirable to investigate the way that creative and less creative art students would respond to complexity (Taylor & Eisenman, 1964). In the Taylor and Eisenman (1964) study, the behaviors of art students rated for creativity by their instructor were studied in two situations. One situation involved them as perceivers, since they were presented with polygons of varying degrees of complexity, as defined by the number of points. The other situation involved the art students as producers, since they were given different colored pieces of paper, scissors, and glue, and were allowed to construct up to five designs in 30 minutes. The results showed that the students rated as creative preferred more complexity in comparison to the less creative students, and also produced more complex designs than the less creative students. Creativity in art was thus related to preference for complexity, which extends the research of Barron and Welsh (1952), Eisenman and Coffee (1964), and Eysenck (1941 c) who all reported that artists preferred complexity. Since it is often said that artists prefer simple designs, the only way to reconcile the research findings with such a statement seems to be the sup-position that the artist might see a great amount of order in what non-artists see as highly complex or disordered stimuli.

While it is of interest to discover that creative artists prefer complexity, for the simplicity-complexity dimension to have meaning it ought to be feasible to study other kinds of people and also find significant preferences for simplicity or complexity. We turn now from the creative artist to a group at the other end of the desirability continuum: hospitalized schizophrenics. Whereas creative artists are highly respected, schizophrenics are almost always considered unfortunate people whose etiology and behavior are frequently studied, but little understood.

It is well known that schizophrenics and other psychotics often have perceptual deficits. Disordered perception in schizophrenics can have various causes (Mettler, 1955) but McReynolds (1960) has claimed that schizophrenics are unable to assimilate percepts. In other words, whereas you and I are able to handle stimulus input adequately, the schizophrenic has a deficiency in his ability to process incoming stimuli. McReynolds (1963; Sidle, Acker, & McReynolds, 1963) has presented evidence consistent with his theory. It is always valuable when someone other than the person who initiated a theory can provide evidence in support of that theory. Also, it is desirable to substantiate a finding by using different stimulus material than that used in the original finding. Consequently, a photograph of the polygons employed by Taylor and Eisenman (1964) was presented to 20 male schizophrenics in a state mental hospital, and to 20 normal male college students. If McReynolds' theory has any validity, we would expect the schizophrenics to choose the simpler polygons as most preferred, because the simpler polygons should be easier to assimilate than the more complex figures. In addition, two poems, one rated as being simple and one rated as being complex, were also presented to the subjects. Consistent with McReynolds' theory, the study (Eisenman, 1965 a) found that schizophrenics preferred the less complex polygons and chose less novelty in poems in contrast to the college students. Thus, when given a choice between simple and more complex stimuli, the schizophrenics preferred simplicity.

Given that schizophrenics prefer simpler polygons, what will happen if a conflict is created by expressing disapproval of their choices? A study (Eisenman, 1966 a) was undertaken to investigate this issue. It is known that schizophrenics react very strongly to disapproval, presumably because they have been sensitized to disapproval during childhood by rejecting parents, especially mothers (Garmezy, 1945). Since schizophrenics are often uninfluenced by group pressure (Gill,

1963, 1965), the successful modification of their aesthetic choices by individual disapproval from the experimenter would imply that change in psychotherapy might best proceed by having a therapist who individually communicates to the schizophrenic and, perhaps, who disapproves of some of the schizophrenic's bizarre thoughts. In the study, (Eisenman, 1966 a) subjects who preferred higher complexity were told that their choices were for figures that were too complex, whereas subjects who expressed preferences for relatively simpler polygons were told that their choices were too simple. In both cases the experimenter explained that complexity or simplicity was based on the number of points on the polygon, and pointed out what he meant on the cards containing the polygons. Schizophrenics responded to this disapproval by changing their choices when given an opportunity to do so, but normal college students did not change when given a second chance to rate the polygons. Experimenter disapproval can modify aesthetic choices of schizophrenics, which has implications for psychotherapy as mentioned above.

Perhaps the kinds of subjects considered thus far seem very distant to the reader, who may not be a creative artist or a schizophrenic. But, all of us have a birth order. We are either the first born child of our parents, or the second, or the third, etc. The research to be mentioned next related birth order to aesthetic preference. The main theories of birth order are those of Adler (Ansbacher & Ansbacher, 1956) who felt that the first born child reacted negatively to the birth of a sibling, which caused the first born to lose his position of "little king" of the family; and Schachter (1959) who theorized that first borns are made more dependent than later borns due to inconsistent nurturance by their parents. First borns later seek to reduce their unmet dependency needs by affiliating with others, and are therefore said to have a greater need for affiliation (Schachter, 1959). Schachter has provided experimental evidence to support his assumptions, including the finding that the first born seems more susceptible to anxiety, presumably because of his early family experience. Support for linking anxiety and the first born together has been provided by the author in research with psychotherapy patients (Eisenman, 1966 b) and with student nurses (Eisenman, 1965 b).

What should be expected of first born subjects when they are given a choice of complexity or simplicity? According to Adler (Ansbacher & Ansbacher, 1956) the first born longingly looks back to the time when the second child was not there and he, the first born, was the "little king." This looking to the past makes for a conservative streak in the first born, and he should prefer simplicity, since preference for simplicity is associated with a more conventional, conforming personality (Barron, 1953, 1963). Unfortunately for us first borns, the author has found that first born subjects preferred simpler polygons (Eisenman, 1965 b) and produced simpler designs (Eisenman, 1964). As Kenneth Ring [2] has said, the outcome of most birth order studies leaves little for the first born individual to cheer about. Since the author's two birth order-complexity studies would be consistent with a view that first borns tend to be less creative (creative people prefer complexity) they add to the list of studies on birth order which make first borns, from the standpoint of adjustment, seem somewhat unfortunate. Perhaps this will change as the birth order variable is investigated more intensively.[3] In the meantime, the only solace for first borns seems to be that they are much more likely to attain eminence (e.g., Rimland, 1964). Thus, we have the somewhat curious finding that while first borns may not be the most well adjusted people within our society, they do seem to be the ones most likely to achieve. Perhaps their greater anxiety serves as

2. Personal communication, November 5, 1965.

3. A recently completed study by the author, "Birth Order and Sex Differences in Aesthetic Preference for Complexity-Simplicity," casts some light on this issue. When both sex and birth order were taken into account, it was found that among females, first borns are more likely to prefer simplicity. But, among males, the first born, not the later born, expressed the greater preference for complexity. The two studies (Eisenman, 1964; 1965 b) which linked simplicity to first borns had samples composed mainly or entirely of female subjects, which may explain why the first borns fared so poorly. Had male subjects been used, it would have been the later borns who would likely have chosen the simpler shapes.

a motivator which makes them talk more in group therapy (Eisen-man, in press, b) and achieve greater eminence due to greater effort expended on intellectual and achievement-oriented problems.

All of the above strikes the author as inconsistent with conservatism, since the highly conservative person constantly looking to the past cannot be expected to be oriented toward achievement. It should be noted that one recent polygon study (Eisenman, 1966 c) did not find significant differences between first born and later born subjects when ratings of "pleasingness" and "interestingness" of the polygons were made. Adequate assessment of conservatism and birth order will occur when variables such as those discussed in Berlyne's (1966) chapter are analyzed for birth order differences, and when the global term "conservatism" is broken down into conservatism in dress, in politics, in moral values, etc. Since conservatism, conformity, practicality, and the like are often inconsistent with artistic creativity (Griff, 1960), the linking of birth order and conservative tendencies has profound implications which invite further research and understanding.

Conclusion

This chapter has stressed how important it is to think through any statement made about art, aesthetics, creativity or related subjects. So much confusion has emerged in past discussions of these fields because authors have not made clear the assumptions on which they were proceeding. While it may seem unkind or downright nasty to say so, this failure to disclose assumptions has likely been due to the various writers not realizing their own assumptions. Creativity researchers seldom comment on whether or not they assume creativity to be field specific or general, though they usually write as if creativity were considered general. If creativity is a general trait, then distinctions between artistic creativity and creativity in other fields are unnecessary. However, if creativity is usually or often field specific, then it will be necessary to specify the kind of creativity one is talking about. Of course, it is quite possible that some personality characteristics, such as openness to new ideas or independence of judgment, are related to creativity in most fields regardless of the demands of that field.

The psychology of modern art can be pursued in a scientific manner. Nevertheless, the reader of *Psychological Abstracts* is aware that most papers written on art, aesthetics, and related topics have been theoretical or speculative essays, rather than empirical studies. The studies reported in this chapter are indicative of the kinds of research which can be undertaken in order to study art scientifically. While we will always need people who will think up bold theories about art, we also need experimentation to test the bold ideas. An important problem is that experimental research must approximate what occurs "out there" in the real world if laboratory findings are to be meaningful. It is this artificiality of laboratory experiments, purposely introduced to give the experimenter control over variables, which has made the more theoretically oriented thinkers question the value of all experimental studies. This is a genuine problem which should not be passed over lightly. For example, Irving D. Harris [4] has suggested, in a personal communication, that the results of my study (Eisenman, 1964) showing more artistic creativity among later borns are misleading. Harris has noticed more creativity in eminent men to occur among first borns, and suggests that the test used in my study taps something necessary for some kind of artistic achievement ". . . but not the constancy and inner re-working inherent in a creative labor of love." Harris has an interesting point, since all laboratory studies impose a time limit on the subject, along with other artificial aspects. All this is not to say that all research is invalidated because artificiality is imposed. Rather, some laboratory findings may be misleading because of the special conditions inherent in scientific research. The researcher must constantly strive to create interesting tasks which will hold the attention of the subject, and otherwise yield valid findings.

Despite the critical comments above, important advances have been made in the study of art, aesthetic preferences, and

4. Personal communication, November 9, 1965.

creativity. We now have some idea of the kind of person who will be creative: one who is independent in his judgments, open to new experience, willing to regress in service of the ego, and able to tolerate a great deal of complexity and inconsistency. These personality characteristics seem consistent with creativity in various fields, and are understood because of recent findings. Thus, recent research points away from hard work and intellectual study as the sole criteria for creativity, and suggests that a liberal outlook and acceptance of one's impulses are equally necessary for creative thinking or achievement.

One of the most exciting aspects of research on complexity is that the simplicity-complexity dimension can be used to assess personal characteristics of artists and give us some insight into personality concomitants of different kinds of artistic productions. And, we can study the aesthetic preferences of people who are not artists: student nurses, schizophrenics, and the ordinary man in the street. Thus, aesthetics can tell us about the artist, or it can reveal important characteristics about non-artists. The exciting thing is that aesthetic stimuli have unlimited use in studying personality. The day should be ended in which the psychology of art referred only to the study of artists. Our art preferences and aesthetic tastes can yield fundamental insights which, after all, is what psychology is all about.

References

Ansbacher, H. L., & Ansbacher, Rowena R. (Eds.), *The Individual Psychology of Alfred Adler.* New York: Basic Books, 1956.

Barron, F. Complexity-simplicity as a personality dimension. *Journal of Abnormal and Social Psychology,* 1953, 48, 163-172.

Barron, F. *Creativity and psychological health.* Princeton, N.J.: Van Nostrand, 1963.

Barron, F. The psychology of creativity. In *New Directions in psychology II.* New York: Holt, Rinehart & Winston, 1965. Pp. 1-134.

Bereiter, C., & Freedman, M. B. Fields of study and the people in them. In N. Sanford (Ed.), *The American college*. New York: Wiley, 1962. Pp. 563-596.

Berlyne, D. E. Laughter, humor and play. In G. Lindzey & E. Aronson (Eds.), *Handbook of social psychology* (2nd ed.). Cambridge, Mass.: Addison-Wesley, 1966.

Birkhoff, G. D. *Aesthetic measure*. Cambridge, Mass.: Harvard University Press, 1933.

Eisenman, R. Birth order and artistic creativity. *Journal of Individual Psychology*, 1964, 20, 183-185.

Eisenman, R. Aesthetic preferences of schizophrenics. *Perceptual and Motor Skills*, 1965, 20, 601-604. (a)

Eisenman, R. Birth order, aesthetic preference, and volunteering for an electric shock experiment. *Psychonomic Science*, 1965, 3, 151-152. (b)

Eisenman, R. The effect of disapproval on aesthetic preferences of schizophrenics. *Journal of General Psychology, Perceptual and Motor Skills*, 1966, 23, 1167-1170. (c) 1966, 75, 315-318. (a)

Eisenman, R. Birth order, anxiety, and verbalizations in group psychotherapy. *Journal of Consulting Psychology*, 1966, 30, 521-526. (b)

Eisenman, R. Pleasing and interesting visual complexity: Support for Berlyne.

Eisenman, R., & Coffee, Sandra. Aesthetic preferences of art students and mathematics students. *Journal of Psychology*, 1964, 58, 375-378.

English, H. B., & English, Ava C. *A comprehensive dictionary of psychological and psychoanalytical terms*. New York: McKay, 1958.

Eysenck, H. J. The general factor in aesthetic judgments. *British Journal of Psychology*, 1941, 31, 94-102. (a)

Eysenck, H. J. "Type"-factors in aesthetic judgments. *British Journal of Psychology*, 1941, 31, 262-270. (b)

Eysenck, H. J. The empirical determination of an aesthetic formula. *Psychological Review*, 1941, 48, 83-92. (c)

Fischelli, V. R., & Welch, L. The ability of college art majors to recombine ideas in creative thinking. *Journal of Applied Psychology*, 1947, 31, 278-282.

Fowler, H. *Curiosity and exploratory behavior.* New York: Macmillan, 1965.

Fromm, E. The creative attitude. In H. H. Anderson (Ed.), *Creativity and its cultivation.* New York: Harper, 1959. Pp. 44-54.

Garmezy, N. Adaptive mechanisms in schizophrenia. *Bulletin of the Menninger Clinic*, 1965, 29, 24-36.

Getzels, J. M., & Jackson, P. W. *Creativity and intelligence.* New York: Wiley, 1962.

Gill, W. S. Interpersonal affect and conformity behavior in schizophrenics. *Journal of Abnormal and Social Psychology*, 1963, 67, 502-505.

Gill, W. S. Attitude change and the schizophrenic. *Psychological Record*, 1965, 15, 289-296.

Griff, M. The commercial artist: A study in changing and consistent identities. In M. R. Stein, A. J. Vidich, & D. M. White (Eds.), *Identity and anxiety.* Glencoe, Ill.: Free Press, 1960. Pp. 219-241.

Guilford, J. P. Creative abilities in the arts. *Psychological Review*, 1957, 64, 110-118.

Guilford, J. P. Traits of creativity. In H. H. Anderson (Ed.), *Creativity and its cultivation.* New York: Harper, 1959. Pp. 142-161.

Hitt, W. D. Toward a two-factor theory of creativity. *Psychological Record*, 1965, 15, 127-132.

Hitt, W. D., & Stock, J. R. The relation between psychological characteristics and creative behavior. *Psychological Record*, 1965, 15, 133-140.

Hochberg, J. E. Natavism and empiricism in perception. In L. Postman (Ed.), *Psychology in the making.* New York: Knopf, 1963. Pp. 255-330.

Kohler, W. *Gestalt psychology.* New York: Liveright, 1947.

Kris, E. *Psychoanalytic explorations in art.* New York: International Universities Press, 1952.

McReynolds, P. Anxiety, perception and schizophrenia. In D. D. Jackson (Ed.), *The etiology of schizophrenia.* New York: Basic Books, 1960. Pp. 248-292.

McReynolds, P. Reaction to novel and familiar stimuli as a

function of schizophrenic withdrawal. *Perceptual and Motor Skills*, 1963, 16, 847-850.

Mackler, B., & Shontz, F. C. Creativity: Theoretical and methodological considerations. *Psychological Record*, 1965, 15, 217-238.

Maslow, A. H. Creativity in self-actualizing people. In H. H. Anderson (Ed.), *Creativity and its cultivation.* New York: Harper, 1959. Pp. 83-95.

May, R. The nature of creativity. In H. H. Anderson, (Ed.), *Creativity and its cultivation.* New York: Harper, 1959. Pp. 55-68.

Mednick, S. A. The associative basis of the creative process. *Psychological Review*, 1962, 69, 220-232.

Mettler, F. A. Perceptual capacity, functions of the corpus striatum and schizophrenia. *Psychiatric Quarterly*, 1955, 29, 89-111.

Mooney, C. M. Recognition of novel visual configurations with and without eye movements. *Journal of Experimental Psychology*, 1958, 56, 133-138.

Mooney, C. M. Recognition of symmetrical and non-symmetrical ink-blots with and without eye movements. *Canadian Journal of Psychology*, 1959, 13, 11-19.

Pine, F., & Holt, R. R. Creativity and primary process: A study of adaptive regression. *Journal of Abnormal and Social Psychology*, 1960, 61, 370-379.

Pratt, C. C. Aesthetics. *Annual Review of Psychology*, 1961, 12, 71-92.

Rimland, B. *Infantile autism.* New York: Appleton-Century-Crofts, 1964.

Rogers, C. R. Toward a theory of creativity. In H. H. Anderson (Ed.), *Creativity and its cultivation.* New York: Harper, 1959. Pp. 69-82.

Schachter, S. *The psychology of affiliation.* Stanford: Stanford University Press, 1959.

Schechter, Naomi, Schmeidler, Gertrude R., & Staal, M. Dream reports and creative tendencies in students of the arts, sciences, and engineering. *Journal of Consulting Psychology*, 1965, 29, 415-421.

Schmeidler, Gertrude R. Visual imagery correlated to a measure of creativity. *Journal of Consulting Psychology*, 1965, 29, 78-80.

Sidle, A., Acker, Mary, & McReynolds, P. "Stimulus-seeking" behavior in schizophrenics and non-schizophrenics. *Perceptual and Motor Skills*, 1963, 17, 811-816.

Stark, S. Rorschach movement, fantastic daydreaming, and Freud's concept of primary process: Interpretive commentary. *Perceptual and Motor Skills*, 1966, 22, 523-532.

Taylor, R. E., & Eisenman, R. Perception and production of complexity by creative art students. *Journal of Psychology*, 1964, 57, 239-242.

Torrance, E. P. *Guiding creative talent.* Englewood Cliffs, N.J.: Prentice-Hall, 1962.

Torrance, E. P. Scientific views of creativity and factors affecting its growth. *Daedalus*, 1965, 94, 663-681.

Wallach, M. A., & Kogan, N. A new look at the creativity-intelligence distinction. *Journal of Personality*, 1965, 33, 348-369.

Welsh, G. S. A projective figure-preference test for diagnosis of psychopathology: 1. A preliminary investigation. Unpublished doctoral dissertation, University of Minnesota, 1949.

Wertheimer, M. *Productive thinking.* New York: Harper, 1945.

White, R. W. Motivation reconsidered: The concept of competence. *Psychological Review*, 1959, 66, 297-333.

PSYCHOLOGY OF POST-FREUDIAN LITERATURE

A. A. ROBACK AND WADE BASKIN

Editorial Note

Sigmund Freud and his followers provided psychologists with a new set of postulates for studying human behavior when they opened up the vast territory previously neglected by researchers who were blind to the unconscious. During the early part of the twentieth century there was gradual acceptance of the view that unconscious desires generate conflicts which find expression in dreams, myths, and works of art. Toward mid-century the existential view of man raised new problems and new possibilities. Together psychoanalysis and existentialism have provided the artist, the reader, and the psychologist with new insights into human behavior and have served as tools for the cultivation of a fruitful field.

Dr. A. A. Roback has shown his penchant for imaginative literature through such volumes as Peretz: *Psychologist of Literature* (Cambridge, 1935) and the extensive survey of Yiddish Literature in the *Encyclopedia Americana*.

Dr. Roback received his B. A. from McGill and both the M. A. and Ph. D. in psychology from Harvard, where he later taught. He served for years as Professor of Psychology at Emerson College and has been Lecturer for the University Extension Division of the State Department of Education in Massachusetts since 1960.

In addition to writing and lecturing on The Psychology of Literature, Dr. Roback has given seminars for graduate students on this topic. He has written and edited many works on psychology and related disciplines, including a *History of Psychology and Psychiatry* and *Present-Day Psychology*, in which portions of the following essay originally appeared.

•

THE PSYCHOLOGY OF POST-FREUDIAN LITERATURE

It is one of the unaccountable curios that although psychology and literature deal with the same subject-matter, viz., imagery, ideas, emotions, feelings, and so on, the psychology of literature has received but scant treatment until very recently; and although there is now available an anthology under the title of *Psychology through Literature* (ed. by Shrodes, VanGundy and Husband) there is no systematic textbook or treatise which covers the growing borderland. When one of the present writers, as a student at Harvard, published his lecture before a Boston audience on psychology and literature [1] four decades ago, the subject seemed a novel one. Only in 1929 did the same title appear over an article by C. G. Jung, which later formed a chapter in his *Modern Man in Search of a Soul* (transl. by W. S. Dell and Cary F. Baynes), and in 1951, a book entitled *Literature and Psychology* by F. L. Lucas opened up the subject on a larger scale.

Since the advent of psychoanalysis, literature and its creators have, of course, come in for a great deal of discussion on the part of depth psychologists, and even before Freud's monographs and articles on artists, including *littérateurs*, stirred the intelligentsia, the serial *Grenzfragen des Nerven- und Seelenlebens* presented studies of a score or more of writers, in which various quirks of talented men were described and analyzed. It was, however, the individual and his behavior that occupied the mind of the, for the most part, psychiatrists. The literary productions were introduced only insofar as they could throw any light on the subject of the sketch. This particular type of study may be called pathography and included among others, mono-

1. Roback, A. A. Psikhologie un Literatur. *Literatur un Lebn*, vol. 1, 1915.

406

graphs on Nietzsche, Poe, Strindberg, Maupassant, Tolstoi, von Kleist and Rousseau.

It was Freud, however, who initiated the new approach to the analysis of art (and literature) through his Leonardo da Vinci and Hölderlin monographs, which set the example for his followers to emulate him in that respect until we now possess perhaps hundreds of books and articles on authors ranging all the way from St. Paul to James Joyce. Apart, however, from the individuals, there is an ever-growing literature on the production as interpreted by psychoanalysis. It is becoming increasingly difficult for a teacher of literature in the higher institutions to be *au courant* with his field without taking account of, let us say, Ernest Jones's *Hamlet and Oedipus* or Hanns Sachs's chapters on *The Tempest* and *Measure for Measure*. As for Dostoyevsky, psychoanalysis seems to dote on him. It will be recalled that Freud thought him the greatest master of fiction, with no exception. One may surmise the reason to be that the Oedipus complex is evident in some of his stories, chiefly the *Brothers Karamazov*.

In our survey of psychology and literature, there is to be considered a field with at least three foci. First, there is the literary problem *per se*, i.e., the interpretation of the content from a psychological angle. There is also the writer who needs analyzing, and perhaps we should consider also the reader. Indeed, the literary critic or reviewer, and even the publisher, are not altogether to be omitted; for although it is true that the latter views the Ms. only as a marketable product, we do know that there are such rare birds as prestige publishers. Furthermore, what determines a publisher or his reader to anticipate a large sale is a possible object of investigation.

Psychoanalysis Takes Over

Since psychoanalysis started as a form of therapy, it is only natural that the individual writer would occupy the center in that sphere rather than literature as such. Prior to Freud, the question as to why an artist should wish to create hardly made sense. In the epigrammatic literature, suggestive hints might occur now and then, but that would only be a flash in the pan. It was taken for granted, as it is mainly today, that writing for a living or for fame is a good enough reason. Naturally every one who is moved to set down his thoughts on paper thinks that bursting into print will be of advantage to him. Yet there are many who write under pseudonyms and many others who will pay to have their works published. Ordinarily it is thought that it titillates their vanity to see their brain-child worrying the brains of others. In some slight way they are affecting the world, and who knows but that even if unrecognized now— so they imagine—posterity will yet accord them their due.

As for the unmistakably gifted, it would never have entered the average man's mind that they are anything but fortunate in enjoying not only the fruits of their labors but the actual creative process. To be sure, the biography of genius is replete with sad and unhappy episodes, but these were regarded more as casual occurrences due to political events or chance relationships. It was Freud who looked for something deeper-going, and out of the unconscious he brought up the conflict which was molesting the artist who, as a result, is seeking to escape into a world of fantasy. The phrase "escape from reality" thenceforth began to take on the aspect of a spell accounting for all creative work. The artist is not a free agent but is driven by a *daimôn*, not (as Socrates thought) implanted by some supernatural power, but a demon engendered by the unconscious forces at war with one another over the heritage of infantile experiences, bound to cause misery to the nascent creator.

Rank's Voluntarism

It would be instructive to examine the various interpretations of the artists by Freud, Rank and Jung. Otto Rank's conception is to be found in *Art and the Artist* (original *Der Künstler*) and *Truth and Reality*, which appeared in English before the German edition. Rank, it must be borne in mind, was the apostle of the Will, with a subtle appreciation of religious values. In the chapter "Creation and Guilt," Rank traces the genesis of willing, and makes the neurotic type out to be a willing on a lower level, practically tantamount to desiring, where external objects and obstacles are involved. A higher willing, which oscillates between a hankering for possessions and the ego-ideal or ought principle, is still fraught with guilt-feeling and can only lead to neurotic tendencies. In his early work *Der Künstler* (1908) Rank sees the artist as partaking of both the normal dreamer and the neurotic, but differing from the latter in that he turns his conflict to advantage and therefore overcomes his shortcomings through sublimation. Rank still is tied to the Freudian apron strings, and speaks of the artist as a narcissist who flaunts his fantasies upon an expectant audience. Employing such dynamisms as displacement and repression in much the same way as Freud, he may still be called a disciple.

In 1928, Rank had already more or less emancipated himself from the parental restrictions of Freud and set up house for himself. Freud had been preoccupied with sexuality and its avowed purpose—reproduction, the creativeness of the individual—but Rank stresses the productive in the universal sense. To quote the author:

> We recognize therefore in the creative impulse not only the highest form of the will affirmation of the individual, but also the most mighty will conquest, that of the individual will over the will of the species represented by sexuality. A similar victory of the individual will over generic will, as I show elsewhere, is represented in the individual love claim, whose psychological meaning lies in the fact that the individual can and will accept his generic rôle only if this is possible in an individual personal way, in the love experience. This represents, as it were, the creativity of the average type who demands a definite individuality for himself and if necessary also creates it, an individuality that sanctions and so justifies and saves his individual will. The creative type, on the contrary, does not content himself with the creation of an individual. Instead, he creates a whole world in his own image, and then needs the whole world to say "yes" to his creation, that is, to find it good and thus justify it.[2]

Rank attributes to this going beyond the bounds of nature,

2. Rank. *Truth and Reality*, (transl. by Jessie Taft). New York: Knopf, 1936, pp. 134-135.

which was meant for reproduction and normal sex behavior, a guilt complex arising out of the diversion of a natural instinct to a glorification of the (creative) will which, the artist fancies, makes a god out of himself—hence his punishment in the form of mental suffering.

Jung's Collective Unconscious

Just as Rank parts company with Freud on the universal *vs.* individual issue in the matter of artistic creation, so Jung objects to Freud's emphasis on the personal, really infantile, and pregenital, traits. The artist is of course a person, but his art, according to Jung, stems from the impersonal, the deeper collective layers.

In his capacity of artist he is neither auto-erotic, nor hetero-erotic, nor erotic in any sense. He is objective and impersonal—even inhuman—for as an artist he is his work, and not a human being.

Every creative person is a duality or a synthesis of contradictory aptitudes. On the one side he is a human being with a personal life, while on the other side he is an impersonal, creative process. Since as a human being he may be sound or morbid, we must look at his psychic make-up to find the determinants of his personality. But we can only understand him in his capacity of artist by looking at his creative achievement. We should make a sad mistake if we tried to explain the mode of life of an English gentleman, a Prussian officer, or a cardinal in terms of personal factors. The gentleman, the officer and the cleric function as such in an impersonal rôle, and their psychic make-up is qualified by a peculiar objectivity. We must grant that the artist does not function in an official capacity—the very opposite is nearer the truth. Art is a kind of innate drive that seizes a human being and makes him its instrument. The artist is not a person endowed with free will who seeks his own ends, but one who allows art to realize its purposes through him. As a human being he may have moods and a will and personal aims, but as an artist he is a "man" in a higher sense—he is "collective man"—one who carries and shapes the unconscious, psychic life of mankind. To perform this difficult office it is sometimes necessary for him to sacrifice happiness and everything that makes life worth living for the ordinary human being.[3]

How does Jung explain the unhappiness of the artist? Again, it is traced to conflicts, but not the kind which Freud and Rank bring to the fore, although in the last analysis it comes to the same thing. It is curious that although Jung is generally obscure and unconvincing because of the many facets in his writing, his essay on psychology and literature, after the many learned citations and illustrations are put to one side, is a clear presentation of the common sense view, viz. that

All this being so, it is not strange that the artist is an especially interesting case for the psychologist who uses an analytical method. The artist's life cannot be otherwise than full of conflicts, for two forces are at war within him—on the one hand the common human longing for happiness, satisfaction and security in life, and on the other a ruthless passion for creation which may go so far as to override every personal desire. The lives of artists are as a rule so highly unsatisfactory—not to say tragic—because of their inferiority on the human and personal side, and not because of a sinister dispensation. There are hardly any exceptions to the rule that a person must pay dearly for the divine gift of the creative fire. It is as though each of us were endowed at birth with a certain capital of energy. The strongest force in our make-up will seize and all but monopolize this energy, leaving so little over that nothing of value can come of it. In this way the creative force can drain the

3. Jung, C. G. *Modern Man in Search of a Soul* (transl. by W. S. Dell and C. F. Baynes). London: Kegan Paul, 1933, pp. 194-195.

human impulses to such a degree that the personal ego must develop all sorts of bad qualities—ruthlessness, selfishness and vanity (so-called "auto-erotism")—and even every kind of vice, in order to maintain the spark of life and to keep itself from being wholly bereft. The auto-eroticism of artists resembles that of illegitimate or neglected children who from their tenderest years must protect themselves from the destructive influence of people who have no love to give them—who develop bad qualities for that very purpose and later maintain an invincible egocentricity by remaining all their lives infantile and helpless or by actively offending against the moral code or the law. How can we doubt that it is his art that explains the artist, and not the insufficiencies and conflicts of his personal life? These are nothing but the regrettable results of the fact that he is an artist—that is to say, a man who from his very birth has been called to a greater task than the ordinary mortal. A special ability means a heavy expenditure of energy in a particular direction, with a consequent drain from some other side of life.[4]

Daydreamer and Artist

Hanns Sachs who had given much thought to the problems of artistic creation, took up the trend of Freud at the stage art was associated with daydreaming, but pursued it to further heights. He, too, recognizes the narcissism of the artist, nevertheless, he draws fine distinctions between the daydreamer and the poet. "The daydreamer is asocial and formless, without regard to continuity and causation, uses words and visual images indiscriminately, and groups everything around the author as the central figure." [5]

Or let us take the following delineation which shows how Sachs had almost specialized in the aesthetic problems and the

4. *Ibid.*, pp. 195-196.
5. Sachs, H. *The Creative Unconscious* (2d ed.) Cambridge: Sci-Art, 1951, p. 39.

artistic technique, and was able to give us a clear-cut picture of the author as compared with his daydreaming counterpart.

The point where poetry and daydreaming disagree almost constantly is in the part allotted to the creator. The day-dreamer is always his own hero, the poet never. Even when he tells his story as though it were about himself and uses a great deal of his own life and character as material, the poet does so in a sense quite different from that of the daydreamer: he is not guided by a wish for self-glorification, but for self-investigation. An author who in his own work indulges in self-flattery has not attained the standard of the artist. This form of vanity, this pleasure in looking at oneself in a beautifying mirror (narcissism) has to be sacrificed when the step is made from the asocial daydream to the work of art. It is the toll which has to be paid for the opening of the gate that leads out of isolation and to a new reunion with men.[6]

But that is not all. The narcissistic author has his heavy load of guilt-feeling which he somehow wishes to lessen, even if it cannot be entirely disposed of, and so he appeals to his audience or public for succor, for it is to their mutual advantage that he has aired out their own daydreams and presented them in such a form that they could enjoy them.

We return to the problem we left unanswered. The day-dreamer uses his fantasy as a means of gaining narcis-sistic gratification for his own person. What happens to this narcissism when the creator has to surrender it in order to win the participation—the readiness to identi-fication—of his audience? Form and beauty of the work appear when this transformation takes place; they make it attractive and enable it to stimulate and dominate the affects. We know that the author needs this to relieve his guilt-feeling. But he does not stop when he once has started on the quest for beauty; he is never satisfied. All

6. *Loc. cit.*, p. 42.

413

the resources of his mind, all the energies of his life are spent unsparingly to achieve higher perfection in beauty for his work. What is sufficient to dazzle his audience does not satisfy his demands. We see here another force at work, one which plays between the poet and his work and is independent of the effect on the audience, even on an ideal audience. The entirely narcissistic character of this force leads to its recognition as the sacrificed narcissism of the daydreamer, reborn as the poet's desire for the beauty of his work. In other words, the form or façade which originally was but a means to an end becomes, after the transformation, a part of the end in itself; the narcissism has been replaced and shifted from the creator to his creation. In this way the poet's work becomes the essential part of his personality; since his narcissism has been transferred to it, it is generally more important than friendship or love or all the rest of life. The poet has to give up a great portion of his narcissism, probably more than average people, but his work wins back immeasurably more of it than others can hope for: acknowledged and enduring beauty, irresistible power over the minds of men, and immortality.[7]

Indeed Jung's demarcation between the personal and the impersonal seems to have been unwittingly made by Sachs when he tells us that

The personality of the greatest of masters—Homer, Shakespeare—has disappeared behind their work. The operator may reserve for himself some little vanities, but the hard and long struggle, the measureless ambition, the alternation between hope and despair, all these indicate his passionate devotion to this work.

Here the line which separates the poet as artist from the hero or "leader" becomes apparent. The leader retains all his narcissism; he too wants to dominate the affects

7. *Loc. cit.*, pp. 48-49.

of his followers, not to relieve his guilt-feeling, since he hasn't any, but in order to use them as instruments for his own purposes, to carry out his plans for his personal aggrandizement. The artist is a leader of men, but through his work, not in his own person. He wants their affects, but without ulterior motive. For the "leader" it does not matter if the affects of his followers are shallow or spurious. All he asks is that they be useful for his purpose. Not so the artist. He cares only for those affects which are deep and genuine; but he is satisfied with the tears and laughter of his audience, and does not even think of making any further use of them. The mean between these types is kept by the author who wants to serve a definite, practical, mostly a political tendency. He certainly has in mind the further use of the affects which he has tried to arouse. But in doing this, he is a "leader" and not an "artist," and nearly always to the detriment of the artistic value of his work. With true artists sometimes the opposite happens; they set out with practical aims in view, but their genius carries them far beyond the initial narrow scope, as it happened to Cervantes when he wanted to ridicule the knight-errant novels. These works are then read and admired long after their "real" purpose has been forgotten.

The two main unconscious aims of the poet—the relief of his guilt-feeling and the replacement of his narcissism— are inseparable. One without the other would be an impossibility. But naturally they are not of equal strength in every case, and we can recognise clearly enough the preponderance of one or the other. It is feasible to make this the principle for dividing all the countless variations of literary schools and styles into two main groups with, of course, transitional forms in between.[8]

It was reserved for Edmund Bergler to come to grips with writers exclusively and plumb their unconscious more search-

8. *Loc. cit.*, 50-51.

ingly than his predecessors, and no wonder he afterwards was obliged to fight figurative duels with a whole succession of reviewers whom he classified and catalogued under not very edifying labels.

Orality and Masochism

In short, according to Bergler, the writer has regressed to the oral stage, or has never progressed beyond it, a stage which is characterized by psychic masochism. These people obtain pleasure out of hurts, grievances, and are collectors of injustice which they receive time and again, themselves being the instigators. The aggression displayed by the writer-masochist is not true to type; it is one which is intended by the unconscious to recoil upon oneself. Of course, it would be a curious sort of analytic interpretation, if the guilt-feeling were missing in such a state of affairs, and it certainly takes its honored place in Bergler's book, for psychic masochism which involves identification with the mother and thus by such partaking both of the mother and himself, the author is able to give and receive at the same time whatever he felt he had not gotten enough from his mother (affection, milk, tenderness) in the infant stage.

But that is not the only source of guilt-feeling. Every writer, affirms Bergler, is a voyeur, a peeping Tom. He must, in order to produce fiction or a play look into the private life of others, at least in his imagination, and that has its counterpart in exhibitionism—both tendencies, the one a reflection of the other, strong in early childhood and somehow associated with orality. Now that the relationships are more or less fixed, we can proceed to the unconscious posturings of the writer in order to exonerate himself. First, he denies he is a masochist but is ready to take the rap for another set of crimes, viz., aggression, which, as has been intimated, is not genuine but only a smoke screen. Next, the writer, who implicates his readers in his perpetration, points to them as equally guilty, and therefore he and they are equally not-guilty. He then proceeds to cover up his *voyeurism* by calling attention to his exhibitionism, for 'peeping' is something deeper-going, more re-

416

gressive and more provocative of guilt-feeling e.g., spying on parents during the sex act.

Acrobatics in Psychoanalysis

It would take too much space to follow the author in all his peregrinations. Given so much latitude as turning from one extreme to the other, from posit to opposite, and leaping nimbly from one limb to another, any conclusion is possible, but Bergler is an excellent writer whose reservoir of illustrations and anecdotes never runs low, and his barbs are never blunted. Hence much of what he says possesses the charm of aphorism; and his astute observations on the editor or critic (as an inhibited or frustrated writer) are acceptable even though the psychoanalytic substructure is questionable. Bergler is not even willing to grant that the writer expresses his unconscious wishes in his stories and verse. What he contends is that the novelist or playwright brings into the open his defences against these wishes and desires. In other words, the fantasies do not appear directly but must be inferred indirectly from the reactions against them or even a further remove, the reaction to the defence against them as shown in the literary productions. But why does Bergler not say that the creation evidences the fight of the ego against the id, and the resurgence of the id?

Perhaps it would be just as well to reproduce a typical passage from the author summing up his thesis.

> With slight exaggeration one could say that the sterile writer is the newest addition to the family of analytical patients. Our acquaintanceship with him is so recent, in fact, that clinical experiences are not even coördinated. The following, therefore, is not the generally accepted psychoanalytic opinion on writers (as yet such a uniformity does not exist), and represents simply my own clinical experiences gathered in intensive and extensive "couch acquaintanceship" with thirty-six writers over a period of twenty years, the typical length of individual treatment being one and a-half to two years.

In my opinion a writer is a person who tries to solve an inner conflict through the sublimatory medium of writing. Whether the writer is successful (in the worldly meaning of the word) is immaterial for psychological evaluation.

The writer's basic *inner* conflict pertains with amazing monotony to the psychic masochist's solution of his relation to the mother image. By mother image we do not mean his relation to the real mother, or even the oedipal mother of his infancy, but to the misconceptions he built up in relation to that giant ogre of the nursery, the preoedipal mother. To this misconception of that "cruel, sadistic" mother, he (the child in the writer) became masochistically attached. This, in adulthood, makes the writer a perpetual defendant indicted before the tribunal of unconscious conscience. To counteract that indictment an alibi is instituted—the artistic creation. The inner alibi goes like this: "I am not masochistically attached to Mother; Mother does not even exist." Thus, in the process of productivity, the writer acts both rôles: that of the "giving" mother and the "recipient" child; he gives himself, out of himself, beautiful ideas and words, thereby establishing autarchy. Whereas any other conflict needs *two* protagonists for unconscious repetitiveness, duplicating the infantile prototype, in the strange psychic economy of the writer's solution he needs but *one* person. The typical neurotic must pay psychiatric fees for his cure, but the writer, if successful, even gets paid for his "self-cure."

Having established his first alibi by achieving autarchy, the writer busily formulates his second alibi. This second alibi is an attack. Accused by his inner conscience of masochistic submission, he counters with aggression. This accounts for the seemingly constant rebellion of the writer, or, to use Elizabeth Bowen's own words? "We must have something to push against."

The third alibi, also unconsciously provided in this battle of the conscience, is a shifting of guilt; guilt rightfully pertaining to the psychic masochism is "fraudulently" entered on the balance sheet of defensive aggression.[9]

Bergler follows out this idea of oral masochism and pseudo-aggression in other literary or reading connections. Take your mystery story fan, for example. What is he but identifying with the omnipotent and omniscient detective, criminal or adventurer? But why is the aggression not real? Because, answers the author, there is the element of uncanniness in it "which is the secondary and masochistic elaboration. But even the criminal, the constant factor is based on the masochistic attempt to overcome the feeling of helplessness stemming from pre-oedipal orality" (pp. 166-167). The actual motivations of the criminal are only the outcome of rationalizations for latent unconscious motives stemming from the child-mother-father relationship and the fantasies resulting therefrom.

It must be said that this is as hard to swallow as the often-repeated thesis that a philanthropist or a humanitarian is deep down a sadist who, on the conscious level, is camouflaging his unconscious motives. It reminds us of the Jewish joke about two business acquaintances who met on a train going West. Asked one of the other where he was bound for. "On my way to Chicago" was the reply. "Listen," said his questioner. "You are telling me you're going to Chicago, so that I might suppose you are bound for Los Angeles, but you can't fool me. I feel sure you are going to Chicago, so why try to string me?"

The Literary Product

Thus far we have considered the creator in the light of psychonalysis; and as has been already stated, the depth psychologist, as a therapist, is concerned mainly with the individual, and studies the productions insofar as they help us to understand the problems of the creator and gain an insight into the

9. Bergler, E. *The Writer and Psychoanalysis*. New York: Doubleday, 1950, pp. 236-237.

solutions he has sought and partially arrived at. But the psychology of literature is something apart from its producers and must be envisaged in relation to life.

Basler has made a similar observation.

> Naturally enough, the application of Freudian theory to literature has been attempted for the most part in an endeavor to psychoanalyze the author. Beginning with Freud himself, one of the chief recreations of the psychoanalytic fraternity has been the study of the artist's personality through the application of psychoanalytic criteria to his works and to the known facts of his life . . . It is the writer's belief that, while psychoanalysis has indeed contributed much, and can contribute still more, to the understanding of individual artists as personalities, the most fruitful employment of Freudian theory by the student of literature lies in the interpretation of literature itself.[10]

Each story, each play, each poem, carries its own message and either fits into or is out of focus with the world such as we know it. It is to be feared that so much significance has been attached to the writer's unconscious that the tale receives practically no attention. It is as though we on the ground floor were so preoccupied peering through peepholes and watching the workmen puttering in the cellar that we completely neglect to observe what is happening in our very midst. Literature may be the fruit of the unconscious tree, but we have a right to examine the different species separately at closer range. There are so many diverse types of literary production even in belles-lettres alone. Is symbolism to be measured with the same unconscious yardstick as realism, and is the psychological tale in the same class as the romantic story? Is it not true that what is permissible in the one case will be decried in the other?

10. Basler, R. P. *Sex, Symbolism, and Psychology in Literature,* Rutgers University Press, 1948, p. 11.

Depth Psychologist Slurs Psychological Fiction

One of the paradoxical features of depth psychology is that it takes little heed of the everyday psychological. In a sense, no specialist will deign to look at what he considers just ordinary. Indeed C. G. Jung surprises us by his statement that the psychologist does not find much of interest in the psychological novel. It is apparently too transparent. What he seeks is the "visionary mode of artistic creation" [11] where there is room for interpretation. It would seem as if the farther away from reality, such as we the readers can gauge, the more advantageous it is for the psychologist (read, the analytic psychologist) to make the most of his ingenuity.

From early Talmudical days, we have known the fourfold interpretation of the Scriptures, the *Pardes* i.e., the literal, the symbolic, the homiletical, and hermeneutical, which afterwards began to be applied to literature; and I daresay that is a great instrument which harmonizes with psychoanalysis, but its superiority is indicated by its keeping within the prescribed levels and not flitting from the one to the other. We can learn much from the story of Red Riding Hood or Jack the Giant Killer in regard to the folk mind or the collective unconscious, but why is Maupassant's *Boule de Suif* not grist to the psychological mill? Is Dostoyevsky greater than Tolstoi because his unconscious revealed more powerful impulses, confirming Freud's basic Oedipus doctrine?

Literary Perversion

An avowed follower of Freud, A. Wormhoudt, admits that "perhaps the most obvious characteristic of contemporary literature which is somehow to be correlated with Freud's influence is its obscurity, even unintelligibility to the average reader" [12] and traces this tendency back to Freud's treatment of dreams. Moreover, Wormhoudt holds that there is a significant relation-

11. Jung, C. G., *Loc. cit.*, p. 180.
12. Wormhoudt, A. Freud and Literary Theory. *Am. Imago*, vol. 6, 1949, p. 9.

ship between the intensity of conflict portrayed and its value as literature.

> The relatively normal person may find his sense of beauty less intense than that of the neurotic, but there is little danger that he will be totally incapable of it. The sublimation of his libidinous and aggressive tendencies has gone far enough to permit the realization of higher values, but not far enough to disturb the psychic balance which is called normality. On the other hand it is true that precisely those works of art which have been acclaimed as the greatest show the most profound sense of inner conflict. *The Iliad, The Aeneid, The Divine Comedy,* and *Hamlet* are but a few of the major examples of this observation.[13]

Why some literature has reached the pinnacle of fame is not easy to answer. All sorts of reasons may be assigned, and one cannot be certain that it all hinges on the intensity of the conflict. Aside from circumstantial reasons—political, social, personal, and even fortuitous, we should not lose sight of such factors as the beauty of diction, the wisdom of the apophthegms, the complexity of the plot, the true characterization of the *dramatis personae.*

Indeed, it seems as if the poet sometimes prolongs (or intensifies) the conflict in order to put into the mouth of the hero or the heroine some more glittering or polished phrases. I think this is particularly true of some of the French masterpieces, *Le Cid,* in particular. A figurative pulmotor is used not to let the sentimentality of the conflict-beset maiden die before the author has had a chance to relieve himself of a plethora of observations couched in antithetic verbiage, which arouses sympathy in the reader for the victim of circumstances.

Freud has exercised a powerful hold on critics as well as writers. Even those who claim moderation and reserve and circumspection end up by capitulating to Freudian demands.

13. *Loc. cit.,* p. 7.

Wayne Burns may serve as an illustration of a critic who makes resolutions only to break them. For he first tells us that

> More specifically, it means that we shall have to desystematize our minds—actually make an effort to clear our minds of the systematic Freudian knowledge we may have spent years in developing. Otherwise we shall inevitably translate rather than follow what the author as artist has written.

All this will be difficult, yet it will enable us to make the fullest use of our Freudian awareness without being overwhelmed by it. We will be free to exploit and control its stimulative powers, to place these powers under the direction of the artist, to do with them what he will. Indeed if we can develop our new-found powers to their ultimate potential, we should be able to follow wherever the artist leads, and thus realize artistic heights and depths that were, until Freud, closed to all but the greatest and most percipient minds, that are still closed to system-bound (including Freud-bound) critics of all schools. Of course we must have a fairly active and well-balanced imagination to begin with, or Freudianism, as W. H. Auden has suggested (*The New Republic*, October 6, 1952) will stimulate us into critical foolishness, or worse. But if we possess this necessary imaginative equipment—and nearly all of us do—we can, with the help of Freudian stimulation, develop an aesthetic awareness that will, in certain instances, carry us beyond the criticism of even the most perceptive non-Freudian critics—beyond, for example, T. E. Eliot's criticism of *Hamlet*, in which he mistakes Shakespeare's psychological subtlety for inferior artistry; then on the basis of this misapprehension, pronounces Gertrude inadequate, the play a failure.[14]

14. Burns, W. "Freudianism, Criticism, and Jane Eyre." *News Letter of the Conference on Literature and Psychology* of the Modern Language Association of America, vol. 11, 1952, No. 5.

But what does he do subsequently? In that very paper he proceeds to show that Emily Brontë, by using words which may have possible sexual connotation in her *Jane Eyre*, conveys to the reader the orgastic state of the heroine, when the missionary "pressed his hand firmer on my head and surrounded me with his arm, almost as if he loved me."

And how does this interpreter arrive at his conclusion?

Jane had been asked in marriage by the missionary St. John Rivers, who thought of her more as a resourceful helpmeet, than as a sweetheart turning into a loved wife. Jane stood under his spell and she relates her emotional experience. She was beginning to soften under his kindness and, she relates, "I was excited more than ever I had been." "My prayers are heard" ejaculated St. John. She heard her heart throb. She was in some sort of ecstasy which made her flesh quiver on her bones. It was a strange and startling feeling which passed at once to her head and extremities. But just as she was on the point of accepting the clergyman's proposal, she thought she heard the voice of her first love, Rochester, and, in response to his call, "Jane! Jane! Jane!" she cried "I am coming! Wait for me. Oh I will come!" Burns underlines some of the telltale words once but the more crucial ones are twice underscored, and because these latter, like "ejaculate" and "I am coming" are sometimes used in a sexual context, the author deduces that Jane is experiencing an orgasm. "In the circumstances she gives in to what she had denied herself with Rochester: her body takes over, so to speak."

The tendency to read sexual connotations and allusions into fiction is generally prevalent among all those who have tasted of Freud's delicacies. Since analogy and metaphor are always at hand, it is the easiest thing to turn almost every noun and verb into a sex symbol. Do such interpreters ask themselves what other imagery the authors might have used in order to express their thoughts? *That* they will not do, since it would spoil their little game; for they are bent on "proving" their case. H. Slochower, e.g., observes very properly that "A striking feature of *Moby Dick* is the almost complete absence of sex" [15]

15. Slochower, H. Freudian Motifs in "Moby Dick." *Complex*, vol. 1, 1950.

yet he soon finds the novel (incidentally Jung thought it to be the greatest American literary masterpiece) shot through with sex allusions. It would take too much space to list all these metaphors and images which Slochower adduces, but the conclusion come to, viz., that Melville was mildly homosexual would require better evidence than such phrases as the latter employs, like "maidenly gentleness," "the masculine sea," "thick walls" and "interior spaciousness." One might take every sentence which one utters that is not a sheer stereotype or catchphrase and discover some possibly remote allusion to sex activity. The rabbinical interpreters of the Old Testament engaged in the same hobby, although in their case there was much greater need; for through such verbal methods were they able to establish laws, which, under a theocratic system and a credo of revelation, had to be deduced from the Biblical phraseology. Between the Talmudic *pilpul* and some of the psychoanalytic fanciful extrapolations, it would seem the former is preferable as more consistent with common sense.

Small wonder, then, that critics and teachers of literature should be divided in opinion as to the merits of the scores of articles undertaking to give us the unconscious inside story of each of the characters in well-known literary works. There are those, of course, that are prepared to accept almost every conclusion a psychoanalytic writer comes to, but there are others more critical and even skeptical. We may even grade them as to positive or negative attitude. There is, e.g., Trilling who attempts to steer a middle course, and while recognizing the value of Freudian psychology for the interpretation of literature, he is not unmindful of the vagaries of some of the psychoanalysts when they turn to literary works.[16] S. E. Hyman goes a step farther in warning against the familiar psychoanalytic method of analyzing the fossilized author and then proceeding to apply the deductions to his characters.[17] W. J. Griffin has elaborated on this objection in an exceptionally well-documented article. He finds that both critics and psychoanalysts have been at fault, for as he says

16. Trilling, L. *The Liberal Imagination*, New York, 1951. The chapter on "Freud and Literature" had already appeared a decade earlier.
17. Hyman, S. E. *The Armed Vision*, New York, 1948.

To call the roll of literary men who have misapplied psychoanalytic theory out of half-knowledge, or a desire to be sensational, or an eagerness to make out a case, would not be enough to explain the situation. Professional psychoanalysts themselves have also frequently been undiscriminating when they have made excursions into the field of literary study. I do not here have in mind the errors into which they may fall through some lack of purely literary training. These may be charitably passed over. I refer to the failure to make reasonable distinctions, to lack of caution and a susceptibility to what are vaguely known as "excesses." In these respects the honors seem to be about even between literary men and professional psychoanalysts.[18]

Griffin pursues his topic, however, with the zeal of a logician to the disadvantage of the psychoanalyst when he observes that

The purpose of analysis cannot be therapy. Coleridge cannot now be retrieved from his addiction to opium nor Poe from his dipsomania; nor can the analyst help Shakespeare to resolve his "deeply rooted conflict with the mother." Yet it is apparently difficult not to adopt the tone of a diagnostician with an eye to improvement of the patient's behavior. Readers of psychoanalytic criticism are frequently irritated by what Charles Baudouin speaks of as an "air of medical superiority."

If the purpose is not control, it is just as clearly not prediction. Presumably, the intention is simply to arrive at an understanding of the author's motivations and meanings. Even conscious motivations are complex; it is unlikely that hidden ones are less so. Yet a common characteristic of psychoanalytic criticism appears to be schematic simplification. It is the besetting sin in such

18. Griffin, W. J. The Uses and Abuses of Psychoanalysis in the Study of Literature. *News Letter of the Conference on Literature of Psychology*, vol. 1, 1951, p. 12.

criticism to make overmuch of the kind of causation that might be centrally important if the end in view were therapy, overlooking the fact that when the purpose which would give certain determinants significance is altered, the significance is automatically altered. We may say that in an author's work we have a set of symptoms, but as Rudolf Eckstein has pointed out, "the symptom is really determined through an unlimited series of causes." The traditional scholar, whatever his shortcomings, cannot fail to be annoyed by readings that find *the* answer to the "riddle" of *Macbeth* in Shakespeare's fantasies of guilt about the death of his son—even if they were reactivated by the death of the barren Elizabeth.[19]

Edel is inclined to caution the critic more than the psychoanalyst, for the latter is surer of his ground and has a greater command of his tools, while the critic lacks the training and is therefore apt to project or misread. Since Edel writes rather from the philosophical than from either the literary or psychoanalytic point of view, he can afford to be neutral and dole out some sound advice to both.

How is the psychological instrument to be used? The literary student turning psychologist for the nonce—unlike his psychological counterpart—must use his newfound tools to gain his own insight into the literary material and then he must bury the tools and write literary criticism or history or biography on his own ground and not that of the psychologist. He must convert and translate into the language of his own field. He is writing, after all, not as a psychologist but as a literary scholar and he must beware of "selling out" his own field or setting down a study that in the end is neither literary nor psychological, bulging with nonliterary terminology. He need not talk about "sibling rivalries" when he can describe quite factually his subject's relationship to his

19. Griffin, W. J. *Ibid.*, pp. 14-15.

brothers and sisters; he need not involve Oedipus when he wishes to discuss fear or guilt or anxiety.[20]

Edel's recent book, *The Psychological Novel 1900-1950* (1955), despite the fact that it deals only with Marcel Proust, Henry James, Dorothy Richardson, Virginia Woolf, and James Joyce, who were somehow affected by a sort of time-complex, is nevertheless illuminating in its distinctions, and replete with significant illustrations, some of which tie in with the early experiences of the writers, thus showing how things of the past keep reverberating in the minds of the authors or artists.

Taking his cue from Proust, he asks "Would all readers read such novels in the same manner?" and answers:

"Thus Proust discovered, as Henry James had done before him, that the writer of fiction can not only represent life but actually can create it. . . ."

After lingering on the commonplace that some people can get extremely excited over a book which others cannot bring themselves to read to the end, he ascribes the difference to the gap between intellectual apprehension and the intensity of feeling in the reading of a book.

Rare are the readers who can achieve a balance between intellectual apprehension of a novel and an intense feeling of it. Yet it is for the feeling as much as the intellectual apprehension that most novelists write their work.

This is particularly true of the modern psychological novel. Here the entire work by its very nature,

20. *News Letter of the Conference on Literature and Psychology* of the Modern Language Association of America, vol. II, No. 5, 1952, pp. 6-7.
20a. Lucas, F. L. *Literature and Psychology*. London: Cassell, 1951.
20b. Lucas, F. L. *Ibid.*, p. 9.

offers us the data in higgledy-piggledy disorder. We are asked to *see into* the characters, to make deductions from such data as may be offered us—and at the same time to live for ourselves the experience with which we are confronted on the printed page. . . . The critical reader who intellectually apprehends a book but has achieved no particular feeling in the process usually has only a ledger-book concept of the work. . . .

At the other extreme is the reader who has felt every page of the work, but can give us no coherent account of the data.[21]

While this is true enough, is it not simply a matter of what experiences the reader has had in the past and what aspirations he has toward the future? As for the author, would it not be safer to say that the true artist writes for himself rather than for the reader?

The most thoroughgoing discussion of the problems involved is to be found in the fascinatingly-written volume, *Literature and Psychology*, by F. L. Lucas. Erudition is the hallmark of Lucas's writing, but it is also distinguished by common sense and an eye for perspective. The psychoanalytic *motif* runs through the whole book like a red thread (many of the illustrations, by the way, drawn from Stekel, whom the author wishes to accord the credit withheld from him on the part of the orthodox Freudians and followers of other depth schools) but the thread is never allowed to thicken into a cord, nor to color the rest of the material. Lucas confesses to a "deep and lasting admiration for Freud's work." [22] Indeed, he believes that "in the long run . . . mankind will have owed yet more to Freud than to Columbus, or Newton, or Darwin, or Einstein; let alone Marx, whose work suffered precisely because he

21. Edel, L. *The Psychological Novel 1900-1950*. New York, 1955, pp. 100-101.

22. Lucas, F. L. *Literature and Psychology*. London: Cassell, 1951, p. 9.

remained (like many other reformers) so crude in his psychology."

This encomium, however, does not prevent Lucas from expressing himself adversely on the endeavors of so many of the psychoanalytic writers.

> To read the bound volumes of *Imago* or *The International Journal of Psycho-Analysis* for, say, the last twenty-five years leaves an impression of great unevenness and a feeling that many of the contributors would have been no worse for a little more skepticism. When we are told, for example, that the scene in the *Odyssey* where Nausica welcomes the hero escaped from the sea represents a birth fantasy; that the princess represents Odysseus' mother; and that the ball she throws to her maidens is a phallic symbol ("I knew it would," said Alice), for such Homeric criticism we can find only Homeric laughter.[23]

Existentialism and the New Literature

The strongest post-war influence on the new literature has been the philosophical movement of existentialism. In his classic confrontation with the chestnut tree, now a familiar image in literary criticism, Roquentin discovers that existence "is not something which lets itself be thought of from a distance: it must invade you suddenly, master you, weigh heavily on your heart like a great motionless beast." [24] Roquentin, the hero of Sartre's first novel, *Nausea* (1938), made his extraordinary discovery when he found himself at the root of a chestnut tree. Suddenly the tree began to move. As he followed the swinging of its branches, he told himself that he was finally going to surprise beings in the process of being born. "The tips of the branches rustled with existence which unceasingly renewed

23. Lucas, F. L. *Ibid.*, p. 8.
24. Sartre, J. P. *La Nausee.* Quoted in *Of Human Freedom* (edited by Wade Baskin). New York, 1966, p. 4.

itself and which was never born." [25] The tree shuddered, but "the shudder was not a nascent quality, a passing from power to action; a shudder-thing flowed into the tree, took possession of it," and he felt existence even in its least perceptible stirrings, "everywhere, infinitely, in excess, forever and everywhere." [26] He left the chestnut tree, walked to the gate, turned for another look.

> Then the garden smiled at me. I leaned against the gate and watched for a long time. The smile of the trees, of the laurel, *meant* something; that was the real secret of existence. . . . Things—you might have called them thoughts—which stopped halfway, which were forgotten, which forgot what they wanted to think and which stayed like that, hanging about with an odd little sense which was beyond them.[27]

The years of anguish and uncertainty that witnessed the incubation and spread of existentialism brought about a re-examination of many traditional assumptions and sounded the knell of anthropomorphism in literature. The trend away from the tendency to view things in terms of their usefulness to human beings and their capacity for reflecting the feelings of human beings was initiated by Sartre's *Nausea* and strengthened by Camus' *The Outsider* (1942). The novel and the drama, which had flourished through successive generations of writers, had been subjected to experimentation time after time. A brief marriage between literature and philosophy was effected by Sartre, who used the stage as the most effective medium for the expression of the tenets of existentialism—for example, in *The Flies* (1943) and *No Exit* (1944). Though the marriage between philosophy and fiction was short-lived, the fascination with things or objects persisted among novelists and dramatists.

Things became the focal point of the writer's attention, as

25. *Ibid.,* p. 4.
26. *Ibid.,* p. 5.
27. *Ibid.,* pp. 5-6.

they had been for Roquentin in *Nausea,* and before that, in the eerie world of Kafka. The human eye—the Medusan Look in the philosophical writings of Sartre—registered, with the exactness and impersonality of a camera, the slightest details of objects and their slightest modifications.[28] It also registered, still impassively and in detail, the outward behavior of people immersed—or lost, caged, or isolated—in a "thingy" world.

The New Novel had been foreshadowed by Freudian-inspired theorists and by existentialists as well as by writers as varied in their techniques as Kafka, Proust, Wolfe, and Faulkner, but the phrase itself was not popularized until 1958, in the review *Esprit.* The School of the Look and the Anti-Novel, a term which Sartre had used to describe Sarraute's *The Portrait of an Unknown* (1948), are also appropriate to the discussion of the writings inspired by an awareness of the gap between man's infinite aspirations and the finite nature of his existence, the unintelligibility of reality, and the irreducible pluralism of life and death. They might also be called "do-it-yourself" novels, for they demand the active participation of the reader in recreating events from isolated hints, glimpses, or impressions of raw materials meticulously chosen by the writer.

The chief representatives of the new novel share a common link of denial rather than of affirmation. Their heroes belong to a very particular species best described by the word "absurd," denoting both a state of fact and "the lucid awareness which certain people acquire of this state of fact." [29] Uncertainty, doubt, despair, anguish, contingency, freedom, all the other elements of the primary situation of the existential creature pass through the novelist's crucible. Robbe-Grillet, Philippe Sollers, and Michel Butor all pursue to its logical end the destruction of the classic novel of the nineteenth century, in which the author acts as an omnipotent God toward his

28. The significance of the Look and the Other is dealt with at length in Sartre's *Being and Nothingness,* New York, 1956, pp. 221-303. (Original, 1943; translation by Hazel Barnes, 1956.)

29. Sartre, J. P. *Literary and Philosophical Essays,* translated by Annette Michelson, New York, 1957, p. 24.

creatures. They differ markedly in style, technique, and diction, but they share a common trait. In their works we see men not as they might appear to God but as they reveal themselves to other men in a concrete situation. Each cherishes his own individuality, yet each steers clear of conventional plots, chronological sequences, or philosophical pronouncements.

In discussing Camus' *The Outsider*, Sartre notes that it does not try to explain or prove anything.

> We remembered, while reading this novel, that there had once been works which had not tried to prove anything, but had been content to stand on their own merits. But hand in hand with its gratuitousness went a certain ambiguity. How were we to interpret this character who, the day after his mother's death, "went swimming, started a liaison with a girl, and went to see a comic film," who killed an Arab "because of the sun," who claimed on the eve of his execution, that he "had been happy and still was," and hoped there would be a lot of spectators at the scaffold "to welcome him with cries of hate." "He's a poor fool, an idiot," some people said; others, with greater insight, said, "He's innocent." The meaning of innocence still remained to be understood.[30]

The new novel tends in general to avoid introspection, moral judgments, preachments. Mme. Sarraute tries to capture imperceptible or barely perceptible elements which anticipate impressions, sensations, emotions, or ideas whereas Robbe-Grillet creates an atmosphere of suspense and troubled but sharp awareness of reality. Neither of them tries, however, to hold up a mirror to society or to offer any criticism of the situations the reader is asked to recreate. The trend during the last decade has been toward abandonment of stock characters—the lover, the hypocrite, the huckster, the salesman, the braggart, the sadist, the saint—in favor of a new start from lower depths, from "the elementary stammerings and visceral shivers

30. *Ibid.*, p. 24.

of people." [31] Though the new novelists prefer to discard many of the philosophical contributions of the existentialists, their fascination with objects still sets them apart from earlier writers. An awareness of the impenetrability, opaqueness, or resistant solidity of things pervades their writings. As Professor Henri Peyre observes, "they resort to objects which mean nothing, signify nothing, and do not lie, as a refuge from what is least to be prized in men: human deceit." [32]

The new theater has adept practitioners in Europe and America, but France is still the center of innovation in this area. At mid-century the French theater gave birth to the new type of drama, which actually traced its antecedents to *Ubu Roi* and Alfred Jarry's revolt against bourgeois values, as early as 1896. A long period of sterility following the death of Jarry ended with the production in 1950 of Ionesco's *Bald Soprano*, an anti-play (in the words of its author) subtitled "The Tragedy of Language."

Ionesco's best known work seems at first to be meaningless but actually has two levels of meaning. Mr. and Mrs. Smith are the protagonists in the one-act play variously called "the theater of the absurd," "metaphysical farce," or "the anti-theater." The sketchy parody of life on the traditional stage draws its material from a manual of English conversation. It is a caricature of conventional drama, replete with "polite drawing-room conversation, melodramatic situations, mysterious asides." [33] Discussing trivial happenings and making trite observations, Mrs. Smith and her tongue-clicking husband behave in a way which at first seems completely natural, but their exaggerated speech and mannerisms raise doubts concerning their reality. The impression that they are wholly unreal soon fades, however, as we realize that their mechanical patterns of behavior resemble our own and that their meaningless clichés are the very ones we hear daily. Members of a perfect society,

31. Peyre, Henri, *Contemporary French Literature*, New York, 1964, p. 206.

32. *Ibid.*, p. 206.

33. Pronko, Leonard. *Avant-Garde, The Experimental Theater in France* (Berkeley, 1962), p. 68.

a society so efficient that it has successfully eliminated all problems, the Smiths are fascinated by banal observations and polite platitudes. Or are they bored? Their meaningless chatter culminates in chaos as they shout nonsense syllables back and forth. The playwright's nondidactic approach places the contradictions of his inner nature under klieg lights and invites the audience to re-examine the question of the meaning of human existence.

Since 1958 there has been a reaction against philosophical dramas, against literary and declamatory plays such as those of Giraudoux and Mauriac, and against social satire. The new "absurdist" plays nevertheless deal with uprooted, anguished creatures who are trapped, "desperately alone, imprisoned in their private hell with no exit." [34] They do not analyze psychological motives, and the audience, befuddled and bewildered, applauds the very absence of serious political and moral issues. Yet the absence of motives and the reduction of feelings and desires to the absurd provides the audience with a moment of introspection and truth. Modern man is forced to start again from nothing—the nothingness of the chestnut tree—and thereby is afforded "a chance to rebuild on new foundations." [35]

It would scarcely be possible within the compass of this paper to do more than to record the various trends, to show that psychoanalysis and existentialism have intrenched themselves in the literary domain, that willy-nilly we must examine their verdicts, although we might appeal to the higher court of reason, if the guilt complex, the judgment of sadism, orality regression, phallic-mother identification, alienation, existential despair, etc., occur to us as preconceived and supported only by the flimsiest circumstantiality.

References

Askew, Melvin. "Psychoanalysis and Literary Criticism." *Psychoanalytic Review*, 51, 1964, ii, pp. 43-50.

34. Peyre, Henri. *Ibid.*, p. 313.
35. *Ibid.*, p. 314.

Basler, R. P. *Sex, Symbolism, and Psychology in Literature*. New Brunswick, New Jersey, 1948.

Bergler, E. *The Writer and Psychoanalysis*. New York, 1950.

Bodkin, M. *Archetypal Patterns in Poetry*. New York, 1934.

Brustein, Robert. *The Theatre of Revolt: An Approach to Modern Drama*. London, 1966.

Bumbach, Jonathan. *The Landscape of Nightmare: Studies in the Contemporary American Novel*. New York, 1966.

Cruickshank, John. "Psychocriticism and Literary Judgement." *British Journal of Aesthetics*, 4, pp. 155-59.

Fiedler, Leslie A. *Waiting for the End: The American Literary Scene from Hemingway to Baldwin*. London, 1966.

Gombrich, E. H. "Freud's Aesthetics." *Encounter*, 26, 1966, i, pp. 30-40.

Holland, Norman N. "Literary Value: A Psychoanalytic Approach." *Literature and Psychology*, 14, 1964, pp. 43-55.

Hyman, Stanley E. *The Armed Vision*. New York, 1948.

Jung, C. G. *Modern Man in Search of a Soul*. Translated by W. S. Dell and C. F. Baynes. London, 1933.

Koestler, Arthur. *The Act of Creation*. New York, 1964.

Lucas, F. L. *Literature and Psychology*. London, 1951.

McElroy, Davis D. *The Study of Literature: An Existential Appraisal*. New York, 1966.

Müller-Vollmer, Kurt. *Towards a Phenomenological Theory of Literature: A Study of Wilhelm Dilthey's* Poetik. The Hague, 1963.

Roback, A. A. "Psikhologie un Literatur." *Literatur un Lebn*, i, 1915.

Roback, A. A., and I. L. Peretz, *Psychologist of Literature*. Cambridge, 1935.

Ruitenbeek, Hendrik M. (ed.). *The Literary Imagination: Psychoanalysis and the Genius of the Writer*. Chicago, 1965.

Sartre, J. P. *Imagination*. Ann Arbor, 1962. Published in France in 1936.

Sartre, J. P. *Being and Nothingness*. Translated by Hazel Barnes. New York, 1956. Published in France in 1943.

Sartre, J. P. *What Is Literature*. New York, 1957. Published in *Situations*, 1948.

Sartre, J. P. *The Philosophy of Existentialism.* Edited by Wade Baskin. New York, 1965.

Sachs, H. *The Creative Unconscious.* 2d edition. Cambridge, Mass., 1951.

Slochower, H. "Freudian Motifs in *Moby Dick*," *Complex*, 1950.

Trilling, Lionel. *The Liberal Imagination.* New York, 1951.

Tsanoff, Radoslav A. "Literary Art and Moral Values." *Rice University Studies*, 50, 1964, i, pp. 91-103.

Wormhoudt, A. "Freud and Literary Theory." *American Imago*, 6, 1949, iii.

Wormhoudt, A. "The Unconscious Identification of Words and Milk." *American Imago*, 6, 1949, i.

THE SCIENCE OF PARAPSYCHOLOGY

J. B. RHINE, PH. D.

Director of the Institute of Parapsychology

Editorial Note

The following lecture was given in the Guildhall of London on October 12, at the invitation of the British Association for the Advancement of Science and Granada Television Ltd. The Granada Guildhall Lectures are given annually under the general title of "Communication in the Modern World." Dr. Rhine's was the first of the three lectures for 1965, the seventh year in the series.

His lecture, along with the two other addresses of the series for the year (one by Alistair Cooke and the other by Vice-Admiral Hyman G. Rickover) was sponsored and published by Granada Television and distributed by MacGibbon and Kee Ltd., London. Permission has been requested and received to reprint the lecture here.

Accounts of the accomplishments of Dr. J. B. Rhine may be found in various editions of *Who's Who, American Men of Science*, and in *Current Biography*, 1945. He is now Director of the Institute of Parapsychology of Durham, North Carolina, a position which he assumed on his retirement in 1965 from 38 years of service at Duke University. In 1950 he resigned his professorship in psychology at Duke to give full time to the Parapsychology Laboratory which, with the sponsorship of Professor William McDougall, he had established in 1935, and which fostered much of the developing work in the new field of parapsychology.

Dr. Rhine was born in Juniata County, Pennsylvania, and received his Ph. D. degree from the University of Chicago. He undertook post-doctoral studies at Harvard and Duke.

With Professor William McDougall, Dr. Rhine established the *Journal of Parapsychology* in 1937, and still serves as editorial consultant. In 1962 he helped to establish the Foundation for Research on the Nature of Man, the organization which sponsors the Institute for Parapsychology. He is a member of the Parapsychological Association and the American Psychological Association. His books are *Extrasensory Perception* (1934), *New Frontiers of the Mind* (1937), *The Reach of the Mind* (1947), and *New World of the Mind* (1953). He edited *Parapsychology: From Duke to FRNM* (1965) and was joint author of *Extrasensory Perception after Sixty Years* (1940) and *Parapsychology, Frontier Science of the Mind* (1957).

•

THE SCIENCE OF PARAPSYCHOLOGY

Under the heading of *psi communication* I shall be dealing today not only with ESP or extrasensory perception but with a more inclusive territory, extrasensorimotor exchange—that is, man's interaction with his environment without the use of sense organs and muscles. The extramotor part of the exchange, known as psychokinesis or PK, is, in fact, quite as important as the ESP function, although not so well known as yet. These two classes of psi communication make up the subject matter of the new science of parapsychology.

Although psi phenomena are old and familiar in human history and folklore, their treatment in a scientific manner is relatively new. Some confusion and uncertainty still prevail even as to just what belongs in this classification and what does not. For that reason it is advisable to mark off at the start where the boundary of the field of study lies.

One characteristic of psi phenomena is that they are identified with personal agency; the study began with strange things that happen to *people*. To qualify as a psi or parapsychical happening a phenomenon must also appear to stand clear of explanation by known natural law; and since, as you know, all the basic natural laws thus far recognized in the sciences are physical, we can say a phenomenon is parapsychical when it is beyond physical principles of explanation.

I might have said "*known* physical principles," but if I had done so I should also have wanted to add "known *psi* phenomena." It seems better to use these terms in their present meaning, without speculating on possible future changes in them, and yet without taking their present meaning as final.

On the other side of the boundary, reports of puzzling occurrences are received that have no recognizable personal connection; these are not, so far as we know, psi phenomena. Also, much of mental life is too obscure as yet for a judgment as to whether or not it is explainable by physics—for example, the fact of consciousness itself, which, though it may well be beyond physical explanation, is not claimed by parapsychology.

The character of psi communication can best be identified in terms of specific examples of representative types of experiences as people have reported them. I have chosen a set of four of these from the collection of over 10,000 made by the Parapsychology Laboratory at Duke. They are selected to represent first the main types of psi exchange and, second, the form which the experience assumed—whether a dream, intuition, hallucination, or a physical manifestation. I am not at all concerned here, however, with the authenticity or evidential value of these cases. The question of evidence will be dealt with later on.

The first case is one of probable telepathy, a telepathic hallucination. Dr. C., an American scholar working in China, wrote me that she was awakened one night hearing her name being called by her mother, who lived in Vermont. Dr. C. was sufficiently wide awake to note the time of what was for her a deeply disturbing experience. In due course she learned that her mother, who was dying at the time of this happening, had been asking for her. This telepathic experience (if that is what it was) could as well have occurred as a dream or as an intuition.

Clairvoyance, too, occurs both in hallucination and in dreams, but the case I have chosen is one of intuition: A Duke professor once received a cable asking him to break the news to friends of the sudden death of their son. But before the professor could touch on the painful news, the father stopped him and told him that his wife had already known of the death of their son and had told him about it three days before. (The day on which the boy had died.) In answer to the question as to how his wife had known, the father could only say, "She just knew."

Precognition is also experienced in the form of intuition, hallucination, and dreams. However, it occurs more often in dreams, and the case I have selected was experienced in that state. Dr. B., a young physicist, told me that at an earlier time when his wife had been employed as secretary to a business executive, she told at breakfast of a dream in which her employer's automobile had been wrecked. In the detailed account which she gave him, the young man who was driving the car was killed and the other occupant, a Catholic priest, received a severe cut on his forehead. Three days later her employer drove to Washington (from Pittsburgh) and while there his car was loaned to a young man and the tragedy occurred as it had been foreseen in the dream.

The fourth type of experience involves a physical manifestation, induced presumably by personal agency, and called "psychokinesis" or "PK," meaning the direct action of mind on matter. A number of natural varieties of these physical cases are reported; some have to do with moving objects like clocks, and others with living things, as in claims of mental healing; however, I have chosen one involving still a third variety—that of static, inanimate objects; this is a simpler type for representing spontaneous PK.

A housewife in Ohio was seated alone in her living room one evening, with no one else in the house, when suddenly she was startled by the falling of two pictures from the wall, about ten feet away from her. The pictures had hung on different walls in the corner of the room, a few feet apart. They were the pictures of her two young daughters. Neither picture was broken, and one was found to have been unhooked from the nail on which it hung, while the other had pulled the nail out

441

as it fell. She thought this was a message of death, and thought of her mother whom she knew to be ill. A few minutes later a telephone call informed her that her mother had, as she had thought, just died.

These four examples of apparent spontaneous extrasensori-motor exchange illustrate, as I have said, the types of occurrence in the main focus of parapsychology today. These are the types indicated by the character of the experiences people say they have had; that is, these are not mere academic artifacts. Rather, they are the natural groupings of phenomena as reported by mankind through the ages. It was with the collection and study of these reports that the investigations in parapsychology began. The occurrences have been so numerous and so universal, and they fall so clearly into these familiar types that they present to those who have studied them an impressive body of puzzling human experiences.

And yet it was not through the collection of these spontaneous happenings that the case for psi communication was established. In challenging accepted explanations, as such cases do by their very nature, they take issue with the basic orthodoxy of modern science. In order to make headway in such a bold confrontation, the strongest possible kind of evidence would naturally be required. The investigation had to be rigorously experimental to survive the controversy it generated.

In turning now to look at the experimental studies in parapsychology I shall have to be selective on account of time. One type of psi will need to some extent to represent all four. One experiment will have to illustrate a large group, and the work of a few individuals stand for that of the entire field. But as general background, many countries, cultures, and continents will be represented.

Parapsychology, like other branches of science, began with methods. In the late nineteenth century many attempts were made in Western Europe and North America to test ESP ability, especially in connection with hypnotism, but without important success. Effective methods had not yet been found.

What was most needed was a measure of chance, the mathematics of probability. Also, the application of this mathematics required a simple testing routine such as card guessing. In the 1870's, however, both of these features, card guessing and mathematics of probability, were introduced by Professor Charles Richet, in tests of clairvoyance conducted with a hypnotized subject, Léonie.

During the first quarter of the present century university laboratories of psychology at Stanford, Harvard, and Groningen admitted the problem of telepathy for a time to the status of acceptable research, but this advantageous foothold was soon lost. The trouble was that, as happened also with Richet, the subjects performed successfully for a time but later ceased to do so. The experimenters did not know at that time how to handle this problem, and the investigation stopped.

When, in 1927, my wife and I went to Duke University to work on this area of problems under your countryman, Professor William McDougall, F.R.S., the favorable situation we encountered made possible a more concerted attack on the problems than had been the case elsewhere.

The first need in our minds was to see if any of the claims for psi phenomena could meet the test of scientific validation. Did any type of extrasensorimotor exchange really occur? In 1927 the main challenge was the claim of mediumship in psychical research circles. The medium was widely believed to be able to deliver information derived from sources beyond her own normal knowledge, presumably from discarnate agencies. This claim led logically to the testing of the medium's own range of abilities, including those needed especially for mediumship—and these were, of course, the psi abilities themselves. However, our frank inability to discover any way to distinguish reliably between a supposed discarnate source and the medium's own combination of capacities led us to pursue the more easily handled parapsychical claims, especially those dealing with telepathy and clairvoyance.

But although the work at Duke began with equal interest in the claims of telepathy and clairvoyance, the emphasis soon shifted to clairvoyance. It was much the simpler of the two to subject to reliable test. Only one subject was involved at a time, and the very necessary precautions were easier to handle. Had we chosen the less advantageous ground of telepathy for a primary attack on the problem of ESP we should not likely have survived the critical attack that followed publication.

Clairvoyance testing, on the other hand, could be reduced to a fairly simple procedure, almost a game. We introduced a special pack of twenty-five test cards with five each of five kinds of geometrical symbols as targets. With these handy cards the tests became exciting rounds of competition between the subject and the laws of chance. The subject was informed of his scores immediately following a test run and was given encouragement whenever he exceeded the chance average of five hits per run. Thus in a fairly spontaneous way the problem of sustaining the subject's interest, which had defeated earlier workers, was at least partially solved. The experimenter's own manifest enthusiasm for high scores communicated itself readily, and every run through the pack was a fresh contest for the subject's ESP ability.

In the atmosphere of unrestrained eagerness of discovery that prevailed, many student volunteers were ready to try their powers on the card-guessing tests the Duke Department of Psychology was sponsoring in the early 1930's. Among the exceptional performers in these tests was a young man (H.P.) with a background of family interest in clairvoyance, who was a Divinity School student at the time. He had continued to be a uniformly high scorer in card-guessing tests over many months of testing when, in the autumn of 1933, the following experiment was conducted, one which we regarded as conclusive.

The subject, H.P., was located in a building 100 yards away from that in which the experimenter with the target cards was situated. A series of twelve runs through the pack of cards was conducted by my assistant, Mr. J. G. Pratt, a graduate student in psychology at the time. The two men worked with synchronized watches; Pratt shuffled the cards just prior to the test and placed them, one at a time, face down in the center of the table for one minute before removal. In this way the 300-trial test of clairvoyance was completed at the rate of fifty trials per day for six days. The results were independently checked from the duplicate records kept by both men. H. P. was found to have averaged 9.9 hits per run of twenty-five trials as against 5.0 to be expected from chance. The odds against chance producing so high a score are of the order of *a hundred trillion to one.*

I then joined Pratt for a confirmation series of half that length, to insure, as is our practice at such an important stage of development, independent supervision of procedure. During the six-run series that followed, in which we both supervised all essential phases of the operation, an average of 9.7 hits per 25 was obtained; and with this score average, even with this shorter series, the odds against chance are of the order of a million to one. The conclusion from this experiment was that extrasensory perception (most probably the clairvoyant type) had occurred.

When a report of the Duke work, entitled *Extrasensory Perception,* was published as a monograph in 1934, a number of attempts to repeat the experiment were made. A fair number of confirmatory findings were reported from other laboratories in the years that followed. This independent confirmation was sufficiently encouraging, since a delicate exploration for a very elusive phenomenon was involved. The search was on for a capacity not yet well enough known that the psychological conditions required for dependable performance could be prescribed. In fact, two major tasks were involved: first, to find others with the capability of H. P., and, second, to provide and maintain the psychological conditions the able subject needs.

Over the years the groping efforts to find or develop able subjects for psi testing have led to explorations in many directions. Time permits the mention now of only one, and I have chosen the most successful and recent of these various attempts. This is the work of Dr. Milan Ryzl of Prague and his method of hypnotic training of subjects to perform in ESP tests. Ryzl's work has been reported chiefly in the *Journal of Parapsychology,* but he has recently summarized it in a monograph awaiting publication. His leading subject, P.S., has performed at less than half the psi efficiency of H. P., but with much more remarkable endurance and an exceptional ability to adjust to visiting observers. This latter feature has made P.S. something of an international exhibit, since he has demonstrated his ability to a considerable number of visiting scientists from different countries. It will be important, of course, to see how far the Ryzl method will work for others and how well it will continue to work for him.

At the Duke Laboratory, however, the main reaction to the experiment with H.P., with the distance between him and the target card, was to advance at once to the most interesting problem of all—that of precognition. Since distance did not diminish the effect of H.P.'s capacity, it seemed logical to expect that ESP might show a similar *independence of time*. The precognition problem was, of course, already in front of us from the spontaneous case material; but it had never before been systematically investigated. Now, in the autumn of 1933, the time was ready for it. The new step needed only that the target order be dislocated in time, and, of course, kept random.

Accordingly, we asked H. P. to try to identify the order of the cards in the pack as they would be after a regular shuffling. As a control for comparison with this procedure, he was asked to guess the order down through the pack without the cards being disturbed until the end of the 25 calls. It was found that H. P. performed at a significant rate with the one method as well as with the other. A wide variety of methods of shuffling the cards were introduced and many other subjects tested. The results, as reported in the *Journal of Parapsychology* since 1938, have added up to a massive body of evidence confirming the hypothesis of precognition.

The precognition test has in recent years become more or less just another routine type of psi test, its use incidental to other research objectives. It has certain advantages: for example, sensory leakage would be impossible, and so too would be any deception on the part of a subject. With the two-experimenter procedure also used in the checking of record sheets, the experimental reliability of this method is about as good as anything could be in the psychological sciences. Precognition testing, too, has already been handled with success by machine methods.

Still another offshoot of the conclusive work with H. P. on clairvoyance occurred at the Duke Laboratory. This was the attack on the problem of psychokinesis. In part this received its stimulus from the spontaneous physical cases like that of the pictures falling. But here again there was a bit of logical support as well. The familiar law of reaction would at least suggest a two-way communication between subject and object, an extra-motor aspect to match the extrasensory. In a word, psi exchange might be reversible. Again, the answer to the question of how to find out came from the world of games.

The first method of the PK research came from games of dice-throwing. As is well known, the player sometimes has the belief that, in a certain state of mind, he can influence the dice by his thinking. We made this belief into a way of testing its own validity. We put subjects to work to try to influence fall-ing dice to a degree that would rule out a theory of chance. There were, of course, some problems, such as those of how to deal with biased dice and how to rule out tricks in throwing them. But it was possible to solve these problems by the design of the test and the technique used, and still to preserve a game-like procedure—one that permitted the subject to de-velop and keep his essential mood.

Overshadowed at first by the ESP work, PK testing has been the slower of the two to spread and develop. It has been mainly confined to the use of target objects in motion, such as dice, beta particles, and steel balls. It has touched but little on living material and has not yet been successful with static inani-mate target objects. In fact, it was fortunate that, as with the ESP research, PK testing began with so simple a test as it did. Even today the other areas (living material and static objects) offer special difficulties that may still be formidable.

Yet in spite of the relatively minor place of the PK research, an unusually conclusive case for that type of psi can properly be claimed, a sort of fingerprint quality of evidence which has emerged as an incidental mark of identification. This is the

447

tendency of the scoring rate to decline on the record sheets in dice-throwing experiments. It was found in 1943 that in one series of tests the subject's rate of success tended to decline on the page from the upper left to the lower right. This "diagonal decline" was more than a mere chance effect. The records of eighteen other experimental series were examined and it was found that this was a highly significant tendency shown even by different subjects, under different experimenters, and with different apparatus. Such a repeated effect could only be produced by a psychological variation in the PK operation itself. Moreover, it has the advantage of being as repeatedly observable in the record books in the Laboratory's files as the strata of the earth's crust are to the geologist. Such evidence is rare in the psychological sciences.

I have left telepathy to the last because it is the most difficult type to investigate. When we began at Duke to divide up the categories of psi communication we found that all the telepathy tests hitherto conducted had been such that clairvoyance could explain the results quite as well as telepathy. The sender had always had an object at which he was looking. Accordingly, we began testing telepathy without giving the sender a series of objective targets or even allowing him to make a record (because this would be available to the subject's clairvoyance or precognition). We found, however, that we then had a very complicated procedure on our hands, especially since we needed to apply the two-experimenter method of safeguarding and double checking.

It was possible, however, in 1946 to demonstrate telepathy under the restricted conditions of this test procedure, and the Duke experiment was confirmed in this country by Dr. S. G. Soal. All the rest of the work loosely called "telepathy" is better designated as "general or undifferentiated ESP (or GESP)." And even the evidence we do have of telepathy should be guardedly defined as psi communication without an objective target other than that of the sender's own organism as he thinks of the target messages the receiver is asked to identify.

Let us look next at these psi types in a more general perspective. The experiments have, in general, confirmed what the case studies first suggested regarding the types of psi. Clairvoyance, precognition, and psychokinesis have now been established sufficiently well for the working needs of a science. The case for telepathy has been carried as far as other sciences of man's nature permit us to distinguish a telepathy target from a clairvoyant one.

Mere establishment of types, however, was not enough. It was necessary in testing for one type to exclude the possibility of any of the other three types contributing to the results. I have already mentioned the difficulty of excluding the possibility of clairvoyance in a telepathy test. A comparable problem arose in excluding telepathy in testing for clairvoyance. The question was asked as to whether precognitive telepathy with the person scoring the record sheets might not be enough to explain the results attributed to clairvoyance. The experimental answer was "no."

There was difficulty, too, over the distinction between precognition and psychokinesis. It required some time and effort to develop a precognition test that satisfied everyone that PK could not have been a factor, and also a PK test that was safe from countercharges of possible explanation of the results by precognition. The distinctions between PK and precognition are fairly well clarified by this time.

On the other hand, these studies have at the same time tended to unify our concepts of the four types of phenomena; these types are thought of now as probably manifestations of a single basic reversible function capable of producing the various phenomena. Precognition is, after all, clairvoyance of the future; and we are not sure what the difference between the targets in telepathy and clairvoyance really means. Finally, PK seems best understood as the reverse of ESP communication. In any case, the two processes are complementary. In this recognizedly hypothetical way workers in parapsychology have come to think of a single basic extrasensorimotor principle of exchange, a unified psi function, of which ESP experiences and

449

PK are simply the surface manifestations. This model of reversible subject-object interaction between person and environment, though admittedly a limited one as yet, is steadily growing with the findings.

The experimental researchers have, however, confirmed the case studies in still more general findings than the identification of types. Even the spontaneous character of the ability itself is only too well borne out in the test situation. As a matter of fact, all the types are, in the laboratory much as in life, uniformly elusive. It is for this reason that psi research has to rely heavily upon statistical method. The individual who has a "psychic" experience is, as I have mentioned, unable to command this gift at will; so we cannot expect that when he comes to the laboratory to participate in experiments he can exercise his ability at the experimenter's command.

But our attention is sharply and hopefully focused on one finding from the experimental studies. This is the fact that the subject does have a certain minimal amount of conscious voluntary control over psi. The tests would be impossible without it. The subjects in every test have to aim at specified targets. The actual psi exchange is, however, unconscious, and the forms of experience are, as stated earlier, intuitions, dreams, or hallucinations, or actual projected physical effects. The fact that all of the findings to date also apply to all of the types of psi supports the current view of a single general psi function which is part of the normal personality.

The biological indications too, although limited, present no difficulty in the admission of the psi function to the science of life. There is no limitation yet known on account of sex, age, or other biological grouping. Psi is, as far as we know, generally potential to the species. It is not pathological. On the whole, the biological picture is still fragmentary, but it offers inviting research questions. The evidence of psi capacity in certain animal species, especially dogs and cats, is good enough to warrant, even to demand, continuing psi research with animals.

We are sometimes asked whether all this adds up to the status of a distinct branch of science. The rational growth of lawfulness and order in the research findings is perhaps fair assurance that we have indeed a beginning branch of science. Its territory has now been well enough marked off that no other neighboring field need be mistaken about it, and, as a matter of fact, no counterclaim or boundary dispute has arisen about the field. The new methodology is in some respects distinctive, but it is readily appraisable and has long been subject to an exceptionally thorough and severely critical examination.

However, the slow emergence of its findings, as well as the paucity of research workers, has indicated that parapsychology is a field of unusual difficulty; it would seem appropriate, therefore, that, along with this outline of progress, a brief review be given of some major difficulties of parapsychology today.

I will not have time to recall the long and bitter controversy over parapsychology. This harrowing trial by ordeal, however, has for some time passed its peak of urgency and can now safely be left to the analysis of history. There is need only to make clear that the exceptional levels of experimental safeguarding which enabled parapsychology to survive this obstacle course have not been abandoned with the cessation of the controversy.

These special precautions have, I think, been evident to some extent in my review. First on the list are the emphasis on safeguards in research, high standards of evidence, and caution in drawing conclusions. *The Journal of Parapsychology* has kept the contested issues in the open by publishing critical articles. A critical Board of Review was kept on the *Journal* staff for a time, to be followed later by two qualified mathematicians—for reading of all manuscripts. The two-experimenter plan has been a special precaution in work of greater importance. These and other measures rightly belong to the efficient methodology of any science, whether or not under special criticism.

If parapsychology has been, as I think, making too slow an advance, two current difficulties are mainly to blame. The first and greater of the two is the major frustration we all encounter in the research itself. This is the fact that, as I have said, psi operates on so unconscious a level that control over it is an extremely baffling matter. The most immediate handicap resulting from this is that it makes it hard for the subject to keep control of his ability even when it is discovered he has it. Most of the leading subjects in psi experiments anywhere in the world played out somewhere along the way. (Among these were not only H. P. himself, but even Ryzl's subject P. S.) The time different subjects were able to work before getting down to a chance rate of scoring has varied greatly; but, of course, we are learning something as we go, even from these frustrating experiences. However, we have not learned enough yet to be able to go back to these earlier subjects and coach them back again to full scale production.

This is not all. The subject knows so little of how he is exercising his ability that he may unwittingly fall into a practice of aiming at the intended target but actually hitting the one just before or the one just after. Or he may mistake one target consistently for another. Or, again, he may persist in missing the targets and make scores below the chance average. If he persists in this "psi-missing" he is, under certain conditions, credited with a reliable diversion of the same ability which normally makes for psi-hitting. For this we have had to develop a quantitative method for the study of unconscious functions.

This psi-missing effect, although psychologically interesting, makes control of psi extremely difficult. It is a kind of unstable differential which, because there is no conscious indication of it, will throw the subject from a psi-hitting level to a psi-missing turn without his knowledge. This difficulty also stands in the way of educating the subject for improved psi performance. Worst of all, perhaps, it discourages the beginning psi worker because it makes it hard for him to get and keep dependable subjects in the conduct of research.

However, some progress on this problem can now be reported as more becomes known about this unconscious ability. We are learning to manipulate even psi-missing. For one example, by setting up an experiment with two parts to it, one part usually drives the subject into a negative response while on the other he goes positive. We can then measure the differ-

452

ence created and use this device as a sensitive measuring technique. We are learning also how to predict which subjects will score above and which below the chance average. There are signs, too, that the barrier of unconsciousness is thinner than was earlier suspected. We may yet break through to a greater degree of conscious control.

The other major difficulty has to do with the fact that psi is quite evidently nonphysical—whatever that really means. It is, of course, this very property that makes this extrasensorimotor exchange unique and interesting; but it also makes for serious difficulty, not in the laboratory as with the unconsciousness of psi; rather, it is with the existing scientific culture. Among the scientific professions of the western world there has grown up a conviction that the universe is physical, and that anything that does not fit the physical picture is unreal and should be ignored if it cannot be disproved. The phenomenal success and growth of the organized scientific professions have given to this adopted image the force of authority that few individuals want to challenge openly. The natural result is a silent boycott of any unassimilable claim that arises, and this is the real opposition parapsychology has now to encounter. The young man who wants to work in parapsychology is subject to the pressure of losing status in stepping out of line. This serious social deterrent, along with the difficulty inherent in the research itself, can explain the comparatively small number of independent and competent individuals who are prepared to venture into parapsychology.

How conclusive *is* the case against a physical theory of psi? The evidence is roughly as extensive as that for psi communication itself. In the very nature of the psi test it is *physical* contact of the sensorimotor system with the environment that has to be screened out. On the other hand, is there any valid evidence at all, of any kind whatsoever, that definitely links a known physical energy to success in controlled psi tests? None such is known, and the prize for such a case would be a fabulous one indeed. It is significant to keep in mind that no one has even attempted a speculative physical theory of any possible testable character that would accommodate the whole range of established psi phenomena. A speculative effort to try to explain only a single type such as telepathy is not worth taking seriously.

The evidence for precognition obviously offers the best way to answer the question of physicality quickly. If one prefers to seek more evidence, the way is now well open. But some of the best controlled experiments ever conducted in any science have been carried out in the precognition research already done. In one of these, in 1941, a colleague and myself participated in a two-experimenter operation with extremely cautious conditions. The experiments that will perhaps most discourage the physicalistically inclined reader are those such as the predictions of target orders at Duke from Yugoslavia and Paris a year ahead and three to four thousand miles away from the target selection.

The exceptional incident, too, adds much to the final judgment. For example, when Dr. K. M. was the subject in the Belgrade series with one-year precognition, he wrote in strong words on the back of one record sheet that this was his worst day ever. The sheet *was* found, when checked a year later, to be so far below chance average that it was highly significant by itself.

Naturally this new concept of psi exchange is a hard one for us all. We are familiar only with physical energies. We cannot think of any other source of energy or influence in nature until some independent mind, with a gift of plausible explanation, does so and tells us how to think about it. Plainly enough we have in these experiments some unconventional, unnamed influence that brings results that are now not to be dismissed.

When such a situation arose in the past, scientists have always invented a new energy concept. The suggestion at this point would be to follow the same precedent, but to do so cautiously and with minimal commitments. If we do have to do with a psi energy, as seems to be the case, it will yield more information about itself as we go on exploring it. It is the only working concept that does fit the present facts, but we can let future research decide its worth.

The main advantage right now is that the characteristic mode of thinking of the natural sciences need not be abandoned. A psi influence or energy is supposedly producing the effect observed. The cause-effect concept need not yet be jettisoned in spite of precognition. The gaps in our present knowledge of the nature of time suggest that judgment be suspended until there are more facts, not only regarding the nature of psi, but also the nature of psychophysical interaction in general.

Finally, I will ask now what we can make of this science of psi communication in terms of implication and application. Where will it fit in and what can we do with it? I will take first the question most often asked: Can we offer a satisfactory general theory of this psi function? Naturally a general theory is one of the goals of any science; but like some other branches, we have not yet reached the stage in parapsychology where the attempt at such a theory is profitable. However, progress toward it in the form of the development of an organized lawful pattern of the findings is definitely encouraging. In the past the emphasis has had to be laid mainly on distinctions of psi types from other phenomena and from each other. Now the search for positive interrelationships with other systems of nature can be more heavily stressed.

For example, before a useful overall theory of psi can be designed, I think we need to know more about the nonphysical energetic factor responsible for the phenomena and how it functions; more, too, should be learned about the place of psi in the organism, the species, and the evolutionary story; and even more about its role in the total personality system. The researchers have, as we have seen, developed a body of organized knowledge about psi phenomena, their occurrence, their interrelations, and their relation to conditions affecting them. But a general theory should also involve their relations to the larger order of nature; and these are problems for the future.

Another frequent question about what we can make of psi has to do with practical application, and a similar answer is appropriate here, too. If we consider only what is known about psi at present, the immediate prospect of dependable application is unimpressive.

We get the same picture if we look back over past efforts of mankind to make use of the psi abilities men have always believed they had. While individuals here and there, as prophets, diviners, clairvoyants and such, developed impressive records of performance, the records are impossible to evaluate in terms of what could be credited solely to the psi element. Moreover, no dependable practice of this type has survived that give a good enough score by the scientific testing standards of today to justify recommendation for dependable use.

The reason, of course, is now a familiar fact of parapsychology. Psi ability seems to be far too deep in the unconscious structure of the individual for him to be able to improve on his performance, instruct others in its use, and maintain it in a dependable way over a long period.

Application, therefore, awaits further basic research. Additional work may bring about more control over the capacity, either through training the individual or in discovering a way of performance; the records are impossible to evaluate in terms of liberating or improving his ability. Devices may be discovered for utilizing not only the usual small uncertain bits of information but also for controlling the psi-missing factor, that elusive, unconscious process by which psi runs amok and produces systematically wrong results. In a word, some formidable problems stand in the way of psi application at present.

Psi communication, then, seems at present a puny, useless thing, viewed against the background of the efficient, elaborate technology of physical communication today. But the index value of the idea, the simple fact that psi occurs, now that this fact has been well established, is quite a different matter—even if no greater control and use of the ability were ever to be achieved. The addition to man's personality of the peculiar properties of psi agency compels a reclassification of the nature of man. Materialist labels will no longer apply to an organism capable of nonphysical exchange.

456

Naturally this has bearing on materialist theories of economics and political affairs that are currently popular in some parts of the world. But it bears equally on mechanistic theories of medicine, biology, and psychology that generally prevail. It liberates these sciences from the confinement of a materialist metaphysics by introducing for the first time a scientific test of the materialist hypothesis that all human agency is adequately explainable by exclusively physical principles.

Far more important at this time, however, is what the facts about psi seem to signify to peoples around the world who are groping for an understanding of man to live by. They want to know whether it is a fact that, as their religious cultures have assumed, a person is more than matter; whether man really has, as he intuitively feels, some distinctive quality that could somehow free his will to some extent from the determinism of the material forces in and around him. In man's long intellectual search for control over his destiny he wants to have the sound assurance of this added personal power over his physical setting, if he can be as sure about it as he has come to be about other facts of life.

This interest has existed throughout the ages, but it has not before had the support of science. Now it is possible through the psi investigations to explore this long hidden side of man's nature. The beginnings that have been made now seem to justify a more inclusive program of inquiry, a composite Science of Man's Nature, designed to integrate all the disciplines that deal with unanswered questions about what is unique and distinctive in the human makeup. In order to pursue this broad program we have established the Foundation for Research on the Nature of Man, an independent organization, in Durham, North Carolina.

But can we reasonably hope to achieve such an undertaking under the shadows of the existing inhospitable orthodoxies of the times? On the one hand, we have never had, and we shall not expect, assistance from the organized religions. This is, I think, understandable. Psi itself is the distinctive communication

457

system assumed in supernatural religion. It is, in fact, the element that contributes to a religious doctrine whatever supernatural quality it claims. In doctrines such as omniscience and omnipotence the respective powers of ESP and PK are obviously enormously extended; this superlativity is the order of divinity. Prophecy, revelation, prayer, seership, and other distinctive experiences of religious life are all readily seen to require an essential psi component to be meaningful. It is, however, in the very nature of orthodoxy not to welcome, let alone support, an experimental invasion of the domain of authority and faith.

On the other hand, on the side of the sciences, the orthodoxy is not opposed, as in religion, to the *methods* of psi inquiry. It has tried in vain to invalidate them, but it objects only to the *results*—to the dragging in of evidence of nonphysical phenomena—because that smacks of the religious superstitions with which science has had its battles in the past. Had parapsychology found only erroneous claims or had psi been even half plausibly explainable by a radiation principle, it would now be in first-rate standing among the established sciences.

Even as it is, however, I can see two favoring circumstances for this Science of the Nature of Man. One of them is a simple historical fact that the history of science affords a logical mandate for parapsychology.

Let us look back, with only a sweeping glimpse, to the time when all the natural phenomena known to ancient man were wrapped in the same fog of religious mystery that encompassed his life. Then the lightning and volcano, the earthquake, and sunrise, were all as much the product of divine agency as his prophetic dreams. But the progressive advance of the physical sciences down through the ages, into and beyond those ancient mysteries, has given man far greater mastery over his physical world than he even credited to his divinities.

Another broad zone of mystery in ancient man's religious outlook covered the miracles of birth, and bloom, of disease, and pain, and death; and, yet, as the biological sciences emerged from the penetration of these mysteries, there developed such control over life and health as completely to overshadow the powers the ancients conceded to their all-powerful deities.

And now as we turn the exploring skills of scholarship upon this remaining zone of the mysteries of man's own hidden nature, problems that must again be taken from the shelf of the supernatural, may we not expect that these inquiries, too, may bring forth from the storehouse of nature the lawfulness needed for an understanding of man himself, greater perhaps and more useful again than the control he once attributed to the heavenly rulers on whom he projected these same powers? Actually, the sciences have *always* surpassed the wildest expectations of their founders as well as the prescientific visions of the religions. We cannot, therefore, hope in this case, even with all the encouragement of history, to anticipate adequately the magnitude of the discoveries ahead of us—if we are allowed to proceed.

Perhaps in this hopeful Science of the Nature of Man we need only to know for the present that this is the *direction* of search for what really distinguishes a man. Fortunately we need not know how great will be the progress on the way. For even if the historic perspective just mentioned be correct, it still remains for its guiding influence to be felt.

But there is another, more obvious, point of optimism as well. Beyond any shadow of doubt the brightest interest in psi communication today is in the fantastic practical benefits it will yield if the difficulties of control and application can be overcome. Thus far I have been assuming only the knowledge we have today. Now for a moment I will consider the reasonable prospect of a moderate advance in improving the degree of effective control of psi communication. I have warned that it is difficult, but I have not said it is impossible.

As a matter of fact we know psi *can* be controlled to some extent, under some circumstances. We could have done little or no experimenting if it could not. I have known still greater control is possible ever since, thirty years ago, I succeeded in building up a subject (H.P. himself) to a pitch of performance in a clairvoyance test in which he made twenty-five hits in unbroken succession. But it was a delicate psychological operation, and it must be kept in mind, too, that H.P. eventually lost his capacity to score above chance in psi tests. The problem of control is first and last a psychological one, but one that should none the less yield eventually to research.

In fact, we already know a great deal about what eventual control will require, but like the unfinished span of a bridge, it does not yet add up to full application. We know of the great importance to psi performance of sustained motivation on the part of the subject. We know that the psi-missing factor, the tendency to reverse direction, must either be brought under control or under some mathematical way of handling that will prevent it from blocking the efficiency of psi.

But, in justice to our science, we must also keep in mind the fact that as yet not even a modest crash program has ever been attempted; no proper teamwork with adequate facilities and reserves of trained personnel has ever been provided. No one can say what could be done if a properly directed and adequately aided program to bring psi under control were to be made.

As a realist, I suspect that the great competition between nations in further extending mastery over physical nature will fully overshadow any mere interest in man himself. Even as I write these words there lies before me the announcement that a large American electronics company is engaging in a program of parapsychological research, with the aim of bringing ESP under practical control. One may infer with confidence that this indicates government interest and that some other government must be suspected to be doing something similar. If that is not the case today, it will be so tomorrow.

As it happens, then, behind the problem of advancing our knowledge of the human beings to whom psi belongs is a powerful practical interest with which we must reckon and for which we can even be thankful. And while this interest is due to nothing more than an overriding urge to get a man on the moon and especially to get one there first, presumably psi communication, if controllable, could be as useful in outer space as anywhere else man goes.

At the very least, one must acknowledge the undaunted readiness of these technological professions for new and unconventional ideas. It is indeed conceivable that their purely practical interest may rocket basic research in parapsychology to an orbit of scientific attention it would not on its own attain within a century.

This is not a note of cynicism, but simple recognition of the way things are. Let us recall that it was a very practical interest in the wine vats of France that started Pasteur's great revolution in medicine; it was not even a physician who led the way.

SUGGESTIONS FOR FURTHER READING IN PARAPSYCHOLOGY

General Reviews and Manuals

The Reach of the Mind by J. B. Rhine. New York: Apollo Editions, 1961.

Challenge of Psychical Research by Gardner Murphy. New York: Harper, 1961.

Experimental Psychical Research by Robert H. Thouless. Baltimore: Penguin Books, 1963.

ESP in Life and Lab by Louise E. Rhine. New York: Macmillan, 1957.

"ESP: What Can We Make of It?" by J. B. Rhine. One of three lectures in *Guildhall Lectures* 1965. London: MacGibbon and Kee, 1965.

Manual for Introductory Experiments in Parapsychology. Durham: Parapsychology Press, 1966. (Multilithed).

Parapsychology, Frontier Science of the Mind by J. B. Rhine and J. G. Pratt. Springfield, Ill.: C. C. Thomas, 1957.

Research Periodical

Journal of Parapsychology. Published quarterly by the Parapsychology Press, College Station, Durham, N. C.

Spontaneous Experiences

Hidden Channels of the Mind by Louisa E. Rhine. New York: Wm. Sloane, 1961.

Relation to Other Fields

New World of the Mind by J. B. Rhine. New York: Wm. Sloane, 1953. Also, New York: Apollo Editions, 1962. (Paperback).

Science and Psychical Phenomena (1938) and *Apparitions* (1953) by G. N. M. Tyrrell, republished by University Books, Inc., New York, N. Y., 1961.

ESP and Personality Patterns by G. R. Schmeidler and R. A. McConnell. New Haven: Yale University Press, 1959.

English Experiments

Modern Experiments in Telepathy by S. G. Soal and F. Bateman. London: 1954.

Reprints of Duke Reports

Extra-Sensory Perception by J. B. Rhine (1934). Foreword by Professor William McDougall. Introduction by Walter Franklin Prince. Boston: Bruce Humphries, 1964.

Extrasensory Perception after Sixty Years ("ESP-60") by J. B. Rhine *et al.* (1940). Republished by Bruce Humphries, Boston, 1966.

From Duke to Foundation

Parapsychology: From Duke to FRNM by J. B. Rhine and Associates. Durham: Parapsychology Press, 1965.

Test Materials

ESP cards with elementary instructions and 25 record sheets.
$1.00 a set. For fuller elementary instructions, see *Manual*
(below) and for more advanced directions, see Chapters 7,
8, and 9 in textbook, *Parapsychology, Frontier Science of
the Mind* by J. B. Rhine and J. G. Pratt. Springfield, Ill.:
C. C. Thomas, 1957.
ESP record pads (50 sheets). Fifty cents.
Manual for Introductory Experiments in Parapsychology. Durham: Parapsychology Press, 1966. (Multilithed).

UNIVERSAL REQUIREMENTS OF A
DWELLING ADVANTAGE

R. BUCKMINSTER FULLER

Professor of Generalized Design, Southern Illinois University

Editorial Note

In a recently published article titled "How Little I Know" (*Saturday Review*, November 12, 1966), R. Buckminster Fuller indirectly criticized editors who attempt to edit his work. We were delighted to have him accept our invitation to prepare a paper for *New Outlooks in Psychology*. We present his contribution, proudly and without alteration, exactly as it was submitted to us.

R. Buckminster Fuller is one of the most extraordinary thinkers of our century. Architect, designer, and philosopher, Professor Fuller has been a visiting professor, lecturer, and critic on many American and European campuses, including the Massachusetts Institute of Technology, the University of California at Berkeley, the College of the Ozarks, Yale, Cornell, and Princeton. Since 1959 he has taught at Southern Illinois University, where he has life tenure. His books include *Education Automation, No More Second Hand God*, and *The Unfinished Epic of Industrialization*. His listing in *Who's Who* mentions scores of his honors and accomplishments. The geodesic dome which he designed to house the American exhibit at Expo 67 has been viewed by millions. One of his most recent creations, a design for a floating tetrahedronal city, could make it possible for men to inhabit the earth's water surfaces.

•

UNIVERSAL REQUIREMENTS OF A DWELLING ADVANTAGE

TELEOLOGIC SCHEDULE

Check list of the
Universal Design Requirements
of a Scientific Dwelling Facility,—
as a component function
of a new world encompassing,
service industry,—
predesigned,
Rather than haphazardly evolved,—
and thus avoiding
a succession of short circuited
and overloaded burnouts
of premature, and incompetent
attempts to exploit the ultimate
and most important phase of
industrialization, to wit,
the direct application of highest
potential of scientific advantage
toward advancement of world living
standards—
to be accomplished by inauguration
of a comprehensive anticipatory
technology scientifically informed
of the probable variables and
possible randoms—
the new volition to succeed
the era of 'survival,'—
that is survival-despite,—
despite preponderant submission
to ignorance,—
ignorance of future probabilities
and general behaviour of nature—
which heretofore 'survival,' tolerated

lethal opportunism, wherein the
progressive deteriorations bred
emergencies which called upon
scientific ability to perform last
minute miracles but only as a
curative dispensation of morbid
inertia.

The universal design requirements of a scientific dwelling
facility are that it accomplish comprehensive advantage for man
over all primitive factors of energetic nature. These factors may
be broadly classified in four parts as follows:

I. Essentially RANDOM and SUBJECTIVE phenomena.

A. Exterior variables—factors of destructive or useful potential; of nakedly intolerable magnitudes, inescapably impinging.

B. Interior variables—factors of destructive or useful potential; of nakedly intolerable magnitudes, inescapably impinging.

C. Exterior constants of relative inertia forgotten through
persistent obviosity and randomly re-encountered.

*II. Essentially ROUTINE and SUBJECTIVE phenomena—
internal to dwelling*—predictably periodic, rhythmic.

A. Inescapable functions of the organic processes, internal to
dwelling and external to man.

B. Inescapable functions of the organic processes, internal to
dwelling and internal to man.

C. Interior constants of relative inertia forgotten through
persistent obviosity, and regularly rediscovered, e.g. furniture to
be lifted with each house-cleaning.

*III. Essentially RANDOM and OBJECTIVE phenomena—
internal to dwelling*—initiative, spontaneously intermittent—
teleologic.

A. Investment of earned increments of lifetime for free will
regeneration of the advantage of life over a priori environment.
Realization of man's potentials as an individual.

B. Implemented and insulated spontaneity of feedback accel-
eration-continuity of the self amplifying individual.

C. Instrumentation of 'home' magnitude, physical realizations
of man's potential as a continuous-man, i.e. a team of individuals
overlapping and weaving around individual birth-deaths and

separate generations, a Total Man who never sleeps, dies, nor forgets.

*IV. Essentially INCISIVE and routine OBJECTIVE phenomena—external to dwelling—*initiating a sustainable complex continuity-design realization of all men's joint potential—teleologic.

A. Investment of earned increments of technical advantage of the science-industry complex in design realization of the complex dwelling facility service.

B. Implementation and insulation of synergetic feedback of higher order accruing to spontaneous group realizations of newly evolving potential.

C. Instrumentation of industrial or institute/university magnitude realization of man's potential as a continuous-man i.e. a team of individuals overlapping and weaving around individual birth-deaths and separate generations, a Total Man who never sleeps, dies, nor forgets.

Note: That I and II above are subjective and defensive and exclusive and that III and IV are objective and offensive and inclusive.

Note: That I defines the outer ramparts and II the inner defenses while III represents the inner initiative-taking and IV the full grown outer offensive—conquest-contact.

Note: That this arrangement is geometrically teleologic, i.e. omni-directionally convergent-divergent-propagative.

Expanded expression of four broad classifications of universal design requirements for a dwelling facility. Original topic of broad classification not repeated and referred to only by number.

IA Structural, mechanical or chemical interception and control of externally impinging factors, either by rejection, reflection, deflection.

Through shunting, channeling, impounding, modulating and/or retiming of volumetric flows of variable external factors of nakedly-intolerable magnitudes.

1. Immunization against aperiodic, energetic interferences,—externally impinging at intolerable magnitudes and heretofore classified as cataclysmic,—because exceeding the practical stress abilities of as yet available technology—However—(new era

467

essence). Since accomplishment of higher physio-chemical stress abilities in, for instance, supersonic flight and snorkle submarine, the stress abilities of technology in general now far exceed the predictable stresses of the hitherto cataclysmic structural interferences—the 180 m.p.h velocity of Antarctic hurricane or Pacific typhoon is now a relatively minor aeronautical velocity-of-interaction of designed structures. External impingements are classified in the order of frequency of probable occurrence and relative magnitudes.

a. Cataclysmic

Improbably annual, possibly 'never,' and least frequent, but of highest stress when occurring

1   earthquake
2   tornado
3   hurricane
4   typhoon
5   avalanche
6   landslide
7   volcanic eruption
8   bombardment
9   forest fire
10 tidal wave
11 plague
12 radio activity
13 lethal gases
14 BW (bacteriological warfare)

b. Dangerous

Probably annual, of borderline 'disaster' magnitudes

1   gale
2   local fire
3   flood
4   pestilence
5   lightning
6   selfishness (self-preoccupation pursued until self loses its way and self-generates fear and spontaneous random surging, i.e. panic, the plural of which is mob outburst in unpremeditated wave synchronizations of the individually random components)
a   vandals

b   marauders
c   meddlers
d   politics
e   fanaticism
f   commercialism
g   materialism
 c. Inclement
 Of high seasonal frequency and of low orders of stress or of naked intolerability
1   fumes
2   hail
3   rain
4   snow
5   dust
6   electrolysis
7   oxidation
8   heat
9   cold
10   epidemic
11   vermin
12   insects
13   fungi
14   minor random missiles
 2. Rejection, or deflection for delayed or immediate use as
 a. energy, admitted into direct work as, for instance, radiation or electronic reaction, or
 b. indirectly into work as, for instance, impounded wind (aeronautical) or water (hydraulic) power
1   piped—for direct use
2   wired—for direct use
3   valved—for direct or delayed use
4   stored—in cistern, tank or battery for delayed use
5   stored—in thermal bank or compost bins, etc.
 IB Dynamic control of internally impinging factors
 1. Interception of and dispellment of the momentum trends of ignorance,—through incorporation of experience informing natural design replacements, realized in physical principles
 2. Interception and neutralization of bacteria by isolation of,—or by direct elimination

3. Elimination of physical fatigue

a. human robotism and drudgery by provision of adequate mechanics of technical advantage

4. Elimination of psychological fatigue (repression) by

a. removal of accident hazard through mechanical adequacy (don't proofing)

b. removal of arbitrary cellular limitations to permit free interaction of living functions

c. provision for selective privacy by push-button sound, sight and smell barriers surrounding any interior space

5. The elimination of emotional fatigue

a. factors stimulating nerve reactions to be automatically controlled in 'neutral' until voluntarily brought into play by the occupant through:

6. Provision of mechanics for wide range in selection of means and degrees of sensible realization of the prosaic or harmonic phenomenon

a. visual

b. aural

c. tactile

d. olfactoral, i.e. taste and smell

IC Control by anticipatory design over exterior constants of inertia forgotten through persistent obviosity and only randomly re-encountered

1. Constants of environment, i.e. the mud forgotten between rains, odorous winds from remote sources, snowdrifting

2. Control devices installed for seasonal duration only requiring inordinate time investments

3. Chemical accumulations (oxides, sludges, fumes)

4. Biological accumulations

a. vegetation, composts, weed

b. insect, animal residues, nestings, general growth changes

5. Surprise emergencies of environmental complex unique to locality, i.e. possible water, oil, gas springs and seepage

IIA Provision for (unselfconscious) (spontaneous) mechanical performance of inevitable organic routines of the dwelling and its occupants with minimum of invested attention or effort

1. Fueling of house (external metabolism)

2. Realignment of house

3. Scavenging of house

IIB 1. Fuelling of occupants (internal metabolism)

2. Realignment of occupants (sleep) by allowed muscular, nerve and cellular realignment accomplished by designed elimination of known restrictive factors.

3. Scavenging of occupants

a. internal, i.e. intestinal, etc.

b. External, i.e. bathing or pore cleansing

c. mental, i.e. elimination by empirical dynamics

d. circulatory: external,—atmospheric control
internal,—as respiratory functions.

IIC Control by anticipatory design over interior constants of relative inertia forgotten by fatigue cloture of feedback sensibilities and routinely re-encountered—(such as heavy furniture to be moved about daily for cleanliness operations, storages to be overhauled to obtain the tentatively retained devices of possible or infrequent use)

1. By provision of adequate occupational-specialty storage means

2. By home employment of travel equipment

3. By dimensional reduction (e.g. of collections of large data to microfilm)

IIIA Provision of ready mechanical means, complementing or implementing, all development requirements of the individual's potential growth phenomena,—allowing the facile, scientifically efficient, no-energy-or-time-loss,—spontaneous development of self disciplined education, by means of

1. Conning, i.e. selectively stimulated awareness of the momentary interactions of universal progressions accomplished by means of facile references to vital data on

a. history

b. news

c. forecasts

calls for a conning facility combining book and periodical library, radio, television facilities, systematically arranged incoming reports on

1 current supply and demand conditions

2 current dynamic conditions-weather-earthquakes—latest scientific research findings

3 social dynamics—surfacing of commonweal problems of comprehensive readjustment to new potentials and concomitant obsolescence factors

4 latest technical reference in

a texts

b movie documentation

c television university (soon evoluting to increasing importance and reliability as the autonomous dwelling facility becomes widely available)

2. Adequate mechanics of personal articulation (prosaic or harmonic) for the spontaneous investment of the imagination-gestating intellectual-increments of experience,—teleology—which trend ever to satisfy the evolving needs—prosaic or harmonic—routine or plus. This category of original articulations also includes the necessity or crystallization of universal progress

a. instruments are tools of communication

1 direct

2 indirect

3 aural

4 visual

5 tactile

a music, writing, drawing, measuring instruments

b wood, metal and chemical working tools

c typewriter

d wire-tape-and-disc-all-purpose-recorder
-radio-phonograph

e easel

f photographic equipment—taking, developing, printing, projection

3. Recreation—appropriate equipment to full physical development

4. Procreation

IIIB Insulation, or isolation, of the instrumental initiatives
Private diaries, tape recordings, films, instrumentally re-corded data as yet incomplete, undigested, ungestated as complete teleologic regeneration.
IIIC Home Magnitude means of displaying, exposing, experimenting and measuring of 'target' or 'trend to target' or 'trend following' assumptions-of-realization-initiative-and-articulation—i.e. 'vital navigation' or 'teleology,' i.e. personal and social and cosmic feedback control. The comprehensive 'frames'—relative to which display, exposure, experiments, measurement and progressive dynamic trend assumptions may be referenced is FOURFOLD

A. Objective Aspect

1. Subvisible (finite)
Microcosmic

2. Geo-visible (de-finite)
Geographical
(visible, near)
Earth

3. Astro-visible
(de-finite) Macrocosmic
(visible, remote)

4. Supravisible (finite)
Comprehensive
Omni permeative

B. Subjective Aspect

nuclear particles
atoms
molecules
cells, genes

crystallographic
biologic
sub-surface
surface
envelope

comets
asteroids
planets
stars
nebula

abstracted 'generalised'
principles
gravity
radiation
number sets
group behavior
    phenomena
probability
transformations independ-
    ent of dimensions
infinity

C. Consolidated Intellectual
    Advantage, or 'Aids'

atomic charts periodic, etc.
spectrographic charts
molecular models
biological slides

globes, maps, geological
    stratification maps
world and local physiological
    data
spectrum charts

star globes
star charts

energetic geometry
devices
(vectorial, formative,
transformative,
number)

IV REALIZATION BY DESIGN

A Priori Design Realization Assumptions
    Asking not
    why, whither, nor whence
    man-life?
    But assuming
    the accumulated experience evidences
    that biological phenomena
    in general
    and man-life
    in particular
    function in universe
    as the anti-entropic,—
    the anti-random,—
    the simple and complex organic,--
    the systematically convergent phases
    of the comprehensive cycling
    of omni energy transformations
    and therefore industrialization
    constitutes the comprehensive,—
    transformative expansion
    of the man-life function in universe—
    and therefore the realization that
    man-life's extension
    into cosmic measurement
    already billionsfolds
    the sensory limits of integral faculties

presages a further successful amplification
of the man-life function in universe
and therefore
that the regenerative ability of intellect
in extension, acceleration, and expansion
of the extra corporeal cosmic-functioning-stature
of the man-life in universe
is realizable
in comprehensive design initiative
relayed through industrialization
and therefore the function of
comprehensive design
is most naturally and effectively
preoccupied with omni-abetment
of the realization in full
of the potentials of the 'individual' complex,—
an organic atomic nebula
identified superficially as man—
man potential includes
regeneratively improving potentials
of sequential derivative orders
of increasing advantage of the organic
over the (random-entropic) chaos growths.
'Individual' man's highest potential
may be realized in terms of full interaction
of all men's potentials—
ergo man's universal function trends
to amplify first the pull potential
of the individual,—
but inherently multiplicative man-life.
Therefore
on first priority
in design consideration
is the full realization
of individual potential
in order to reach the second derivative,—
full realization for all individuals.
Keys to design realization

are the anthropological measurements,
of the limiting factors
of corporeal man,
beyond which extra-corporeal articulation
of the integral faculties
may be accomplished by extension in principle
through atomic-complex trains,
and energetic transformations
to cosmic stature advantage.
Universal conditions of design realization
commence with the static and dynamic
dimensions of man
and his basic behaviour involvements
of which there exists a wealth of data.

The whole program of realization is to be considered in the following order which breaks into two primary categories or phases: (1) the initial work to be undertaken by the individual prior to his engagement of the aid of associates and (2) original and initial work to be undertaken by the first group of associates. These two phases may be subdivided as follows:

IVA Research and development by initiating individual (prior to inauguration of design action and development action involving full-time employment of others).

Inauguration of a general work pattern as a natural pattern coinciding with best scientific procedure to wit:
Preliminary
Initiation of diary and notebook
Initiation of photographic documentation
Initiation of tactical conferences

PHASE I, INDIVIDUAL

1. Comprehensive library study of accrued developments within the pertinent arts
a. past
b. contemporary

2. Listing therefrom of authorities available for further information
a. local, personal contact
b. remote, correspondence
3. Pursuant to information thus gained, calling at suggested local laboratories
a. university
b. industry
c. setting up of informative tests for first-hand knowledge in own laboratory
4. First phase of design assumption
a. consideration of novel complex interaction unique to project
b. preferred apparatus from conceptive field
c. design of appropriate flowsheets
5. Flowsheets submitted to
a. those competitive specialists who have proved helpful in step b and c
b. industrial producers of similar equipment and assemblies
c. make informative tests for closure of gaps supporting assumed theory
6. Submit specifications and drawings of general assembly and unique component parts for informative bids by manufacturers
a. second redesign of flowsheet based on available and suggested apparatus, price information, etc.
7. Prepare report consisting of diary of above supported by photographic documentation and collected literature—with trial balance conclusions of indicated economic advantage (which, if positive, will inaugurate Phase II)

Pertinent arts to be studied by the initiating individual include:
1. Anthropological data
2. Energetic Geometry, the philosophy of mensuration and transformation, relative size
3. Theory of structural exploration
4. Theory of mechanical exploration
5. Theory of chemical exploration
6. Energy as structure

7. Dwelling process as an 'energy exchange'
8. Dwelling process as an 'energy balance sheet'
9. Theory of structural complex
10. Theory of service complex
11. Theory of process complex
12. Theory of structural and mechanical logistics
13. Theory of complex resolution

PHASE II, COLLECTIVE

IVB Design and development undertaking—involving plural authorship phase and Specialization of full-time associates
Consideration of Relationship of prototype to industrial complex by constant review of principles of solution initially selected as appropriate to assumptions
Adoption of assumptions for realization in design of pertinent principles and latest technology afforded
1. Comprehensive survey of whole sequence of operations from original undertaking to consumer synchronization
Realization strategy #1 by individual (Phase I)
Realization strategy #2 by associates (Phase II)
a. Physical tests in principle of the design assumptions' unique inclusions not evidenced in available data
b. General assembly drawings (schematic) providing primary assembly drawing schedule reference
c. General assembly assumption, small scale models and mockup full size
d. Primary assembly, sub-assembly and parts calculations (stress)
e. Trial balance of probable parts weights and direct manufacturing costs (approximately three times material costs; includes labor, supervision and inspection) and forecast of overall cost magnitudes, and curve plotting,—at various rates of production, ratioed to direct costs per part and 'all other costs,'—i.e. 'overhead,' tool and plant 'amortization,' 'contingencies,' 'profit'
f. 'Freezing' of general assembly and its reference drawing
g. Drawing for first full size production prototype com-

479

mences in general assembly, primary assembly, sub-assembly and parts

h. Budget of calculating and drawing time is set with tactical deadlines for each

i. Parts drawing and full size lofting and offset patterns

j. Prototype parts production on 'soft tools' commences

k. sub-assembly and primary assemblies with 'obvious' corrections and 'necessary' replacement (not 'improvements' or 'desirables' which must be deferred until second prototype is undertaken after all-comprehensive physical tests have been applied)

m. Photography of all parts and assemblies

n. Full assembly completed and inspected—cost appraised with estimates of possible 'improvement' savings to be effected

o. Static load tests

p. Operational tests

q. Assembly and disassembly tests

r. Photography of all phases

s. Packaging and shipping tests

t. Estimates of savings to be effected by special powered field tools

u. Opinion testing

v. Final production 'clean-up' prototype placed in formal calculation and drawing with engineering budgeted with deadlines

w. Parts cost scheduled by class 'A' tools and time

x. Production tool layout fixed

y. Production tools ordered

z. Production dates set

a' Lofting and offsets produced of full-size-test 'masters' and templates

b' Fabrication of special jigs and fixtures

c' Production materials ordered

d' Production tool-jig-fixture tune-up

e' Parts and assembly testing

f' Field operation scheduling

g' Field tools ordered

h' Distribution strategy in terms of initial logistic limitations i' Field tests with special tools

j' Field tools ordered or placed in special design and fabrication

k' Test target area selected for first production

l' Production commences

m' First field assemblies with power tools

n' Maintenance service instituted and complaints

(1) alleviated
(2) analyzed

o' Plans for new yearly model improvement run through all or previous steps—for original production

p' Cycle repeated

2. Production and distribution velocity assumptions

3. Plotting the assumed progressive mass-production curves to determine basic velocities of new industry

4. Tensioning by crystalline, pneumatic, hydraulic, magnetic means

5. Compressioning by crystalline, pneumatic, hydraulic, magnetic means

6. Consideration of manufacturer's basic productions forms, —relative to proposed design components for determination of minimum steps, minimum tools, and minimum waste in realization

7. Establishment of priority hierarchies of effort

8. Time-and-energy-and-cost budgeting

9. Assumption of industry responsibility for field practices. not only in mechanical and structural, but in economic design

10. Designing for specific longevity of design appropriate to anticipated cycles of progressive obsolescence and replacement ability as ascertained from comprehensive economic trend curves

11. Designing with 'view to efficient screening of component chemicals for recirculated employment in later designs'

12. Maxima and minima *stated* and *realized* performance requirements per unit of invested energy and experience and

capital advantage of tools and structures employed and devised

13. Logistics assumptions compacted shipping considerations as original design requirement in

(a) nesting
(b) packaging
(c) compounded package weight
(d) relationship to carriers of all types
(e) field delivery
(f) field assembly
(g) field service and replacement

14. Consideration of tool techniques
15. Consideration of materials' availability

(a) at time of design
(b) in terms of world economic trends
(c) in terms of world potential

16. Consideration of materials ratio per total design
17. Elimination of special operator technique forming
18. Elimination of novel special soft tool designing
19. Numbers of

(a) types
(b) repeat parts
(c) sub-assemblies
(d) primary assemblies

20. Numbers of forming operations
21. Number of manufacturing tools by types
22. Schedule of forming operations included on parts drawings
23. Decimal fraction man hours per operation
24. Designed-in-over-all one-man-ability at every stage of operation
25. Schedule of design routines and disciplines
26. Establish a parts inventory of 'active' and 'obsolete' drawings—from beginning

27. Establish a 'parts' budget of 'required' designs of 'parts' for assemblies and major assembly and general assembly and molds

28. Drawing dimension standards

29. Establish a numbering system of controlled parts

30. Establish purchasing techniques, jig and fixture, lofting techniques

IVC Industrial Magnitude means of etc.

This section repeats all content of IIIC except at Industrial magnitude instead of at Home magnitude.

PUBLIC RELATIONS To run concurrently with all phases of IVB

1. Education of public

Rule 1: Never show half finished work

a. General magnitude of product, production, distribution. But no particulars that will compromise latitude of scientific design and production philosophy of IVB

b. Publicize the 'facts,' i.e. the number of steps before 'consumer realization'

c. Understate all advantage

d. Never seek publicity

e. Have prepared releases for publisher requests when 'facts' ripe

I'd like to mention an individual and his experimental work that has been recently and deservedly much discussed. I speak of Dr. Benjamin Bloom and his book on *Stability and Change in Human Characteristics*—Wiley & Sons, publishers. His book reviews effectively a number of case histories of individuals from birth up to the university graduate-student years, approximately the first twenty-six years of life. The studies have been made in relation to periodically and uniformly administered IQ tests. I am going to talk about these case histories of Dr. Bloom's in the light of other scientific explorations, for instance the explorations that are being made by the neuro-physiologists, exploring the human brain with electrodes and thus discovering many important electrical wave patterns.

Gradually a number of patterns in the brain have been positionally identified with respect to specific cell groups, as related also to specific types of thought, expressions, and actions of individuals. Through this physiological exploration a great deal is now known of the patterning of brain events and functions. Apparently we start life with a given total brain cell capacity, component areas of which are progressively employed in a series of events which are initiated entirely in the brain of the individual by pre-set chromosomic "alarm-clocks." Put your fingers in the palm of a newborn baby's hand and the baby will close its tiny hand deftly around your finger. If you try to withdraw your finger, the baby's hand responds instantly to the withdrawal tension which you exert and it opens its hand. Its *tactile* apprehending organism is apparently operative in superb coordination at birth. Days later the "alarm clock" calls the hearing function into operation. Days later the babies "see" for the first time. One by one the brain's alarm clocks and the chromosome "ticker tape" instructions inaugurate use of the child's vast inventory of inter-coordinate capabilities and faculties. The child is not in fact *taught* and cannot be taught by others to inaugurate any of these capabilities. He teaches himself—*if given the chance*—at the *right time*.

Parents, as you know, have for eons thought that they were going to have to teach their children how to develop, function by function—to walk and to talk—but gradually it has been discovered that was not the case.

Now, we are entering a much more up-to-date phase of humanity on earth. We're beginning to learn a little bit experimentally about a child's extraordinary capabilities. What you can get from Dr. Bloom and the neurologists is the information that the set of "alarm clocks" that go off by the time a child is four years old, govern fifty percent of the total capacity of the child to improve its IQ at any later date. If not properly attended to and given the chance to function, despite the brain's alarm clock inauguration of progressive capabilities in those first four years, the brain mechanism can be frustrated and can shut off the valves of those specific capacities and capabilities to learn, then or later on, in the specific areas. The capabilities need not necessarily be employed to important degree immediately after inception, but must upon inception be put in use and kept in use as active tools in the human coordinating capability else they will squelch themselves; that is, "shut themselves off," not necessarily irreparably, but usually so.

The next thirty percent of the total capacity of children to learn has been put into action by the time they are eight. Thus eighty percent of the total capability to self-improve IQ capability thereafter has been put in operation by eight. By age thirteen, ninety-two percent of the total capability has been self-started into usability. Between the years thirteen and seventeen the final eight percent of the total capacity to coordinate and apprehend; to comprehend and teleologically employ the input data, has been brought into operation. From seventeen on, the most the young people can possibly do is to conserve the one hundred percent capacity to further improve their IQ. We'll take those figures and plot a curve of the rate of inauguration of the capacity to learn, starting the curve at zero years and plotting fifty percent of the capacity by four, another thirty percent by eight; another twelve percent by thirteen, and the final eight percent by seventeen. Next we plot the curve of state and federal funds in aid of education as applied at those same age levels. We find that somewhere around three billion Federal and State dollars a year are applied to the "higher education" period from seventeen years onward, while approximately no government dollars are applied to help the birth to eight years periods when eighty percent of the critical educational capacity is being established, which if not properly set in use and kept in use will be closed off. The great bulk of government educational funds is being applied "after the horse has fled the barn." There was a little cartoon received with the papers about our Conference—a picture of the teacher, and a problem of multiplication chalked in white on the blackboard; along came the supervisor and gave the teacher a machine, an audio-visual aid, which projected the same multiplication problem in black figures upon a white screen—a new tool but no difference in technique.

I have what ought to be a surprising, even startling thing to say, which is that inasmuch as the period of greatest educational capability development is before four years old, the home is the primary schoolhouse—and kindergarten is the high school. Dr. Bloom makes this clear.

Given an adequate set of variable factors characterizing the environmental conditions experienced by a human individual from birth to seventeen years, Dr. Bloom can tell you within one percent what the individual's IQ will be at seventeen years of age.

Human babies are born helpless, and stay helpless longer than the babies of any other biological species. If, up to four years old, that young life has experiences leading to its mistrust of the competence and spontaneous inclination of the older life to look out for it, there is a breach of basic *trust:* its parents have a certified school drop-out on their hands.

Nothing that I say is meant to tell you that the individuals whose spontaneous employment of their innate capabilities has been curtailed or abandoned, due to childhood frustrations, cannot later on "find" themselves. Determined and reinspired individuals have occasionally found ways of reopening their abandoned cortexial faculties.

Besides trust, there are two other conditions of critically controlling importance during the first four years: (a) *autonomy* and (b) *initiative.* The new life has to have an area that is really its own. All life tends to guard its minimum regenerative territory. This is apparently a basic ecological requirement of all living species. The child needs a minimum "territory" that is its own—its own room if possible—at least its own bed. This is autonomy.

The third prime factor affecting the one-to-four year old is *initiative*, which must not be frustrated when it starts making experiments. The child may want to experiment with gravity and inertia by just knocking things off tables—this gives him basic information. He must be able to make many such experiments in order to learn about the way the universe works. The child must have experiences which indicate the coherence of materials and things. What can he trust when he has to grab something to stop his fall? To find out he needs to tear many things apart. Newspapers need only be torn a few times to show

486

that newspapers give poor tensional support. Looking for adequate tensional coherence, the child will soon want to pull good vellums or silks apart. Children mustn't be stopped thoughtlessly as they go through their basic explorations, by virtue of which in due course they are going to start putting things together. They must take everything apart first and then learn how to put things together. Thus they learn to coordinate spontaneously. If parents break up that exploratory *initiative* by too many "dont's" or punishments, or by having things in the child's environment that are dangerous and by which the child gets hurt so frequently as to discourage its further exploratory initiative, then that child will probably be an early school "dropout."

In the four year to eight year period of child development, something comes in that is in a sense close to music which governs the ability to improve his IQ during those three critical years. The most important factor is the *speech pattern of the parents*. If the parents take the trouble to speak clearly, to use their language effectively, to look for the better words, the children are inspired to do likewise. If the parents' tones of voice are hopeful, thoughtful, tolerant, harmonious, again the children are inspired to think and speak likewise. If the parents are not parroting somebody else, but are quite clearly trying to think and are trying to express themselves, nothing encourages more the intuitions of the young life to commit itself not only to further exploration but to deal competently in coordinating its innate faculties. However, if the parents indicate that they are not really trying, or worse, relapse into slang clichés, slurred mouthings, blasphemy, anger, fear, intolerance indicating an inferiority complex which assumes an inability of self to attain understanding by others, then the four-to-eight-year-older becomes discouraged about his own capability to understand or to be understood. If the proper books are on the family shelves, if there are things around the house that make it clear to the child that the parents are really trying to educate themselves, then the children's confidence in family is excited and the children too try to engender the parents' confidence in their—the children's—capabilities.

We witness then that the children intuitively differentiate between parents who try to employ their minds and brains instead of relying only upon their muscles, cunning, or deception in the struggle to survive. The children who intuit that their parents have chosen to use mind over matter (of course unconsciously and without formulating such words) are inspired to employ their best innate faculties to highest effectiveness and most spontaneous coordination of the factors favorable to success.

I've just come from Caracas, Venezuela, a very beautiful city of two million inhabitants. We don't have many cities in the United States that size and none more beautiful. We have heard much about bombings and political troubles in Venezuela. The beauty of the scene at first belies the reputation. You have also heard much of the petroleum generated wealth of Venezuela and its capital city Caracas. From the Caribbean port of Caracas you climb by automobile through tunnels in the mountains to enter a high and beautiful inland valley in which the city of Caracas is situated. The city runs about fifteen miles along the three thousand foot altitude valley bottom between two winding mountain walls rising on either side another three thousand feet above sea level. They are green growth covered mountain walls. There are no snow peaks on them. Clouds frequently hang lacily along the mountain tops. The clouds sprinkle frequently enough to maintain lush growth everywhere. A river bed winds through the valley intertwining with sculptured ribbons of expressways. Year-in, year-out, and the year-round, the temperature ranges only between seventy and seventy-five degrees Fahrenheit.

The Caracan rich have had enough money to build extraordinarily modern office buildings, apartment houses, hotels, universities, hospitals, and expensive residences. A few rich homes are on the hillsides.

In most cities, the slums run horizontally out behind, and are hidden by, the larger buildings. But with the opulent buildings of Caracas filling the entire valley floor, the only place left for the slum blight to spread was onto the rising slopes of its flanking mountains. In Caracas you can see the slums all along the hills. With the shacks constructed on the rubble and leftovers of yesterday's changing materials the different slum areas draped over the lower mountainsides have the color effects of patchwork quilts. They make a deep impression. They disclose the large proportion of poverty as yet unbenefited by the energy wealth released by Venezuela's petroleum. I was asked to meet with educators there in Caracas; much of my meeting was with the university students and those successful citizens who thoughtfully and wisely take responsibility for the general advancement of public education. First telling the Caracans of Dr. Bloom's findings regarding environmental effects on IQ capabilities, I pointed out to them that the "real school houses" are the homes in the slums right there on the hillsides. None of the slum shacks have running water. There are no sewer lines and no bathrooms or inside toilets. Getting sanitary waste disposal and bathrooms into those slums would up the IQ capabilities fifty percent in a short space of time. A bathroom isn't just a piece of machinery. It is intimate to the fundamental routine of cleanliness, morality, and clean thinking. The ability to cope with filth-bred fungi bacteria and their ravaging, through sanitary waste disposal and ready-to-hand soap and running water, has many subconsciously important relationships to the scheduled inaugurations of the progressive cerebral capabilities of the new life as disclosed by Dr. Bloom and his colleagues. Whether the older life really wants more life, and whether the environment manifests that the older life is going to try to make its arrangements to foster life more adequately deeply effects the "unfolding flowers" of the cortexial "gardens." There are a million people sitting on those Caracas hillsides who are looking right at all that modern plumbing in the valley and the bombs of resentment explode first in their hearts over their incapability to adequately foster their children. Bombs going off in Venezuela are all to do with this. Of course illiterates are easy to incite to political revolution. But after the revolution there are no more sanitary facilities. So revolutions follow revolutions with never a sanitary gain.

Despite the poverty of those slums, they bristle with the TV antennas. Secondhand TVs are connectable with civilization by wireless. Secondhand plumbing needs billion dollar water and sewer line developments—and hillsides double the time and cost. In all the slums of the world, the TV antennas bristle. There is therefore a wireless hook-up directly to the mothers and children who watch their televisions avidly. Whatever comes over the TV to the children and parents is the essence of education for better or worse. Television is the great educational medium. It is the number one potential emancipator from ignorance and economic disadvantage of the entire human family's residual poverty stricken sixty percent. I pointed out to the Caracans that their educational problems would not be solved in their universities but through sanitation in their slums and through educational TV advancements of high order.

The little red school house was a worthy conception of our forefathers. The older life always identified education with higher possibilities of economic and cultural success. Wanting their young life to have a better break of fortune than they—the parents—had experienced, they put their children on highest priority in the communal mandates upon their political leaders. Thus *education* has become the most obviously acceptable political objective. Politicians who set about to get high educational facilities for their constituents were most likely to succeed. Thus the educational system has become a political football. The enormous appropriations for education, however, go primarily into building programs—on a "millions" for buildings and a "thousands" for the teachers basis, approximately ten for the buildings and one for the teachers. In fact, education is a good way for politicians to keep the construction business going in bad times. So the construction business lobbies for education. The construction industry is the political pay-off system of least visible corruption. The great Appalachian poverty program has turned out in the end to be only a road contract bonanza for that branch of the construction industry. We don't need more brick. We don't need more Georgian architecture symbols. We need more wholesomely attractive and efficient sanitary facilities and superbly conceived television educational documentaries. Early schools, with few to educate, had only one teacher. Teachers were scarce because even public literacy was minuscule. It seemed appropriate to bring all the children together in one place to hear that rare individual—a teacher. It was nice for the mother to be able to have the children out of the house for a little bit in order to have a chance to get the house clean. This did not mean that she did not love her children—but it was very nice to get them out for a while. There was therefore a babysitting function of the school. But mothers didn't like to say that it was babysitting, because they didn't want to seem to be getting something for nothing so they called it school. It also seemed desirable for the children to have social experience which the walk or ride to and from school and the children's proximity—drilling and playing together—provided. However, the least favorable environment for study is a school room and closely placed desk prisons. Dr. Einstein did not sit in the middle of Grand Central Station in order to study math and physics. He went into seclusion to study as does any logical human—in his private study or laboratory.

Let's return to Bloom's basic proclivities of the new life. The child wants his autonomy. The maturing student wants his privacy—his special place. We have learned by experimental work in education at Southern Illinois University of the IQ capability favoring that is attainable with a little individual, private roombooth with a windowed door which "belonged" to each student. When he first entered he found in his private "room" all kinds of desirable items. He had his own telephone directly and privately connected to his teacher. He found a good dictionary; wall charts of the periodic table of the elements; a world globe; a wall-mounted chart of the electromagnetic spectrum; his private typewriter, and other items conducive to thought and study. He did not feel inclined to go out of that room in order to find an environment more favorable to study. However, he was not allowed to go into that room unless he was going to study. It became a privilege to be allowed to go in. He was not allowed to smoke in there, or to listen to music in there unless he had a music course. He could go outside his private study and there were places to smoke, places to have music, places to be social—to do anything else he wanted except study, calculate, and write. It became an obviously realized privilege to be allowed to go into his private study. The student found that when he was in his private study his reflexes become progressively conditioned, by association with that environment, to give himself spontaneously to study, calculation, and writing. He found himself producing. His mind really began to work.

So I don't see any reason why, with television reaching not only the children in their private homes in the slums but children in the privacy of their homes everywhere, why we should not bring education—school—to where the children are. That is a surprise concept—the school by television *always and only in the home* if possible in a special room in the home. Try to remember your first experience in going to school. You suddenly find that there are the inflexible coupled chairdesks. You fit uncomfortably into yours. The next kid has one. Everyone is pinned into his desk. One of the children psychologically escaping his lock-up wants to go to the bathroom. You say maybe I'll go to the bathroom too. You try to escape to the bathroom. It has horrid smells. I immediately resented and as yet resent these stupid little bullpen desk-chair "strait jackets" where you are put on exhibition as they ask you to say things in front of others so that if you venture an original thought the others can laugh. This is conducive to showmanship and rote learning but not to self-teaching and study. I think within the next ten years we are going to have to give up school houses. Your new educational media are going to make possible bringing the most important kinds of experiences right into the home.

Let's be honest; if you want to send the children out for babysitting, send them out for babysitting. Send them out for social experience, to learn to lead parades or whatever you want them to do, but don't let's confuse our objectives. Give them a chance to discipline their own minds under the most favorable conditions. That is in their very own special private environment. We'd better mass produce "one pupil schools"; that is, little well-equipped capsule rooms and send them to all the homes; or we can design special private study rooms for homes. There are many ways we can do that. We'd better build that into the new life.

PSYCHOLOGY AND SPACE EXPLORATION

A. A. VOLKOV, V. G. DENISOV, E. S. ZAVJALOV

Editorial Note

The adaptation of the human organism to conditions of long-term space flights poses a number of complex problems. Of immediate concern to psychologists are the effects of weightlessness or partial weightlessness on cosmonauts in the course of interplanetary flight. Though the psychology of space exploration is still in its infancy, the human factor comes into sharper focus as the tempo of world space activity increases, revealing the possibility of sensory, neuromuscular, and emotional disturbances which limit the activities of the cosmonaut. Study of the psychophysiological disturbances experienced by both American and Russian cosmonauts has led to the conclusion that engineering psychology can contribute to the design of a spaceship in which the human operator performs essential functions with minimum effort and maximum efficiency.

The article reproduced here originally appeared in the Russian-language journal *Voprosy Psikologii* (Problems of Psychology), Moscow, No. 5 (Sept.-Oct., 1965), pp. 5-17. The translation, titled "Features of the Control of Spaceship Systems by the Human Operator under Conditions of Change in Gravity," was prepared for the Joint Publication Research Service of the U.S. Department of Commerce as a service to the various federal government departments. We present it here in the belief that it offers an objective account of current research in the field of psychology and space exploration.

PSYCHOLOGY AND SPACE EXPLORATION

In recent years the advances made in cosmonautics and the expansion of the flight programs of manned spaceships have resulted in a marked increase in the interest of specialists in engineering psychology in the problems of the interaction between the operator and the technical control-system devices in a spaceship under the unique and often unusual flight conditions not encountered in terrestrial practice. Here of particularly great importance is the operator's work to control the spaceship and its systems under conditions of altered gravity: in the presence of high overloads over parts of the ascent to orbit and descent from orbit as well as during weightlessness or subgravity (partial weightlessness) in the course of orbital or interplanetary flight.

We will dwell briefly on the physics of the gravity effect itself. Gravity is construed as the action of gravitational forces of attraction. The force of attraction is the greater the larger the masses of the interacting bodies are. It decreases in inverse proportion to the square of distance between these bodies.

In theory, the gravitational field of any heavenly body is infinite. In reality, however, it is always possible to find points in outer space where the force of the gravitational field of a given heavenly body can be infinitesimally small. Therefore, for example, it is possible to disregard the gravitational pull of the Sun with respect to a spaceship flying in the neighborhood of Earth even though the mass of the Sun is 332,000 times as large as the mass of Earth. Moreover, it is also possible to find points in outer space where the gravitational pulls of two or several heavenly bodies are mutually balanced. It is said that static weightlessness exists at these points. A body placed at such a point in outer space will weigh nothing (Fig. 1).

The flight of an artificial satellite along a circular or elliptical orbit results in dynamic weightlessness, since the centrifugal force of inertia balances the gravitational pull of Earth (Fig. 2).

The human organism has been adapting itself over millennia to the conditions of existence on Earth, where the level of

494

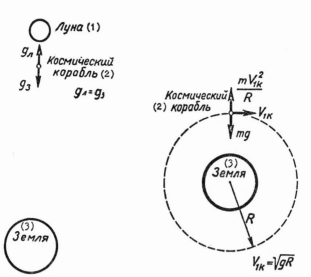

Fig. 1. Condition of Static
Weightlessness.

1 -- Moon; 2 -- Spaceship;
3 -- Earth.

Fig. 2. Condition of Dynamic
Weightlessness.

2 -- Spaceship; 3 -- Earth.

gravity is 1 g. During a spaceflight it has to undergo the state of subgravity (fraction of g) or complete weightlessness. Hence, specialists in space psychology, biology, and medicine have logically been confronted by the question of how man will tolerate a prolonged stay in a state close to weightlessness, and how this will affect his working capacity.

It is worth noting that the prolonged effect of conditions of subgravity and weightlessness on man has not previously been investigated.

The most radical means of investigating the prolonged effect of weightlessness on the human organisms is the development of orbiting stations. The plan of one station of this kind, according to foreign reports, provides for testing six subjects over a year and providing biomedical data with an 85-percent significance level and data on human working capacity with a 70-percent significance level (Watkins [25]).

At present fairly extensive studies have been made of man's condition under conditions of momentary weightlessness (30-

495

50 sec.) during the flight of aircraft along a parabolic curve as well as during more prolonged weightlessness in the course of the first manned spaceflights. These studies revealed disturbances in a number of functional systems of man (cardiovascular, analyzers, higher nervous activity, etc.). Some of these disturbances were also observed in cosmonauts during the spaceflight (G. S. Titov, P. R. Popovich, A. Shepard).

The article will not examine man's condition in the presence of overloads, since it has already been sufficiently studied and comprehensively elucidated in the literature. The principal attention here will be devoted to the effect of weightlessness on the spaceship operator, since it accompanies man in spaceflight.

The possibilities of sensory disorders in man in outer space were discussed by K. E. Tsiolkovskiy as early as 1911. Experimental confirmation of these effects we find in Diringshofen [22], Ye. M. Yuganov et al. [16], L. A. Kitayev-Smyk [7, 8], and others.

While flying through outer space, the man inside the spaceship not only lives but also, with the aid of different technical devices, performs the professional functions of the cosmonaut. We would hardly be mistaken in assuming that the profession of the cosmonaut as the operator basically is reduced to manipulating different systems of the spaceship. Thus, the control of the spaceship is the most important component of the varied in-flight activity of the cosmonaut. Hence, the features of the cosmonaut's work to control the spaceship and its system, the interaction between the operator and the technical facilities of the spaceship, have to be specifically considered.

The piloted spaceship together with its equipment is a complex multi-loop control system in which the operator participates [11]. In this system, the operator is essentially "separated" from the devices and mechanisms he controls, and actually he does not control them directly, but merely the instruments used to monitor them. Thus, specifically encoded information is "wedged in" between the operator and the device he controls, and the operator faces the problem of decoding this information. Besides, the effect itself which the operator exerts on the process he controls—on the device he controls—also is mediated by a system of different technical connecting links.

If such intricate control systems as the spaceship systems are designed without taking into account the possibilities for their control by the operator, in the hope that the operator will somehow "come to some accommodation" with any system, then, as experience shows, the operator will not always be able to successfully perform his control functions (particularly under the specific conditions of spaceflight). Selection and training alone, such as have previously been done with respect to relatively less intricate systems, are not enough to assure an effective control work by the operator in a spaceship. It is becoming clear that, for this purpose, the control machines and devices themselves should be so designed that they can be successfully "controlled" by the operator. This has given rise to the need for a scientific substantiation of technical control facilities and hence also to the need to investigate the psychophysiological possibilities of the operator with respect to control and to measure these possibilities while subjecting the operator to specific conditions of spaceflight, and primarily to prolonged weightlessness (Denisov [5]).

The features of spaceship control systems and the nature of performance of the operator with respect to these systems, of course, largely depend on the type and purpose of the spaceship. At present there still does not exist any universally recognized classification of manned spaceships. Nevertheless, it is possible conditionally to distinguish between the following basic types: circumterrestrial satellite vehicles, stations in outer space, interplanetary spaceships, and military rocket-planes. The following typical control systems for these maneuverable (and non-maneuverable) vehicles may be enumerated: (1) Control of orientation of the vehicle with respect to some celestial body and stabilization of the selected direction; (2) Control of the vehicle to the point of junction; (3) Control of vehicle for landing purposes, following its descent from orbit; (4) Control during correction of vehicle's flight trajectory in order to fulfill the tasks of space navigation or tasks of interception; (5) Control of vehicle's observation devices.

Moreover, it must be considered that the spaceships of the future will contain fairly complex life-support systems in whose functioning (control, adjustment, monitoring), along with automatic devices, a major role should be fulfilled by the cosmonaut-operator. This equally pertains to the steady progress in communications systems; a new type of communications, the so-called telecode communication, will play a significant role in future spaceships.

A special role in astronautics is occupied by control systems in which the operator will fulfill the role of not only some one or several "links" of control, but also that of being a "control object" himself. Such a role may be fulfilled by the operator in the event of emerging from the spaceship into outer space in order to perform scientific research, or preventive or repair operations while wearing a special spacesuit with an emergency locomotion system which is connected to the control system, or while wearing the spacesuit on the surface of the moon or another planet.

Under such conditions, it is necessary to solve a number of new problems unique to cosmonauts alone, namely: what should be the optimal angular and linear velocities and accelerations of the operator? where and how should impulse thrusts be "applied" to the operator to enable him to perform a particular operation? what should be the proper sequence of his movements while wearing the spacesuit? what are his possibilities for self-orientation in space and determination of distances to objects while in outer space? and many other problems.

We will now consider the aforementioned types of control systems and point out their features that exert a marked influence on the psychophysiological potential of the operator when he joins in the control work.

a) *Spaceship Orientation System*

The concept of the control of the spaceship's orientation in space includes, first, stabilization of this orientation, i.e., the implementation of a program under which the hull of the spaceship will assume a definite position (orientation) with respect to some reference point (e.g., Earth); second, the change in the stabilization of the spaceship—the conversion from one stabilized orientation to another. The Vostok spaceships, for example, while orbiting, are oriented by the astronaut with respect to Earth in such a manner that their longitudinal axis is tangential with respect to the trajectory of the mass center, while the vertical axis is oriented in the direction of a plumb line linking the spaceship's mass center with the Earth's center.

An examination of the orientation control system of the spaceship gives reason to believe that, on the whole in the psychophysiological respect, so far as the operator is concerned, this system greatly differs from the stabilization system of modern aircraft. The differences consist in that the former system employs indicators (optical orientators) which markedly differ from the known aircraft instruments (gyrohorizon and compass); the design features also are different. The operator's work to control orientation takes place under the unusual conditions of complete dynamic weightlessness and dynamia which accompany orbital flight. From the standpoint of dynamic characteristics the orientation control system of the spaceship may be characterized as a control system of a slow process, which places the cosmonaut under unique conditions which, by contrast with the conditions of a fixed time limit or time deficit, may be termed conditions of time "surplus."

b) *Control System for Approach of Spaceship to and Junction with Space Station*

In the next few years the interplanetary flights of manned spaceships will take place from an intermediate orbit, the so-called assembling orbit, at which all the parts of the rocket system—including the manned capsule itself—will be assembled following their separate delivery from Earth.

A similar problem arises with respect to heavy manned permanent stations orbiting around Earth.

At present no systems for controlling the approach of a spaceship to and junction with a space station have yet been completely developed or tested under real flight conditions. True, intensive research and development work on the design of such systems is already under way.

499

It is assumed that the elements to be assembled should be launched into orbit over a short distance from Earth and their orbits generally should not be coplanar. Earth-based homing systems will subsequently assure the issuance and transmission of instructions for bringing these elements together (we will call the element carrying the crew the spaceship and the other element, the station) to a distance of 30-50 km. which assures reliable performance of the automatic spaceship-borne system for controlling the approach between spaceship and station to a distance within the operating radius of the contacting system, which functions with the participation of the operators at this distance.

The rate of approach between the elements over the last segment of distance prior to actual physical contact should not exceed several meters a second (this rate will determine the time of approach, which should not be too long). As the relative distance shrinks to zero, the relative velocity should decrease to the minimum assuring an impact-free coupling of the spaceship to the station, yet at the same time sufficient to trigger the locking attachments. At the moment of contact, when the relative mutual distance is close to zero, the relative angular position of the spaceship with respect to the station must be fully definite, and the relative angular velocities may not exceed the extent permitted by the contacting units.

These operations require the preservation of the acuity of vision; they demand of the operator spatial, contrast, and color vision. While working on the final stage of approach the operator has at his disposal a time of the order of five to six minutes. Under the unusual conditions of weightlessness during approach between spaceship and station, the operator's tasks are new and exceptionally complex. They are much more difficult than the most intricate tasks encountered by the crews of aircraft flying in close formation or refueling in mid-air. The scarcity of time and the overloading of the operator with information incoming via many control channels may cause sharp shifts in the operator's actions and lower the reliability of his performance. Some incoming signals may be overlooked and immediate responses to the situation at any one moment may

500

be delayed. Considering, moreover, the exceptional emotional tension under which the operator performs his functions, manipulating the approach and contact control system must be regarded as a highly intricate and laborious task requiring the mobilization of his entire psychophysiological potential.

c) *Control Systems for Correcting the Spaceship's Flight Trajectory*

Control over the spaceship's flight trajectory may be required during prolonged interplanetary spaceflights following the precise determination of the locus of the spaceship in the course of navigational calculations, as well as during the performance of tasks associated with the interception of space targets, moving along the orbits of artificial Earth satellites by means of manned satellite spaceships.

In all such cases a wide range of maneuvers of the spaceship is required.

These maneuvers are fundamentally different from the maneuvers performed by ordinary land-based transportation vehicles. Whenever the direction of travel of a land-based vehicle has to be changed, a force directed at an angle to the axis of its motion must be applied to the vehicle. Thus, to gain altitude, the pilot changes the position of an airplane by means of rudders in such a way that the lift on its wings is greater than in horizontal flight. By contrast, were a merely accelerating or a merely braking force to be applied to a spaceship, it would change not only the orbital velocity of the spaceship but also the form itself of the orbit, along with a change in the apogee and perigee of the orbit. Hence it is clear that a maneuver in outer space must be calculated in advance.

Thus, when correcting the spaceship's flight trajectory, the operator, with the aid of information devices, should compare the actual position of the spaceship with the specified position, produce instruction signals and, in accordance with the extent and direction of these signals, apply the required control effects to the spaceship via the controls.

The spaceship's trajectory control system should be so designed that its component indicators will reflect without delay the operator's actions in controlling the ship. This will make it possible to greatly enhance the precision of steering, which is of major importance under these flight conditions.

d) *Control System for Spaceship-Borne Observation Instruments*

Observation by the operator of different objects located outside the space ship (during approach in space, landing, etc.) by means of the unaided eye alone is difficult. To this end special instruments, chiefly of the optical type, must be used in the spaceship. The performance of the optical instrument may in no way be considered separately from the work of the operator. Here again we are dealing with the unified "man-and-machine" system. In fact, during the observation of objects by means of an optical instrument, the resolution threshold depends on both the resolving power of the optical instrument and the resolving power of the operator's eye. The search for targets in space and on planets and the discrimination, identification and complete analysis of these targets (time and precision characteristics) depend equally on the psychophysiological potential of the operator under the conditions of prolonged weightlessness, adynamia, optokinetic stimuli, on his training and readiness, and on the characteristics of the optical instrument itself such as magnification, drop in magnification (on change-over from the regime of search to the regime of detailed examination of the object), the regimes of observation assured by the design of the instrument (scanning without tracking and scanning with tracking, with halting of image in the field of view of the instrument), the design and location of the controls of the instrument, etc. Moreover, allowance must also be made for the external conditions of the observation of objects (nature of the object, its illumination, range of contrast, nature of the medium across which the object is scanned, etc.).

Semiautomatic—with the operator's participation—control systems on board the spaceship, which also are called cosmonaut-spaceship systems, usually operate on the principle of "track monitoring," or "compensation monitoring." These two principles are explained in Fig. 3; usually they may be distinguished according to the indicator devices employed. The upper diagram in this figure shows the track monitoring system, from which the operator perceives the magnitude of the output and input signals of the system. The operator's task lies in reducing to a minimum the mismatch between the target pip and the tracking pointer of the controlled object, with both the pip and the pointer being mobile. The lower diagram in the Figure shows a compensation-monitoring type system in which the operator sees only the mismatch between the perturbing effect and the system output.

As spaceflight experience indicates, the cosmonaut-operator performs simultaneously the functions of controlling several spaceship systems. The operator's functions in the complex control system are reduced chiefly to the following: compensation monitoring of many pointer needles, operations of control over the regulable parameters of the control object, mathematical and logical analysis of the information provided by the instruments and signaling devices, generalization of the results of control and their comparison with the plan of actions, development of a decision on controlling the object, and implementation of this decision by means of the controls by manipulating them correspondingly.

The study of the psychophysiological possibilities of man as an operator under conditions corresponding to flight in a changed gravitational field may in its general features be reduced to the following: (1) study of the general condition of the operator's organism; (2) investigation of the functioning and interaction of his sensory analyzers; (3) investigation of the operator's motor acts while controlling the instruments; (4) clarification of the fundamental differences between the functional characteristic of the operator under spaceflight and terrestrial conditions. This last aspect is determined by the circumstance that so far the operators have been trained in their particular skills while on Earth. Finally (5), determination of changes in functional characteristics of the operator during a prolonged flight, since a temporary stay under flight condi-

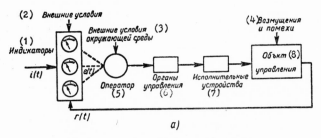

Fig. 3a. Track Monitoring System.

1 -- Pointer needles; 2 -- External conditions; 3 -- External
conditions of ambient medium; 4 -- Disturbances and noise;
5 -- Operator; 6 -- Controls; 7 -- Actuating devices; 8 --
Control object.

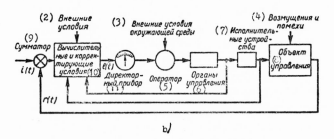

Fig. 3b. Compensation Monitoring System.

1 -- Executive instrument; 2 -- External conditions; 3 -- External conditions of ambient medium; 4 -- Disturbances and
noise; 5 -- Operator; 6 -- Controls; 7 -- Actuating devices;
8 -- Control object; 9 -- Adder; 10 -- Computing and correcting conditions; 11 -- Directing instrument.

* * *

tions may yield characteristics (owing to the resources of the
human organism) which cannot be extended for a longer time
period.

Of particular importance is research into such functions of
the operator as the monitoring of one or many indicators,
determination of angular dimensions, angular velocities and
distances in the landmarkless conditions of outer space, recognition of the shapes and colors of observed objects, and perception of sound signals and oral commands. This requires the
investigation, under spaceflight conditions, of such functions of

504

the visual analyzer of the brain as accommodation, convergence, color and depth vision, the process of adaptation of the analyzers to the changed conditions of gravity, and fusion processes.

It has been established that the stay of humans under conditions of prolonged weightlessness is accompanied by vegetative disorders. Prolonged weightlessness may lead to motion sickness which, particularly when present in pronounced form, reduces the reliability of man as a "link" of the control system. Nausea and vomiting lead to a sharp depression of the tonus of the nerve system, dysfunction of the analyzers, and changes in the cardiovascular and respiratory functions of the human organism. Vegetative disturbances and the motion sickness syndrome are explained variously by different investigators; in particular, they are attributed to the weight loss of the otoliths, resulting in a sharp decrease in their inhibiting effect on the semicircular canals, and also to the cumulative effect of Coriolis accelerations on the vestibular apparatus (Khilov [14] Vozhzhova [1], Voyachek [2]). The motion sickness syndrome may arise not only on irritation of the vestibular apparatus but also during the flickering of different objects in the field of vision of the astronaut (optokinetic stimuli), as well as during the displacement of internal organs (Voyachek [2], Khilov [14]). Symptoms of motion sickness also appear on irritation of the sensory nerve endings in the muscles or via the conditioned-reflex pathways. The state of motion sickness alters the long-established system structure of the interconnections and interactions between the different analyzers (visual, vestibular, motor) which had previously become firmly established under conditions of the Earth's constant gravitational field. The customary visual stimuli required for spatial orientation are absent during a spaceflight. Owing to the change in the character of muscle activity, the flows of proprioceptive afferent impulses become perturbed; conditions enhancing vestibular sensitiveness arise and at the same time the inhibitory effects on the vestibular apparatus diminish or disappear. Vestibular and optokinetic stimuli (flickering of objects in the illuminated field) may be active against this background.

Thus, we are dealing with interaction disturbances in the

505

system structure of the analyzers, leading to autonomic-system disorders, along with symptoms of motion sickness (Yazdovskiy et al. [17], Komendantov and Kopanev [9]).

A man who remains in the state of weightlessness over a prolonged span of time, may be influenced by adynamia. All living matter on Earth is constantly under the action of the forces of terrestrial gravity. Gravity affects a number of man's physiological functions, and particularly the activities of the supporting-motor apparatus. Under the conditions of terrestrial gravity the vertical position of the human body is conditioned by continuous neuromuscular activity and the organism expends a considerable amount of energy on compensating for the effect of terrestrial gravity. Under the conditions of a prolonged spaceflight the muscle work of the organism sharply diminishes, both owing to the lack of muscular effort required to perform physical work and owing to the lack of need to maintain the vertical position of the body. This results in a marked lightening of the load on the cardiovascular system, since the need for muscle work is absent and the heart's work to move blood through the circulatory system is eased. This state of relative muscle inaction and decrease in the load on the cardiovascular system is accompanied by changes in metabolism. Changes also occur in the flow of nerve impulses continually arriving at the brain from the osteomuscular and cardiovascular apparatuses and other organs, and these changes may in turn affect the neuro-psychical reaction (Lebedev [10]).

The short-time effect of weightlessness on man is often accompanied by illusions of spatial position. L. A. Kitayev-Smyk [7, 8] performed observations on 193 pilots and parachutists and established that these illusions were absent in only 25 percent of them. In 16 percent of cases a feeling of falling, tumbling, accompanied by fear, had initially arisen, but after some time was superseded by a sensation of pleasant lightness, soaring, emotional excitement, and joy. In 52 percent of cases the subjects sensed a change in the direction of terrestrial gravity rather than the lack of this gravity, i.e., felt themselves to be lying prone, supine, on a side, etc. Illusions of this kind lasted for 25-30 seconds and their emotional coloring was not so strongly pronounced as in the former case. In seven percent of cases the subjects experienced both the illusion of falling and the illusion of spinning in space, accompanied by a marked fear and by complete disorientation in space. In persons with flight experience the illusions of spatial position were expressed much less markedly. The dynamics of the psychical and vegetative disturbances on repeated exposure to temporary weightlessness pointed to man's ability to adapt himself to the conditions of weightlessness. Thus, the psychical reactions disappeared following 5-20 exposures of this kind, and the vegetative reactions, following 40-50 exposures. Thus, in the presence of temporary weightlessness, man rapidly develops adaptation responses. Illusions of spatial position were observed not only in experimental flights of aircraft along a parabolic curve but also in astronauts. Thus, G. S. Titov, P. R. Popovich, and A. Shepard, once their spaceships were inserted into orbit, displayed momentary illusions of spatial position. It seemed to them that they were in an unnatural overturned position (Gazenko [3], Sisakyan et al. [12], Sisakyan [13], Laughlin [23]).

Acuity of vision may decrease with the onset of weightlessness. Monty and Richard [26], on testing 36 subjects in the presence of temporary weightlessness, found that the sharpness of vision drops six percent. Some of the subjects reported seeing a violet halo around glowing objects.

The disturbances observed in this case in the visual analyzer may be due to the change in vegetative processes both in the brain centers and at the periphery of the visual analyzer, particularly owing to the reduction in the tonus of the individual eye muscles (the inferior exterior and inferior rectus muscles as well as the ciliary muscles). During weightlessness, changes in color vision may also take place. A study of color perception in weightlessness revealed an enhanced perception of colors, chiefly of yellow (Kitayev-Smyk [7]).

The allegation made by the astronaut Gordon Cooper that, during his orbital flight, he saw little houses and other objects on the Tibetan Plateau, apparently indicates disturbances in visual perception and chiefly in depth vision. According to Warrey [20], this was caused by the change in the afferent

507

influences of impulses from the muscles. Similar states are sometimes observed in divers and lead to loss of spatial orientation and occasionally a tragic outcome. Something of the kind has been observed by the author in monkeys (macacus) placed in a darkened cage and deprived of all customary stimuli. There exist reports that military pilots, on being placed in cabin training device of a spaceship under conditions of simulated weightlessness for 30 hours, generally retained their spatial orientation and problem-solving ability and alertness. Some individuals, however, displayed visual and tactile hallucinations and irregularities of behavior.

The state of neuromuscular coordination under conditions of weightlessness may be of major practical significance, since the success or failure of the operator's performance depends on the precision with which he performs his movements. Certain investigators believe that motor coordination changes insignificantly during temporary weightlessness (Gurfinkel, et al. [4], Yuganov et al. [16]).

On the other hand, studies by Beckh [18] and Gerathewohl [19], performed under conditions of parabolic flight, revealed disturbed motor coordination. The subjects, when under visual control, could not draw crosses with a pencil within specified squares. Considerable dispersion of hitting targets with the pencil was particularly marked during the transition from positive acceleration to the state of subgravity.

These discrepancies in findings are clearly attributable to different techniques of investigation and conditions of experiment, as well as to the different degrees of difficulty of performing specified experimental motor acts and perhaps also to differences in the degree of training of the subjects for performing experiments in the state of weightlessness.

Under spaceflight conditions, Soviet astronauts, while attached to their chairs, successfully performed a number of important professional functions associated with control (orienting the spaceship, etc.) as well as making log entries, taking motion pictures, and carrying out other operations.

A series of experiments has been carried out to determine the operator's potential for performing different types of activity under spaceflight conditions. The effectiveness of the manipulation of levers and different tools (monkey wrenches, screw drivers, etc.) in the absence of friction was investigated. The experiments were performed in the presence of minimum friction of the support on which the subject was located (friction coefficient 0.0015). In the presence of insignificant friction, pushing and pulling of levers proved to be virtually impossible. Maximum effort was required in order to change the position of the lever without changing the position of the subject himself. The efficiency of the effort applied by the operator changed sharply compared with his efficiency under normal conditions. It was 27 times as low during pulling, 18 times as low during pushing, and one-third as low during rotational movements. The magnitude of the compressive and tensile effort exerted with both hands did not change markedly [21]. In the process of determining the possibility of visual control over encounters between spaceships it turned out that the acuity of visual determination of angular quantities by the operator when calculating the velocity and distance of the object encountered amounts to three minutes, while the resolving power with respect to angular velocity for an observation time of 10 seconds was 0.3 angular minute per second [26].

During the last few years a large number of studies have been and are being performed to determine methods of maintaining the normal vital activity and working efficiency of the human organism under the conditions of prolonged spaceflight. Such methods include employment of drugs with a tonic effect on the human organism, employment of physical exercise and massage to maintain the tonus of the muscles and vessels, and creation of artificial gravity. This last method is the most radical. The solution of the problem of the expediency of creating artificial gravity largely depends on the manner in which human subjects will withstand experiments with the prolonged effect of weightlessness. Nevertheless, by now requirements are already being drafted for the conditions of artificial gravity that may be created during spaceflights.

The distinguishing feature of these conditions is that, since artificial gravity will be created by spinning the spaceship about one of the axes of inertia, the magnitude of the centrifugal force of inertia determines the level of artificial gravity. Moreover, while moving through the cabin or moving his head and extremities, man will be exposed to the Coriolis forces of inertia.

An analysis of the effect of human factors [24] on the selection of the design parameters of a spaceship in which artificial gravity is created by rotation, indicates that the upper limit of the angular velocity (ω) of spin may not exceed 0.4 1/sec. Then the artificial gravity should not exceed 0.9 g; the lower limit of the artificial gravity may not be less than 0.2 g. Given an optimal configuration of the spaceship, the cabin should have the shape of a cylinder positioned parallel to the spin axis; a second, symmetrically positioned cylinder should serve as the counterweight; the creation of an artificial gravity of 0.9 g requires a spaceship spin radius of 60 meters for $\omega = 0.4$ 1/sec.

Thus, during a prolonged spaceflight the operator working in the control system of the spaceship may encounter certain difficulties, primarily due to the unaccustomed conditions of gravity.

The tasks of engineering psychology lie not only in investigating the possibilities of man as a link in the spaceship control system, but also in developing efficient measures contributing to the successful implementation of the functional duties imposed on the operator.

Bibliography

1. Vozhzhova, A. I. "Data on the Problem of the Prophylaxis and Therapy of Experimental Motion Sickness." Dissertation, Leningrad, 1946.
2. Voyachek, V. I. *Voyennaya Otolaringologiya* (Military Otolaryngology), Medgiz, 1946.
3. Gazenko, O. G. "Certain Problems of Space Biology," *Vestnik AN SSSR* (Herald of the Academy of Sciences USSR), No. 1, 30, 1962.
4. Gurfinkel, V. S., Isaakov, P. K., Malkin, V. B., Popov, V. I. "Coordination of the Pose and Movements of Man Under

Conditions of Increased and Reduced Gravity," *Byulleten'* *Eksperimental'noy Biologii i Meditsiny* (Bulletin of Experimental Biology and Medicine), 11, 12, 1959.

5. Denisov, V. G. *Kosmonavt Letayet na Zemle* (A Cosmonaut is Flying on Earth), Moscow, 1964.

6. Kas'yan, I. I., Kopanev, V. I. "State of Weightlessness and Artificial Gravity," *Izvestiya Akademii Nauk SSSR, Seriya Biologicheskaya* (News of the Academy of Sciences USSR: Biology Series), 1963.

7. Kitayev-Smyk, L. A. "Certain Sensory Disturbances of Persons in Gravity-Free Conditions," *Aviatsionnaya i Kosmicheskaya Meditsina* (Aviation and Space Medicine), Moscow, 1963.

8. Kitayev-Smyk, L. A. "Human Reactions to Weightlessness," *Problemy Kosmicheskoy Biologii* (Problems of Space Biology), 3, AS USSR Press, 1963.

9. Komendantov, G. L., Kopanev, V. I. "Motion Sickness as a Problem of Space Medicine," *Problemy Kosmischeskoy Biologii*, Vol. II, 1962.

10. Lebedev, V. "Adynamia in Spaceflight," *Aviatsiya i Kosmonavtika* (Aviation and Astronautics), 9, 1963.

11. *Pervyye Kosmicheskiye Polety* (The First Spaceflights). Anthology, edited by N. M. Sisakyan and V. I. Yazdovskiy, AS USSR Press, Moscow, 1962.

12. Sisakyan, N. M., Yazdovskiy, V. I., Volynkin, Yu. M., et al. "The First Manned Spaceflights," *Mediko-Biologicheskiye Issledovaniya AN SSSR* (Medico-Biological Research of the AS USSR), 1962.

13. Sisakyan, N. M. "Biology and the Conquest of Space," *Aviatsiya i Kosmonavtika.*

14. Khilov, K. L. "Genesis of In-Flight Motion Sickness," *Tezisy Dokladov Vsesoyuznogo Soveshchaniya po Aviameditsine* (Theses of Reports of the All-Union Conference on Aviation Medicine), Leningrad, 1939.

15. Tsiolkovskiy, E. K. *Svobodnyye Prostranstvo* (Free Space), *Sobrannyye Sochineniya* (Collected Works), 2nd Edition, AS USSR Press, 1954.

16. Yuganov, Ye. M., Kas'you, I., et al. "Sensory Reactions and

the State of Spontaneous Movements Under Gravity-Free Conditions," *Izvestiya AN SSSR, Seriya Biologicheskaya*, 1961.

17. Yazdovskiy, V. I., Yemel'yanov, M. D., et al. "Weightlessness and the Vestibular Apparatus," *Aviatsiya i Kosmonavtika*, 12, 1962.

18. Beckh, H. J. "Experiments with Animals and Human Subjects Under Sub- and Zero Gravity Conditions During the Dive and Parabolic Flight," *J. Aviat. Med.*, 25, No. 3, 235, 1954.

19. Gerathewohl, S. J. "Comparative Studies on Animals and Human Subjects in the Gravity Free State." *J. Aviat. Med.*, 25, 412, 1954.

20. Warrey, W. "Weightlessness Effects on Cooper," *Aviat. Week. Space Technol.*, 78, No. 24, 1963.

21. Celertano, J. T., Alecsander, H. S. "The Use of Tools in Space," *Amer. Rocket Society*, 19, 145, 1961.

22. Diringshofen, H. "Sensory Physiological Observations on Transition from Acceleration to Weightlessness," *Raketentechnik und Raumforschung*, 2, 1959.

23. Laughlin, G. P., McCutcheon, E. P., Bapp, R. M. "Physiological Response of the Astronaut." Results of the First United States Manned Suborbital Space Flight, February 20, NASA *Manned Spacecraft Center*, 1962.

24. Loret, B. J. "Optimization of Space Vehicle Design with Respect to Artificial Gravity," *Aerospace Med.*, 24, No. 5, 1963.

25. Watkins, H. D. "Weightlessness Study Program Analyzed," *Aviat. Week and Space Technol.*, 2, No. 2, 1964.

26. Monty, W., Richard, A. "Vision and Unusual Gravitational Forces" *Human Factors*, 5, No. 3, 1963.

NEW OUTLOOKS IN PSYCHOLOGY

Edited by Pat Powers
and Wade Baskin

The attainments and distinction of those who have contributed to this much-needed volume enhance its value as a contribution to the literature of psychology. Contributions range from José M. R. Delgado's pioneering statement on the control of the human brain to F. Buckminster Fuller's insightful speculations concerning the universal requirements of a dwelling advantage. Contributors were asked to pause in their research long enough to acquaint the general reader with recent findings, to identify research trends that hold promise for the future, and to suggest directions for productive study. They were encouraged to focus attention on emergent issues, exciting discoveries, and promising experiments. Each contributor was given sufficient latitude to move freely over familiar ground and into peripheral areas.

The publication of such a comprehensive work represents an important step toward the solution of the manifold, complex problems generated by technological advances that are rapidly reshaping the face of the physical universe and impinging from all sides on the destiny of man. This book will be welcomed by specialists and students in the broad field

(Continued on back flap)